IMPERIAL
PAGAN

PAUL STRACHAN

IMPERIAL PAGAN

ART AND ARCHITECTURE
OF BURMA

UNIVERSITY OF HAWAII PRESS

HONOLULU

Published in North America by
University of Hawaii Press
2840 Kolowalu Street
Honolulu, Hawaii 96822

Published in the United Kingdom by
Kiscadale Publications
23 Lauriston Gardens
Edinburgh EH3 9HH

Published in hardcover in 1989 under the title
Pagan: Art and Architecture of Old Burma

Printed in Singapore

Library of Congress·Cataloging-in-Publication Data

Strachan, Paul.
  [Pagan]
  Imperial Pagan: art and architecture of Burma /
  Paul Strachan. p. cm.
  Previously published as Pagan. 1989.
  Includes bibliographical references
  ISBN 0-8248-1325-1 : $29.95
  1. Buddhist art and symbolism—Burma—Pagan. 2. Pagan
  (Burma)—Civilisation. 3. Pagan (Burma)—buildings,
  strucctures, etc.
  N8193. B93877 1990
  704.9'494391'09591—dc20

CONTENTS

ACKNOWLEDGEMENTS

I SPENT 1986 in Burma and returned for a shorter period in 1987. Whilst there inexplicably I found myself to be the object of a hospitality and kindness that I had never before believed was within the reach of mankind. In the village of Pagan itself I found, far from the ignorance and obliviousness that is normal amongst communities dwarfed by great monuments, an aura of silent respect and interest for all that is about. Thus, firstly, I thank the people of Pagan for offering a vision of their noble ancestors.

I am also deeply grateful to the following: the Department of Religious Affairs who encouraged and assisted me in all possible ways during my visit. In particular I thank Daw Khin Khin Su, the Director of Research, and the Deputy Minister U Kyi Nyunt and his wife Daw Aye Myint for their generous offerings of time and encouragement; my two Sayagyi in Burma U Than Htut, former Director General of the Culture Department, and U Maung Maung Tin, formerly a lecturer in Burmese at Mandalay University, both of whom now are now members of the Burma Historical Commission; at Pagan, to the late U Bo Kay, former Conservator of Pagan Monuments, who spent half century in the study and preservation of the monuments, and to his disciple U Aung Kyaing, whose energy and integrity have refused to diminish in the face of many practical difficulties.

However, at Pagan my greatest debt does perhaps lie with the local people. From old men tilling the worn fields who paused to tell me about a monument's history, to swarms of eager children who insisted on taking my photographs for me. I particularly wish to thank Ko Kim Maung Way of Taungbi Village who accompanied me on many of my visits to the more distant monuments and whose sharp eyes located many a feature that would otherwise have eluded me. Thanks also to Saya U Aung of the Sithu who often took me on his evening walks to read epigraphs, his wife the Sayama, their daughter Ma Maw Ma Aung and niece Ma Khin Khin Soe.

In Mandalay, the last royal capital of Burma and heir to so many of Pagan's great traditions, I am particulary grateful to the monk U Thutalin-gara and his friend the wood carver Tampawaddy U Win Maung. I also wish here to acknowledge the debt I owe to Dr Myo Myint, who, when he visited London and then back in Burma with his wife Daw Tin Tin Win, constantly strove to encourage my interest in his country's art, and to U Myo Myint's colleagues from Mandalay University Ko Ni Tut and Ko Kyaw Thi Ha; also a note of appreciation to Ko Wunna and all his family.

I thank: John Marr, my academic supervisor at SOAS; John Okell, also of SOAS; Patricia Herbert, British Library; Zunetta 'Mathanda' Liddell; Luke Hoyer Millar; Sebastian Kinsman; the Ross-Gills of Arran; Cath Liston, my great-aunt, who loaned me her Arran cottage where I produced this book. I am indebted to London University's Central Research Fund and to the Spalding Trust who financially assited my 1987 visit to the monuments. Pierre Pichard of the Ecole Française d'Extrême Orient at Pondicherry has generously permitted me to use the architectural drawings intended for his own *magnum opus*, a complete inventory of the Pagan monuments, whose publication we await with impatience. In 1987 I was at times fortunate enough to accompany Pierre on his rounds about Pagan and Salé. Anthony Aris, of Serindia Publications down in London, well deserves a mention here, for without his initial interest and encouragement this book would probably never have been done. Finally a word of appreciation to my parents and family who gave me much support and encouragement during those years of study.

Paul Strachan ဘုန်းမြင်
Edinburgh, February 1990

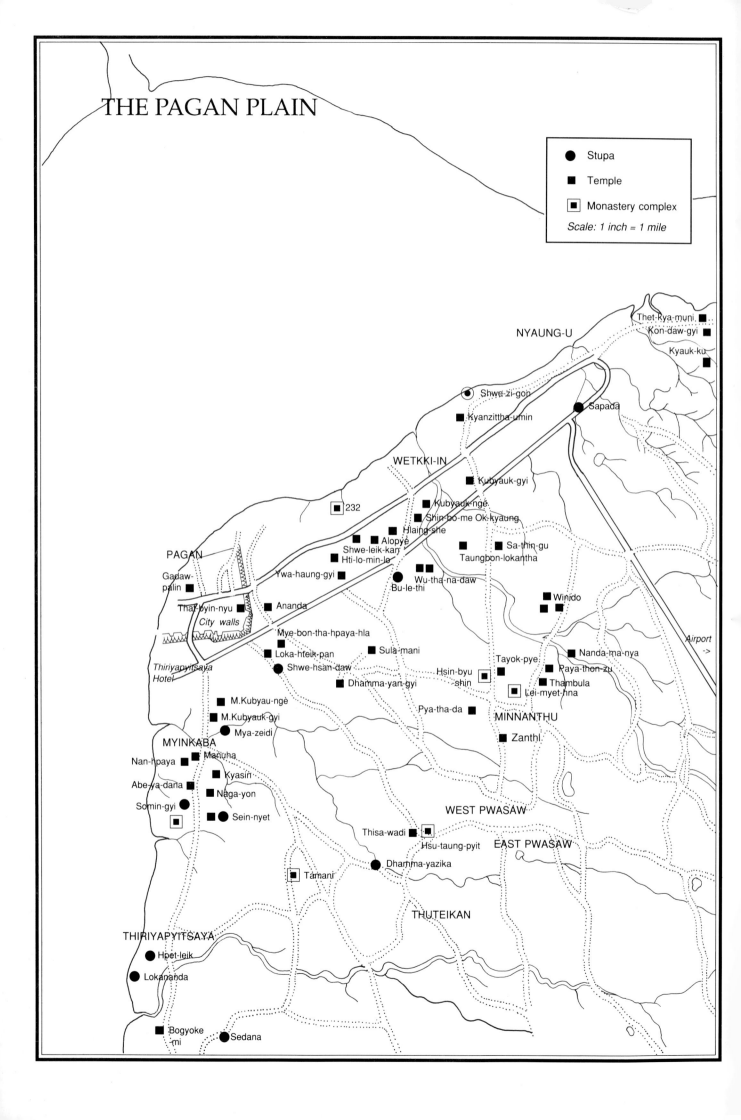

THE PAGAN PLAIN

Stupa ●
Temple ■
Monastery complex ▣
Scale: 1 inch = 1 mile

NYAUNG-U

Thet-kya-muni ■
Kon-daw-gyi ■
Kyauk-ku ■

Shwe-zi-gon ◉
Sapada ●
Kyanzittha-umin ■

WETKKI-IN

Kubyauk-gyi ■

▣ 232

Kubyauk-ngè ■
Shin-bo-me Ok-kyaung ■
Hlaing-she ■
Alopyè ■
Shwe-leik-kan ■
Hti-lo-min-lo ■

Sa-thin-gu ■
Taungbon-lokantha ■

PAGAN

Ywa-haung-gyi ■

Gadaw-palin ■

Wu-tha-na-daw ■■
Bu-le-thi ●

Winido ■ ■

That-byin-nyu ■ Ananda ■
City walls

Mye-bon-tha-hpaya-hla ■

Loka-hteik-pan ■

Sula-mani ■

Tayok-pye ■
▣ Hsin-byu-shin

Nanda-ma-nya ■
Paya-thon-zu ■
Thambula ■
▣ Lei-myet-hna

Airport →

Thiriyapyitsaya Hotel

Shwe-hsan-daw ●

Dhamma-yan-gyi ■

Pya-tha-da ■

MINNANTHU

M.Kubyau-ngè ■
M.Kubyauk-gyi ■
Mya-zeidi ●

Zanthi ■

MYINKABA

Nan-hpaya ■
Manuha ■
Abe-ya-dana ■ Kyasin ■

Naga-yon ■

Somin-gyi ●
▣ Sein-nyet ●

WEST PWASAW

Thisa-wadi ■ ▣
Hsu-taung-pyit

EAST PWASAW

▣ Tamani

Dhamma-yazika ●

THUTEIKAN

THIRIYAPYITSAYA

Hpet-leik ●

Lokananda ●

Bogyoke mi ■ Sedana ●

THE PAGAN - MYINKABA VILLAGES AREA

Scale: 2.5 inches = 1 mile

TAUNGBI

Irra Inn

Upali Thein ■

Hti-lo-min-lo ■

● Bu-hpaya   ■ Gu Bizat

Nga-myet-hna ■

Maha-bodhi ■

PAGAN

■ Gadaw-palin

Archaeology Department Museum

■ Pitaka-taik

Tharba Gate

Old Museum

■ Ananda Ok-kyaung

■ Ananda

■ Shwe-gu-gyi

● Nga-kywe-na-daung

■ Pa-hto-tha-mya

■ That-byin-nyu

Nat-hlaung-kyaung

City walls

■ Mi-nyein-gon

■ Myin-pya-gu

Thiriyapyitsaya Hotel

■ Hsin-pya-gu

■ Pa-tha-da

■ Mye-bon-tha-hpaya-hla

● Scovell's Paw-daw-mu

■ Loka-hteik-pan

● Mingala-zeidi

■ Pe-nan-tha-gu

■ Thein-mazi

● Shwe-hsan-daw

Dhamma-yan-gyi ■

■ Loka-ok-shaung

■ M. Kubyauk-ngè

■ M. Kubyauk-gyi

■ North Gu Ni

● Mya-zeidi

■ South Gu Ni

MYINKABA

■ Manuha

■ Nan-hpaya

■ Kyasin

Abe-ya-dana ■

■ Naga-yon

Somin-gyi Stupa ●

Somin-gyi Monastery ■

When the Lord Buddha thus smiled, from his four eye teeth rays of six colours issued forth and went up as far as Brahmalok; while down below the rays penetrated all earth, water, and air; across all the four quarters of the thousand million universes they went; and then the rays entered into the Lord Buddha's mouth again. The Lord Anan seeing this miracle, bowed down and put on his head the soles of the Lord Buddha's feet, and then lifting his joined hands questioned him thus: "What reason was there that my Lord did smile thus? For without reason Buddha's do not smile". Thus did the Lord Anan ask.

Thereupon the Buddha spake to the Lord Anan thus: "Anan, hereafter a sage named Bishnu, great in supernatural power, great in glory, possessing the five transcendental faculties....shall go up to Brahmalok; and departing from Brahmalok, shall come down to be in the city of Arimaddanapur (Pagan), and shall bear the name of King Sri Tribhuwanadityadhammaraja and shall uphold my religion". Thus did the Buddha tell the reason of his smile to the Lord Anan.

PART ONE

Introduction:
The Western Discovery of Pagan

The whole, as seen from the river, might pass for a scene in another planet, so fantastic and unearthly was the architecture.

Henry Yule, 1855

THIS WORK is in all senses an introduction to the art and architecture of the Pagan Dynasty. It is perhaps the first 'art history' of the three periods into which the art of the dynasty may be divided, according to transition in style, conception, and, to a lesser extent, iconography. Such a work has been conceived as being of use to both the scholar and the more interested visitor to Pagan. This is always an awkward balance, but it is hoped that in addition to guiding the traveller about the city and its many monuments, it will explain something of the dynastic art's origins and evolutions and something of the monuments' functions and the conceptions underlying their construction, in greater detail than a pocket guide book, whilst lacking the cumbersome nature of a more detailed and encyclopedic study.

No complete study in English of the dynastic art and architecture of Pagan has been attempted before. What scholarship that exists is often confusing or even contradictory in its conclusions. Furthermore, 'art history', that is, the analysis of style, its origins and end, the transition of motif and form, has, as a discipline, never been applied to the art of the Pagan dynasty. An assortment of learned articles on the ethnography, epigraphy, orthography and iconography of the period and one major three-volume analysis of the Early Period, by G.H. Luce, were the main contribution of colonial period scholarship. Even the Archaeological Survey of India was scant in its exploration of the city and in the various reports running through the colonial period it appears that resources were applied to conservation rather than exploration. Unlike the French and Dutch parts of South East Asia, there was little attempt to record systematically and analyse the monuments found here. It has not been till this decade that the Ecole Française d'Extrême-Orient have applied their own more systematic and meticulous tradition of archaeological analysis in recording the city's monuments in their entirety.[1]

This book has been built upon over a century of Pagan studies by Westerners. Even today, numerous monuments have escaped study, and in the following chapters significant omissions are numerous. (It was not until the sixties, over one hundred years since the first analysis of the monuments by Henry Yule, that the

highly significant Lokha-teik-pan temple was discovered by the *Bohmu* Ba Shin and his group.[2]) This work represents a reorganisation of existing scholarship, a reinterpretation of many past theories that have not worn well with time, a more balanced periodisation, and, to a limited extent, the introduction of a number previously unpublished monuments. Thus, this book is perhaps little more than a synthesis and revision of existing work, attempting to guide and encourage, rather than to define and state.

Much work remains to be done at Pagan, not just in restoration and conservation, but in exploration and study. In the past, historical research at Pagan has mainly involved the translation and study of contemporary epigraphy, indeed, a valid and elucidating source for understanding contemporary events, society and religious life.[3] It is intended that this book will 'introduce' the possibility that the monuments themselves, all 2,217 of them, are an equally valid and elucidating source for an understanding of the dynasty in all its aspects. Through the study of these temples and stupas; their origins and development; the cosmology and the conceptions behind them; their ornament within and without; their forms, and the functions that related to these forms, a vision of all that Pagan was begins to unfold itself.

G.H. Luce, the doyen of Pagan studies, spent a lifetime of research and study in Burma and produced a life's work named *Old Burma- Early Pagan,* a work that is encyclopedic in scope and erudite in its scholarship, that Luce himself likened "to a torso without head or feet".[4] For, though three volumes were filled with meticulous analysis of Pagan's history, iconography and architecture, only the 'Early Period' and part of the 'Middle Period' were included, in other words up to the completion of the great and mysterious Dhamma-yan-gyi temple in the mid-12th century: the end of the experimental phase in architecture. Luce's masterpiece, together with the great corpus of his learned articles, are much referred to in the following chapters. It is to Luce that any student of Burma's early history, art and archaeology is indebted and here it must be emphasised that without Luce's pioneering work the writing of this book would never have been possible. Any pioneering study, by its nature, must err in places, and though certain of Luce's

*No.1: the Shwe-gu-gyi, c.1855
by Colesworthy Grant from
Yule's Narrative*

conclusions may be questionable, and indeed are questioned and reinterpreted above, this does not lessen the debt owed to Luce by any student of these periods.[5]

The story of the western discovery of Pagan is of some interest and a necessary prelude to the chapters that follow—that in a sense are the sum, or synthesis, of these earlier discoveries.

Marco Polo, in the late 13th century, as member of the Mongol emperor Kublai Khan's entourage, was most likely the first European to learn of the city. In 1298 he was to dictate, whilst in prison in Genoa:

> You must know that at the end of fifteen days journey lies a city called Mien (Burma) of great size and splendour, which is the capital of the kingdom. The inhabitants are idolators and speak a language of their own. They are subject to the Great Khan. And in this city is a very remarkable object of which I will now tell you.[6]

Marco Polo goes on to describe great gilded towers and the finials of monuments, "...and round the whole circuit were little gilded bells that tinkled every time the wind blew through them", just like the *hti* of Burma today.[7] Marco Polo may not have physically visited Pagan; however, in December 1283 when the Mongols engaged the Burmese forces at Nga-saun-gyan in the north and defeated them, it was this battle that Polo witnessed and described in some detail in *The Travels*. As a direct consequence of the Great Khan's victory he wrote: "And from this day forward the Khan began to have elephants in plenty."

In 1795 Michael Symes led a diplomatic mission, from the Governor General of India to the Court of Ava, and travelled up the Irrawaddy, from the coast to the capital, passing Pagan and noting it in his account.[8] Symes was most likely not the first European to spot Pagan from the river, for at least two centuries before this Western mercenaries had been in the pay of the various kings and dynasties operating in the region.

However, such men of action were rarely men of letters and left no record of their impressions of the former capital. By the middle part of the 18th century, early envoys from the East India Company had begun to visit Ava, though they barely gave the former capital a mention in their various reports and narratives. Pagan was not a significant staging post on the river route, and even today steamers stop upstream at Nyaung-U and not at the village itself. Thus in 1795 Michael Symes recorded his impression:

> Leaving the temple at Logahnunda (Lokha-nanda), we approached the once magnificent city of Pagaham. We could see little more from the river than a few straggling houses, which have the appearance of having once been a connected street: in fact, scarcely anything remains of ancient Pagaham, except its numerous moulding temples, and the vestiges of an old brick fort, the ramparts of which are still to be traced.[9]

On his return journey Symes actually visited some of the temples and mentioned the regilding and restoration operations in progress, for it was at this time that King Bodawpaya sent the Crown Prince, who took the title 'Prince of Pagan', to supervise the restoration of the city.[10] It is significant that the Burmese themselves discovered the significance, symbolic, historical or artistic, of Pagan, and commenced restoration work there, exactly a century before the British were to introduce 'archaeology' to the region.

It was close to Pagan that one of the final engagements of the First Anglo-Burmese War of 1826 was fought; Colonel Havelock in his history of the campaign noted of the monuments:

> The sensation of barren wonderment is the only one which Pagaham excites. There is little to admire, nothing to venerate, nothing to exalt the notion of the taste and invention of the people that the traveller might have already formed in Rangoon or Prome.[11]

Pagan's significance was to await recognition from the West. Indeed, only with the recognition of the antiquity and past glory of Pagan, would contemporary Burmese civilisation gain some credibility with the envoys visiting the Burmese court during this period.

John Crawfurd, in his account of the 1827 expedition, mentions that his party stopped off and toured some of the ruins. Crawfurd was no antiquarian and his observations are general; though the monuments did impress the envoy of the value of Burma's demised civilisation, he was to write: "The vast extent of the ruins of Pagan, and the extent and splendour of its religious edifices, may be considered by some as proofs of considerable civilisation among the Burmans."[12] A number of Crawfurd's observations are of some interest today to the historian of Pagan, for example, he counted some fifty-three inscriptions stored in the hall of the Maha-bodhi Temple (the temple itself he likened to that of a neat English parish church).[13] In 1835, Captain Hannay, on his way to survey amber mines to the north, mentioned in his narrative that the monuments "were covered with jungle on top", and in 1837 a Rev. Kinncaird visited Pagan.[14]

It was in 1855 that one Scotsman, Henry Yule, commissioned in the Bengal Engineers, visited the old capital on his way to Ava where he, as the envoy Phayre's secretary, like Symes, was to visit the Court in the aftermath of the Second Anglo-Burmese War of 1852. With Phayre, Yule disembarked and explored the city, instantly recognising the historical and architectural significance of the monuments. Using his skills as a military engineer, he surveyed a number of the principal monuments and recorded his explorations in his *Narrative of the Mission to the Court of Ava in 1855.* Captain Linnaeus Tripe, who accompanied Yule, possessed a very early camera and took the first photographs of Pagan and the artist Colesworthy Grant made a number of sketches, which with Tripe's photographs, were reworked to create colour illustrations for the *Narrative.*[15]

Yule was thus the first foreign visitor, possibly since Marco Polo, to recognise the importance of Pagan and he wrote in the *Narrative:* "Pagan surprised us all. None of the preceding visitors to Ava had prepared us for remains of such importance and interest." [16] Yule and his party were the first Westerners to realise the importance of Pagan and convey it to the rest of the world together with the drawings, sketches and written descriptions of the monuments that he included in the *Narrative.*

Following this visit, Dr Emil Forchammer, a roving German archaeologist, came to Pagan in 1881, only five years before the absorption of Upper Burma into the British Empire.[17] It is uncertain whether Forchammer's visit was a response to Yule's pioneering, albeit brief, study, however, Forchammer presented a detailed report on the Kyauk-ku-ohn-min temple near Nyaung-U that was printed by the Superintendent of Government printing in 1891, along with the publication of reports on various other monuments throughout Burma.[18] It seems strange that Forchammer should carry out so articulate a study of such an obscure, though by no means insignificant, temple. One may wonder if, perhaps, as this temple is closer to the old landing stage at Nyaung-U than the Pagan village sites, whether Forchammer only had time for one study, executed with a Teutonic exactness.

The next visitor to Pagan was also German, though less academically inclined than Forchammer, Fritz von

No.2: the Dhamma-yangyi, c.1855, by Colesworthy Grant, from Yule's Narrative

Nöetling, an expert on oil matters, who used to holiday in Pagan whilst preparing a report on the Yenangyaung oil fields not far to the south of the old city.[19] These holidays were mainly spent in detaching glazed plaques from the Mingala-zeidi, Dhammayazika and Somin-gyi stupas, in addition to removing various Vishnu sculptures from the Nat-hlaung-kyaung, that eventually found their way to the Berlin Völkerkunde Museum.[20]

The Teutonic exactness of Forchammer returned to Pagan in 1899, though in this case it was a destructively inclined exactness, with the arrival of the so-called 'Doctor' Th. Thomann, and his party of fellow Germans.[21] Though Thomann may be credited with producing the first book on Pagan, he may also be credited with systematically dismantling some of Pagan's finest mural paintings, which he subsequently launched on the Euro-art markets of the day, eventually to be sold to the Hamburg Ethnographical Museum, at no slight discount on the original asking price. Today, one may see the scars of Thomann's work on the vault of the Wetkyi-in Kubyauk-gyi: tattered newspapers, used to lift the sections of plaster off, remain stuck to the vaults and the sawed cuts, in neat lines, reveal Thomann's method of cutting loose the murals in rectangular sections. Thomann and his group visited other temples too, at one, the Paya-nga-zu group, their names are scrawled upon the wall.[22] Fortunately, though belatedly, Thomann's activities were arrested by the District Commissioner of Myingyan. The road from Pagan to Myingyan is of comparatively recent construction and news of the German's activities took some time to reach the Commissioner. The German party was subsequently expelled from Burma, though much of their loot had been sent ahead, thereby escaping confiscation. The present location, or even existence, of the Wetkyi-in paintings is not known and the murals taken from the Thein-ma-zi temple which are now at Hamburg are little displayed.[23] Happy will the day be when these treasures are returned to their rightful places on the walls, vaults and soffits of these now denuded temples.

Tragically, thieving from the monuments continues to this day, for so long as dealers can command high prices from wealthy collectors, 'greed' will drive less fortunate local people to thieve and vandalise. Luce in 1948 lectured:

> Germans alas were not the only vandals, though they were the worst. I have myself met more than one globetrotter, bag in hand, "souveniring" among the ruins. There used to be statuettes, and small objects of dedication in the temples; one never sees them now.[24]

Nowadays, the Burmese Government, anxious to save what remains of their early civilisations, have banned the export of antiquities, yet still they pass out to the thickly carpeted galleries of more affluent places, in the protected baggage of the diplomatic community. Perhaps those that connive to rob Pagan of her riches

should mind the dreadful curses placed upon those who take from a work of merit, and mind that Thomann suffered a tragic death in mysterious circumstances.[25]

In 1886 Upper Burma was annexed, and by 1900 the region had been pacified and the British regime turned their eye to the archaeological possibilities of Burma. In 1901 Lord Curzon, the Imperial Viceroy, came to Burma. A highly cultivated man, Curzon was quick to realise the full value of Burma's Buddhist civilisation. In Mandalay he commanded that the royal palace should be conserved, and the drinking club set up by the conquerors, in one of the throne rooms, be removed elsewhere.[26] Curzon stopped at Pagan on his way upstream and ordered the construction of a museum there, the original Ananda Museum. In the year following this fortuitous visit, the Archaeological Survey of India set up a 'Burma Circle' under the directorship of Taw Sein Ko who contributed each year to the Survey's *Annual Reports*.

Taw Sein Ko, of Peking Lodge in Mandalay, a Chinese in the Indian Civil Service, was responsible for inaugurating the western discipline of archaeology into Burma. In his reports his interpretations are highly Sino-centric: *chinthe* are Chinese, stupas are of the Chinese type as are palaces. Though he did acknowledge that Buddhism was of Indian origin, his tributary mentality permitted little else to have seeped through from that direction. However, under his directorship (1901-15), temples were repaired, reports that are now valuable sources on lost structures were published and some exploration was carried out. It was under his directorship that the first list of the monuments was prepared with the assistance of the old and venerable headman of Pwasaw, U Tin U. On their rounds together Taw Sein Ko would ask U Tin U the name of a monument, U Tin U would pause in deep thought and, rather than disappoint the official, invent some apt name.[27] These spontaneously invented names for many of the less well known monuments remain in use today and are followed in the monument descriptions that are discussed in Part Two of this work. Taw Sein Ko wrote the first tourist guide on Pagan, for by this time Pagan was opening up to the traveller:

NOTES FOR TOURISTS

Express steamers, which ply up and down the Irrawaddy twice a week, do not actually touch at Pagan, but at Nyaung-U, which is five miles distant from the Pagan Circuit House. There is a good circuit House at Nyaung-U, where the Post and Telegraph Offices are situated. At both circuit houses, the Khansamah can supply meals. Ferry boats, which start from Myingyan, call daily at Nyaung-u and Pagan (Sundays excepted), and Pagan can be reached from Nyaung-u by these boats. The journey can also be made by country boats, by bullock carts, or on horse back, according to the inclination of tourists.[28]

It was with the arrival of a Frenchman, Charles

Duroiselle, in 1915 that a sounder archaeology at last came to Burma. Duroiselle, a Pali scholar, commenced the immense task of both exploration and conservation, not just at Pagan but at other sites, particularly the former Pyu capital of Sri Ksetra. Duroiselle attempted systematically to measure, analyse and assess the monuments, publishing his reports and memoirs in the publications of the Archaeological Survey of India. Perhaps his finest work was his 'memoir' on the Ananda Temple.[29] However, Duroiselle should primarily be remembered for his translation of a number of the lithic inscriptions in *Epigraphica Birmanica*, which he edited with C.O. Blagden, and which ran from 1919 onwards. Blagden is a name also to be remembered in any story of the introduction of archaeological and historical studies in Burma; he brilliantly deciphered the Pyu script for the first time, after eight hundred years of disuse, in addition to exploring the great wealth of Mon lithic inscriptions.

Despite Duroiselle's work, much remained to be done; the emphasis was very much on epigraphy, and though the old Ananda Museum had been set up, it mainly housed inscriptions collected for safe storage there. Comparatively few of the monuments had actually been explored; whole areas, like mural painting and iconography, remained undocumented—the task of research, at Pagan, had barely begun; yet, despite lack of resources and manpower that lead to ill-thought restoration in the case of Hpet-leik, it was not a bad start, and Pagan was perhaps lucky to be in the care of a Pali scholar..

Duroiselle was followed by a number of highly competent Burmese directors, particularly Mya , Lu Pe Win and Bo Kay, yet though a system of numbering had been devised, and the job of conservation continued, exploration at Pagan remained limited and our knowledge of the monuments and their significance expanded little. For example, though the approximate location of the palace is known, the site has never been dug. Likewise, the Dhamma-yan-gyi enigma remains unsolved despite recent discoveries.[30]

In 1912, a group of young Cambridge aesthetes, that included E.M. Forster, nurtured by Bloomsbury, and all former Cambridge Apostles, set sail from England to take up academic appointments of various sorts in the colonies.[31] Thus, Gordon Hannington Luce came from Cambridge to Burma to teach at the Government College in Rangoon. Burma was lucky. Luce soon became besotted by the country and was to dedicate his life to the study of the literature, languages, history and art of old Burma. Though neither an archaeologist, nor expert in oriental languages by training (he read Classics and English at Cambridge), Luce was quick to master not only the Old Burmese and Mon epigraphic sources, but also the Chinese sources relating to Burma. A poet by calling, compassionate by nature, he took a Burmese wife and had little love for the club society of the colonials. Luce never belonged to the Archaeological Survey, though he worked closely with them, and after the foundation of a

university at Rangoon in 1920, where he lectured first in English and then in Burmese and Far Eastern History, Luce's personal research into Pagan history, reinforced by a study leave spent at the Sorbonne under Louis Finot and Paul Pelliot of the Ecole Française d'Extrême-Orient, was prolific and enormously productive.[32] Luce trained his servant in the art of making rubbings and sent him off to search round the districts for previously unknown inscriptions.[33] Luce saw the clue to an understanding of Pagan in the study of languages and literature and as Professor Tinker said:

> The erudition he now employed was quite amazing. He ranges over so many texts that the reader not so well equipped linguistically is left breathless. If his main sources are Chinese, he also demonstrates his mastery of Greek and Latin texts as well as considerable familiarity with Pali, Sanskrit, and even of the Tamil, Malay, Arabic and Persian languages. This polymath was also his autodidact. Languages which other men require a lifetime to master became his linguistic tool within a few years.[34]

Linguist Luce was, and it is in this role, together with his brother-in-law U Pe Maung Tin and his friend *Bohmu* Ba Shin, that his name will be remembered. Luce was not trained as an art historian; indeed this discipline developed late in Britain, and, thus, late in her colonies. In his encyclopedic study of 'Early Period' Pagan, a work that represented the findings of a life's research, Luce was to set out one of the most difficult stories a historian could ever attempt to tell. Unlike so many scholarly works, it is a work as beautiful as that which it explains; if there are inaccuracies and errors they are outweighed by a high degree of exactness and insight elsewhere. If, at times, his Cambridge aestheticism shines through, with gorgeous prose-poetry, it is a joy for the reader and hardly a distraction. Luce was a 'romantic', yet he combined his romanticism with scholarly precision, erudition and insight. Though he has since been much criticised by Burmese scholars for his belief that Pagan culture was extracted from that of the Mons, he may easily be excused for this.[35] Likewise, though in his assessment of many of the monuments he ignores the process of evolution of style, form and motif, and bases all on either epigraphy, or perhaps his muse, he must still be honoured for offering a foundation upon which works such as this may be built.

With the outbreak of the 1939-45 war, archaeological work stopped and Pagan was, as in 1826, to come close to being the site of a major last battle, on this occasion between the advancing allies and the retreating Japanese. Fortunately, the temple-studded plain escaped the attention of heavy artillery and aerial bombings, in other words the inevitable destruction that modern warfare would bring. This escape was due to the direct intervention of Luce at the allies' headquarters and Luce has been remembered in a

Burmese poem which compared him with Shin Dis-apramuk, who intervened with the Mongol Khan to save Pagan from destruction at the end of the 13th century:

And we, like orphaned children,
Were helpless to protect Pagán—
Singly stood Pramuk Velu,
A fortress like Mount Meru,
Guarding Pagán's golden rayed
Temples, stupas, arches, sikharas.[36]

Pagan folk still talk much of their great *saya*, re-membering how, in his explorations, he would always circumvent a field for fear of damaging a crop.

Since Luce, little that is original on Pagan's art and architecture has appeared. His disciples and friends, whom he trained or encouraged for the task, have continued his work though much hampered by lack of resources and encouragement.[37] With Burma's in-dependence, exploration has tended towards the Pyu sites and as a consequence surprisingly little remains known of the material culture of the Pagan periods. Dr Than Tun, a Burmese historian, has contributed much to our knowledge of Pagan's history, social and economic life, in, firstly, a brilliant doctoral thesis and then a series of articles published in various learned journals, through the detailed study of epigraphic sources.[38] Meanwhile, at Pagan, the work of conser-vation and restoration continued under the direction of the Burma Archaeology Department.

In 1975 a disaster of tragic and monstrous pro-portions struck the city that had so narrowly escaped destruction in the last war, in the form of an earth-quake. Entire temples, like the Bu-hpaya, were demol-ished, the superstructure of the Gadaw-palin was completely destroyed, perhaps the worst sufferers were the numerous Konbaung period structures, like the Upali Thein, whose brickwork was less sound than that of the Pagan periods and cracked in many places ruining the once vivid mural paintings. Thus, in addition to restoring a vast number of already decayed monuments, the department was faced with the task of initiating a number of large scale building opera-tions. Fortunately, UNDP / UNESCO came to Burma's assistance with funds and expertise and rebuilding has proceeded not only speedily but accurately, following the original designs.[39] Following from these restora-tions, UNESCO have sponsored the Ecole Française d' Extrême-Orient to assist the Archaeology Department in the ambitious scheme of making a complete inven-tory of all the monuments, with the intention to publish the plans, photographs and descriptions of each monument in the near future.[40] This vast work will greatly assist the scholar of the future in a study of Pagan architecture, and record less well-known structures in case of future destruction. Thus, there is some hope for the art history of Pagan.

No.3: G.H. Luce

1
The Rise of a Dynasty at Pagan

AT PAGAN there are over two thousand extant Buddhist monuments scattered across the arid and dusty plain. Built mainly of a red-baked brick, they glow like rich jewels, elevating believer and non-believer alike.[1]

Though Pagan's origins are in the mid-9th century, the large scale construction of temples did not begin until the mid-11th century under the first historical ruler Anawrahta (1044-77).[2] In this unlikely place, with the lowest rainfall in all Burma, the first Burmese Buddhist civilisation, on an imperial scale, grew up. Nurtured with the teachings and philosophy of the Buddhist faith that at this time underwent a royally promoted purification, the early Burman rose above tribalism and formed a nation, the first 'Union of Burma', composed of ethnic groups such as the Mon, the survivors of the Pyu, the Arakanese and others.[3] Each race lent something of its own cultural life, indigenous or alien, to the young Burmese. Pagan must have been a cosmopolitan place: here, the North Indian of Bengal met with southern Tamils and Singhalese, the Chinese diplomat with the Cambodian merchant, the Mon monk with the Hindu brahman and the Arakanese consort with the Indian concubine.

Pagan: Arimaddanapura, 'the City of the Enemy Crusher', or Tambadipa 'the Land of Copper', are some of the original names of old Pagan used in the lithic inscriptions.[4] Pagan itself, as a name, is first written in an inscription erected before 1050 on the Panrang River in Annam, it talks of the city of Pukam, and in Burmese 'Pukam' is not actually written until 1196, in a stone inscription.

Suggestions that once the plain of Pagan was afforested and that the trees were cut during this period to fire the kilns that baked the brick, thus causing a climatic change, would seem to be ruled out, for other early inscriptions refer to the city as the Tattadessa or 'parched land'. In other brick-based cultures, for example Mohenjo Daro in the Indus Valley, deforestation may have been responsible for some climatic change, and it is likely that the original Pagan was once a greener place.[7] Tree planting in Pagan times was a meritorious activity and many a lithic inscription mentions the planting of shady fruit-bearing trees about a dedication, from which the clergy might gain shelter in addition to sustenance. No kilns for brick baking, have been found, though a little to the south of Myinkaba village there are artificial depressions, most likely caused by the digging of clay. However, a number of the bricks used during the Pagan dynastic periods were marked with the name of the place of their production—riverside locations, as far south as Minbu and as far north as Monywa on the Chindwin;

places of more abundant firewood, and conveniently close to the water for transportation.[8]

The original site of the city was on the inside of a bend in the Irrawaddy's course. The city walls meet the river on the up and downstream side of the bend, thus the broad river formed two sides of the capital's defences and water from the river filled the moat.[9] These walls are still traceable. The river's erosion has depleted the part of the city that was close to the river's banks, washing away many temples and their treasures. Starting close to the present Irra Inn, the walls curve inland to the Tharba Gateway, through which the Pagan main road now runs, along to the massive That-byin-nyu, and round it on its outer side, to continue back to the river, meeting it close by to the old Circuit House.[10] The moat is now dry, yet its course may still be followed along the outer side of the tumbled walls. Within the walls stood the palace for which there is the date 1101/2, in the reign of Kyanzittha (1084-1113), as documented in an elucidating inscription found near the Tharba gate.[11] The inscription also describes in some detail the Brahmanic rituals used in the ceremonial construction of the palace. The walls are older; Duroiselle, the first archaeologist to seriously work in Burma, dated them to c.850, as did the chronicles.[12]

There would have been other palaces before Kyanzittha's, possibly at the village of Thiriyapyitsaya, south of Pagan, on the road to Chauk, as is told by many of the local Pagan people to this day.[13] Nothing survives. Built of wood, such structures perish quickly in so harsh a climate. Indeed, Pagan was a city of wood. The empty spaces between the surviving pagodas were once filled with richly carved wooden architecture: elaborate wooden monasteries, rest houses, and, of course, the homes of the people who once populated the city. The few fragments of wood-carving that survive, and depictions of wooden architecture in the mural paintings of the time, give some impression of the brilliance of the Pagan woodcarvers craft, a tradition that has continued in Burma up to the present.[14] One may wonder whether the Pagan Burmese, perhaps leading a nomadic or migratory existence before settling in this strategic location, first came to express themselves artistically in the medium of wood before progressing to stone.

Unlike the older Pyu city of Sri Ksetra, where the entire population and the land that they cultivated, were within the bounds of the walls, at Pagan only the king, court and certain crown service groups were quartered within the now more limited confines of the city walls. Burma, by the 11th century, was a more secure place to live in as the artisan and mercantile population, not to mention the sacred monastic communities, could be safely accommodated beyond the city's defences. This sets the pattern for later Burmese cities right up to the foundation of the last royal city of Mandalay in 1856.[15]

The city is located at the heart of the 'dry zone' with one of the lowest annual rainfalls in Burma. Despite the inclement climate and problems of water supply (that continue there to this day), the location of the administrative and military nerve centre of a rapidly expanding young empire here was excellent. In command of the Irrawaddy river, sited just a few miles downstream from its great tributary the Chindwin, that flows down from India and Assam, Pagan stood midway between the delta trading ports of the Mons and the China road, between the river and overland routes to India, and the scattered trails that still weave through the hills to the east, to the remainder of South-East Asia.[16] Pagan was the crossroads for traders as well as armies—contemporary inscriptions refer to Pagan as the 'hub' or, *kharuin*.[17] Thus, the dynasty's art and architecture reflected the multitude of cultural cross currents that met here with indigenous elements. Though Pagan may be said to have undergone a process historians name as 'Indianisation',[18] elements of indigenous culture survived and integrated with the imported. Indeed, 'Indianised' states had for several centuries evolved to create their own unique variant forms of Indian-based religious and cultural life. Thus, Pagan received not only a direct input of Indian artistic forms, from the mid-11th century onwards, but also an adapted version from the hands of the pre-Pagan Mon and Pyu kingdoms, whose cultural life had been incorporated into that of Pagan, before the rise of the city to statehood.[19] Pagan was to rise above being a mere syncretism, her art is never hybrid, for Burmese convictions rose to mould the imported into shapes that satisfied their own temperaments.

The Pyu have been said to be the first wave of a migration of the Burmese people, possibly, according to Luce, from the Nanchao region of north-west China.[20] Luce believed that, further to this, from the 9th century onwards, a second migration of the Early Burmese took place. Their settlements expanded in central Burma, where they learnt, under the tutelage of the Pyu, how to cultivate wet rice, and developed urbanised states, particularly in the area known as the 'rice bowl of Burma' around Kyaukse. One of these states was Pagan, who rose to be the dominant settlement, and established precedence over her rivals. However, as Pagan's early iconography and architecture indicates, there was little difference between her and the Pyu's cultural life. It may be questioned whether there was a clear racial distinction between the Pyu and Burmese, and surmised that Pagan succeeded Sri Ksetra, and the other early city states, in the political vacuum left by the Nanchao raid of c.732.

Influenced by Indian conceptions of statecraft and government brought to the emergent city-power by brahmans from India, no doubt attracted by the riches service to so great a state would bring, Pagan was to develop into an empire under the military prowess of Anawrahta (1044-1077). It would, though, be a grave mistake to assume that Anawrahta was the first king of Pagan-Burma. He was most likely an exceptionally capable chieftain, from a long line of forebears, whose good accumulation of *kamma* enabled him to unify Burma, just as Asoka had once done in India. Theravada Buddhism assisted Anawrahta in his territorial conquests. The later chronicles make it clear that any conquest was inspired by motives of Buddhism, usually an attempt to secure some powerful relic, or a set of rare scriptures. However, most likely the motives were more economic and Anawrahta sought, in addition to the riches of the Mon canon, the riches of her seaports.[21]

The chronicles, not always a reliable source, tell how Anawrahta, moved by religious zeal and under the influence of one Mon Theravada monk, Shin Arahan, requested a set of the Tipitaka, the Theravada Buddhist scriptures, from the Mon king, Manuha of Thaton. He was refused and therefore seized the scriptures by military force and brought them to Pagan together with the captive king, Manuha, and his court, not to mention artists and artisans.[22] Once returned to Pagan, and under this Mon influence, he set about eliminating heterodox sects in favour of Theravada Buddhism, and commencing what was to be one of the greatest temple building eras in the history of mankind. As there is no lithic evidence to support such a theory of 'pious motivation' the raid may be said to be simply an act of aggression on the lucrative delta ports, capturing much needed manpower for resettlement in Upper Burma, in addition to gaining access to the international maritime world of the period.[23] Possibly, according to Luce, Anawrahta sought to intervene in a Cambodian campaign against Pegu.[24] The significance of the raid is that it led to an injection of Mon culture into Pagan that was to have a profound effect on religious, and moreover literary, life after 1260. It is, though, misleading to think of the Mon as Theravada purists, whilst possessing the literature of the Jatakas, as seen in the carvings of the original Kalyani Thein and the plaques of the Thagya Pagoda; Brahmanic and Mahayanist elements had been incorporated into Mon culture, for not inconsiderable amounts of Vaishnaivite sculpture have been found in the Mon country.[25] It must be emphasised that Mon cultural influence on 11th century Pagan extended to literature only, not the visual arts as has been originally supposed.[26]

By the advent of the Middle Period, in the reign of Sithu II (1113-70), the empire extended from Katha, in the north, to Thaton and possibly even Mergui in the south.[27] Arakan was never fully incorporated into the empire, yet paid tribute, and was claimed by Pagan; the chronicles mention a marriage connection between Anawrahta and a princess of the Vesali kingdom, which may well have been the Vesali of ancient Arakan.[28] Through the construction of pagodas, and enshrining within them clay votive tablets bearing his seal, Anawrahta, at the outer limits of the empire, indicated the extent of his territories.[29]

After the conquest of Thaton, Anawrahta marched on the old Pyu capital of Sri Ksetra.[30] The Pyu had remained a potent cultural force in Burma and Anawrahta may have regarded the Pyu as his dynastic and cultural forerunner. To differentiate ethnically between Pyu and Early Burman is deceptive. Pagan dates back to Pyu times, and was originally one of many city states, existing contemporary to the great Pyu centres, practicing wet rice cultivation in central Burma. Moreover, the fall of Sri Ksetra in 832-5 to the Nanchao does not necessarily imply the annihilation of the Pyu and their civilisation. Whilst at Sri Ksetra, Anawrahta opened the massive Baw-baw-gyi stupa and removed the relic to take it back for re-enshrinement at his own capital, leaving behind, within the Baw-baw-gyi *tabena*, some of his own signed votive tablets.[31] This was symbolic of the absorption of the old Pyu heartland into Anawrahta's renewing empire.

Pagan's religion and art were not suddenly imported wholesale from the south after the Thaton raid of 1060. Indian religions had been professed in Burma for at least three centuries prior to this date. Coexisting without struggle, the Theravada, Mahayana and the Brahmanic cults have left their remains in the cities of the Pyu, Mon and Arakanese. The Pyu fell to the Nanchao Chinese in c.832-5, and there was a power vacum into which the Early Burmans stepped, absorbing elements of their culture. It is around this date that the Pagan city walls were built (850) and as late as 1113 a Pagan quadrilingual inscription still uses the Pyu script together with the Mon, Pali and Early Burmese scripts.[32] The Pagan temple type is derived from the early brick temples of the Pyu capital of Sri Ksetra, such as the Be-be and Lei-myet-hna temples, where radiating arches and a voussoir type brickwork, of the same kind used at Pagan, are to be found. The Pyus were fine workers of bronze and makers of exquisite jewellery. They passed on all this to Pagan.[33]

There are no surviving temples from these early times in the Mon country, for the relentless monsoon rains of the delta have simply dissolved all early brickworks. To suggest that the Early Pagan temple type is Mon cannot be substantiated. Luce goes so far as to describe the Early Period as the " 'Mon' period".[34] This assumption is based on the fact that the Old Mon script was used for the glosses on temple walls that narrate pictorial scenes, and on terracotta plaques illustrating 550 Jataka tales. Whilst Mon culture was doubtless a significant literary force in Early Pagan, there is no substantive evidence to suggest that the Mons originated the type of brick temple found at Early Pagan. The main contribution of the Mons to Pagan was this Jataka literature, and their language that was used to narrate it. This literary tradition was combined with the Pyu temple building tradition, more contemporary South and North Indian decorative

currents, and the courageous and aspiring spirit of the early Burman—the daring quest for an architectural ultimate that embodied his search for an escape from *samsara*, and thirst for *nibbana*.

More significant than the assimilation of the federation of Mon port-states, such as Bassein, Twante and Thaton, after Anawrahta's 1060 conquest, was the opening up of Burma to the influences of the older Theravada country of Ceylon, and possibly to a lesser degree, South Indian artistic influences. For the conquest of Thaton gave Pagan access to sea, and thus to Ceylon. It is known from contemporary epigraphy that Anawrahta assisted his fellow Buddhist king, and contemporary Vijaya Bahu I (1055-1110) in the defeat of the Saivite South Indian Cola, who had occupied that sacred isle bringing about a wane of its Pali Buddhism, and in the re-establishment of the Theravada faith there.[35] It would seem that whilst Ceylon possessed the *pitaka*, they lacked the *bhikkhu*. Monks exchanged missions as well as diplomats, occasionally monks were diplomats, and in addition to monks women were exchanged between the two courts. Thus began a tradition of cultural exchange and periodic renewal between the two countries that has continued up till the present time.[36]

At Pagan, new Pali texts were introduced from the late 11th century onwards—this is apparent in the subjects chosen by the painters of murals. From the reign of Anawrahta, few temples, as distinct from stupas, were either built or survive. However, at Kyauk-ku-ohn-min, which, along with the Nan-hpaya, may be attributed to his reign, some mural painting does remain, triad panels of the Buddha with his two foremost disciples, Mogallana and Sariputta, which are repeated identically across vaults and soffits, the uppermost being polychromed coffered mouldings. These are intended to portray the moment of the delivery of a *sutta*, or discourse, by the Buddha. At this early stage, other than Jataka estampages, pictorial illustration of the events of the Buddha's life had not yet been applied to broad narrative cycles on temple walls, though, again at Kyauk-ku, the Pagan artist was attempting to release the principal scenes from the life of the Buddha, from the eight or nine scenes presented together in a cycle on a votive tablet, to individual stone reliefs. With the maritime opening, left by the removal of the Mon hegemony of the seaboard, new, purified texts arrive at Pagan and are deciphered and expounded by the monks to the artists who disseminated their message or story on the wall space and statuary of temples.

By the time of the next great reign after Anawrahta, that of Kyanzittha (1084-1113), not only was the Pagan artist in possession of more detailed texts on the life of the Buddha, and past buddhas, namely the *Nidanakatha* and *Buddhavamsa*, which seemed to be the most popular narratives for pictorial exposition at Pagan, but also his competence as painter, or sculptor, had improved.[38] For example, examine the great leap in the sculptor's skill from the Kyauk-ku reliefs, to those at the Naga-yon, or, alternatively, note the sudden liberation of the painter's brush from the tight triad panels of the Kuyauk-ku vaults to the broad, freize-like narrative of the Pa-hto-tha-mya.[34]

Towards the end of Anawrahta's reign, the system for numbering the Jataka changed from a Mon recension to the Ceylonese recension, and under Kyanzittha (1084-1113) a revision of the *pitaka* or scriptures, again on a Ceylonese model, is noticeable in the choice of subjects employed in contemporary painting schemes.[40] By the time of Rajakumar's temple building activity, at the turn of the 11th to 12th centuries, and his supervision of the Myinkaba Kubyauk-gyi construction work in 1113, the wider range of texts that were selected for translation into the medium of painting, demonstrates the great progress of scholarship at Pagan. Pali studies were, perhaps, the legacy of Ceylonese contact. Just as Anawrahta had sent *bhikkhu* to Ceylon, when the faith was on the wane there, in the face of South Indian Saivite pressures, so too the Ceylonese assisted Burma in the establishment of a purer canon at Pagan.[41]

Ceylon was not alone in the development of Pagan's religion and art. North India was also in contact with the young empire. Kyanzittha's supposed bride, Abeyadana, has been said to be a Bengali princess, with Mahayanist inclinations, and the painted decorations in the temple named after her are said to confirm this connection.[42] For at Pagan, South and North Indian artistic elements met, as did the Theravada and Mahayana, with the Brahmanic somewhere in between. Burma's art grew from these disparate elements to achieve a distinctive style and type, that never becomes dominated by any of these cross-cultural elements. Pala Bengal was Mahayanist, and though the Mahayana must have been tolerated at Pagan, and, though there are numerous examples of Mahayana elements in Pagan's art and architecture, the dominant religious movement, as is clearly expressed in contemporary literature, was Theravada Buddhism. However, Pagan's Theravada art selected and took what it fancied from the Mahayana art of contemporary North India, together with what vestiges of the Pyu Mahayana tendencies that remained, not to mention Hindu elements (themselves absorbed into the art of Buddhism at a far earlier stage in its development) and adapted such disparate elements to suit current Theravada tastes. Thus, a full cycle is evident: Mahayana temple forms and designs, and even practices, were applied to magnify the rational of the orthodox Theravada religion and state. Past scholars have exaggerated the place of the Mahayana in Pagan's religious life, and in the descriptions of the monuments that follow below in Part Two, constant reference is made to the fact that the Mahayana entities were secondary, by their iconographic position supporting the Theravada, and were often merely decorative.

A stable, well run empire encourages trade, and that brings about prosperity. Immigrant Indians came to serve the court as ritual major-domos, astrologers, artists and artisans and the such like, and Theravada

Buddhism, being an essentially tolerant creed, naturally let them practise their respective religions without hindrance. Outside the court orbit were other Indians—merchants and pedlars, scions of distant trading houses, plying the web of routes that converged on Pagan.[43]

The Pagan Palace inscription refers throughout to the vital role of brahmans in the palace's ceremonial construction.[44] The earliest surviving temple found at Pagan is the Nat-hlaung-kyaung and is dedicated to the Hindu deity Vishnu. There is no dichotomy in this side-by-side existence of two religions which in their essences were once opposed to each other. Nor was Pagan a religious syncretism. Elements of Hinduism were absorbed to support Buddhism, not to challenge it. Most likely, the priests of the Nat-hlaung-kyaung were the king's personal brahmans who supported the king in his mission to propagate Buddhism, as in contemporary art, where in certain instances, such as the Buddha's 'Descent from Tavatimsa', Indra and Brahma physically support the Buddha.

Marshalled through their duties by Indian brahmans, who had a monopoly on the rituals that dominated the life of the inner city that was the palace, kings were styled as avatar of Brahmanic deities in the service of Buddhism. Kyanzittha, as part of his personal propaganda, presented himself, in his panegyric inscriptions, as an avatar of Vishnu reincarnated in kingly form to propagate the *dhamma*. To promote the religion, or *sasana*, a Pagan king's royal duty lay in the construction of monuments to his religion's founder, the Buddha, in some cases enshrining actual relics of the lord himself.[45] The building of temples and other edifices, the feeding of monks and a cycle of court life based on meritorious activities thus became obligatory for any credible monarch. This accounts for the magnificence and profusion of temples at Pagan. Monarchs, motivated by a mixture of genuine piety, statecraft and a desire for credibility, became obsessed with temple building. The original reason for building a temple or stupa was not only to enshrine a precious relic or image, but to glorify and propagate the faith, whilst bringing untold benefits to man in his quest for *nibbana*, and thereby earn the merit that ensures release from the sufferings of this world. By the Late Period at Pagan, such instincts had, perhaps, become politicised. However, it would be unnecessarily cynical to suggest that a city of such outward visual glory and inner spiritual power was the product of political preoccupations.

The merit accumulated by royal temple building activities was part of the national interest. Temple building secured the release of the king's subjects as well as the king himself. The humanitarian objective of 'sharing' merit is constantly underlined in the inscriptions that detail such dedications. The king was often styled as a *bodhisattva*, a future buddha: incarnate in this world to assist mankind in their quest for salvation.[46] Kings were thus addressed as *hpaya*, the same appellation used for a sacrosanct object of worship, whether it be an image of the Buddha, a stupa or a monk (who is the living embodiment of the *dhamma*). This concept of the king as 'Champion of Buddhism' is based on Indian models that originate with the first Buddhist emperor, and unifier of India, Asoka Maurya (272-232 B.C.).[47] Like Asoka, Early Pagan kings viewed themselves as *cakkavatti* or 'Universal Monarch', the temporal equivalent of a buddha, and, whilst supporting the faith, found the faith supported them, in their drive for an imperial end. Other conceptions of the Pagan monarch included the belief that the king was *dhammaraja* or 'king of the *dhamma*' or *kammaraja,* a king whose power is based on the accumulation of merit from past existences. Finally, in the chronicles there is mention of a *sangharaja*—a monk-king who is the embodiment of total sacred and temporal power.[48] These conceptions of kingship were an integral part of contemporary statecraft, and, to prove the validity of such titles and appellations, a king was required to build stupas and temples—this in part explains the multitude and magnitude of royal monuments on the Pagan plain. Other people, members of the royal family or household, merchants and officials, likewise followed the royal example to enhance their own, and their family's accumulation of merit. They hoped not only to better their circumstances in this existence, but also the next, and ultimately hoped to be present here on earth when the next buddha, Mettaya, comes, so as to receive instant and effortless enlightenment through the hearing of the *dhamma* from the actual lips of a buddha.

The Burmese fixation with earning merit is often expressed in the dedicatory inscriptions. Here the foster mother of King Klacaw expresses her sentiments:

> ...desiring to escape the misery of the round of rebirths and to attain salvation in the presence of the Lord Buddha Metttaya and desiring the numberless beings in the Avici hell below (to come) up to the firmament above, and (that) the countless world systems across, might all attain salvation made a cave and also a four faced pagoda. She also made three sets of Pitakas and a great summit monastery...[49]

In the following chapters some discussion will be made on the role of the future buddha, Mettaya, in the religious life of Pagan and the application of this cult figure on the religious architecture of the old city. Here, it must be initially emphasised that it was upon this future buddha that the people of Pagan rested their hopes of salvation. Gotama had come and gone and it was their own ill luck, or ill *kamma*, to have missed him. Though a great corpus of teaching was left behind and disseminated by the *sangha*, the attainment of an enlightened state, *nibbana*, was no easy task. Thus, most Pagan people looked to Mettaya for ultimate salvation, and it was often a fervent prayer that they may be reborn, as a man, contemporary of the next great teaching buddha, Mettaya.

Merit earning occurred at all levels of society and was not just the prerogative of the ruling cast that orbited itself about the king's person. Though Pagan society was hierarchic, with castes defined by occupations living within their own unit—for example, there would be a residential quarter for masons and another for musicians—all sectors of the population were arranged towards the national objective of making merit. The lowest of the casts were the *hpaya kywan* or 'pagoda slaves', who were hereditarily bonded to a dedication in order to maintain it, and its incumbents, into posterity (*hpaya kywan* were formally abolished in 1947). Thus, Pagan society was rigidly organised around temple building occupations and the maintenance of the various dedications.

Michael Aung Thwin believes that Pagan economically declined in the 13th century, prior to its fall to the Mongols in 1287, as a result of such pagoda building preoccupations.[50] Along with a temple, glebe lands, villages and slaves were endowed for perpetuity to maintain the dedication. These lands were exempted from taxes. Endowments increased and revenues dwindled, ultimately weakening the state's authority. However, Late Period monuments show no sign of prevalent decline, rather they are emblematic of a supreme self-confidence. This is curious, for usually in a decadent society there is a collapse in aesthetic sensitivity, or taste, combined with a slackening in the quality of craftsmanship. No such movement is evident in the arts of Late Pagan. Further, there does not appear to have been a sudden cut-off, certainly none of the customary *fin de siècle* slip downwards, and temples continue to be dedicated well into the meridian of the next century.[51] The physical arrival of the Mongols would seem to have affected Pagan little and despite the political imbalances that the Mongols brought about Pagan remained a cultural centre, possibly even up to the present. From one inscription it is known that the *thera* Disapramuk travelled to the court of the Mongol Emperor and persuaded him that an agriculturally productive Burma would be of greater value to his hungry horsemen than an ecologically raped Burma.[52] The presence of exotically clad Mongol cavalrymen on the streets of Pagan seems to have aroused more interest than shock: one artist painted such figures on the soffits of the Kyanzittha Umin cave-temple; they are curiosities, not fiends.

Thus, Pagan did not physically 'fall' in 1287, when the Mongols entered into the *tattadesa*. Though the regime was politically destablised, and some tribute and booty must have been removed, life seems to have carried on at Pagan, little changed, well into the 14th century. Dedications continued: monastic land endowments increased and temple-monastery complexes continued to be built and lavishly embellished with ornament. What devastation one finds nowadays, disembowelled Buddhas and the such-like, was either the work of Shan hordes, treasure hunting during anarchic phases in the Early Ava period, or, possibly, the work of underpaid Mon or Burmese armies moving up or down the Irrawaddy valley during the 17th and 18th centuries.

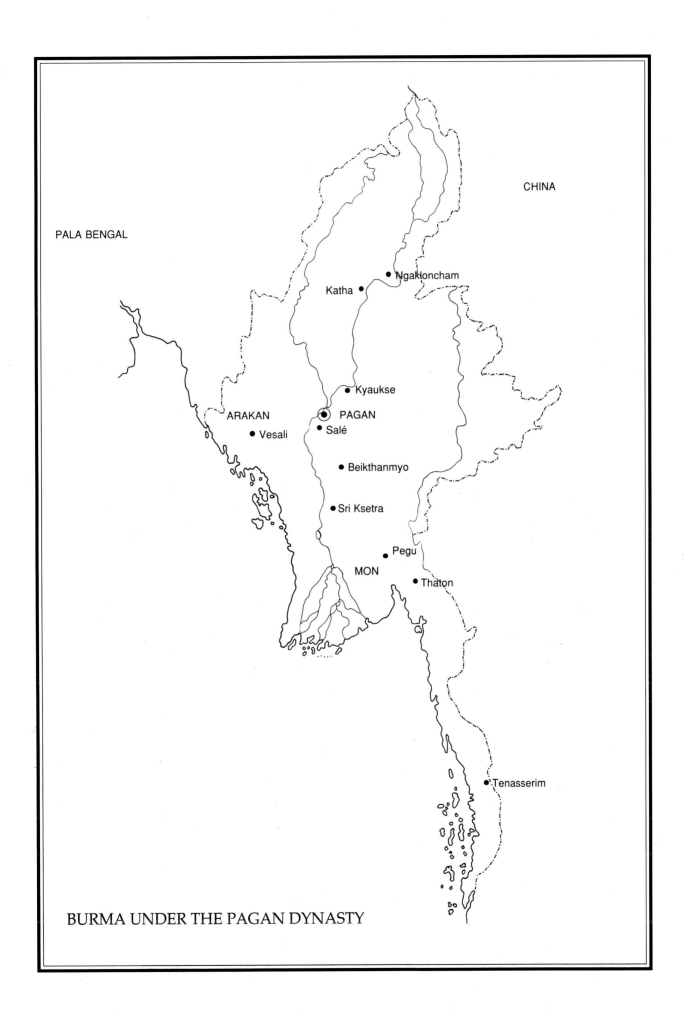

CHINA

PALA BENGAL

● Ngaktoncham
Katha ●

● Kyaukse
◉ PAGAN
● Salé

ARAKAN
● Vesali

● Beikthanmyo

● Sri Ksetra

● Pegu
MON
● Thaton

● Tenasserim

BURMA UNDER THE PAGAN DYNASTY

2
The Pagan Temple and Stupa

No.4: stupas and temples from the Mingal-zeidi

AT PAGAN, the three arts of painting, sculpture and architecture should be viewed as one. Sculptor, mason, and painter attempted to collaborate in the creation of a unified whole. In the early temples, like the Myin-pya-gu, this is less apparent, mural paintings, decorative or didactic, tend to be secondary to to the architecture, almost an afterthought. With the building of the Lokha-teik-pan in the first quarter of the 12th century, the idea of the arts in unity, working together to enhance doctrine, state faith and pay homage to the Buddha is embodied.

Religious monuments at Pagan take a variety of forms and little survives of the great monastic complexes, palace apartments, rest houses and other sacred structures, and nothing survives of the original secular or domestic architecture, all of which had been made from wood. Remaining are the fundamental Buddhist monuments, which were usually made from baked brick though occasionally stone. In Part Two, a selection of monuments representative of the various periods, and movements within those periods, is presented, with a more detailed analysis of each monument's architecture and iconography. Here, the principal architectural forms, their origins and the conceptions behind their construction shall be outlined in brief.

STUPAS

Pagodas or stupas are solid structures that enshrine a sacred relic or a particularly potent image of the Buddha. The ground plan is usually square, though a five-sided type develops in the Late Pagan Period. The base is terraced, three or five times, and the terraces rest on an elaborately moulded plinth. The terraces reflect the tiered slopes of the cosmic mountain, Mount Meru, a Brahmanic conception that had been, by this time, absorbed into Theravada Buddhism. The stupa, taken in its original essence, is a giant reliquary designed to contain some part of the mortal remains of Gotama, the Buddha. By the time that Buddhism had reached Pagan, the stupa had developed, in its conception, as a structure; in addition to enshrining the mortal remains of the Buddha (and a number of Pagan stupas claim the distinction of enshrining such contents) they might also enshrine a particularly potent image of the Buddha, usually made from the most costly of materials. Alternatively, the stupa might hold copies of the scriptures or other precious items. Many of the original inscriptions explicitly describe this enshrinement process as this excerpt, translated by Dr Than Tun, details:

On Wednsday 22 December 1227, (the following) are

13

enshrined in the *cetiya*: the bodily relics of the Lord; the image of the Lord made from the branch of the sacred banyan tree: the image of the Lord cast in gold; the image of the Lord cast in gold; the image of the Lord in ivory bezoar; and the image of the Lord made of sandalwood. (Underneath) all these were spread gold cushions and silver cushions and these are covered with gold umbrellas. Parched rice of gold, parched rice of silver, gold chandeliers and silver chandeliers are also offered. When these gems are enshrined the relic chamber is closed with bricks. After this wonderful figures of deva and various beings are made with stucco.[1]

The stupa is not merely a protective structure built about certain sacred objects. It is a symbol of the Buddha and his *dhamma,* or sacred teachings—to a Buddhist the ultimate of architectural structures. Though there is a common symbolism with the Brahmanic Mount Meru, the stupa is more than simply an architectural imitation of this cosmic mountain: it becomes, in its own right, the cosmic mountain. Mount Meru, the celestial abode of the Hindu pantheon, was the template upon which the architect philosophers of early Buddhism modelled their monuments. Just as certain of the Hindu gods, who would normally reside on the slopes of Mount Meru, were (and remain) incorporated into the defence strategy of Buddhism, and indeed were iconographically worked into the cosmically orientated layout of the stupa, this most fundamental architectural form, though conceptually Buddhist in origin, was designed according to Brahmanic cosmological thought. On Pagan stupa exteriors, Brahmanic deities were fixed at strategic points and sealed within the inner chamber, or *tabena*, to guard the relic or sacred image. The stupa's terraces and structural elements, likewise, reflected the hierarchically ascending slopes of the great mountain.[2]

The terraces served a practical as well as a symbolic function; they acted as an open air gallery from which the pilgrim could view pictorial depictions of fundamental texts, usually the Jataka, the 550 tales of Gotama the last buddha's former incarnations; each tale illustrating a major event in each of his 550 past lives. These scenes were stamped onto compact terracotta plaques that, with one exception, at Hpet-leik, were glazed.[3] In the late 11th-early 12th centuries, when kings were attempting to purify the existing Buddhism of Old Burma, stupa terraces proved a convenient location for the display of a didactic art form. As part of a long-established Buddhist ritual, the male devotee would ritually circumambulate, or make a *pradaksina*, about the stupa, using the terraces, and learn something of his religion's history from these delicate, usually delightful, stamped scenes that were, as an art form, rare and pure, akin to the reformed faith they sought to imbibe. The inclusion of complete Jataka sets on stupa terraces continued through all three periods of dynastic art, on major, usually royal,

dedications, notably the pentagonally-planned Dhamma-yazika (1186)[4] and the equally magnificent Mingala-zeidi (1268).[5] On a number of lesser stupas, like those that flank the Hsin-pya-gu[6] (Late Period), the last ten Jataka were included—the *Mahanipata*.

On each of the Early Period stupas' faces medial stairways cut through the terraces and lead to an upper platform from which the *anda*, the either concavely or convexly-shaped superstructures, rises from an octagonal band set within the upper terrace. Within the core, beneath the ground level, was the sealed-off relic chamber, or *tabena*, the spiritual epicentre of the stupa.[7] In these were enshrined not only physical relics of the lord, if the dedication was important enough to have obtained, perhaps by force,[8] such precious items as a tooth or hair, but also images, made of costly materials ranging from sandalwood, to gold, ivory and glass,[9] and palm leaf, or even gold plaque, manuscripts.[10] Other inclusions in the *tabena* were votive tablets, often bearing the seal or signature of the donor, miniature versions of a stupa or temple and images of Brahmanic deities to protect the *hpaya*. Often several *tabena* were included in a stupa and those smaller monuments, that were split open by the 1974 earthquake, display these now opened chambers at various levels. If, as was often the case, the stupa was re-encased at a later date by another outer one, it may be surmised that, as dedications were constructed not only for the salvation of the donor, but also wife and family, and, as in contemporary Burma the descendents of a donor continue to maintain and offer to that dedication, a descendant may have been responsible for the re-encasement of an ancestors' earlier work of merit.[11]

In the great royal stupas, like the Early Period Shwe-hsan-daw, or Late Period Seddana-gyi, either to reduce the volume of brick required, or to foil intruders, seemingly anticipated judging by the epigraphy, labyrinthine systems of compartments were included, creating a structure that, if viewed from an imaginary cross section, resembles a honeycomb. It remains uncertain whether the enshrinement took place upon completion of the temple or at its foundation. Passages that enter into the interior appear to have been hewn by the *tabena-sha*, or 'treasure hunters' of later times. So it would seem that enshrinement, as with today, occurred at the dedication of the work. However, in original Indian stupas, where the *harmika,* or relic casket, was placed between the *anda* and finial, it may be presumed that the sacred items were inserted after the completion of the main structural body.

This tradition of placing the *harmika*, which originally had acted as a reliquary casket, between the *anda* and finial had survived in Ceylon, Nepal and other Buddhist countries; and, though the *harmika* is depicted in early Pyu stone reliefs,[12] it had been phased out of Burmese stupa design by the time of the rise of imperial Pagan in the 11th century, to revive during the Late Period—the visual consequence of a new phase of Burma-Ceylon relations.[13] The *anda* itself was covered with stucco, with moulded lotus petals, often with *kirtimukha* masks forming a band about its upper part, once dazzlingly highlighted with polychrome. The whole stupa itself was mirrored at the terrace corners with mini-stupa obelisks; these spread out on each of the descending terraces, in each of the cardinal directions. In some Middle Period works, like at Sein-nyet,[14] and Late Period versions, notably the Mingala-zeidi,[15] the *kalasa* pot, normally associated with Early Period temple plinths, and found in the tympana of the Nan-hpaya exterior window pediments, replaces the mini-stupa.

Originally all Pagan's stupa and temple exteriors were covered in protective plaster, whitewashed with a lime-based coating, and the stucco ornament was enlivened with bright colours. The pious trustees of the more popular establishments continue to perennially pour lime over their charges' surfaces.

The *anda* is surmounted by the *amalaka*, a finial that symbolises the lotus bud, from which the crowning seven-tiered finial, *chattravali*, was placed. Original finials, called *athwat* in Old Burmese, we know from the dedicatory inscriptions[16] were made of copper and one was recently found in a temple undergoing local restoration near Chauk and is presently being kept in a local monastery near there.[17] The *hti* that crest the monuments of Pagan nowadays, have been placed there by local devotees who have faithfully acted as the custodians of the Pagan monuments over the centuries, in spite of the sparseness of their own despoiled resources. However, these modern *hti* bear little resemblance to original finials. From pictorial depictions that date from these times, it is apparent that stupas were decked with long banners that must have gracefully flapped in the breeze, as they flowed out like vinous stems from about th lotus bud, in a similar way to the delicate peepal runners stemming out from about the lord's aureole in the terracotta tablets of the period.[18]

The stupa is the physical embodiment of the *dhamma*, not just the supreme teachings of the last historical Buddha, Gotama, but also the sacred laws that govern the workings of the universe. Further to this, the stupa is a physical embodiment of the Buddha himself. Burmese people call a stupa *hpaya* or 'Lord' and the same generic term is used when referring to an actual image of the Buddha, or to the living embodiment of the *dhamma*—a monk, and, in past monarchic periods, to a king, who was viewed, according to contemporay conceptions, as a future Buddha or *bodhisattva,* called *hpaya-lon* in Burmese.[19] Thus, these non-functional structures, with neither an accessible interior, nor a distinct and regular ritual function, are the ultimate architectural form of a Buddhist society. If they are fewer in number, on a colossal scale, to the temples, it is perhaps because of their very 'specialness'; for the construction of so powerful a monument required a highly confident donor. In a number of cases, a donor included with a temple dedication small stupas within the same enclosure. Possibly the explanation why stupas are so outnumbered by *gu* temples is that in a time when ritual practices involving colourful visual displays, such as music, dance and the daily ablution and adornment of the humanly treated image, the stupa was a less functional architectural instrument for the enactment of an anthropomorphically orientated religious life. However, countless mounds in the Pagan area contain the crumbled fragments of stupas and the earliest Buddhist dedications at Pagan dating from the 9th century were stupas based on the bulbous Pyu type.[25]

TEMPLES

The *gu,* or cave, was a more popular form of dedication than the stupa; they appear to be countless in number, dotted across the plain and seemingly reaching out into infinity in each direction. Their prototype are to be found at the old Pyu capital of Sri Ksetra (the modern village of Hmawza near Prome), where the Be-be and Lei-myet-hna *gu* temples (7th-8th century) have the same type of voussoir brickwork and radiating arches as those employed on the Pagan temples. The Pyu type is, in plan, based around a solid, or at least inaccessible, central block: there are thus four faces and each face symbolises one of the last four buddhas of this *bhadrakalpala,* or time period, the west-facing buddha being for Sakyamuni, the buddha Gotama, who is generally known as 'the Buddha', the most recent buddha to manifest in the present time cycle. Receded into the block at the cardinal points were niches, each of which contained an image of one of the buddhas.

The Pyu model, known in modern Burmese as *lei-myet-hna,* or four faced, is derived from North Indian prototypes and came to Burma by an overland route. Possible antecedents may be the early Nagari temples at Bhuvaneswar, that date from the 7th century. The earliest *gu* at Pagan is generally said to be the Nat-hlaung-kyaung, most probably built in the early 11th century, which is a Vaisnavite dedication. Its tall elevation and thickly-moulded, upwardly-emphasised *sikhara,* follows from the Early Nagari examples.[21] The Nat-hlaung-kyaung plan is, though, based on the Pyu central block, or *lei-myet-hna,* that carries the *sikhara* superstructure, and in execution the work shows many traces of Pyu building techniques. Thus, by the rise of Anawrahta, an indigenous building tradition, evolved to express the tenets of Buddhism, manifested itself, for the first time at Pagan, in the form of a non-Buddhist dedication, onto which more recent North Indian developments are added.

Temples, in Burmese, are called *gu*, or cave, and must be thought of as artificial caves.[22] They, like the stupa, are *hpaya* or 'lord'. The *gu* temple's function differs from that of a stupa and, at least in the Early Period, they are intended to evoke the spirit of the early Buddhist caves of North India.[23] Like real caves, often the homes of hermits, they are places for devotion, ritual and meditation. The Hindu concept of *bhakti*, the emphasis on an intense relationship between the devotee and an anthropomorphised object of worship, that had influenced the development of the Mahayana in India, was applied to the early cave temples of Pagan.[24] Thus, in the Early Period temple, the architects created an interior scheme directed towards the inducement of a spiritual experience, or *bhakti*. This does not necessarily imply the pre-eminence of Mahayana cults at Pagan, rather, the Theravada monarchs directed their builders to create schemes that were psychologically conducive to spiritual experience at a time, as clearly stated in contemporary epigraphy, when the religion was undergoing a state-sponsored purification, which in Theravada lands occur periodically, and is the duty of a pious and proper ruler to organise.[25] The Early Pagan builder, zealous in his attempts to propagate the Theravada, felt no constraint when it came to borrowing forms and concepts from the Mahayana. Pagan *gu* are mystical, yet never esoteric. In fact, they represent an exoteric movement. By the Middle Period this tendency towards the atmospheric in architecture was to be phased out, the Theravada process of purification and conversion having been completed. *Bhakti* ceased to determine architectural design and a more rational tendency, with a preference for luminosity, displaces the dark mystical Early Period *gu* interior.

The *gu,* like the stupa, could contain sacred relics, images of the Buddha, made from precious and costly materials, or precious manuscripts. Such enclosures were protected by Hindu or even Tantric guardian figures, that could include images of contemporary members of the royal family, courtiers and soldiers.[26] Before the shrine was sealed devotees would throw gems and various other precious items into the shrine.[27] All this would be bricked up, never to be seen again and the donations were recorded on stone in-

scriptions that often meticulously detail the costs.[28] The significance of this enshrinement was that the relics and valuable images, the actual *hpaya*, emanated a force out from the central mass that benefited not just the donor and his immediate circle, but all mankind. In addition to within the sealed *tabena*, further images were placed in recesses on the outer sides of the central block, usually made of brick and stucco, for large stone blocks are not easily quarried in this part of Burma.[29] In the Early Period, the half-facing recess of the Pyu, and Nat-hlaung-kyaung, was cut into the block and formed a complete cella unit, however, by the beginning of the 12th century the original Pyu type, namely the *lei-myet-hna*, was reverted to, with exceptions.[30] Precious gems were placed with the spiritually sensitive areas of the body: within the head, chest, abdomen and upper arms (this accounts for the widespread vandalism and disembowelment of so many temple images). Pagan Buddhists measured the sanctity of a *hpaya*, whether it be an entire structure or an individual image, in terms of the expense lavished on it. The more expensive an image, the more merit earned and, thus, the *hpaya* became more sacrosanct and beneficial for mankind. The spending of one's wealth on creating a potent *hpaya* was in itself a symbolic act, reflecting the Buddha's own act of renunciation and the Vessantara Jataka.[31] The hoarding of treasures within the *hpaya*, thus increasing the *hpaya*'s potential, was therefore an act benefiting all who would worship the image. In one known instance, an outer image actually encases an inner one made of a more valuable material: like in the Lotus Sutra, buddha emanates out from buddha.[32] Likewise, as discussed above, stupas may be periodically re-encased, structure radiating from structure.

Just as the conceptions behind these two types of monuments are shared, the design of a *gu* is related to that of the stupa. Stupa motifs or *zeidi*, were placed at

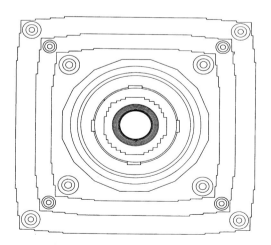

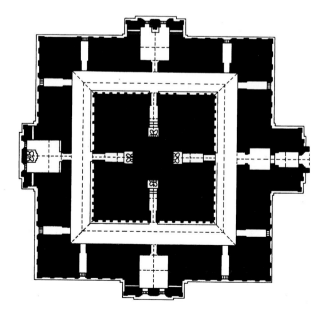

Fig.1 above: Sein-nyet Nyi-ma stupa plan
Fig.2 right: Myin-pya-gu plan forming a lei-myet-hna

various points on the temple terraces and a stupa finial crested the *sikhara*. The *sikhara* is, in essence, no more than an evolved adaption of the stupa *anda* and *chattravali*, crowning, like a *jatamukuta* diadem, the *hpaya*. The *sikhara* was, though, not always preferred on temple superstructures and following the Pyu, who do not seem to have used this form on their temples,[33] a current runs through our periods where a stupa, either concave or convex in shape, rose from a temple's terraces; in the periods after the Pagan dynasty ones this form was to become established as the norm.

Thus, both temple and stupa have a common symbolism and cosmology, each being *hpaya*. They differ in function, for the *gu* is conceived as a cave-like house for an image before which daily rituals were enacted and, judging by the pictorial schemes on the interior walls, they served a didactic role, at least in the early, proselytisin, part of the Pagan dynastic periods. Didactic or devotional, most likely both, the Early Period *gu* was an impressive instrument of the Buddhist faith at this time in Burma.

To understand something of the devotional life that went on within the *gu* a quotation from one of the contemporary inscriptions is illuminating. In this excerpt, translated by U Pe Maung Tin, the donor records the offerings of provisions for the slaves, responsible for the enactment of the daily rituals going on about an anthropomorphised image of the Buddha or buddhas:

> Let my Lord, the Elder consider all these slaves, fields, cattle and gardens that I have offered to the cave and the monastery. Let him repair the cave, monastery and hall of the Law, should they fall into ruins...The offering of betel to the Buddha is 10 nuts per day, 300 per month, 3600 per year...135 baskets of paddy are for all the pagoda slaves who sleep in the cave, drummers, xylophonists, and *naracana*.[34]

In another inscription, also translated by U Pe Maung Tin, the requisite objects that the actual image required were listed in detail:

> The requisite things are for the lower Buddha his wearing apparel- 1 outer robe, 1 inner garment; for the upper Buddha his wearing apparel: 1 embroidered inner garment, 1 gold couch, 1 apartment for his dwelling place, 1 high cot complete with bed covers and pillows, 1 betel box, copper oil lampstands, copper spitoons, 1 big copper kettle, 1 elephant lotus from which the bell is hung, gold bowls, silver bowls, 2 pestals....[35]

As U Pe Maung Tin notes, the Buddha in this dedication, was attired not in royal regalia, as was common at this time, but in an attitude of royal ease wearing only his under-robes, relaxing as if at home as a real king might.[36] Thus, the now spartan brick *gu* interiors should be regarded in this light: cluttered with regal objects and requisites, a clamour of activity as food offerings were shuttled from the kitchens down passageways crowded with chanting devotees, to be offered to the rousing din of xylophones, drums and castanets, amidst the lustrous blaze of brightly coloured wall paintings, gilted furnishings and flapping banners and hangings. Like in certain of the popular shrines of Burma today, the usual plain, seated, Buddha image, found in the deserted temples of Pagan today, would have been bathed, perfumed and dressed with the finest and most costly of garments.[37]

The Early Period temples are composed of two units: the hall and the shrine, which are usually orientated in an east or north-facing direction, though there are numerous exceptions, and it would appear that the Pagan architect was less concerned with cosmologically arranged orientation than his Indian counterpart. The hall may be said to be the Indian *mandapa* built up and covered with a vault. At Pagan's first surviving temple, the Nat-hlaung-kyaung, there is a *mandapa*, the only extant one at Pagan and now solidly restored by the Archaeology Department.[38] In other temples this paved area, projecting from the front, is transformed into a hall that would protect assembling devotees from the sun's glare. By the construction of the Shwe-gu-gyi in 1131, temples tend to be raised above subsidiary constructions on a plinth and this was to become the standard pattern for most middle-to-large size temple dedications.

Between hall and shrine, whether set in a recess or cella, is an ambulatory that runs continuously around the central block. In the Early Period the two architectural units were separated: joining arches regulate the units. Within, the shrine or cella deepened from the niche recess on the central block's east face, that at the Nat-hlaung-kyaung held an image of Vishnu, and in the Pyu types an image of the Buddha, or buddhas. In the Early Period temple the niche is cut into the central block which is opened out to form a cella. Thus, the devotee is admitted into a previously closed sanctum to participate in a spiritual communion with the *hpaya*. Buddhism was being consciously developed into a popular movement by the Early Pagan kings, and their preceptors, at this time. Temple planning, though aiming, at least in the Early Period, at creating a spiritually charged atmosphere, in no way marked an esoteric movement, as was then current with the Vajrayana Himalayan kingdoms, or maritime South-East Asia, rather, it was exoteric. The creation of a cella and the role of this unit in contemporary religious life may be said to be comparable with the development of the *garbha-greha* in Indian temples.

The psychological role of light in the Early Period temple is of some interest. The quantity of light permitted to enter each architectural unit of the building was skilfully managed. Entering from the glare of the outside into the cool, balanced light of the hall, one crosses into the ambulatory and makes a *pradaksina,* or ritual circumambulation, about the central block. Here, the light is rationed by elaborately perforated windows, yet is sufficient enough to follow

Clockwise from top left:
No.5: re-encased stupa S. of Myinkaba
No.6: hidden arches in the Nat-hlaung-kyaung
No.7: pitaka taik — Late Period
No.8: stupa forms in stucco relief — Pa-hto-tha-mya
No.9: gateway to enclosed sanctuary west of the south
Kyanzittha Umin

the scenes and glosses of the mural paintings. Having completed the *pradaksina,* the shrine is faced and within the almost pitch-dark interior a massive image of the Buddha awaits worship. Secret skylights and long, narrow ducts pass through the mass of the superstructure, to throw a gentle beam of filtered light on the 'Enlightened One's' face.

This Early Period temple type was to be phased out by the early 12th century when the Pagan builder unconsciously reverted to the cosmically-orientated ground plan types of the Pyu *lei-myet-hna.* The distinction between hall and shrine gradually becomes reduced, though rarely eliminated, and the temple's components become balanced into a unified whole, an integration evident both from the exterior and interior.[39] The admittance of light was no longer rationed and it is easy to forget that this is supposed to be an artificial cave. This architectural movement is a reflection of prevalent religious beliefs. The dark, mystical Early Period *gu* interiors, that were contrived to inspire a personal devotion, as part of a national movement directed at propagating a purified form of Buddhism, were no longer required, for the process of purification had been completed by the reign of Sithu I (1113-1155) when, architecturally, the transition into the Middle Period takes place.[40] There was, by this time, less need to psychologically spur the believer with architectural inducements. *Bhakti* had given way to a more rational Theravada philosophy. In temples, lighter environments came to be preferred, and the predominant architectural tendency was in the upwardly directed possibilities of the exterior, or elevation, rather than the mystical possibilities of the 'cave' interior.

From the four-face type a five-face type (*nga-myet-hna*) develops. Though not very common, a number of examples are to be found dating from the late 12th century and continuing to occasionally be built up to the present. This pentagonal scheme represents an extension of the four buddhas of this time span, or *bhadrakalpala,* to include the future buddha Mettaya. Mettaya's cult was popular at Pagan, judging by a number of finds of his image in bronze, and may be associated with the contemporary kingship cult, in that kings self-styled themselves as *hpaya-lon,* or *bodhisattva.*The ultimate expression of this theme was the magnificent Dhamma-yazika stupa near the village of Pwasaw built by Sithu II in 1196.[41]

The inscriptions, the great bulk of which belong to the Late Period, that recorded each dedication offer much valuable information on the monuments of this time. A large dedication centred around a stupa or temple would have monastic complexes attached, rest houses for visitors and accommodation for the pagoda slaves and monastic servants. Few monastic structures survive from before the Late period, however, from the mid-12th century onwards such dedications abound. Water tanks were dug and groves of shading palmyra planted. All this was built and laid out with astonishing speed, often within a year. Entire villages, and the

lands connected to them, were dedicated and their tax-exempted incomes were offered into perpetuity for the maintenance of the establishment.[42] Musicians were also offered to play music to the *hpaya* and slaves were responsible for the ritual washing of the image and daily offerings of food and flowers. These hereditarily-bonded slaves were also responsible for the general upkeep of the shrine and to serve the monks, who themselves were living *hpaya.* The senior monk resided within the inner enclosure in a brick house known as *kala kyaung,* or 'Indian Monastery', possibly because the craftsmen who built them were Indians. The form of this type of structure may be described as a 'block house' on account of their shape. The junior monks, novices and other members of the community lived in the outer enclosure. Attached to brick structures, that most likely acted as *pitaka-taik,* were lean-to wooden halls, or *dhamma-yon,* used for the preaching of sermons.[43]

These now desolate enclosures should be viewed as once having been the centre of a hub of activity, revolving around the glorification of the *hpaya* and scholarly pursuits, and the larger establishments, particularly in the outlying Minnanthu and Pwasaw areas, were akin to the ancient Buddhist universities of India, such as Nalanda. Inscriptions make mention of the fact that a set of the Pali canon, the Tipitaka was more costly than the building of a temple itself.[44] A donor could also choose whether to have the 'cave' painted and in accordance with the advice of the monk who was to receive the dedication formulate a suitable programme of subjects to be illustrated.

The great dedications were usually offered by a senior member of the court or the royal family. Often dedications were made by women, widowed and anxious to earn merit for their loved ones. Those lacking the financial resources to build their own *hpaya* could join in the national preoccupation with earning merit by serving a dedication and its monks; voluntarily, as *kappiya,* or involuntarily, as a hereditarily-bonded slave—*hpaya-kyawn.* It would be mistaken to think of these pagoda slaves as pawns in the merit-making process of the higher classes, for a major dedication was built with all mankind's salvation in mind, not just the royal donor's, and the benefits of a lesser one extended out to the donor's family circle.[45] Pagan society was hierarchically regimented into occupation-defined groups and all groups were bonded and socially immobile whether part of the crown and military sector or agricultural and services sector. It is arguable that life as a pagoda slave could have been a good deal softer than in the service of the crown.

No.10: detail of the Ananda Ok-kyaung bronze image of the buddha Gotama

3
Images: Style and Iconography

THOSE IMAGES uncovered so far at Pagan, whether in the medium of sculpture or wall painting, are, to say the least, diverse in their iconographical and stylistic origins. It is in a study of the images found at Pagan that the pattern of the city's cultural and religious life may begin to be comprehended. Currents, cross-currents and sub-currents ebb and flow, contriving to throw the dogmatic iconographer or generalist off course. To say Pagan sculpture is 'Mon derived' is to deprive the Pyu of their true place in Burma's art history; to say Pagan sculpture takes its origin from the Pyu excludes the potent input of Pala influence that occurred during the Early Period. Likewise, the finding of miscellaneous portable Tantric images does not necessarily indicate the dominance of this sect at Pagan. Nor does the positioning of Brahmanic images in Buddhist temples imply that Pagan's religious life was syncretistic.

In the past art historians have tended to generalise Pagan images, of whatever medium, to a single characteristic style. It is possible, though, according to the presentation of an image's physiognomy and physiology, to detect three mainstream styles. These styles correspond approximately to the three architectural periods into which the dynasty's art has been divided: Early, Middle and Late. In the words of the woodcarver Tampawaddy U Win Maung:

> Images for worship between the 11th and 13th centuries of the Christian Era are defined as Pagan Period. Although 'Early Pagan', 'Middle Pagan' and 'Late Pagan' periods can be distinguished.

Dissemination, evolution and transition, in style and iconography, during these periods, for sculpture, is usually related to developments in mural painting. Thus, the story of Pagan's iconography can be applied to both mediums of sculpture and wall painting. However, the one difference is that usually mural paintings are subsidiary in importance to an actual image. Murals have a twofold purpose: to emblazon an interior with joyous colour and lively design and to tell a story. That is, an art that can be both decorative and didactic in purpose. Sculpture too can be didactic, when placed in subsidiary positions, however, the most commonplace central image of a shrine, usually the buddha Gotama, seated defeating the evil one, Mara, in *bhumisparsamudra* or, more rarely, standing in *abhayamudra*, or in other 'combination' *mudra*, was integrated with the architectural scheme as the principal object of devotion or *bhakti*.[1] Such icons

were usually 'larger than life', colossal in scale, and conceived so as to awe the beholder. In the Early Period, the effect of such colossal images was increased by the subtle, yet dramatic, play of light, whereas mural paintings tended to be subsidiary, in position and purport, to the colossal central icon.

Many of the principal images set in the great niche-like shrines of Pagan's temples date from after our period, for example, the principal image of the That-byin-nyu.[2] In some cases, Ava period inscriptions tell of the donor's horror at the destruction wrecked by Mongol, Shan or, perhaps, indigenous hordes in the 14th century, and thus felt compelled to restore the heart of their civilisation to something of its former grandeur .

MEDIA

The manner in which a work of sculpture was to be portrayed depended on the medium that was used. Pagan has always been impoverished of stone; the very costliness of this material must have prohibited its general use in temple construction. Slabs of firm sandstone were available for single reliefs, though these are rarely over a metre in height. Pagan workmen had little laterite to use, and, with the exception of the relief depictions of Brahma on the Nan-hpaya piers, did not possess the skill of being able to create great sculptural scenes from interlocking relief sections as was the practice in the remainder of South-East Asia and in parts of India. Some steatite, known in Burmese as *andagu,* was available, which the Pagan carver turned with miraculous dexterity into minute portrayals of the Eight Scenes in imitation of Pala models. Marble was also rare at this time, though some images, lesser in size and late in our period, survive in this brittle medium. It seems that the great marble quarries of Kyaukse, used by Konbaung and contemporary craftsmen, had yet to be opened. Bronze casting was being skilfully practised at Pagan by the end of the Early Period. However, many of the bronzes that have been uncovered are of a portable type and stylistically and iconographically belong to other regions, exotic mementos carried home by returning pilgrims and itinerant scholars, or possibly the object of private devotions for visiting merchants or political refugees. An indigenous bronze casting tradition did, though, exist in Burma: at Sri Ksetra, once capital of the Pyu, and at Vesali, the ancient capital of Arakan. It was probably the Arakanese bronze casting tradition that made the greatest impact

I, previous: bronze Buddha in profile,
from Myingyan c.1100-1150
II, left: That-byin-nyu from north-west
III, right: view north-east from Pwasaw
IV, next: the Dhamma-yan-gyi at dusk

V, left: view to the west with the Mingala-zeidi in the back-ground
VI, right: dawn over Pwasaw
VII, next: the That-byin-nyu from the Ananda at sunset

at Pagan. Though Pyu inscribed bronzes have been found at Pagan, they are cruder in workmanship and execution when compared with their Arakanese counterparts and iconographically detached from mainstream Indian traditions. The Pyu impact was in silver and gold smithing—virtuoso filigree and repoussé work, surprisingly little of which survives at Pagan.[4] By about 1100, the Pagan craftsman had mastered bronze casting and was competent enough to create images whose radiant beauty are capable of softening the stoutest of stoics. Perhaps their finest examples from this period are two standing *vitarka* images, one in the Ananda monastery and the other in a shrine near Chauk.

The Pagan builder's forte was brick which he lavishly coated with stucco, moulding it into myriad forms and motifs, energetic designs and satisfying symbols. As stone was rare and bronze, on a monumental scale, both costly and impractical to cast, the Pagan brickmen, ever adept in their master craft, created colossal images from these available materials. The inexpensive nature of these materials was compensated for by the precious items held within them. Likewise for decoration, the advent of a new repertoire of decorative motifs, with the Kyauk-ku-ohn-min and Nan-hpaya temple stonework, was rapidly translated into the medium of stucco, a local tradition well mastered by the Pyu.[5] Often these colossal images of brick and stucco were structurally strengthened with a wooden post passing through the middle of the body, perhaps emulative of the central pole of early Buddhist stupas. In a number of examples, mainly from the Late Period, the lower part of the face was carved from a stone block that projected out from the back wall of the recess and about which the brick and stucco was worked.

The medium in which the Pagan genius was perhaps once best expressed was wood. The sinuous lines, bestial configurations and floral fantasias of the mural paintings that glorify the plastered walls of numerous brick temples, reflect and recreate the wood carved surfaces of contemporary timber structures. Motifs, forms-figurative and forms-abstracted, were all common to the three Pagan decorative mediums—stucco work, painting and wood carving. Little carved wood now survives with the exception of carved doors and the odd lintel[6] Though Luce illustrates a number of carved images in his volume of plates, they stylistically date from the first Ava Period.[7] The only wooden images that may definitely be attributed to the dynasty itself are the two original standing images of buddhas in the Ananda (south and north shrines), constructed from interlocking timber components, those in the Naga-yon, and two *dvarapala* in a temple south of Salé.[8] Fragments of timber beams may still be found spanning the corridors of *ok-taik* and, more rarely, as part of image pedestals. Little else of this frail medium has survived sack and pillage, sun and flame, or the rabid entomological life of this *tattadesa*.

Other media in which images and the sacred texts might be presented, whether as icons or ornament, symbolic presence or instruments of instruction, were the textile, glassware, terracotta estampages (often glazed) and possibly lacquer.[9] Few textiles have been discovered to date at Pagan; some minute fragments of paintings on cloth may be seen in the museum there and recently Pierre Pichard of the E.F.E.O. discovered a larger, though fragmented, piece in temple No.315 which is at present undergoing restoration in Italy.[10]

THE BUDDHA AND BUDDHAS

Gotama is one of a long line of buddhas who have revealed themselves throughout the history of the world; at Pagan the precise number was taken to be 28.[11] These buddhas, with the exception of Gotama, are non-historic and stretch back in time to the moment of the world's creation. The world's existence is divided into a number of time spans, through which these successive buddhas have periodically manifested themselves. Such time units are called *kalpa* and each may last for many thousands of years. Gotama, who was the 'Sage of the Sakya' (the Himalayan people into which he was born) or Sakyamuni, is the first 'historical' buddha who lived c.500 B.C. and was the third buddha to appear in the present *kalpa*—the *bhadrakalpa*. He was preceded by three other buddhas and there is one buddha yet to manifest himself: the 'Future Buddha'—Mettaya. Thus, the Buddhas of this *bhadrakalpa* are: Kakusandha, Konagamanda, Kassapa, Gotama and the buddha to come, Mettaya.

This cosmic succession of Buddhas presented the Pagan artist with five possible iconographic arrangements:

1. Gotama—the Buddha and his Legend.
2. Gotama with Mettaya—the Buddha and future buddha.
3. The four buddhas that have so far manifested themselves in this *bhadrakalpa*.
4. The five buddhas of this *bhadrakalpa* including Mettaya.
5. The 28 buddhas of all times.
6. Mettaya—the future buddha, alone.

In addition to these arrangements, a number of supportive figures, drawn from the Hindu and Mahayana pantheons, may combine with Gotama. In the preceding discussion on architecture, the buddhas of this *bhadrakalpa* have been mentioned with reference to temple and stupa ground plan designs. Symbols are common to all mediums in Pagan's art; the *lei-myet-hna* and *nga-myet-hna* schemes for architectural ground planning have a direct correspondence to pictorial representations of these fundamental iconographic items.

THE BUDDHA GOTAMA

The buddha Gotama is the most commonplace and fundamental icon of Theravada Pagan. Usually intended for the central image of a temple's shrine, he may be portrayed in a variety of *mudra* and *asana* that had developed in India during Gandharan and Mathuran times. When his image is placed centrally in a temple shrine, Gotama is generally portrayed in the *bbhumisparsamudra*, the moment when, as *bodhisattva*, Gotama defeated Mara, the personification of evil, and touched the earth to call it to witness his supreme victory and enlightenment—Buddhahood. This vision of a struggle with, and victory over, evil, was a favourite theme in the pictorial imagery of a temple, and the Buddha was often portrayed on a colossal scale, surrounded by paintings which elaborately detailed this fantastic struggle, and the ultimate rout of Mara's host.

Either nomadic hill men or perhaps warring Mons and Burmans in later times, their lust for booty unleashed by political instability and economic arduousness, were responsible for the disembowelment and decollation of nearly all these colossal brick and stucco temple images. For within these *hpaya,* donors sealed treasure of various sorts, the presence of which somehow increased the potency of the image for the believer, through its very costliness. Such enclosures, ritually positioned, not only increased the image's credibility but paid honour to the 'Supreme Teacher'. Just as treasures were also enshrined within the *tabena* of a temple or stupa, so it was within an image. In a colossal image, that acted as the main icon in a temple, the usual place for concealment were in the cranium, the heart, the abdomen and in each of the upper arms. This again reflected architectural conceptions, with often several *tabena* included at various levels within the structure. Such a metaphor of *hpaya* radiating out from *hpaya* is well attested in sacred texts and at Pagan was illustrated in the multiplication of the Buddha's image to a maximum of 100 on terracotta votive tablets. Thus, *hpaya* emanates from *hpaya* in a cosmic radiation. Likewise, small stone reliquary stupas might encase others, and in certain examples actual stupas re-encase other stupas. Likewise, a brick and stucco image may encase, not only precious gems, but another image within it.[12]

The Pyu and Mon were naturally well acquainted with so fundamental an icon as Gotama at his supreme moment. It would seem that in these pre-Pagan city states a number of Buddhist and Hindu cults and sects co-existed, one of which was the Theravada sect which rose to prominence at Pagan, where it was to undergo a purification under the supervision of the Ceylonese. A variety of images of Gotama Buddha date from these early times which are stylistically derived from the art of the Gupta Period of North India (5th century A.D.). The Mon art of this period was more closely related to the art of Dvaravati in Southern Thailand, adopting a humanistic radiance that recalled earlier phases of Indian art, notably the work of the Mathura period (1st-3rd century A.D.). At Sri

*No.11 upper left: Pyu stucco work from Sri Ksetra
(Hmawza Museum)*
*No.12 lower left: Gotama and Mettaya, found at Kyasin
temple Pagan, and close in style to Pyu types*
*No.13 upper right: the Buddha in bhumisparsamudra,
Pagan museum, c. reign of Kyanzittha*
*No.14 lower right: Late Period buddha in
bhumisparsamudra, Pagan Museum*

Ksetra the Buddha's images are far closer to the more contemporary Guptan work, less benign and more overbearing in their appearance. It would appear that at Sri Ksetra, an indigenous Buddhist and Hindu iconography had by the 8th century evolved often radically to depart from the established iconographical norms of Indian art.[13] Thus, Gotama may be portrayed with his left hand touching the earth rather than his right, or, as Ray has elaborated, Hindu deities are portrayed with attributes that are deviant from the dogmas of Indian iconography.[14] Sri Ksetra was a matter of a few days downstream sail from Pagan and, as with architecture, the fundamental elements of Pagan's iconography were directly derived from this indigenous Pyu tradition, reinforced by a new wave of influence from 11th century Pala India. Though North Indian religious life had by this time evolved to the 'Greater Vehicle' or Mahayana, the Old Burmans felt no constraint when it came to borrowing from the Mahayana artistic and architectural vocabulary and repertoire, imitating this contemporary aesthetic whilst retaining their own long-standing doctrinal and iconographic traditions, that during the great reign of Kyanzittha, underwent a purge of any deviant elements.

Thus, it may be said that, at Pagan, the monumental appeal of Pyu art combines with the humanistic appeal of Mon art, and a third ingredient blends to create the moving yet succinct Early Pagan Buddha: the art of the Pala dynasty of Bengal, who had succeeded the Guptas by the 8th century as the political and cultural force in North India. Pala art reached Pagan in the form of two portable mediums, bronze and terracotta, brought back from Bodh Gaya and the holy places of Buddhism by pilgrims, merchants and monks. Cultural exchange was, though, two way, votive tablets from Burma are to be found in the Calcutta Museum and it is known that Kyanzittha, and possibly also Nadaungmya, sent missions to restore the Vajrasana Temple at Bodh Gaya.[15] The introduction of Pala-derived Mahayana art into Theravada Burma does not appear to have doctrinally unsettled the people of Pagan. Images of the Buddha in *bhumisparsamudra*, crowned or uncrowned, in Pala Bengal had, by the 11th century, evolved to represent Aksoba, one of the five Dhyani Buddhas. The original intention behind this portrayal of Gotama, the historical Buddha, had thus, by the 11th century, been displaced in Mahayana lands.[16] In Theravada Burma the original significance of *bhumisparsa* portrayal had remained, whilst any Mahayana connection this portrayal might have accrued was soon ignored, if ever realised. Thus, as with contemporary architectural design, the Theravada eclectically borrowed from the Mahayana to enhance their own faith, that by this date was doctrinally opposite to the Mahayana. Likewise, many a motif or form, deployed in painted mural decorations, originated from the art of Northern Buddhism and was modified to suit Theravada tastes. The presence of *bodhisattva, sakti,* and other Mahayana and Tantric divinities has in the past confused some scholars, leading them to suggest that the ritual practices and philosophies associated with such imagery had been incorporated into the religious life of Pagan.[17] However, as will be emphasised throughout this work, such images are secondary to the fundamental image of Gotama and the Pali texts that tell his story and illustrate his teachings.

The Pala idiom, in which Gotama was portrayed in 11th century Pagan, particularly when bronze or stone was the medium, is distinctive: the physiognomy sharp, with accentuated features, perhaps even slightly stylised, or, in Zimmer's words, "deficient in true plastic life," a style that propagated the then, in North India, prevalent concept of Lokottara—the divine aloofness of a Buddha.[18] Though a Pala type of physiognomy and physiology certainly became imbued in the early Pagan aesthetic, the radiant spirituality of Mon-Dvaravati art, and that very Guptan boldness, strength and power of Pyu art wielded a potent indigenous influence in the formation of an Early Pagan style of portraying the Buddha, as indeed was the case iconographically. To borrow again from the immortal prose of Zimmer, this time from his characterisation of Burmese art:

> simplicity and composure, a sober cleanliness of contour that rejects exuberance of ornament and detail, and a cool pure atmosphere, nicely balanced between a dignified graceful emptiness and a sweet inward spiritual life.'[19]

The characteristics of the Pagan buddha have been elaborated upon with the more technical eye of the woodcarver Tampawaddy U Win Maung, and his description might also be applied to images portrayed in other media, here in L.E. Bagshawe's translation:

We can describe the points common to the Indian style as follows:

1. The *hman-kin* or *ushnisha,* the mark of omniscient wisdom, is present. The *hman-kin* is flat and is placed a little behind the top of the head. It usually takes the form of the pipal leaf or a lotus bud, and it was a frequent practice to decorate it with jewels set in it.
2. The top of the head (*mani-daw*) is small but raised. The hair is represented by an arrangement of small rounds (*ywe-lon-tan*).
3. There is no separate representation of the head band, called *thin kyit.* The front hair line takes the form of the *thin kyit.*
4. The forelock (*uhna-lon*) is incised.
5. The length of the ear is only eight fingers breadth, from the top of the eyebrows to the chin, and does not reach down to the shoulder. Inside the ear (the hollow of the ear) is hollowed out. There is no boundary between upper and lower parts of the ear; it is all in one piece. The tip of the ear leans a little forward.
6. The eyebrows, the eyes, the base of the nose, the mouth and the chin all slant upward, going outward from the central line.
7. The tip of the nose is curved, and comes below the wings of the nostrils. Its bridge is sharp and its ridge is marked.
8. The eyes are shaped as a parrot drinking.
9. The upper lip is long and thin; the lower lip is thick and short.
10. The chin is distinct and rounded, coming to a point in front.
11. The neck is wider at the base, and the three folds can be seen distinctly.
12. From the hairline to the brow (*myet-hmaung*) to the tip of the nose is one unit; from the brow to the tip of the nose is the same; from the nose lip to the chin is again the same. One third of the face belongs each to the area of the eyes and to the area of the mouth.
13. The ears are set towards the back of the head and in front of them is a wide area of the cheek.
14. From the top of the head the hair falls to a little above the point of the chin.

However, U Win Maung's characterisation of the Pagan image refers mainly to the Early Pagan image, as he notes particularly those dedicated by Kyanzittha in his various temples.

By the mid-12th century, bodies broaden and become shorter, whilst faces grow round, and the crown of the head flatter; the lips thicker, the jowls deeper; the Pagan buddha become less succinct in its expression, whilst more benign. Stone relief images, in contrast to terracotta ones, dating to before the succession of Kyanzittha are more rare. A number of monoliths, *dhyanamudra,* with one exception, which is *bhumisparsamudra,* have been found in the Pagan area; examples of which may be seen in the west hall of the Dhamma-yan-gyi; in one of the Dhamma-yazika shrines; in two of the small temples in the Shwe-hsan-daw enclosure; one at the Loka-nanda and one in the museum, excavated from the Shwe-hsan-daw. Luce mentions in his description of the Dhamma-yan-gyi that the one found there dates from the Ava Period.[20] However, Luce's assumption, based on a recently damaged ink inscription to the image's right, refers to the restoration, or re-dedication, of the image, not its manufacture. As U Aung Kyaing makes apparent, these monoliths, most commonly found at dedications associated with Anawrahta, are by their squatter shape, with short necks and awesomely bold faces, comparable with certain of Anawrahta's terracotta plaques. Further, there seems to be a clear stylistic connection with the Gupta-derived work of the Pyu.

No.15: head of bronze buddha in abhayamudra
from the Ananda Ok-kyaung

No.16: painted textile fragment found in temple 315

GOTAMA BUDDHA: MUDRA

The significance of the *bhumisparsamudra* image, often surrounded or backed by a painted scene of the 'Attack and Defeat of Mara', the evil one, has been made mention of. This scene, to a Pagan follower of the Theravada, was perhaps the most important image of the buddha Gotama, representing their lord at the moment of his enlightenment. In certain temples, particularly in the Early Period, the main buddha is depicted standing in *abhayamudra* (Fearless) or *vitarka* (Elucidating), or sometimes in a combination of these. A number of the standing *mudra* are not easily identifiable and appear to be indigenous variations of Indian originals, the most notable examples of which are the Ananda standing images that appear to project some form of compassion gesture. Such standing images were particularly favoured by Kyanzittha, who enshrined them in three of his temples. In the Middle and Late Periods colossal standing images as the principal image of a shrine, in any medium, become extinct.

'Iconic' *mudra*, that is, the gesture used in images, that, by their place in a temple were the objects of people's offerings and supplications, were, with the exception of the standing ones favoured by Kyanzittha, normally Earth Touching ones. Other *mudra*, such as *dharmacakrapravita* (Turning of the Wheel of the Law) take their place in subsidiary reliefs or mural paintings, as part of a didactically intended narrative, for example, the *dharmacakramudra* is always employed to signify the Buddha's first sermon in the Deer Park at Sarnath. Occasionally the *dharmacakra-mudra* was applied to a colossal image, as at the Mye-

bon-tha-hpaya-hla, but in such cases remained part of the *bodawin* or 'Life of the Buddha', at Mye-bon-tha in a reduced narrative of four massive scenes about the four sides of the temple's squarely planned, central core, or *lei-myet-hna*.

Another *mudra* that is a significant aspect of Gotama's iconography, yet never used as the main icon of a temple, is the *dhyanamudra*. In the Naga-yon ambulatory *dhyana* reliefs alternate with *bhumisparsa* reliefs as part of a clear, textually-derived symbol-narrative. As has been mentioned above, a number of monoliths, apparently dating from the reign of Anawrahta, have been found about Pagan in this *mudra*.

Finally, there is the *pralambanasana* posture, that is sometimes described as 'Seated in the European Manner'. This type also was well known to the Pyu and Mon, and was commonly stamped onto votive tablets.[21] The earliest *pralambanasana* portrayal in stone, at Pagan, is to be seen in the relief series in the Naga-yon hall, and another version may be found in the That-byin-nyu ground level ambulatory (north east section). Its greatest manifestation was at Kyasin temple where two *nirodha* buddhas, each in *pralam-banasana*, flank the Buddha in a portrayal of the 'Miracle at Savatthi'—a scene also found at temple No.218 and the Myinkaba Kubyauk-ngè.[22]

There are many iconographic curiosities at Pagan, some of which are comparable with similar Pyu finds, for example the *bhumisparsa* buddha with his left hand touching the earth. In the Ananda there are several reliefs in which one hand touches the earth, or is folded across the lap, whilst the other is placed, palm inwards, across the chest in a gesture indicative of *karuna,* or compassion.[23] Also of interest are a number of smaller finds in which both hands are raised in a double *mudra.*[24]

BUDDHA AND BODAWIN

The stylistic and iconographic origins of the image of the Buddha or buddhas have been discussed in detail above; what is of further interest is the diffusion of these diverse influences at Pagan and the formation of a distinct Pagan style and type of Buddha—a cross of indigenous tradition and the latest of contemporary North-East Indian developments—and the gradual and corresponding expansion of the Buddha legend, or *bodawin* as it is called in modern Burmese, as portrayed in sculpture and in wall painting, in response to incoming Pali texts from Ceylon. It has been noted that there was no single Pagan style in sculpture, but rather, three styles that chronologically correspond to the three styles discernible in Pagan's architecture. The process through which the Pagan buddha image, and the portrayal of the associated story, grew through the interaction of the indigenous and alien require some degree of analysis.

Pyu monoliths and reliefs of the Buddha abound, however, no find from this time, in monolithic form, depicting the great events of his life have as yet been discovered.[25] The Pyu did, though, have a tradition of portraying the chief events of the Buddha's life in the medium of the votive tablets. Many of the 'Pyu type' have been found at Pagan, indicating the source for the legend may have again been indigenous, rather than a direct import. What the Pagan sculptor was to achieve was a removal of these scenes, from their miniaturised portrayal on votive tablets, to become isolated relief scenes in themselves as part of ambitious and, in Burma, unprecedented sculptural programmes.

The Pagan votive tablet differs from the Pyu type in that there are eight scenes (*atthatthana*) instead of nine; in Pyu tablets an additional scene was included, which depicts the Buddha, seated, holding an alms-bowl, beneath the central Earth Touching Buddha.[26] Such tablets encapsulated the essential elements of the Buddha story, in an easily portable form. Often these were stamped by hand, and on the reverse side were signed by the reigning monarch, to be carried to the remotest outposts of the empire, not only revealing the geographical limits to which royal attempts at propagating the religion extended, but also demarcating, for the historian, the actual limits of the empire itself. Alternatively, tablets were enshrined within a stupa or temple; their presence then being symbolic rather than proselytisive.[27] It was recently revealed that Anawrahta had actually bonded tablets between the bricks of his Shwe-hsan-daw to form a spiritual defence field throughout the fabric of his dedication.

Numerous tablets of the Pyu type, and often inscribed in the Pyu script, have been uncovered at Pagan, and not always depicting the Buddha. Mettaya, Lokantha and other Pyu cult deities have been found here in votive tablet form and were to be absorbed into the religious life of Pagan as *dvarapala,* or door guardians to the Theravada sanctuaries.[28]

Replacing the Pyu votive tablet type was the Pala Eight Scene one. Pyu buddhas, as found in this medium of terracotta, are broad in physique, with rounded heads, whilst the Pala versions have pinched bodies and sharpened facial features, which become commonplace during the reign of Anawrahta. In addition to terracotta finds, a number of small carvings, named *andagu* in Burmese, most likely steatite, have been found; these finely carved works have often been claimed as being direct imports from Bengal, however, none of this geological type have as yet been found in Bengal.[29]

The Pyu Votive Tablet: Nine Scenes

	parinibbana	
Nalagiri Elephant		Descent from Tavatimsa
	THE BUDDHA *bhumisparsamudra*	
Deer Park at Sarnath *dharmacakramudra*		Twin Miracles *dharmacakramudra*
Parileyyaka Monkey *pralambanasana*		Nativity
	Sujata's Offering	

Pagan Votive Tablets: Eight Scenes

	parinibbana	
Nalagiri Elephant		Descent from Tavatimsa
	THE BUDDHA *bhumisparsamudra*	
Deer Park at Sarnath		Deer Park at Sarnath
Nativity		Parileyyaka Monkey
	Crouchant Animals or Mara's Daughters	

The Pala versions tend to be carved from a jet black steatite, whilst the Burmese *andagu* versions are hewed from a stone that is paler in colour and not found in Bengal.[30] From these intricate, though slight, estampages in clay the *atthatthana,* or Eight Scenes, were to be transferred to the more viewable mediums of stone sculpture and wall painting, as part of didactically conceived iconographic programmes at a time when Pagan monarchs were actively purifying and propagating the Theravada faith.[31] Involved in this religious movement were the Ceylonese who provided the necessary texts that were quickly disseminated through artistic portrayal in readily digestible mediums such as stone, wood and paint, at a time when illiteracy was widespread and temple construction proved quicker and less costly than transcription.

The earliest datable temples at Pagan (from the mid-11th century) do not date from the foundation of the city (c.850). Various portable images, bronze or terracotta, of Gotama or other 'deities', often inscribed in the script of the Pyu, and in some cases identical to finds from the Sri Ksetra area, thus predate the great era of temple building to the century and a half of the city's pre-imperial existence. The pattern of 'sculpture in architecture' is traced in some detail in the descriptions of the monuments that follow in Part Two. Here, the general trends will be outlined and the evolution of the Buddha, image and story, will be briefly traced.

The Nat-hlaung-kyaung is said to be Pagan's oldest surviving temple and is dedicated to Vishnu.[32] Arranged about the exterior, perhaps once enclosed by a lean-to corridor, are a set of stone reliefs, their condition now much worn, depicting the manifestations of Vishu. These seem Gupta in style, stocky figures, plastic, yet never fluid; monumental, yet never overbearing. In the temple's interior are brick and stucco figures of Vishnu, again poor in condition, yet enabling a glimpse of the fine stylisation of the deities apparel and the smooth plasticity of their form. Is this the work of the indigenous Guptan-derived Pyu tradition or the work of immigrant artists? The temple itself was the place of worship for the Indian community who traded and guided kings through the complex web of court life. The actual temple's architecture and the style of these reliefs is more akin to the indigenous Pyu tradition than prevalent Indian developments. Indeed, it may be said that by the early 11th century, when this temple may be said to have been built, such a style was well out of fashion in contemporary India and, thus, found here, was a survival from Pyu days. The Vaisnaivites, court Brahmins and traders who built the temple must have employed local men.

Two Buddhist temples at Pagan, said to date from the time of Anawrahta, provide a clue as to the sources for contemporary sculpture: the Nan-hpaya and the Kyauk-ku-ohn-min.[33] In these temples, contemporary by the style of their workmanship, stone carving emerges at Pagan with so perfected a finish and sumptuous effect that some scholars have been led to conjecture that this was the work of immigrant sculptors. Indeed, Luce illustrates some Bengali door jambs that are not dissimilar to the Kyauk-ku ones.[34] How-

ever, as U Bo Kay emphasises, the Brahma reliefs in the Nan-hpaya are, in physiognomy, Mongoloid rather than Aryan, to him an indigenous portrayal of the human, or supra-human, form.[35] Whatever the origins of this fine carving, dating to the middle part of the 11th century, it remains notable that there is a great discrepancy between the style of this essentially decorative and ornamental work, virtuoso in its design, and the contemporary manner of portraying buddha images, which is far cruder in execution, as may be seen on the *bodawin* reliefs within the Kyauk-ku itself. Thus, it may be surmised that there were two ateliers working alongside each other at Early Pagan, the one dedicated to architectural ornament, whose legacy of motif and form was inherited by the stucco worker, and the other attempting to portray the principal events of their lord's life. Curiously, at this stage, there seems to have been little connection between the two studios.

So at Kyauk-ku, with neither technical nor stylistic recourse to the stone work on the front, and then about two decades later in the Naga-yon, programmes, in the medium of stone carved in relief form that portrayed the chief events of the life of the Buddha were attempted. These reliefs represent, stylistically and iconographically, an indigenous development that clearly reveals the increasing mastery of the Pagan artisan over the medium of stone that was curiously unaffected by the fine architectural stone work of the Nan-hpaya and Kyauk-ku-ohn-min. The surviving scenes at Kyauk-ku are outlined in this monument's description that follows in Chapter Four.[36] According to Forchammer's report of 1890 there were once fragments of a number of other reliefs, perhaps shattered by an earthquake, scattered across the cave's floor.[37] It would thus be mistaken to suggest that there was a progressive expansion in the quantity of scenes to be depicted from Kyauk-ku to the Naga-yon. What is notable is the increasing adeptness of the sculptor's hand after the Kyauk-ku reliefs, seen firstly in the Naga-yon, and then in the Pa-hto-tha-mya, leading ultimately to the Ananda reliefs, dating to around 1105. With the construction of the Ananda, under the supervision of Kyanzittha, local knowledge of the Buddha story and its sculptural possibilities had considerably expanded: in the outer ambulatory a total of eighty scenes were executed, in a style directly derived from that of the Naga-yon and evolved to an aesthetic perfection.[38] Thus, in the Early Period, a natural progression in the Pagan sculptor's technical ability is evident in the successive construction of three major temples.

Compared with contemporary Indian works the Kyauk-ku reliefs are crude, almost parochial parodies, they even lack the visual impact of Pyu sculpture. However, here are the architectural backgrounds (*tage*) found on votive tablets, and no doubt mirroring contemporary trends in wood. In the Naga-yon hall, the carver's hand is surer of itself, no doubt in the intervening period he had practised much with wood.

Here is an easily defined Early type: the figures bold yet approachable; a balance between the hierarchic and the human, the elevated and the compassionate. Again, architectonic forms dominate the *ta-ge*, an essentially indigenous device; what is of recent importation is the expanded subject matter. By the reign of Kyanzittha (1084-1113) the Pala influence, in physiognomy and physiology, is certainly evident, indeed, to such an extent that it has been claimed that these images must be the work of visiting Bengali artists.[39] Such a hypothesis is unlikely, the indigenous evolution is clear and, though a Pala manner of interpreting face and body is present, the Ananda reliefs lack the aloofness of their Indian counterparts. The all-encompassing sweetness, enveloping warmth and benign sense of welcome expressed so succinctly in the Ananda reliefs may be derived from the gentle art of Mon-Dvaravati, together with a touch of that Pyu taste for monumentality. A further development from the sculpture of the Naga-yon hall to the Ananda is in the reduction of the narrative to the predella—all emphasis is on the Buddha, raised, or elevated, to a supramundane scale. Luce noted a number of reliefs in the Ananda cross-passages that illustrate scenes identical to those in the outer ambulatory, these he convincingly explains are rejects from the main series on account of their expressive freedom and lack of symmetry.[40] Kyanzittha sought an art that was to be educative through its human appeal, but never through familiarity. Kyanzittha, like any proper Buddhist king, was concerned with order:

> Predellas he approved: a large Buddha above, in one or other of the accepted poses; below, a small predella, to identify the scene. But the means to do so are often meagre: four monks in worship hardly suffice. And though the total effect of such a relief may please, or even move the devout, it gets monotonous. If the architectural background forced some unity on the design, it also numbed movement, life and action...The

tendency has been to petrify religious sculpture in a lifeless hierarchic groove; and by cutting out distance, chiaroscuro and perspective to confine it to two-dimensional decoration.[41]

Luce's interpretation is valid, however, what he ignores was the Pagan conception of the Buddha. Though anthropomorphically depicted, he was never to be represented on the human scale and usually his image in temple shrines was colossal, that is, supramundane. When it was physically impossible to depict a Buddha on a colossal scale his 'might' was expressed by the reduction of gods, men and events to a lesser size. Though super-human in his physical dimensions, the Buddha's compassion embraces all, a sensation readily conveyed by the moving nature of Kyanzittha's images. The scene where the *bodhisattva* Gotama cuts off his hair is quite dynamic: an energetic and potent image, hardly monotonous.

The Ananda relief style, the product of a clear, local evolution, refreshed by a wave of Pala influence, was to be short lived. Though a number of stone reliefs from this period, and later, are to be seen in the Pagan museum, the main events of the Buddha's life were rarely depicted in stone relief after this period, and never again on the scale of the Ananda series. In the Myinkaba Kub-yauk-ngè, there is a stone relief series that dates to the Late Period, however, this seems to be an isolated survival of an Early Period tradition.[42] Though the Buddha legend remained a central theme in mural paintings, the scarcity of good stone made such programmes unentertainable. Maybe, Kyanzittha's purification completed, there was less need for so didactic an art, and the more decorative medium of painting, or less costly and more rapidly produced, stucco work tended to replace stone relief scenes.

Intermediary between the three standing shrine images of the Naga-yon and the four colossal standing figures of the Ananda, in each case constructed from wood, are the four bronzes of the Shwe-zigon

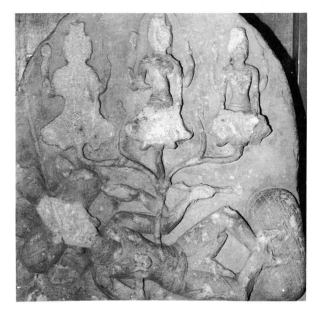

which again suggest that the Pagan sculptors' idiom evolved locally, and was not the work of immigrant artists. The quality of casting of these images is very fine. Like other standing images from the Early Period, the robes hang with striated folds, the bodies are curvaceous, with a thin waist and broad, well-rounded hips. Again, they achieve a compromise between aloofness and compassion. Considering that these are among the earliest bronzes from the Pagan dynastic periods, with little other than a few Pyu bronzes pre-dating them, the sudden advent of skilful and large scale bronze casting at Pagan is prodigious (these images average over 3.5m high). It is easy to surmise that this was the work of visiting bronze casters, yet, in style and form they correspond to contemporary local work in stone. Smaller versions of this type of standing bronze image of the Buddha, in *vitar-kamudra*, may be found in the Ananda Kyaung-taik and in one monastery near Chauk. These exquisite images are the ultimate manifestation of the Pagan bronze casters' genius: smooth whilst rich, sensitive whilst strong, sweet yet succinct—the finest visual expressions of Kyanzittha's brilliant reign.

The Pala wave of influence in Buddha images was short lived; by the start of the Middle Period, c.1120, faces broaden, bodies seem shorter, squatter and quite stout by comparison. Standing Buddhas, as individual portable works, such as bronzes, or as temple icons, no longer seem to be in vogue, unless when required in a scene from the *bodawin*, now generally expressed in paintings or stucco, not stone. The often colossal seated images in brick and stucco, that fill the temple shrines, are neither human nor hierarchic; an integral component of the temple design, these brick and stucco projections were no longer conceived to con-duce, assisted by tricks of light and shade, some metaphysical relationship between *hpaya* and devo-tee. Conversion and purification now completed, the 'true' faith firmly established, temple icons had less need to create an impact; a token, perhaps standard-

Clockwise from top left:
No.17: imported crowned buddha found at Pa-hto-tha-mya, of Tantric origins
No.18: scene from Ananda bodawin, with the Buddha in a mudra expressing compassion, early 12th century
No.19: gold Buddha (Archaeology Department)
No.20: Vishnu anantasayin, Pagan museum
No.21: Indra, in nat shrine at Shwe-zigon

ised, presence replaces the tactile pull of Kyanzittha's images. Some conventional *bhumisparsa* buddha stele, usually of sandstone, from the Middle and Late Periods do survive, whilst little in bronze from these otherwise artistically prolific, periods remains. Stucco carvings of the eight *bodawin* scenes were, in varying scale, conveniently included along the eight wall faces, between the transepts, of the temple shrine outer wall. In certain instances the *bodawin* was arranged along the inner wall, in place of the *lei-myet-hna* or four cosmic buddhas, for example at South Gu Ni or at Mye-bon-tha, where the *bodawin* was reduced to an essential four scenes, or 'potted life'.[43] There is still some intensity about these lesser images, for stone is a more expressive medium than piled brick coated in plaster. One head in the Pagan Museum expresses the Late Period image succinctly, the all-pervasive smile is both human and divine, approachable, its supra-mundane qualities instantly recognisable.

The development of the *bodawin* in sculpture, whether stone or stucco, was paralleled in mural paintings. Approximately contemporary to the Naga-yon hall reliefs, similar scenes were painted along the outer walls of the Pa-hto-tha-mya and Myin-pya-gu ambulatories.[44] In the Late Period, a painted version of the *bodawin*, as in stucco versions reduced to either four or eight scenes, proved a popular alternative to a sculptural medium.[45]

By the end of the Late Period, such an equilibrium between the tactile and the aloof, that had reached its high point around 1100, becomes increasingly displaced by a sentimentalising tendency towards the cherub-like sweetness that was to characterise the art of the Ava periods. As in wall paintings from this period, sinuousness displaces tension; they charm with humour and some wit, they do not move the beholder with the intensity and spiritual radiance of the Early Period image.

CROWNED IMAGES

In the periods of Burma's art that follow those of the Pagan Dynasty, large crowned and seated images of the Buddha in *bhumisparsamudra* were frequently placed as the main image of a temple. In the Pagan Period crowned types were rarely used for the main image, though a number of portable bronze crowned images have been found.[46] Images of Gotama, the Buddha, crowned and royally adorned, are often confused with those of Mettaya who may be depicted in a similar manner. The principal difference between these two is in the *mudra* and type of regalia. Gotama, though crowned, retains his monk's robes and is seated in a characteristic earth touching pose.[47] Mettaya wears a bejewelled costume, adorned with much finery, and his hands are placed in his lap, in *dhyanamudra*. In the case of some Pyu Mettaya images which have been found at Pagan, the posture used, common to seated *bodhisattva*, is *lalitasana*.[48] If

crowned, Gotama, or Jambupati as some scholars refer to him, though the term is not generally used in Burma, may be confused with Mettaya; in turn Mettaya may be confused with the *bodhisattva* Lokantha, a version of the Mahayana *bodhisattva* Avalokitesvara.

The earliest images of Gotama crowned, wearing his monk's robe and subduing Mara, in *bhumisparsamudra*, found in the region, are Arakanese, from the pre-Pagan site of Vesali. Pamela Gutman has published this version and other crowned images from Arakan and discusses the adaption, from Pala prototypes, of their physiognomy and physiology to suit local tastes.[49] No Pyu crowned version of Gotama is known, though other crowned figures, *bodhisattva* and Hindu divinities, abounded in Pyu centres.[50] Gotama, in royal costume, may well have found his way to Pagan by way of such Arakanese bronzes. Likewise, Luce identifies an Arakanese type close in style to a bronze from the original Maha-muni shrine of Mettaya.[51] Images and their iconography are always interchangeable and the later Jambupati images may well have been adaptions of Pyu Mettaya versions. Stone tablets, called *andagu*, that may have been copied from Pala models, also show an image of Gotama crowned. The Jambupati image thus may have come to Pagan, either directly from Bengal, in the case of votive tablets, or indirectly, in the case of bronze castings, through Arakan.

What was to evolve was a distinctive image of Gotama crowned, that has since become a highly venerated type of image for Buddhists throughout the Theravada world. Essentially this representation is a merging of the Buddha and *cakkavatti* conception, both are concerned with the *dhamma*, in the Buddha's case sacred *dhamma*, in the *cakkavatti* case temporal *dhamma*; and each is associated with the *cakka* or 'Wheel', and each ranks a stupa for burial.[52] This envision of the Buddha as a princely figure, though popular amongst the Arakanese, earlier and contemporary to the Pagan Dynasty, was not to develop in Burma till later and at Pagan it is confined to portable bronze or *andagu* images.[53] In no temple or shrine does a permanent Jambupati image feature as the central icon. However, from the inscriptions, we know that it was popular to dress and adorn images with fine royal garments. The plain and unadorned image one finds in today's deserted temples, was thus originally royally regaled, and was treated, as epigraphy details, with the reverence due to an actual king, ritually bathed and perfumed on a daily basis, entertained with music and dance, and attended by slaves, bonded to serve into perpetuity.[54] No doubt coronets and other jewellery, long since pilfered, embellished these images, as is the practice in a number of popular shrines today. The inscriptions that record the dedication of these lavishly maintained images were usually explicit that they were in honour of the last buddha, Gotama. By honouring Gotama a path was prepared to salvation—Mettaya.

METTAYA

The buddha Gotama had left the world; those that were not fortunate enough to have been his contemporary and hear the *dhamma* from his lips would have to wait through countless rebirths in the hope that they would be in this world, as a man, when the next and final teaching Buddha was to come, Mettaya.[55] Though Gotama had left mankind, the legacy of his fine example (*buddha*), his teachings (*dhamma*) and the order of monks to continue his example and propagate his teachings (*sangha*), the path to salvation, as conceived by the people of Pagan, and indeed many a Burman to this day, was not an easy one. King Sithu I expressed this in the poetry of his Shwe-gu-gyi temple inscription dedicated in 1131:

> ..Rarely, rarely in this world
> are Buddhas born; and to be born a man
> Is hard, and hard to bear the Buddha's law.[56]

It was Sithu's prayer that he might be present, by virtue of this meritorious deed, when Mettaya comes, for to hear the *dhamma* from the mouth of a buddha is to instantly attain enlightenment, a preferable option to the long struggle that he would otherwise be required to pursue. Anawrahta likewise looked to Mettaya for salvation and wrote on the back of one of his votive tablets:

> I, King Anawrahta the Great, have cast this image of the Buddha. May I, by virtue of this act of merit, gain the bliss of *nibbana* during the dispensation of Arimettaya.[57]

Mettaya thus became a popular cult figure at Pagan, and, by the Late Period, countless inscriptions clearly state that, whilst building a *hpaya* in honour of Gotama, the Buddha, the donor's thoughts were directed towards Mettaya upon whose advent they pinned their hopes.[58] Devotion to Mettaya, at Pagan, did perhaps go beyond that of being a sub-cult, to become a significant religious movement in its own right. It would, though, be inaccurate to regard this religious phenomena as a Mahayana one, this was a local movement within the Theravada framework. Mettaya had been worshipped by the Pyu who passed the cult on to Pagan.

In no other Buddhist country, Mahayana or Theravada, did the cult of Mettaya cause so radical a departure from established architectural forms. The *nga-myet-hna,* or pentagonal form of architectural ground plan, achieved some measure of popularity in the Late Period, including the patronage of the King Sithu II, who built the highly ambitious Dhamma-yazika stupa in 1196, which surely is the ultimate architectural manifestation of the Mettaya cult.[59] Likewise in sculpture, *hpaya* is placed alongside *hpaya.* In the museum of Pyu art at Hmawza, near Prome, two stone slabs feature representations of the five buddhas of this *bhadrakalpa*, which includes Gotama beside Mettaya, who is uncrowned. This pictorial equivalent of the architectural *nga-myet-hna* is known in Burmese as *hpaya-nga-zu:* 'the Five Sacred Lords'. This arrangement of the five buddhas, treated in an identical manner, is an indigenous Pyu iconographical development. Though five buddha arrangements, the *jina* or *dhyani* buddhas, were part of the Mahayana belief system, neither a pentagonal architectural form, nor the simultaneous depiction of past and future buddhas, in identical *mudra*, was part of the Mahayana iconography.[60]

Also unearthed at Sri Ksetra is a small stone relief depicting Gotama, in his customary *bhumisparsamudra,* alongside Mettaya, who is bejewelled and apparelled in the costume of a *cakkavatti,* or 'Universal Monarch'.[61] A near-identical work has been found at Pagan, again underlining the fact that Pagan took its version of Buddhism, and its art, from the Pyu.[62] Images of Gotama and Mettaya together are, though, rare at Pagan, possibly one of the last interpretations of this theme are the twin Earth Touching Buddhas in the west facing shrine of the Dhamma-yan-gyi temple; this pair, by their style, may be dated to the Early Ava Period.[63] In this instance Mettaya is seated in the *bhumisparsamudra*, as is Gotama, and neither is crowned nor royally adorned. Mettaya was likewise depicted in this iconographically abnormal manner, as buddha manifest, rather than *bodhisattva,* in the *hpaya-nga-zu* of the Pyu, and the images in the shrines on each of the five faces of a *nga-myet-hna* stupa or temple are likewise treated identically in the *bhumisparsamudra,* without any form of differing attributes for the future buddha.[64]

A possible textual source for either the Pyu or later 'buddha beside buddha', or Gotama alongside Mettaya, may be derived from the *Saddharmapundarika Sutra,* or 'Lotus Sutra', a Mahayana work of great importance, that describes the ultimate moment when the two buddhas meet and sit together.[65] Elements of the Mahayana had become infused into the religious life of the Pyu, whilst the great purification of the Early Period had suppressed any such Mahayanist tendencies in contemporary religious life; iconographic elements, such as 'buddha meeting buddha', from the Mahayana, were rarely to recur until this highly curious Ava work at the Dhamma-yan-gyi.

Despite this *hpaya-nga-zu* connection, Mettaya was conventionally portrayed, in full *bodhisattva* garb, not as an icon in a shrine, singly or part of a cycle in a *nga-myet-hna* architectural complex, but as a *dvarapala,* or 'door keeper', usually made of stucco and brick, or painted on the wall, flanking the entrance to a shrine.

SUPPORTERS OF THE BUDDHA

1) Bodhisattva and Dvarapala

Though Avalokitesvara was known to the Pyu, the *bodhisattva* that at Pagan was most widely portrayed, with the exception of Mettaya, was Lokantha, himself a form of Avalokitesvara. Lokantha was followed in Pyu times, as a number of finds from the Sri Ksetra area testify, and his image was directly transplanted from the Pyu to Pagan. The earliest figures of Lokantha found at Pagan are on the estamped votive tablets signed by King Anawrahta: "This image of Lokantha has been cast by the great king, Sri Aniruddhadeva, by his own hands in order that he might win liberation."[66]

In these images the *bodhisattva* poses in *lalitasana*, with hands raised in the *varadamudra*, seated on a double lotus throne; he is ornamented with fine jewellery and crowned with a *jatamukuta* crown. The *bodhisattva's* figure is set within a trefoil niche, carried by pillars and surmounted by a *sikhara* finial, about the pavilion are relief stupas, bulbous like those of the Pyu, and five in number—the *hpaya-nga-zu*.

Other Lokantha depictions found at Pagan are made from bronze, some cast locally and some imported. The image found in 'Scovell's Pawdawmu Pagoda' in 1920 may be compared with a similar work found in 1915 at the Paung-gu temple at Myinkaba.[67] In their apparel and appurtenances these images are quite similar: *jatamukuta* crown, enveloping lotus stems and princely ornaments; however, the Paw-daw-mu image is far cruder in execution than the other, the lines less sinuous, the surfaces lacking in the smooth plasticity of the Paung-gu find. The Paung-gu image is most likely an import from the northern Buddhist world, whilst the other is of local manufacture.[68]

Lokantha, the local variety of Avalokitesvara, existed alongside Avalokitesvara himself, and other gods of the Mahayana pantheon, in Pyu Burma. Avalokitesvara bronze images, standing in the *tribhanga* pose, with the figure of Amitabha Buddha in his headdress, have also been found at Pagan, as have images of Tara, however, it is in the medium of painting that the northern gods make their most frequent appearance.[69] In the following descriptions of the monuments, the positioning of the *bodhisattva* in a *dvarapala,* or guardian, role is frequently noted. These visually impressive figures, royally regaled, sometimes multi-armed, riding their *vahana* and accompanied by their *sakti*—the best preserved example of which is in the Myinkaba Kub-yauk-gyi—are iconographically subjugated to the central icon of Gotama, and the portrayals of his life and past lives. At Pagan, these figures are borrowed from the Mahayana world to support and protect the faith as *dvarapala,* and were not themselves icons.

Lokantha may also support the Buddha together with Mettaya, again the earliest examples of such triads are to be found in votive tablets that date back to Pyu times.[70] In such instances, to accurately discern the one *bodhisattva* from the other is difficult, and it is questionable whether the tablet's donors made such a distinction. The most colossal rendition of this theme during our periods may be found in the little known temple No.315 (Taungbon Lokantha), where, set in recesses, emulative of caves, on the north and south sides of the central block, are two such *bodhisattva*, seated in *lalitasana*. Lokantha survives today in Burma; when priest or layman is asked the significance of this god invariably the answer is "Nat".It was Anawrahta himself, who, on his tablet that bears this triad, wrote by hand, "King Anawrahta, who conforms to the *true* doctrine, is the donor of this tablet."[71]

2) Mogallana and Sariputta

The two chief disciples of the Buddha do not make an immediate entry into the iconography of Pagan. From the Late Period, and up to the present times, their inclusion, whether painted or as sculpture, had become near mandatory. In the Early Period, other triads, arranged about a central buddha were popular: the *hpaya-thon-zu* or 'Three Sacred Lords', Lokantha and Mettaya, as discussed above, and Brahma and Indra. Mogallana and Sariputta's earliest painted depiction is in the Pa-hto-tha-mya temple (c.1080).[72] At the Lokha-teik-pan (c.1130), the two disciples are prominent in the painted backdrop to the Buddha, their clean shaven heads, shadowed by haloes, in three-quarter profile. This arrangement was to continue with little variation to the end of the period and in later periods of Burma's art. The two disciples may also appear flanking the Buddha in scenes such as the 'Twin Miracle' or the 'Taming of the Nalagiri Elephant' from the *bodawin*. In the Abe-ya-dana (c.1080s), two brick and stucco figures flank the Buddha in attitudes of devotion, these doubtless depict Mogallana and Sariputta.[73] These premier followers of the Buddha were generally included in the votive tablets and bronzes from all of the Pagan periods and after, ever pious and adoring.[74] In the Ananda west shrine (c.1105), Kyanzittha extended this human theme to include himself, with his co-reformer, Shin Arahan, the contemporary equivalents of the two original disciples of the Buddha.

3) Gavampati

No image of this figure has yet been found at Pagan, however, he is referred to in a number of inscriptions and he is used as the prophetic spokesman in Kyanzittha's panegyric inscriptions.[75] In the Tharba Gate inscription Lord Gawampati is referred to alongside the "golden Buddha" and "four thousand one hundred and eight lords of the church of whom our lord, Shin Arahan, was the leader."[76] Gavampati was one of the Buddha's disciples, and is mentioned in the Pali scriptures, however in Burma, as Luce notes, in some mysterious way he becomes associated with Ganesa.[77] The question arises: was the disciple Gavampati depicted as Ganesa, or was he portrayed as a monk? In India, Ganesa is also called Ganapati—possibly the word Gavampati is a derivative of this.

Gavampati is also referred to as 'Lord of the Cattle' and is said to have been patron of the Mon merchants.[78] More likely this figure was the mysterious 'Fat Monk'.

4) The Fat Monk

In the Pagan Museum are a number of curious stone images of a pot bellied figure. These images have been found in relic chambers throughout South East Asia: in Burma at the old Bo-ta-taung pagoda, in modern Rangoon, at Sri Ksetra, Pegu and Mandalay. Arakanese versions have also been found, whilst a number of similar examples have been located in Thailand. This figure seems to have enjoyed a wide following, though his cult has not survived till today. Identifications have been various: Kubera, or the Shan-Thai 'Mahakachi', the Chinese Mi-lo Fo, or even Mettaya.[79] Luce believes, along with U Mya, that this image represents Gavampati, so often referred to, yet without a surviving image, for Gavampati too was a monk and his cult extended to the Mons as well as the Burmans.[80] However, U Aung Kyaing, in a recent article, identifies the image with the Thai Mahakachi.[81]

5) Brahma and Indra

In certain instances four-headed Brahma, on the left, and Indra, crowned with a *jatamukuta,* on the right, flank the Buddha, and thus a further triad is formed. This triad was established in the early periods of Buddhist art and as a combination, supporting the Buddha, in no way contradicted the tenets of the Buddha's teaching, that had originally marked a rejection of Brahmanism. At Pagan, this triad is usually to be found in scenes depicting the Buddha's Descent from Tavatimsa.

As an individual figure, Brahma is more frequently found than Indra, the most obvious example of this are the fine stone reliefs that face the piers of the Nan-hpaya Temple (1060/70). Other early examples may be found in the Vaisnavite Nat-hlaung-kyaung temple and painted above the *dvarapala-bodhisattva* guardians in the Myinkaba Ku-byauk-gyi, where they essentially continue the *dvarapala* role on a higher plane. Another part for Brahma was his insertion into panels within an image's pedestal, first done at the Ananda, and then more prominently at the Mye-bon-tha-hpaya-hla, where sandstone figures of the deity symbolically bear the mass of the Buddha. Isolated images of Brahma have also been found, old photographs of the Shwe-hsan-daw show him on the terrace corners, once again protecting the *hpaya*. Of these some were saved and are now in the Pagan museum.

Indra appears rarely as a single figure, even as a *dvarapala*. Only one known image of him from this period is to be found in the Nat shrine in the precincts of the Shwe-zigon; much regilded, the god bears his attributes of *vajra* and conch, is crowned with a *jatamukuta* and is clad in a loincloth. Indra, or Sakka, was to be incorporated into the Burmese national pantheon of spirit gods, the Thirty Seven Nats, as Thagya-min, in later periods. There is little visual or literary evidence to suggest that this incorporation occurred during the Pagan period and the present position of this image, in a Nat shrine of recent construction, is coincidental.[82]

6) Other Deities of Brahmanic Origin

Ganesa, with an elephant head and human body, was a deity known at Pagan and, like Sakka, became incorporated into post-Pagan spirit cults under the name of Mahapenni. Like Brahma, Ganesa guarded the terraces of the Shwe-hsan-daw; what fragments that survived, noted by Ray in 1932, are now lost.[83] Though Ganesa's image has not been found at the Pyu sites, a number of minor images have been found at Pagan, when, according to Luce, they were often placed in relic chambers—again the Brahmanic bulwarking Buddhism.[84] In painted form, Ganesa appears in the Abe-ya-dana tondi.

Vishu had his own temple at Pagan, the Nat-hlaung-kyaung, and here a set of stone reliefs depict his various avatar and there are two, now headless and much battered, brick and stucco images of the deity in the ambulatory; the main image, a depiction of Vishnu *anantasayin*, is now lost.[85] This was the temple of the local Indian community and, though Vishnu was a popular deity, amongst both Pyu and Mon, his image at Pagan does not appear to have been enrolled as a supporter of the Buddha. However, Kyanzittha, self-styled *bodhisattva*, claimed transmigral descent from this deity in his panegyrics.[86]

There is no surviving Siva temple at Pagan, though one large and finely carved image of the god is now in the Pagan museum. This was noted by Phayre at the Nat-hlaung-kyaung, and recorded in his description of this temple, which is included in Yule's *Narrative*, and Thomann in his book, the first book on Pagan, photographed it in situ in the Nat-hlaung-kyaung.[87] Ray describes it as being stylistically of South Indian origin from the 12th century.[88] An inscription in Tamil, that also dates from the later part of the period and records the dedication of a new *mandapa* for the temple confirms this later South Indian connection.[89] Possibly the temple's dedication widened to include the Siva cult in the later periods, an inter-denominational chapel for the Indian community. Alternatively, the image may have been simply stored there, out of sight, lumped with other Hindu images in their appropriate residence: 'The Shrine Confining the Devas'. Siva also appears, mounted on various *vahana* in a series of painted tondi in the Abe-ya-dana.

PART TWO

4

The Early Period, c. 850-1120

In all artistic media, movements of motifs, forms and subjects rarely pass abruptly; their passage wears smoothly into time, often unhindered by geographical or political considerations, whilst their origins remain unclear, and their ends uncertain. To formalise into patterns that have one date for the start and another for the finish into what may be called periods, styles or schools, is thus a highly unsatisfactory pastime. Yet, for a work such as this, such generalities, in the name of an order comprehensible to the reader, may be excused.

Art and architecture does, though, at Pagan, pass through a variety of phases, and often with a remarkable speed and fluidity. In an attempt to follow such movements it has been necessary to break our story into three periods: Early, Middle and Late. Just as 'Early' does not necessary imply 'Birth', whilst 'Late' most certainly does not imply 'Decay', neither does 'Middle' indicate a 'highpoint'.

Pagan art grew gradually from its Pyu foundations, and the first stupa monuments to be discussed are those of Pyu period and extraction. This 'Early Period' may be vaguely dated from the said foundation of Pagan, around 850, and continues through the architectural explosion that dates in the reign of Anawrahta, to 1131 when the Shwe-gu-gyi was built by Sithu I and the dynasty had become more firmly established in the second quarter of the 12th century. From this time onwards a new architectural style had clearly displaced an earlier one of differing aesthetic and spiritual values. So broad a period as the Early Period may be broken down into further sub-periods, which in turn may be broken down, until one arrives at the conclusion that no two works are the same and that, really, each temple itself represents a decisive moment in the growth of Pagan's artistic traditions. The majority of the 'Early Period' monuments discussed below date from the beginnings of the city-state's imperial mission under Anawrahta. The story of Pagan before this time must be told by an archaeologist, not an art historian.

As has been discussed in Chapter 2, past historians have tended to categorize the Early Period at Pagan as a 'Mon Sub-Period'.[1] However, the examination of the visual evidence that follows disclaims any such suggestions. Firstly, and most obviously, because there are no Mon temples with which to compare the Early Pagan temples. Secondly, because the Early temple and stupa at Pagan seem to clearly follow from a prototype, originally devised on Gupta Indian models, that had evolved over the past three or four centuries

under the tutelage of the Pyu, at their old capital of Sri Ksetra, where a variety of brick temples, dating to before the rise of the Pagan dynasty to political predominance in the region, attest to the direct architectural connection between these two civilisations. Further, despite the fall of Sri Ksetra in the 9th century to a Chinese raid, the Pyu, with their great building and sculptural traditions, do not appear to have become either culturally or demographically extinguished. As epigraphy reveals, Pyu, as a language and script, was still important enough to be included in a major royal dedication dated to 1113 and groups of Pyu people were formed into individual communities at Pagan.[2]

Pagan, a more northerly city-state, that was most likely founded at a date contemporary to numerous Pyu city-states dotted across Middle and Upper Burma, may well have absorbed the displaced Pyu population of Sri Ksetra between the 9th and 10th centuries. Indeed, it could be convincingly argued that Pagan itself was a Pyu city and the notion of a Burmese migration from Yunnan after the fall of the Pyu might be spurious.[3] The successful territorial expansion of this one city-state, under the leadership of Anawrahta in the second half of the 11th century, may be seen in the light of being one of many such states dating from Pyu times which had achieved suzerainty over its rivals. Indeed, the oldest monuments at Pagan, like the Nga-kywe-na-daung, are clearly of the Pyu stupa type and dating to before the 11th century, and the Early Pagan temple, such as the Nat-hlaung-kyaung or Nan-hpaya, are also, by their structural design and workmanship, clearly the heirs of the Pyu ones at Sri Ksetra. Likewise, sculptural finds from before and during Anawrahta's reign are of the highly individualised and locally evolved Pyu tradition that had, through its isolation, departed from Indian iconographic stereotypes.[4]

This chapter is perhaps the most problematic one of this work. Lack of chronological data leaves one to speculative guesswork and the twilight world of hypothesis. Yet the Early Period is surely the most exciting period of Pagan's art and architecture to explore, on account of its diverse and enigmatic nature. This is no doubt why past historians have tended to concentrate their researches on the 11th and early 12th centuries. So diverse is the artistic life of this period that it is impossible to generalise. For example, one may argue that the greatest architectural mistake of the period was the general use of the half vault, which was remedied in the subsequent periods, yet the Early

VIII, previous page: the Ananda temple
IX, above: detail from the 'attack and
defeat of Mara' in the Myinkaba
Kubyauk-gyi
X, right: dvarapala - bodhisattva in the
Abe-ya-dana shrine
XI, upper right: mural painting of the
Buddha and disciples in the Myin-pya-gu
XII, lower right: princely figures, Pa-
hto-tha-mya
XIII, next: detail of Mara's warriors in
the Myinkaba Kubyauk-gyi 'attack and
defeat of Mara'

XIV, above left: Nan-hpaya window stone work
XV, above right: Early Period buddha image
XVI, left: tondo showing a manifestation of Shiva in the Abe-ya-dana
XVII, right: tondo with dancing couple found on the window steps in the
Myinkaba Kubyauk-gyi
XVIII, opposite: Pa-hto-tha-mya front from the east

Period well knew the three-quarter and full barrel.[5] Likewise, the variety of architectural forms never ceases to surprise; as soon as the art historian attempts, for reasons of simplicity, a generalised temple design scheme, countless exceptions spring to mind. It thus only remains to be said that one should enjoy the glowing creations of the Early Pagan genius for their own sake, as people then would have done.

Most of the temples included in this chapter are in the vicinity of Pagan village, the furthermost to the south being the Hpet-leik and to the east being No. 315 between Wetkyi-in and Minnanthu. By the Late Period temple construction had expanded, on an often ambitious and elaborate scale, to more distant localities like the Pwasaw villages, Minnanthu and Nyaung U. The descriptions of the monuments that follow in this chapter and the next have thus been arranged chronologically, though in many cases with great reservation, whilst in the two final chapters, on account of the greater proliferation of monuments, it has been necessary to break the chapter into geographical zones within the Pagan plain.

No.1657 BU-HPAYA   ဘူးဘုရား

The Bu-hpaya was completely demolished by the 1975 earthquake and has now been rebuilt, albeit unacademically, from the donations of devotees. The Bu-hpaya's bulbous shape suggests Pyu origins and similar bulbous types are to be found at the Pyu capital of Sri Ksetra. Sited within the city walls, and perched high on the river bank which, gradually, has become undercut by the monsoon spates, it must once have been set more inland. The Bu-hpaya may be contemporary with the building of the city walls, c.850.[6]

No.1603 NGA-KYWE-NA-DAUNG
ငကွဲငါးတောင်း

This is an early stupa of Pyu type, most likely dating from the 9th century when the Pyu fell to Nanchao invading armies and refugees came to Pagan, bringing with them elements of their culture. Early examples of the Pagan glazier's art may be seen here, or perhaps the work of immigrant Pyu craftsmen. The Nga-kywe-na-daung was believed to be Chinese in origin by Taw Sein Ko, indeed Pyu contacts with China were strong and they may have learnt ceramic glazing from them.[7] The brickwork is cruder than the long, thin, tight-fitting bricks that are used from the mid-10th century onwards. The sanctum, which is hollow and accessible from above, was explored by the pioneering archaeologist Bohmu Ba Shin, but treasure hunters had preceded him.[8] A little further down the bullock cart track, past the Pa-hto-tha-mya, other examples of this type are to be found in the grove to the fore of the

Mi-ma-la-kyaung. Luce compares them with the Tibetan chorten.[9] There is only one other glazed stupa from the Early Period, or, indeed, any other period at Pagan, the Shin-pa-hto.[10]

XVIII: dvarapala-bodhisattva painted on south pilaster of the Myinkaba Kubyauk-gyi shrine arch

No.22 left: Bu-hpaya from the river bank
No.23 right: Nga-kywe-na-daung from east

No.1600 NAT-HLAUNG-KYAUNG

နတ်လျှောင်ကျောင်း

This enigmatic temple possesses a variety of names, their usage depending on the religious viewpoint of the speaker. Nat-hlaung-kyaung, 'Shrine Confining the Devas', which indicates the triumph of purified Buddhism over the Brahmanic, is the name used by most Burmese people today. Nat-daw -kyaung, 'Shrine of the Sacred Devas', is a term less in favour, though more ancient, as it implies that the Hindu images of this temple remained objects of devotion, and were not 'confined' here, as the verb *hlaung* might suggest.[11] Finally there is another redundant, though perhaps most revealing name, Nat-hlè -kyaung, 'Shrine of the Reclining Deva', which denotes the former presence of a Vishnu *anantasayin* image that was once the centre-piece of this temple.[12] Later Burmese people are a little embarrassed at having a Vishnu temple at the very core of their first great Buddhist empire. The Early Burmans were less bigoted and different cults may have peacefully co-existed at Pagan. To describe this temple as the 'Nat-hlaung-kyaung' is not strictly accurate, for this implies that heterodox images were rounded up and stashed here out of harm's reach. In fact, the sculptural and painted visual contents of this temple were part of a complete Vaishnaivite iconographic programme that was included contemporary to the temple's actual construction. On the exterior the Vishnu avatar stone reliefs are, by the style of their carving, clearly derived from the Guptan sculptural tradition.

This would have been the temple of the Brahmans, in the pay of the king and court, and the Indian merchant community at Pagan. Buddhism makes little allowance for the pomp and ritual so needed by the state, and thus imported Brahmans filled this gap.[13] Taw Sein Ko dated this temple to the reign of the non-historical King Thugyi (931-964) and generally tradition assigns this temple as being one of the most ancient at Pagan, though there is no direct evidence to prove this other than that in the manner of its construction there seems to be a logical link between the Pyu *lei-myet-hna* type, as seen on the actual Lei-myet-hna or Be-be temples at Sri Ksetra, and the Early Pagan temple type. At a glance, the Nat-hlaung-kyaung does not seem to date a great distance before Anawrahta's great outburst of building activity.

An inscription in Tamil associated with this dedication records the gift of the *mandapa* by a Vaishnaiva saint from Cranganore, in Malabar, in the 13th century. This may account for the *mandapa,* which has now been restored, but not the temple proper. The temple's high plinth (about 1.5m high) and the lack of a hall, as in other Pagan temples, would suggest the existence of some form of *mandapa* dating to before the 13th century, possibly with a timber hall extension as found in so many Late Pagan *ok-taik.* With its high plinth and profiled *kalasa* pot moulding running

about the plinth in a continuous band, various Indian connections have been put forward. Some scholars have suggested, on account of the style of the sculpture, a North Indian origin,[14] whilst others suggest, on account of the stone threshold, jambs and lintel, a South Indian origin.[15]

The terraces rise steeply, with the mouldings tightly bunched together, producing the effect of an upwards thrust. The superstructure does not conform to the more customary superstructure type that became popular at Pagan from Anawrahta's reign onwards, which have a square base and curved, tapering edges, first introduced into the Pagan architect's repertoire with the building of the Nan-hpaya in c.1170. This stupa crown for the *hpaya* had been the usual capping form in Pyu days.[16] With an inverted base and dramatically serrated mouldings, it creates a highly effective crowning stroke. There is a compactness and upwardly directed elevation to this temple, lacking in the Pyu versions, which must come from contemporary Indian designs current between the fall of Sri Ksetra and the rise of Pagan. The tradition of positioning a circularly or polygonally based stupa as the diadem—*jatamukuta*—upon the temple, was not to be displaced, from the mid 11th century onwards, by the then introduced squarely based *sikhara*; Early temples such as the Abe-ya-dana or Pa-hto-tha-mya continue this Pyu tradition, whilst in the Late Period and after the stupa type of superstructure enjoyed a vogue that was eventually to render, until the early 19th century, the *sikhara* extinct.

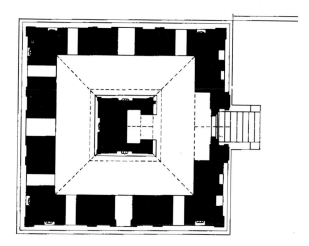

Nat-hlaung-kyaung
No.24 upper left: from west
No.25 upper right: brick and stucco Vishnu figure set
in inner ambulatory wall
No.26 middle: a Hindu deity carried by garuda above
shrine with painted decoration around
Fig.3 ground plan (EFEO)

On the front, the pediment arrangement, which reflects the Indian *torana,* has been much damaged. Notable, though, is the cinquefoil arch rising from pilasters. This is sometimes called a 'flame pediment' and at Pagan is to be found here for the first time. The earliest cinquefoil *torana* found in Burma is in the museum of Pyu art at Hmawza; it acts as reredos to an image of the buddha Gotama and dates from before the 9th century. The cinquefoil *torana* becomes a significant decorative feature on the Pagan temple and combines with the *makara* motif, above the capitals, and the motif of a deity, said to be Laksmi, at the apex. The cinquefoil *torana* is repeated within the temple above the central niche, here, rising up from the pediment, are the flame-like spinodes that become the hallmark of later Pagan architectural decoration. There is, though, as yet, no *makara* placed in the lower curves of the arch. In fact, this arch feature here is far closer in design to the Pyu version than the Early Pagan ones.

A second feature of Pagan architecture that starts off from here is the use of the semi-circular radiating arch hidden within the structure. The Early Pagan architect, like his Pyu masters, understood the structural possibilities of the arch, yet refused to acknowledge its aesthetic appeal, skilfully using it wherever necessary in concealed positions. This type of radiating arch, with voussoired brick patterns, was known to the Pyu, as a visit to the remains at Sri Ksetra will demonstrate. The Nat-hlaung-kyaung is the first surviving example of these Pyu-derived engineering skills at Pagan. Some controversy surrounds the origin of the voussoired brick arch, with suggestions ranging from South India to China, from ancient Mesopotamia to the North of India. Yet in no civilisation before our period was this form mastered with so much accomplishment as it was in Burma. Might it not be possible that the early Burmese evolved it for their own purposes—an indigenous development?

Square in plan, the Nat-hlaung-kyaung was intended as a gallery for sculpture. Relief scenes depicting the avatar of Vishnu were placed in niches around the exterior walls. Seven of the original ten survive.[17] These stone reliefs are, by the style of their carving, clearly derived from the Gupta sculptural tradition. Possibly an outer ambulatory was once attached to this now exterior wall, running about forming a second corridor about the inner cella and acting as a gallery for the sculpture.[18] This is plausible, yet there remains the *kalasa* profiled plinth moulding which would normally run along an exterior wall. Alternatively, looking at the cornice level of the present exterior, the incomplete nature of the brick-work might well indicate that a vault, possibly the frail half-barrel, that in so many early Pagan cases has collapsed, once sprung from here. This would have made the interior far darker, indeed, almost like an Early Period temple.

On entering from the *mandapa,* that would once have been covered by either an awning or wooden hall not unlike the *dhammayon* of the Late Period, one passes across a stone threshold, through stone jambs and beneath a lintel of the same material: this stone is geologically unlike any other found at Pagan and one may wonder whether it too was imported like this temple's priests. On the inner side of this flat arch is a second arch, this time a broad pointed one, its curve rising from the floor. In plan, the shrine instantly recalls the Pyu *lei-myet-hna* and the inclusion of an east-facing central recess seems to initiate the Early Pagan movement of cutting an inner cella out of the central block that carries the superstructure above.

The central recess originally contained an image of Vishnu. Yule and Phayre, when they visited the temple in 1855, noted a large size, free-standing figure lying on the floor and suggested that this would originally have been placed in the recess.[19] However this figure, now to be seen close by in the new Archaeology Department museum, is of Siva not Vishnu. The original main image, that would have filled the broad central niche facing the porch as the old name Nat-hlè-kyaung implies, would have represented Vishnu sleeping beneath the serpent, the Vishnu *anantasayin*, which is now believed to be in Berlin. This arrangement, as Luce notes, was popular in Pyu and Old Mon times, a further indication of the Nat-hlaung-kyaung's early date.[20] To the north of where the reclining god would have lain, the stucco tentacles of the sea serpent may be seen. Was this then a brick and stucco scene, as found in this position in so many other Pagan temples, or did stucco simply provide a graphic backdrop to a stone relief? On the upper sections of the recess, flanking above where this image would have lain, were originally two figures. On the north side, bejewelled and seated in *padmasana*, is a figure that seemingly floats upon a lotus flower carried upwards on a sinuous stem. On the opposite side of the recess a similar figure has now disappeared, whilst his vegetal vehicle remains. Early paint-work may also be seen on the underside of the recess arch—geometric designs and naturalistic painting. Set into the pilasters that carry the pediment over this recess are niches, the lower of which are now empty and no doubt once contained some species of *dvarapala*.[21] To the south, a figure does, though, remain set in a trefoil niche—Garuda bearing a deity, Vishnu perhaps?

Further paintings, now faint but in no way invisible, may be seen on the vaults and inner wall: geometric designs of interwoven, circular motifs on the soffits and above and panels of presumably Vishnu, flanked on each side by devotees or sub-deities. These repeated panels are close in style and format to the repeated Buddha triads of the Early temples such as Alopyé or Myin-pya-gu.

Brick and stucco standing images of four armed Vishnu, now in a battered condition, were bonded to each of the three remaining inner walls, about the central core. These figures too, recur throughout the period, in style and form transmitted into the guardian figures of shrines that often are called *bodhisattva* though in fact *dvarapala*. Their beauty, despite the damage that has been wrought against them, has diminished little.

Thus, to conclude this description of the Nathlaung-kyaung temple, it may be said that here, either before or during the reign of Anawrahta, was a temple built by indigenous craftsmen in the Buddhist bricktemple building tradition of the Pyu, for Hindu priests imported to serve a Buddhist monarch.

No.1030-1 EAST AND WEST HPET-LEIK
အရှေ့ အနောက်ဖက်လိပ်

East and West Hpet-leik stupa-temples, situated in the village of Thiriyapyitsaya, were restored by the Archaeological Survey of India between 1907 and 1915; they were more concerned with economy than the correct recension, in good light, of the priceless Jataka plaques found here and the restoration of the vaulting in a manner commensurate with the temple-stupa's original appearance.[22]

Said to pre-date the time of Anawrahta, the two stupas each have the *harmika*, between *anda* and finial.[23] The Pyu, as is evident from one relief sculpture of a stupa in the museum at Hmawza, knew about the *harmika* though none from this period have survived on an actual structure. Those to be seen around Pagan, for example the Sapada or Sein-nyet Nyima, date from the reign of Sithu II (1174-1211), and it is at this time that the two Hpet-leik *harmika*, each so different in their respective profiles, may have been added to the existing stupa structures. If the assumption that these are pre-Anawrahta works is to be believed, then Anawrahta must have added the series of Jataka plaques that illustrate scenes from the Buddha's former existences. Of these scenes 546 have been uncovered and each bears a single scene stamped onto an unglazed terracotta plaque. As there are two stupas at Hpet-leik there would have been two cycles, making a total of 1,100, over half of which are lost or remain buried. In addition to the discovery of these plaques, a number of votive tablets, signed by Anawrahta, have been found.

The original structures were a combination of the *gu* and the stupa, perhaps the prototype for the Myin-pya-gu, in which there is also a covered ambulatory running about the base of the stupa.[24] On the east section of the east stupa the original vault survives, and remarkably, is a three-quarter barrel vault and not the lean-to type that has commonly been associated with the Early Period; this too is like the later Myin-pya-gu, where there is a full barrel. These ambulatories were intended as galleries for the Jataka series and have now been rebuilt with concrete.

Taw Sein Ko in 1907 mentioned that two traces of wooden pillaring were visible.[25] Now lost, these would have carried the original timber shelter over a *mandapa* type extension or shrine platform to the west side of E. Hpet-leik and the east side of W. Hpet-leik, that is, facing towards each other. Though wood fragments are no longer visible the post holes are. Curious is the absence of shrines, or places where shrines would have been, usually at the cardinal points about a stupa. There are, though, some medial steps leading up through the ambulatory vault, breaking the inner 'gallery' wall space, on the west side of the east stupa and the north side of the west stupa. East Hpet-leik also has an extension to the east, something like a hall, not dissimilar to the one on Gu Bizat.[26]

The glazed tiles on the Nga-kywe-na-daung pre-date Anawrahta's reign, yet, here at Hpet-leik the glazier's art was not applied.[27] On later terracotta Jataka series, the plaques were finished with a glaze. However, at this stage in the development of Pagan's art the glazer's craft was yet to be applied to Jataka plaques. Possibly so large a glazing operation could not have been afforded by Anawrahta, alternatively this ancient craft had fallen into disuse, to revive with the building of the great Shwe-hsan-daw stupa in the same reign.[28] These Jataka scenes would originally have been recended in order, according to the textual source popular at that time, which was a Mon adaption of the Ceylonese model. The ordering has become muddled in their present relocation in poorly lit, concrete galleries running about the base of each pagoda. The actual numbering of each scene or plaque differs from no.497 onwards from the Ceylonese recension. Though the script used for each plaque's title and number is in Pali, by the recension the literary source is Mon. With the building of the Ananda (c.1105), the numbering changes, to follow the Ceylonese system.[29]

The style of the scenes depicted also suggest that this lovely fresh art originates from the Mon south, passing up the Irrawaddy valley through the hands of the Pyu. The bold, clear forms and well-defined outline are reminiscent of art from the Dvaravati Period in Thailand. Fragments of the Jataka, in stone relief, have been found at Thaton, at the Thagya-hpaya and Kalyani *thein*, these depict the Mahanipata or last ten Jatakas. Here at Hpet-leik, these scenes, that are charming in their naivety and simplicity, were possibly executed by artisans brought to the capital after 1060 from the South who were unacquainted with the glazer's craft, so well known to the Pyu.

No.1568 SHWE-HSAN-DAW

ရွှေဆံတော်

Here, at the epicentre of the Pagan area, is the first architecturally developed Pagan stupa. Popularly believed to have been built by Anawrahta and believed by Luce to have been built by him to enshrine the 'Sacred Hair Relic', or *shwe-hsan-daw*, brought back to Pagan after the raid on Thaton, which had been 'presented' to him by the king of Pegu.[30] The Shwe-hsan-daw is not only a giant reliquary, built to hold a prize, but a monument to a successfully completed military campaign and symbol of Pagan's transition from the parochial to the imperial.

Anawrahta built four other great stupas that may pre-date this one: at Myinkaba, the Loka-nanda near Thiriyapyitsaya village to the south (now encased by a more modern version); at Tuwin-daung mount to the east; on top of the Tan-chi-daung mountain to the west, across the Irrawaddy; and fourthly, the great Shwe-zigon to the north, near the modern town of Nyaung-U. Pagan villagers will tell that these pagodas, at the old city's limits, were built to demarcate the city and protect the capital from each quarter.[31] This is a credible hypothesis for at the old Pyu capital at Sri Ksetra, there survives a similar arrangement in which massive stupas stand on the outside of the city perimeter, facing the cardinal directions, presenting a cosmic forcefield to defend the city-state from each direction. The Shwe-hsan-daw dates from this great stupa building era and stands in the centre of Anawrahta's demarcated area. Curiously, it is little worshipped today, whilst the other demarcating stupas are popular places, for pilgrim and villager alike, and have been much rebuilt over the years, whilst the Shwe-hsan-daw remains much as it was in Anawrahta's time.

The Shwe-hsan-daw is the first stupa in Burma, pyramidally-shaped, with tall and steep terraces, that have medial stairways. An octagonal banded moulding is set between the five square planned terraces and the rising, concavely-shaped *anda*. The entire elevation's form is full and self-confident, far removed from the early bulbous type of the Pyu. The most notable innovation in stupa design that came in with Anawrahta was the rejection of convexity in favour of concavity in the design of a stupa's *anda*. This sets the prototype that was generally to be followed for the next nine hundred years of Burmese stupa architecture. The *amalaka* and *chattravali*, or tapering neck, and lotus bud onto which the *hti*, or parasol finial, would have been fixed, surmounts the dome. Well-defined bands run round the tapering *amalaka*, contrasting the smooth texture of the *anda*. The present *hti* is the latest of many replacements (a former one lies on the ground to the south of the pagoda where it fell after breaking off in an earthquake).

Hindu deities that had been incorporated into Pagan's Buddhism were strategically placed on the

terrace corners in a protective role. Fragments of the guardian Brahma's head, from this monument, may be seen now in the Pagan Museum, whilst other, less well-preserved fragments are scattered about the stupa garth and terraces. The assignment of the Shwe-hsan-daw to the reign of Anawrahta is definite as clay votive tablets bearing his seal have been discovered here. This stupa was a powerful cosmic symbol at the very centre of Anawrahta's expanding empire.

The stupa is not only a great reliquary but also a symbol of the Buddha. The ultimate Buddhist expression, the symbol merges with the reality and the stupa itself becomes the 'lord' or *hpaya*. It is also a cosmically arranged diagram. Here the five terraces imitate the slopes of Mt. Meru, the cosmic mountain that is the abode of the *deva*. A cosmology that is essentially Hindu in origin had thus been absorbed into Buddhism to support it. Like the Brahmans on whom the king depended, a pagoda with its Brahmanic cosmology that determined ground plan and elevation, was also dependant on a cosmological system for the protection of its sacred contents, which the original Buddhism of the Buddha was a reaction against.

Located on the west side, third terrace to the north of the medial flight of steps, a small arched opening is visible. Visitors to Pagan are not recommended to enter this passage for it leads to a maze of tunnels and chambers where fresh air is short and bat droppings have turned noxious, not to mention the dangers presented by usual curses and tales, confirming the efficacy of these curses, of those who never made it. However, in December 1987, accompanied by Ko Kim Aung Way from Taungbi village, I entered the tunnel with the aid of a powerful torchlight and a ball of string, and learnt much about how Anawrahta's architects built a stupa. Firstly, the question came to mind—what was the purpose of this passage to the exterior,

was it the route by which the relics and sacral objects were carried, after the completion of the stupa for their enshrinement in the *tabena*? Or, alternatively, was this the work of the *tabena-sha,* or treasure hunters, who were known to cut passages through masses of brick in search of the treasury? The answer must be the latter, for the tunnel has jagged edges and no vault, and the present neatly arched exit is the work of the restoring Department.

The first real discovery, made by Ko Kim Aung Way, was that votive tablets had been bonded into the mass of brick work at measured points, each tablet positioned horizontally, with the image and scenes facing outwards. These were spotted in a fissure off the tunnel that had been hacked out by the *tabena-sha,* who, also aware of their existence, and hoping that Anawrahta might have inserted some gem or other precious item with them, had hewed a crack of about an arm's length through which a line of tablets can now be viewed. Doubtless Anawrahta's intention had been to enhance the spiritual-force field effect by bonding tablets into the brick mass around the stupa. The purpose of this may have been twofold: firstly, to protect the relics and secondly, to enhance the beneficial effects of this work of merit that radiated out from the stupa's spiritual centre or *tabena.*

The tunnel, after crossing a downwards shaft, then ended with a second shaft leading down. We worked our way down this (about 1.5m) to a ledge and then down the same depth again to enter a small low-ceilinged chamber, beneath the ground level. This chamber contained a number of openings, each with a stone lintel. Passing through one of these, we entered into a further chamber with further openings and short passages radiating out, and passing through one of these, we were faced with the same again, and so on. Thus, there is a series of chambers conceived, like a maze, to confuse the *tabena-sha* . Alternatively, these were conceived as brick saving devices. It remains unclear which of these chambers, if any, was

the *tabena,* though we found a number of fragmented votive tablets, and Luce illustrates others that have been found here. Other, now broken, stupas in the Pagan area reveal that often a series of *tabena* were included at various levels. Caution, or rather fear, prevented us from penetrating the interior further, though a number of local informants mentioned that there was a stone *tabena* chest to be found down there.

As at Hpet-leik, a Jataka plaques series was included by Anawrahta in his dedication, of which only a few fragments survive now. Unlike the Hpet-leik ones these are glazed, the first glazed series in Burma, beginning a tradition that continues throughout the history of Burma's art. Some of the missing plaques may have been taken by von Nöetling to Germany.[32]

The earliest known representation of the double-bodied lion (*min-o-thi-la*) that guards the corners of most pagodas and some temples of later times are to be seen here making their debut.

Within the Shwe-hsan-daw enclosure are scattered a variety of stone almsbowls and parasols that are of a later date. The area, paved with stone, a rare commodity at Pagan, contains some interesting *gu* temples that in Pagan times were called *gandhakuti* or 'perfumed chambers' on account of the aromatic scents offered to the Buddha. Such shrines were subsidiary, used for devotional rituals and here were built at a later date within the Pagan Period; note the way they are orientated, contradicting the East facing norm. In two of these are very curious monoliths of the Buddha seated in *bhumisparsamudra,* believed by Luce to belong to the Ava periods.[33] A further monolith of this type and style was excavated by the A.S.I. in the Shwe-hsan-daw enclosure, and a number of others of this type, though in *dhyanamudra,* are be found in various other Pagan locations.[34] U Aung Kyaing presents a convincing hypothesis for a dating contemporary to Anawrahta for these monoliths, indeed in the art of Ava there was nothing of these images bold intensity, and they seem far closer in style to the early images of the Pyu, and certainly earlier than the Kyauk-ku reliefs.[35] To the south-west of the enclosure is a long, low-lying, single level brick vaulted building; this, the Shin-bin-thaly-aung, is likewise a later addition, and will be discussed in greater detail in Chapter Six.[36]

No.27 top left: Shwe-hsan-daw
No.28 middle: West Hpet-leik
No.29 far left: Jataka plaque from East Hpet-leik
No.30 left: three-quarter vault on west section of west Hpet-leik ambulatory
No.31: detail of Jataka plaque from West Hpet-leik

No.1587 PITAKA-TAIK
ပိဋကတ်တိုက်

The chronicles describe how Anawrahta brought back from Thaton thirty sets of the Tipitaka (c.1060) and it was in this building that the precious manuscripts were housed.[37] Though the validity of this story may be questioned, scriptures of a sort did start arriving at Pagan during the reign of Anawrahta, most likely from Ceylon, the homeland of Pali Buddhism, which was diffused into Upper Burma through the hands of the Mon. Ceylon became accessible to Upper Burma with the taking of the coastal ports by Anawrahta following his 1060 campaign. This building has, despite a later remodelling, always been associated with Anawrahta and its site is not distant from where the palace, put up by Kyanzittha in 1102, must have been sited.

Such texts were sacred and costly items, in fact it was cheaper to build a monument than to copy a set of the Tipitaka.[38] Anawrahta thus required a type of building that would protect the delicate palm-leaf manuscripts from the dangers of the elements. Firstly, it was necessary to place them in a detached and enclosed structure to protect them from the periodic ravages of municipal fires.[39] Secondly, a dimly-lit interior was required to protect the leaves from the damaging effects of harsh sunlight. Finally, it was necessary to ensure that the vault would be tight against rainfall.

The architectural solution to these requirements was an adaption of the Early Period *gu* arrangement. There is a central cella surrounded by an ambulatory: the ambulatory serves to reduce the amount of light admitted to the cella. The plan is a square one and there were originally three entrance openings facing east (two of which have now been claustured) and three perforated window openings to each of the three remaining walls. The texts would have been taken from the cella to be studied in a nearby monastery-school. The interior itself is now empty and something of a disappointment. The finest feature, though, are the window perforations, each carved from a single piece of stone. These are not dissimilar from the perforations found in 12th and 13th century *ok-kyaung* and one may wonder whether these beautifully designed apertures were added at a later date as has so much else, or whether the window work on later monasteries drew on the Pitaka-taik as their source.[40]

In 1783, the Konbaung monarch, Badon, sent his crown prince, who traditionally took the title 'Prince of Pagan', to Pagan to supervise the restoration of several monuments. The Konbaung hand is clearly evident in the Pitika-taik's exterior: the plinth balustrade, with its punctuating obelisks and three curvacious step supports, are typical of this period as is the five-tiered *pyatthat* made from brick and stucco, with winged corner ornaments and a square based finial. The Pagan Period builder was familiar with the *pyatthat* form though it was generally associated with

wooden pavilions or *ok-taik* emulations of this form.

Symes visited the Pitaka-taik in 1795, when the restorations were still in progress:

> We walked from the palace of the Prince of Pagan to see the Piedigaut Tiek, or Royal Library: ...It consists of one room, with an enclosing virando, or gallery, surrounding it: this was locked, and as we had brought no special order for seeing it, the person who had the care of the library said that he was not at liberty to open the doors, but assured us that there was nothing in the inside different from what we might see in the virando, where a large number of chests, curiously ornamented with gilding and japan, were ranged in regular order against the wall. I counted fifty, but there were many more....[41]

No.1240 MANUHA

မနူဟာ

> "Plot I never so shrewdly, it may not be !" Then stricken with remorse he built a monumental Buddha seated with legs crossed, and a dying Buddha, as it were making a *parinibbana*.[42]

The Manuha temple is so named after the captive Mon king, Manuha, who is said to have built it in penance after Anawrahta had finally eliminated his dharmic powers.[43] The block-like form is close to the Kyauk-ku-ohn-min, that may be contemporary, and also contains a similar monumental seated image of the Buddha entirely filling the interior. The *makara-*

No.32 *above left: Pitaka-taik*
No.33 *left: the buddha reclining in the Manuha*
No.34 *above right: Manuha temple*
No.35 *above: Pitaka-taik window perforation*

torana pediment over the entrance is later in style, the multiple tall and narrow spinodes with the figure of a deity in the central and highest spinode do not seem to date from the reign of Anawrahta when Manuha is said to have been imprisoned at Pagan. This more developed type of pediment makes its debut with the Naga-yon Temple in the 1090s and evolves from then onwards. The rows of stupas on the roof with their long necks are likewise of a later date. If the temple does date from shortly after the 1060 Thaton raid then the exterior must have been substantially renovated during the Middle or Late Pagan Period.

The colossal central image is flanked by lesser, though by no means small, images to each side, set in equally claustrophobic recesses. All three portray the buddha Gotama in the *bhumisparsamudra*. On the west side, at the back, is another colossal image: a *parinibbana* scene with the Buddha reclining, his head directed towards the north. It is possibly the earliest colossal reclining image at Pagan, if an early dating for this temple is to be accepted, though the *parinibbana* was a standard component in the votive tablet miniaturisation of the *bodawin*, whether stamped by Pyu hands or Anawrahta's.

The four colossal images' facial type do though suggest that the Manuha temple may well belong to the Early Pagan Period: taut faces, with long and sharp noses and accentuated chin closely resemble the Pala influenced physiognomy that were at this time being applied to the buddhas of Anawrahta's votive tablets.

No.1239 NAN-HPAYA

နန်းဘုရား

This small, compact and in all senses 'perfect' *gu* temple is also said to date from the reign of Anawrahta and if so, must be the first free-standing Buddhist 'cave' at Pagan.[44] One tradition, though a spurious one, assigned this temple as being the palace of Manuha, the captive Mon king.[45] Taw Sein Ko questioned whether it was indeed a Buddhist temple, for there is no image enshrined and the stone reliefs of Brahma on the piers were to him evidence of a Hindu connection.[46] However, the central pedestal could have born an image of the Buddha, possibly life-size and standing, for there is a skylight above that would have illuminated a figure of such dimensions.

The Nan-hpaya and the contemporary Kyauk-ku-ohn-min temple are the only two temples at Pagan where stone was widely used. It is a soft sandstone of warm hues and satisfying texture. The quality of masonry in both of these temples is very fine: note the way the blocks tightly integrate with each other with practically no use of mortar. The main structure is actually brick, the stone work being a facing for aesthetic or protective purposes and imitating the form of bricks. It would seem strange if this stone facing was originally completely whitewashed over,

with its ornament polychromed and gilded as was usual in Pagan temples. On close examination on the exterior, and moreover the interior, ornament polychrome traces are still evident.

The exterior composition is simple in its conception, perhaps even slightly restrained. The porch and its pediment are now lost, the masonry at the base indicating the one-time existence of such a porch, extending outwards from the east facing hall. The hall has a window placed at the medial points of its north and south walls. Windows on the Nan-hpaya are perforated so as to filter or ration the quantity of light admitted. Each is surmounted by a pediment carried on single pilasters with an undramatic capital between pilaster and pediment. These cinquefoil pediments are low-lying, unlike the soaring later types with heightened spinodes. The tympana, between the lintels and cinquefoils, contain a *kalasa* pot, a motif from India, that was also applied here on the Nan-hpaya in profile form along the plinth. This window arrangement is repeated for the shrine, where there are three openings to each side of the three open sides of the base. As for the actual stone perforations, these are made up of a diamond pattern, something like a trellis. In subsequent temples, like the Abe-ya-dana, various perforation designs alternate with each other, in an attempt to dispel monotony. However, there is little monotony to be experienced at the Nan-hpaya.

Running in continuous bands round the base are the plinth mouldings; the central one is the same *kalasa* pot in profile, first found at Pagan on the Nat-hlaung-kyaung. Above this, at the level of the pilaster bases, runs a subtle dado frieze carved from the stone bricks. The dado is comprised of a band of tondos, each

tondo framing the figure of a *hamsa*, a mythical aquatic bird of Indian origin. This motif is often repeated in mural paintings, for example, the Myinkaba Kubyauk-gyi, and acquired great popularity in later times. Here at the Nan-hpaya, the *hamsa* too makes its Pagan debut. On the upper part of the exterior wall, beneath the entablature, is the *kirtimukha* frieze. Of breathtaking beauty, it also has been chiseled from the surface of the stone bricks either before they were laid or once in position. This work is contemporary with the Kyauk-ku-ohn-min stone work, where a near identical vocabulary of decorative motifs was employed. The style of stone carving at Kyauk-ku is also close to the Nan-hpaya's, though, perhaps on account of the greater scale of the Kyauk-ku, the stone carved ornament on its exterior is less delicate whilst bolder and more visually impressive. The Kyauk-ku-ohn-min door jambs are claimed to be traceable to similar jambs in Bengal and a convincing argument has been presented to suggest that this stone work was the work of immigrant artists from Bengal.[47] However, U Bo Kay presents an equally convincing argument for an indigenous derivation, for the Brahma reliefs' physiognomy within the Nan-hpaya is Mongoloid not Indo-Aryan.[48] The other Pagan decorative motif that becomes widespread and may be seen here ornamenting the pilasters, that also is later translated into the stucco medium, is the corner pilaster featuring the downwards pointing **V** incorporating a *kirtimukha*.

After this time, exterior temple ornament would rarely be carved in the medium of stone again, perhaps on account of the rarity of this medium, and these innovative motifs and forms were translated into the medium of stucco, a medium in which contempo-

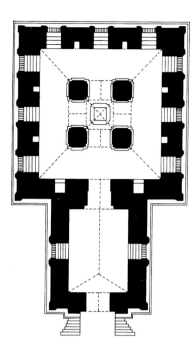

No.36 far left: Nan-hpaya, east
No.37 left: Brahma relief, Nan-hpaya shrine
Fig.4: Nan-hpaya ground plan (EFEO)

rary artists were more familiar as Early Pagan had absorbed the Pyu stucco working traditions into its own artistic life. So, the question recurs, from whence did the artists who worked here and at Kyauk-ku come? Were they local men working in a local tradition of which there are no other vestiges? Or, perhaps, the work of Mon artists transported as booty by Anawrahta back to his capital, as the chronicles tell? Alternatively, was this was the work of imported Indians who modified physiognomy to suit the local taste? Whatever, it must be noted that there is a dichotomy between the prodigious virtuosity of this atelier, who were concerned with ornament, and Anawrahta's Buddha images which are far cruder in their execution and surely the work of different hands.

The hall vault is masked by two simple crenellated terraces and over the shrine a third one runs beneath the *sikhara*. The medial openings protruding about the base of the *sikhara* are sky-lights. Rising from the steep, horizontal lines of the base moulding is the *sikhara,* a vertical stroke countering the horizontality of the temple's sub-structure. The east face retains the sunken round and square panels that were originally a feature of all four faces. If this work does belong to the reign of Anawrahta, and there is no reason to invalidate this tradition, then this must be the first *sikhara* of this type at Pagan, unlike the Pyu type found on the Nat-hlaung-kyaung. Again, the origin of this form is unclear, it does not seem to have been known to the Pyu so it may well have been an import from India. On Anawrahta's votive tablets similar forms are to be seen, acting as a reredos to the central figure. Anawrahta at this time rejected the Pyu type of

tablet that had included nine scenes from the life of the Buddha, in favour of the more regular Pala type with eight scenes, and tablets from Bodh Gaya have been found from this time at Pagan.[49] This type of *sikhara* with square base and curved, tapering, upwards and inwards panels, something like the *jatamukuta* or crown ornament, was the current form used in contemporary north-east India. It may have been carried to Burma in this portable medium to influence temple design. This whole superstructure is set well within the low-lying terraces and there is none of the steep, energetic climb of the Nat-hlaung-kyaung.

The plan is a simple two unit, one of hall and one of shrine. The *sikhara* is carried by four freestanding piers. The space between them is directly beneath the central mass above. Sky-lights transmit a dim light down onto the empty pedestal upon which the Buddha must have stood. Freestanding, it may have been made of bronze. Here, the central core of the Nat-hlaung-kyaung and Pyu prototypes is hollowed to create the cella framed by the four massive piers. It is the next logical step in the evolution of the Pagan temple, after the Nat-hlaung-kyaung and the first Buddhist one. Immediately above the restored pedestal is an upper open space with four openings that pass through the base of the *sikhara,* here is also a cornice running about the four sides of this upper open space. However behind this, in the vault between the two west piers, is a further aperture. It may be conjectured that, originally, the image stood between these piers, and not to the centre, and that the upper space, inside the base of the *sikhara,* was in fact an attic, with boards covering the opening held by the cornice. The present pedestal, as has been noted, is a restored one and it is uncertain whether the original would have stood in this position.

Perhaps the finest feature of the whole temple are the stone relief carvings of the Hindu deity, Brahma, characterised by the four heads at right angles to each other. There are four of these Brahma reliefs, one on the inner face of each pier looking into the cella towards where the image would have stood. The carving of these reliefs is of outstanding sumptuousness, their production a prodigious moment for Pagan. Carved from not a single slab but from stone blocks that interlock, they are reminiscent of the stone-carving techniques of Java or Cambodia. Brahma is carried on a lotus cushion that extends sinuous stems to encompass his body with lush buds. Set within a semi-circular arch, framed by curvacious line carvings and surmounted by a richly-carved *kirtimukha* frieze, this manner of treating Brahma in relief on stone was never to be repeated again in Burma, though Brahma, the god, who has been met earlier at the Nat-hlaung-kyaung, was a well known deity to the Pyus and Old Mons. Always, Brahma is secondary to Buddha; it would be a grave mistake to suggest that the Nan-hpaya was a Brahmanic temple.[50]

The pediments that span between the piers, masking the arches, are related to the ones on the exterior, which are cinquefoils with spinode ornamentation first found at Pagan at the Nat-hlaung-kyaung, but a form known to the Pyu. Here the cinquefoil pediment is developed to the next stage in which it is superimposed upon a tiered arrangement resembling a *pyat-that*. This arrangement was, by the end of the Early Period, to be applied to exterior window ornamentation, for example at the Myinkaba Kubyauk-gyi. Interesting here is the inclusion of leogryphs on the lower horizontal protrusion. This device was, though, not to be repeated in later renditions of this form.

On the remaining three sides of the four piers that same **V** feature of the exterior pilasters is elaborated. The carver's chisel self-confident, his creations hang down as if richly textured banners. Fragments of mural paintings may be seen in the hall vaults: these must be among the earliest surviving paintings in Burma.[51]

No.154 KYAUK-KU-OHN-MIN

ကျောက်ဂူဥမင်

A sense of indescribable loneliness overcomes one here...

Forchammer[52]

A remote and desolate spot, difficult to get to, still today a place favoured by hermit monks, and perhaps easiest reached by boat. The cave is set into the steep side of the ravine and tunnel passages lead from here into the hillside to dark and silent cells that would have originally been used for meditation.

Dating the Kyauk-ku is difficult. The block-like form, with a superstructure of three receding terraces and surmounting stupa finial, resembles the Manuha, which is also of arguable dating but may be said to originate from the reign of Anawrahta. Each of these temples contain a colossal seated Buddha which fills the interior. At Kyauk-ku, two massive freestanding piers on the interior are repeated in form in the projecting inwards and outwards masonry that flanks the porch. This arrangement reminds one of the four piers forming the cella in the Nan-hpaya at Myinkaba

No.38: Kyauk-ku from across the ravine

(c.1060-70). Likewise, the use of stone and manner of carving on the dado and *kirtimukha* friezes, not to mention the splendid door jambs, are very similar to the Nan-hpaya. The Nan-hpaya and Kyauk-ku-ohn-min must be near contemporary and possibly the two earliest Buddhist temples at Pagan.[53] The Kyauk-ku may also be compared with the Manuha which may also be said to date from around this time and is also composed of a block-like arrangement.[54]

The window openings, one to each side of the projected outwards masonry of the round arched porch, are perforated with roundels and have a simple rectilinear stone lintel, not dissimilar to the flat pediments of the Pa-hto-tha-mya.[55] At the Nan-hpaya, the windows have diamond perforations and cinquefoil pediments. The stupa finial on the upper terrace is a later replacement like those that have been added to the Manuha.

The door jambs have been compared with those at Bangarh in West Bengal, but the Kyauk-ku ones are different in style, though outwardly comprised of similar forms. The receding planes of the jambs bear guardian deities or *bilu*, as they are known in modern Burmese, and are prototypes for later guardians that hold a club across their breasts.[56] Such figures are carved in low relief across the right angle of each receding jamb, their clubs indented out of the angle, and half the body to each side of the jamb. Note the first depiction of the nude female in Burmese art on the east side of the entrance on the lowest tier. Also making a debut is the *kinnaya*, a mythical bird with exotic feathering and the head of a human. Framed by a square on all tiers of each of the jambs is the figure of a deity, or adorant human set in profile, bearing offerings carried on the palm of the hand of each arm raised to the level of the head, their heads are crowned like a *bodhisattva* or perhaps a temporal prince. They face in towards the shrine to which they lyrically offer their gifts. Such figures about a porch too become a constantly recurring theme in the subsequent art of Pagan transferred to the more applicable media of stucco.

On these jambs is a marvellous wealth of detail: adorers, guardians, grotesques and myriad other characters, not to mention a mass of decorative motifs and devices. Memories of Romanesque jambs on the church porches of Medieval Northern Europe cannot help but come to mind. These figures and motifs arrive in Burma at this moment, from where is uncertain, and are to be carried on through the Burmese artistic tradition for the next eight centuries in the media of stucco, woodcarving and mural painting. Elaborated door jambs themselves never feature again after the Kyauk-ku-ohn-min.[57]

Before entering, also note the dado above the plinth mouldings with its richly textured frieze of bud-like cusps, so similar in carving to the non-Brahma surfaces of the piers that carry the *sikhara* of the Nan-paya, where the downward tapering **V** is interspersed with an upwards projecting bud and stem. Likewise closely related to the Nan-hpaya, moving to the upper portion of the wall across the smooth surface of closely interlocked stonework, the eye meets a sumptuous band of *kirtimukha* motifs running beneath the entablature. The draping lines of bobbles link the *mukha* as they loop beneath. Here, the workmanship is sumptuous; these are tasty berries waiting to be picked. The same craftsmen that were employed on the Nan-hpaya must also have worked here. They employed a treasury of decorative and figurative motifs; the Old Burman, always short of stone, was to transfer their legacy into the Pyu stucco working tradition, a medium in which the Old Burmese felt more at home.

In plan, the Kyauk-ku is a single unit with two colossal piers carrying the vault, rising in the space between the east wall, from which one enters, and the image, which entirely fills a recess, cut into the hillside to the west. The colossal image, made from stone, is framed by a further two pier-like projections from the west wall that form the image recess and carry the full barrel vault above. On the north and south side of these projections are lateral door openings with a flat arch and horizontal pediment. There are also image niches positioned on the outer faces of these west pier blocks. These portals lead to subterranean passages that pass deep into the hillside, some of which have been blocked by earthfalls; here the tunnelling is of brick. Like the Nan-hpaya, the vaults and main mass of this whole temple is made from brick, the stone being a facing, protective against the elements and aesthetically satisfactory in effect. In addition to the two perforated openings on the east front there is a third opening on the south side, this, though, was not balanced by one to the north on account of the hill's slope behind. Lighting was not restricted to these windows, though, on the north side, in the aisle-like area created by the piers just above the opening that leads into the tunnels, is a small aperture set high in the vault casting a dramatic spot of light down into this otherwise dim corner. The stone ornament of the exterior is matched by equally fine work in the interior, for example about the bases of the piers are the same upwards tapering **V** work of those at the Nan-hpaya and the dim light has preserved the original polychrome work. The vault, as has been noted, is a full barrel one, preserved on these are the mural paintings described by Luce as 'Mon style' though, as he notes, lacking the customary Mon glosses.[58] On the soffits and lower part of the vault over the main image there are panels of polychromed stucco mouldings, their content characteristic of the first half of the Early Period, the triad of Buddha adored by Mogallana and Sariputta. On the remainder of the vaults are painted panels, without a moulded coffer beneath. There are further painted Buddha images on the inner sides of the main image recess. The colossal image, about 6.5 m high, and made from stone, at least on its exterior surface, has already been compared with the Manuha image. Colossal images were built by the Pyu and

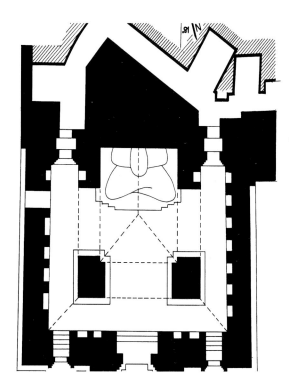

Kyauk-ku-ohn-min
No.39 upper left: kirtimukha frieze on exterior
No.40 middle left: dado on exterior
No.41 lower left: door jambs in porch
No.42 above: 'the tonsure', stone relief in the shrine
No. 43 above right: 'the dream of Maya', stone relief
Fig.5: ground plan (EFEO)

51 EARLY PERIOD

possibly Arakanese and remain popular with the Burmese up to present times. Symbolising the supremacy and omnipotence of the Buddha in an anthropomorphic form, the beholder, Buddhist or not, is certainly humbled.

Set in niches to each side of the monolithic piers that carry the entrance arch, are fragmented stone relief sculptures of scenes from the life of the buddha Gotama or *bodawin,* placed in three tiers of niches on the north, south and west walls.[59] If the assumption that this temple dates from around 1070 is to be believed, then these twelve relief scenes must predate those found at the Naga-yon that also depict the *bodawin*. In style and iconography they are similar to the Naga-yon reliefs though somewhat cruder, for these are the earliest depictions of this theme in Burma, with the exception of votive tablets.[60] The sculptors who worked these reliefs were less experienced and less confident than the sculptors who ornamented the exterior. These reliefs are the work of an indigenous atelier, who were in the next thirty years to grow into an accomplished school in their own right, whose greatest work, following on from these reliefs and the Naga-yon work, were the 80 scene *bodawin* in the Ananda. The Kyauk-ku relief's condition is now poor and the light inside the temple even poorer. Since my visit and study of these reliefs in 1986 and 1987 certain of them have been stolen; stylistically unique, it should not prove hard to track them to the usual western emporia.

Forchammer noted, in 1916, a *parinibbana* scene, which can no longer be found, in addition to a number of wooden crowned figures, like the ones in the museum, which by Luce's time had disappeared.[61]

No.1493 MYIN-PYA-GU

မြင်းပြူ

Both *gu* temple and stupa are symbols of the *hpaya* or Lord; thus each possesses a common symbolism. Though the *gu* temple develops from the stupa and forms a distinctive architectural type, the stupa conception is carried on in the *gu*. The 'cave' is a hollowed recess into the central block, comparable with the base of a stupa, where relics and other sacred items are enshrined. The cave temple differs in function from the stupa, being a place for devotional practices rather than a functionless cosmic monument. In the Myin-pya-gu, there is an architectural compromise between the two types: *gu* and stupa return to become one and the same. The Myin-pya-gu does, though, have a prototype, the Hpet-leik cave-stupas, generally assigned to Anawrahta, where there was a similar, though less unified, attempt to combine these two fundamental forms and where the earliest three-quarter barrel vault may be found.[62]

The base is low-lying, squashed by the mass that rests above. In fact, it is like a subterranean basement. To each of the four sides a central unit projects outwards. On the west side, this forms the entrance porch, whilst at the others, a square chamber lit by two window openings, and entered through a low arch from the ambulatory. The base walls to either side of the projections have only one opening. The rhythm created by the play of window units is 1-2-1. Like the near-by and near-contemporary Pa-hto-tha-mya, the articulation of the architectural elements breaks the monotony of a grid-like arrangement of horizontals and verticals.

Unlike the Pa-hto-tha-mya, there is no balanced contrast between a severe lower unit and sumptuous upper unit. Equilibrium, achieved by means of balanced contrast between lower and upper units, has here been sacrificed for effect. The base is depressed by the imposing superstructure which rises with the usual three terraces and a concavely-shaped stupa (not the *sikhara* of the *gu* temple). The terrace planes themselves recede inwards at the corners, forming an upwards movement. However, overall, this is a horizontally emphasised structure, with a downward movement. One is almost magnetically attracted by this downwards pull of the mass into the secret interior of the shrine.

The interior is dark, there are bats and one fears snakes; when eyes are adjusted the power and energy of the 'cave' becomes apparent. The ground plan is square, with the ambulatory running around the central mass [plan on page 16]. At the medial points, cardinally positioned, a narrow passage leads into an even darker cell that is receded out of the central block. Each cella contains a large image of one of the last four buddhas of this *bhadrakalpa*. This is the *lei-myet-hna*, the four face type, a cosmic symbol that dates from Pyu times and was revived at Early Pagan.

This 'four face' type, with the four medial shrines receded into the central mass, was the prototype for the Ananda 'Greek Cross' type of ground plan, whilst medial projecting units on the exterior were to develop into the arm-like halls of the Ananda that reach outwards in all four directions.[63]

The four enshrined, earth touching Buddha images are lit from a sky-light placed above the medial projections. What is interesting is that an inaccessible, continuous passage runs above the ambulatory round the temple. This is a clerestory, the main function being to reduce mass and carry the superstructure's thrust down onto the outer base wall. Through the clerestory, a spot of light, which enters from one of the sky-lights at each medial point on the exterior, crosses, to reach down a long duct and beam a faint glimmer of light on each buddha's face. Of the main ambulatory, the most significant feature is the use of the full barrel vault, a fact that casts dispersion on past beliefs that the Pagan builder only knew how to build a half or lean-to type of vault. Hpet-leik, the prototype for this temple-stupa, featured a three-quarter barrel vault.[64]

The four main buddhas have suffered much, but are still remarkably effective, as one feels one's way through the darkness into the shrine passage to be confronted by these massive figures, squeezed into the narrow confines of their cells, lit dramatically from above by a torch-like beam of light. On the shrine walls are painted panels, each containing the ubiquitous triad. Treasure hunters have cut passages into the core from these shrines.

Of the four units that extend outwards at medial points on the exterior, three appear to have shrine chambers, the west one serving as a porch. The south unit contained a standing Buddha arrangement (the Buddha's head is now lying in the ambulatory). Another feature that brings to mind the Pa-hto-tha-mya are timber lintels on the window insides.

The ambulatory inner wall is lined with trefoil arches each containing an image of a *bhumisparsa* buddha made from brick and stucco. Not to be missed are the mini-leogryphs that carry the pilasters of each trefoil, these are early examples of *chinthe*. The south-east wall section niches contain some Early Period versions of recumbent and standing images. The style of these images is far less polished than those at the Pa-hto-tha-mya or Naga-yon, but then the media differ for these are made from brick and stucco, whilst the others are carved from stone. It would seem that these are the earliest brick and stucco images at Pagan. However, at Sri Ksetra, one temple does have a similar arrangement of stucco buddhas set in niches along a line. In physiology and physiognomy, these images are broadly built and squat-shaped, faces are block-like, not at all like the Pala derived images that Kyanzittha favoured. In fact, they seem far closer to the Anawrahta monoliths that have been found in several places about the plain.[65] On the inner wall corners traces of stucco *bilu* are evident.

In the spandrels between the trefoils are painted figures of *deva* playing music and bringing offerings to the buddhas. The ambulatory vault is painted with geometric designs, in this case, broad, vertical and multi-coloured stripes, each filled with rondos. On the inner soffit there is a painted band filled with stupas and floral work; the darkness of this monument has preserved the rich and vividly coloured pigments. These early paintings seem as fresh as the day they were painted. These enchanting scenes are of heavenly beings bringing offerings of lotus flowers to the lords. On the outer walls are panel scenes, their condition now too fragmented to enable accurate identification but according to Luce the Jataka.[65] It would therefore be a mistake to suggest that, at this early date, mural painting was more decorative than didactic.

No.44: Myin-pya-gu

No.1605 PA-HTO-THA-MYA

ပုထိုးသားများ

...this Mother of Theravada Temples, so full of beauty without and scholarship within.

G.H.Luce[66]

By the building of the Pa-hto-tha-mya, an architecture that is balanced and self-confident has manifested itself at Pagan. Luce reckoned this temple, along with the Myin-pya-gu, which stylistically shows a number of parallel developments, to date to the short and historically uncertain reign of Saw Lu (1077-84), between the reigns of Anawrahta and Kyanzittha.[67] If so, then temple design and building techniques have made a prodigious leap from the time of Anawrahta. Further, there is no real evidence to support Luce's hypothesis, which he presents on the grounds that the mural painting content of these temples reveal the arrival of new Pali texts from Ceylon at this time. It would seem more logical to place these works within the long reign of Kyanzittha, when temple building passed through a variety of stages, when a variety of ground plan types and elevations were experimented with, producing an architectural epoch of stunning diversity.

In any case, the Pa-hto-tha-mya is a supreme symbol of the advance of the Theravada Buddhist faith at Pagan by the third quarter of the 11th century, and the fragmented and much decomposed paintings on the ambulatory walls do represent new advances in Buddhist scholarship that reflect an increasing scholarly exchange with Ceylon. However, if iconography and the textual sources for mural paintings are the criteria for dating an Early Period temple, then the Pa-hto-tha-mya must be placed before Kyanzittha's Naga-yon and Abe-ya-dana. Architecturally, the Pa-hto-tha-

mya is a considerably more articulate and sophisticated work than either of these two temples. Another criterion for dating Early temples is the evolution of the upper shrine and here, unlike the Naga-yon and Abe-yadana, four upper shrines were included, which places this work far closer in dating to the Myinkaba Kubyauk-gyi of 1113. Another temple that seems to belong to this type is the half ruined Gu Bizat which also has horizontal pediments and a grid-like exterior surface design.[68]

Sited close to where the palace must once have stood, within the compass of the city walls, the Pa-hto-tha-mya is orientated with the main image facing eastwards. The front has a double pediment framing the porch arch. Developed on from the Nat-hlaung-kyaung and Nan-hpaya, this front form is now treated with a greater firmness, though it has yet to develop that soaring quality that is the hallmark of Middle and Late Period pediments. This pedimental arrangement is repeated on the side entrances of the hall. Above, the entablature is elaborated with bulbous stupa reliefs (perhaps suggestive of Pyu ones?). Similar stupas were repeated, in the round, along the terraces and, as obelisks, feature on the corner pedestal blocks.

The window openings, like at Kyauk-ku, have no cinquefoil pediment. A flat lintel balances off the strongly delineated verticals of the pilasters. The architect's conception was of a grid arrangement: an equilibrium has been achieved through the play of verticals and horizontals. Likewise, note the delineating emphasis of plinth mouldings, with *kalasa* pot in profile, matched by the firm line of the entablature above. The shrine base walls are comprised of five square units, each containing the flat-topped windows framed by pilasters. Here, stone is no longer used for the perforations but, rather, brick in stark grid patterns of squares. The central unit of each side is projected outwards, breaking any monotony the grid

arrangement might produce. Exterior ornament is sparse, possibly there was once stucco work that has since perished. Here, there is none of the rich surface texture of the Nan-hpaya or Kyauk-ku-ohn-min but rather, an overall effect of sumptuousness achieved through the articulation of architectural elements rather than ornament.

The severity of the base is contrasted by the sumptuousness of the crenellated terraces and *sikhara*. Square blocks strengthen the elevation at the corners; these may once have been crowned with copies of the central *sikhara* motif or mini-stupas, their outer faces are adorned with the *sikhara* stupa form in relief. Obelisk *kalasa* pots were placed on the terrace corners. Unlike the Nan-hpaya, there is now only one terrace masking the hall vault. Over the ambulatory vault two further terraces rise to meet the horizontal bands of mouldings incised into the dome, varying in width and shape, that work up in a crescendo to form the crowning *sikhara*. At the medial points on the lower second of the shrine terraces are block-like upper shrines, detached from the base of the *sikhara*. Alongside the dormer stair exit on Alopyé,[69] that gives the impression of being an upper shrine when viewed from the ground, and if the Pa-hto-tha-mya work predates Rajakumar's Kubyauk-gyi,[70] which may be presumed so, then these upper blocks mark the beginning of the Pagan builder's movement from a temple with the shrine on the ground, to the Middle Period development of an upper shrine, the greatest, in scale, example of which being the That-byin-nyu.[71] These upper shrines do, in fact, contain images, which, made from brick and stucco, have been much damaged. Original stucco does, though, remain on the terraces, too delicate to be noticed from the ground beneath, with moulded or possibly carved *cakka* running along the terraces.

The *sikhara* with its splendid onion shape may be derived from the Indian *gavaksha* or horseshoe arch found at Ajanta and other early Buddhist sites. A dodecahedron, its smooth surface is punctuated with vertical ribs that contrast the horizontal play of the dome's mouldings. Inverted at the base, the *sikhara* wells out to taper back in. Over this a broad octagonal band nips this flow before the cresting finial bursts upwards.[72]

This interest in equilibrium is reflected in the ground plan. It is a play of squares. From the porch, extending outwards from the east wall, one passes through the hall, a perfect square, with door openings instead of windows on the north and south sides, under the base wall arch, flat as was normal in Kyanzittha's temples,

No.46 upper: Pa-hto-tha-mya upper shrine
No.47 middle: dharmacakra buddha in
Pa-hto-tha-mya shrine
No.48: lower: Jataka plaque from Shwe-zigon terraces

and into the ambulatory passage. Facing is a second arch leading to the once again square shrine, positioned beneath the *sikhara*. The shrine arch is framed by a splendid brick and stucco pediment arrangement, with a spinode cinquefoil superimposed upon a hierarchic scheme of horizontal tiers, reminiscent of the *pyatthat*, rising to a relief *sikhara* and finial. The ambulatory inner wall on the remaining three sides also have similar medial pediment arrangements, on the north and south sides framing a through-wall opening, like at the Naga-yon, and on the west side framing an image recess. This type of spinode pediment superimposed onto an elaborate system of tiers from which *sikhara* and finial rise in relief has been met with earlier at the Nan-hpaya;[73] in later temples, most significantly the Kubyauk-gyi at Myinkaba, this pediment scheme is applied to exterior decoration.[74]

The ambulatory paintings are in poor condition, though they may be among the earliest in Pagan. They do not dominate the interior. They are secondary to the architecture and Luce described them as "devotional wallpaper".[75] Around this time, c.1080, new texts were coming to Pagan from Ceylon and as scholarship rose in standard, under the stimulus of new literature, the painter was offered new themes and concepts. With the assistance of a good torch, most of the scenes are traceable. On the outer wall starting from the east wall south section, that is from the hall arch opening, and working about the outer wall, moving in a clockwise direction, are the following scenes from the *bodawin*, the original textual source for which was the *Nidanakatha*.[76] The scenes are painted onto a band broken by the window openings and niches. Some of these niches contain relief sculptures. Above are rows of identical Buddha triads rising high on the wall. There is a painted dado beneath the *bodawin* band and further foliate work about the niches, window openings and above the *bodawin* band beneath the triad panels. Of further interest is the inclusion of wooden lintels visible on the inside of the window recesses, such lintels were also used at the Myin-pya-gu, which is generally identified as being contemporary with this temple. Nearly all of the *bodawin* scenes have been identified by Luce, through the study of the glosses:[77]

1. *bhumisparsa* buddha.
2. *dharmacakra* buddha.
3. faint.[78]
4. Nativity.
5. Prophecy of Kaladevila.
6. Brahmans examine the Bodhisattva's auspicious signs.
7. Miracle under the rose-apple tree.
8. Boat race.
9. Archery contest.
10. Bodhisattva enthroned beneath pavilion with retinue.
11. Leaving the palace on a chariot: the Four Omens.
12. Bodhisattva in the Garden.
13. Return from the Garden.
14. Princess Kisagotami worships the Bodhisattva who

presents her with pearls.
15. Bodhisattva watches dancing girls performing.
16. The Departure: the Bodhisattva's horse is carried by the *deva*.
17. The Tonsure.
18. Practising austerities,
19. The Alms Round.
20. Visit of King Bimbisara.
21. Bodhisattva seated with hermits.
22. Sujata's offering of milk-rice.
23. The Buddha eats the milk-rice.
24. Approach to the Bodhi tree (?).

East Wall (North Section)—the scenes here are too faint to trace now and the glosses illegible.

On the ambulatory inner wall, in place of the sculptures set in niches that one finds at the Naga-yon, is a second band of paintings. Here too, the scenes are portrayed in a broad and expansive manner. The subject for this series would seem to be derived from the 28 buddha theme (*Buddhavamsa*) that was so popular throughout the Pagan Period and was also portrayed on the inner ambulatory wall at the Naga-yon in the medium of sculpture.[79] However, here, perhaps because this temple was earlier than the Naga-yon, the painted figures do not directly correspond to the text, though there is the same alternation between the *dharmacakra* and *bhumisparsa* buddhas, but without the predella scenes.[80] The Pa-hto-tha-mya series further deviates from the Naga-yon, and the text its sculptures follow on the east wall, south of shrine arch, where the 'Twin Miracle' and 'Descent from Tavatimsa' have been included, and the east wall, north of arch, where there is a *parinibbana* scene. Perhaps, if the Pa-hto-tha-mya does pre-date the Naga-yon, an accurately detailed *Buddhavamsa* text had yet to arrive and be interpreted by the painter.

The shrine contains a colossal image of the Buddha in *bhumisparsamudra* that is lit from a skylight set in the superstructure, which is hidden by the upper shrine, like at the Myinkaba Kubyauk. Squeezed behind the image, pressed into the space behind his colossal limbs are smaller buddhas, thus there is a triad.[81] There are through-wall light openings from the ambulatory, like at the Naga-yon, and the vault here is quadpartite. Some of the niches on the north, south and west cella walls contain stele. These reliefs, mainly *bhumisparsa* buddhas, are significant in the telling of the story of Kyanzittha's sculpture. Stylistically more advanced than the Kyauk-ku ones, the carving now less crude, the bodies smoother and better proportioned, the faces polished, yet spiritually radiant, there continues an interest in a relief's reredos background, which was to reach a high point at the turn of the century with the Ananda relief sculpture.[82] They seem to date, by their style, from around the time of the Naga-yon hall sculptures.[83]

No.1 SHWE-ZIGON

ရွှေစည်းခုံ

The Shwe-zigon has been described by Luce as "the most 'national' of all Burma's pagodas", for the Shwe-zigon, to many Burmese people, is the objective of any pilgrimage to Pagan.[84] Its precincts are littered with the shrines and *zayat* of subsequent periods and the Shwe-zigon remains to this day a 'growing' monument as donation is heaped upon donation by pious earners of merit. This fact, and the incorporation of Burma's most historic *Nat* shrine into the enclosure, make the Shwe-zigon as much the territory of the anthropologist as the art historian. Though the stupa itself has suffered the wrath of the angry earthquakes that periodically ravage Pagan and despite the multitude of later additions the lower part of the *anda* and terraces are original whilst the upper part of the *anda* and finial were restored by King Bayinnaung (1551-81).[85]

The chronicles record how Anawrahta built the lower terraces and Kyanzittha completed the work by adding the superstructure.[86] This is quite possible, though Kyanzittha in his inscriptions make no mention of this earlier start, perhaps out of policy, for he is believed to have usurped the line of Anawrahta.[87] Kyanzittha set up a palace close by the Shwe-zigon site, at a place known as Jayabhumi or 'Land of Victory', and, according to Luce, the modern name Shwe-zigon is a corruption of this Pali word.[88] The building work must been recommenced shortly after Kyanzittha's coming to power in 1084 and before the Tharba Gate Inscription of 1102/3 that refers to his new palace.[89] Later inscriptions also refer to the Shwe-zigon as Kyanzittha's work of merit, and the Prome Shwe-hsan-daw inscription, a panegyric that lists the main events of the reign, mentions the Shwe-zigon, not under its present name, but with a long Pali name, that by its language was distinctly Theravada and to Luce marked the triumph of the Theravada over other practices in Burma.[90]

The first stupa on a massive scale attempted at Pagan was Anawrahta's Shwe-hsan-daw (c.1070) which is quite different from the Shwe-zigon, being composed of a pyramidal arrangement, with steeply climbing terraces that sharply recede at the corners, and a tall elegant superstructure. The Shwe-zigon returns to the more massive type favoured by the Pyu and the grace of the Shwe-hsan-daw is sacrificed for the solidity of a bastion. The Shwe-zigon's form is closer to Anaw-rahta's earlier *zeidi* at Myinkaba whilst the broad and straight-sided *anda* is far less curved than the Shwe-hsan-daw's. Thick, circular mouldings run round the tapering neck or *chattravali* and a short, well-rounded *amalaka* or lotus bud finial crests this, though these upper sections were the outcome of later restoration work. 'Bastion' the Shwe-zigon certainly was, it is to the modern Burmese the ultimate symbol of the triumph of the 'purified' Buddhism propagated by the Early Pagan kings.

There are three terraces rising steeply to an octagonal band from which the bell-shaped *anda* rises. This is the standard arrangement in Burmese stupas. The terraces are tall and thickly moulded with panels indented to hold Jataka plaques and are crenellated. There are medial stairways and the terraces carry a blend of the *kalasa* pot and miniaturised stupa finial to mark the corners. The upper terrace has a direct copy of the main stupa at its four corners. The terraces recede inwards on five planes. It is a heavy and massive arrangement, and, with the Shwe-hsan-daw, the prototype for most later stupas in Burma.

Double-bodied lions guard the corners and *makara* protect the stairways, however these accessories are of later addition. At the cardinal points facing the stairways are free-standing 'perfumed chambers' or *gandhakuti,* each with a tall *sikhara* rising above them. Within these essentially *gu*-like structures are standing figures of the Buddha. These images are similar in style to those used at the Naga-yon, which was also the work of Kyanzittha, who seems to have particularly favoured this standing type of image. The four Shwe-zigon buddhas, symbolising the four past buddhas of the *bhadrakalpa*, are all in the same *mudra*, the *vitarkamudra*. The arrangement of one standing image to each of the cardinal points, in emulation of the cosmic succession of buddhas through this time-span or *kalpa*, heralds a similar arrangement at the Ananda, Kyanzittha's greatest work, though in the Ananda the *mudra* differs. At the Shwe-hsan-daw, the 'Perfumed Chambers' are not cardinally arranged, nor do they orientate themselves in the direction of the stupa, and by their architectural style are later additions. Most likely at the She-hsan-daw, as one often sees today, the images and their sacral appurtenances were sheltered by timber *zayat*-like structures, whilst here at the Shwe-zigon more permanent structures were cardinally arranged about the stupa. Cast of bronze, the four buddhas are, in fact, the largest surviving bronzes from Pagan, and by their style chronologically between the images in the Naga-yon and the Ananda. Thus they must date to around the time of our epigraphic date of 1102 for the Shwe-zigon. These images provide a vital clue in our understanding of the evolution of the Early Pagan style of portraying the Buddha and act as further substantiating evidence for the belief that the sculptural style that manifested itself in the ambulatories of the Ananda after 1105 was the logical conclusion of an indigenous evolution, and not the work of craftsmen imported from India.[91]

The shrines, rest houses, *zayat* and other structures, as has been remarked, are of later date. The Shwe-zigon, with its numerous images, inscribed bells, stone inscriptions and other paraphernalia of the Burmese pagoda, is a 'national' museum of Burmese art, covering each period that followed the Pagan dynastic one up to the present.

Towards the south-west corner is a modern building containing two figures of guardian deities. These are

Nats. Probably of a later date, their mythology is incorporated into the history of the pagoda, as told in the chronicles and by word of mouth down to the present, and their origins are a mixture of indigenous folklore and Hindu iconography.[92] In form, these squat, club-bearing figures may derive from the guardian deities at Kyauk-ku-ohn-min and represent the next step in the development of the standard Burmese *bilu* or ogre. They are close in style to those that guard the Shwe-saw-lu pagoda in the Yimabin township, which also dates from the Early Ava Period.

In the south-east part of the broad Shwe-zigon enclosure is another Nat shrine, contained within a modern, low-lying, building. These are the 'Thirty Seven Nats', the Burmese national pantheon of spirit gods. Their origins, deep in Burma's animistic past, metamorphosised during the various waves of Buddhist penetration from India; they have become the quasi-historical figures of today's pantheon. The ones in the present collection are copies, the former collection was bought up, parcelled in the pouch and is now said to be in Italy—an immense loss for Burma, not to mention for the art historian and anthropologist.

Closeted in a dim chamber at the east end of this unattractive building is a free-standing stone image of Thagya-min or Indra. Stylistically, it dates from the Pagan Period with its curvacious hips and regalia, quite unlike the images of Thagya-min that became widespread in later periods. This is the earliest known figure of Indra in Burma; before this date he is usually seen in a supportive role, along with Brahma, in the Buddha's Descent from Tavatimsa.

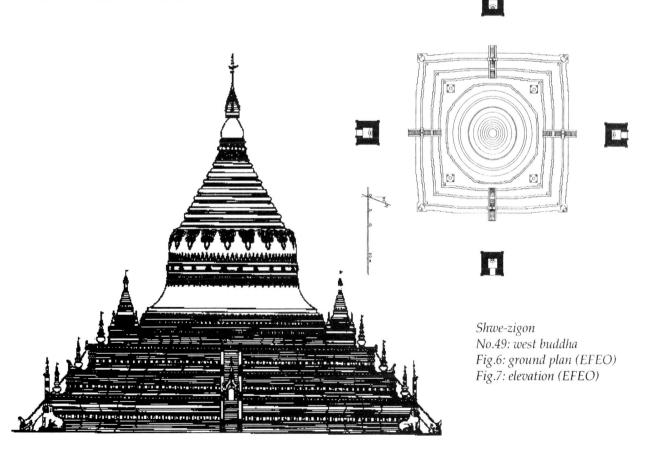

Shwe-zigon
No.49: west buddha
Fig.6: ground plan (EFEO)
Fig.7: elevation (EFEO)

No.1202 ABE-YA-DANA

အပယ်ရတနာ

The Abe-ya-dana is sited to the west side of the Myinkaba-Thiriyapyitsaya road, opposite and orientated in the same direction as the Naga-yon, northwards, in the direction of the palace that Kyanzittha was to build in 1102/3. It is not only close to the Naga-yon in its proximity and orientation, but also in form and style. They must be near contemporaries and are connected in the legends told in the chronicles.[93] Luce suggests that Abeyadana, Kyanzittha's queen, who may have built this temple that shares her name, may have been Bengali in origin, which to Luce explained the Northern Buddhist nature of certain of the paintings on the interior walls.[94] However, this is conjecture and there is no real proof to back so undocumented a connection. The neighbouring Naga-yon's paintings are less heterodox in character; if the two temples were built simultaneously it seems strange that their paintings are not more similar in content, though stylistically they are close. Possibly as Kyanzittha became increasingly submerged in Theravada dogma the Tantric and Mahayana artistic elements of the Abe-ya-dana became unacceptable. It should, though, be noted that despite the presence of Mahayana, Tantric and Brahmanic deities, the essential Theravada texts remain prominent in the painting cycles and the *bhumisparsamudra* Buddha, the most sacred of Theravada icons, remains the primary object of worship, central in the shrine of this supposedly Tantric temple. Other, seemingly alien, iconographic elements support the Theravada, they do not contradict it. Such colourful, decorative figures embellish the temple, filling awkward spaces at the corners and between niches and openings; it is unlikely that they were themselves actual focal points for people's devotions. Whilst this dimly-lit temple must certainly have offered its visitors a mystical experience, it was not an esoteric one as Tantric counterparts could be. Rather, it was an exoteric experience, conducive to conversion, not exclusion. Iconographic elements, seemingly incompatible with Pali Buddhism, have been borrowed by Early Pagan's reformers to reinforce their purifying mission without contradicting the import of their message.[95]

The architecture of the Abe-ya-dana appears to be less mature than the Naga-yon's, which may indicate a dating earlier than has been originally supposed.[96] Also, far less light is admitted to this interior than to its counterpart across the way. If the development of Pagan architecture is to be measured by a gradual increase in the luminosity of temple interiors, then this, too, would suggest that the Abe-ya-dana may slightly pre-date the Naga-yon.

The front has a projecting porch that must have been faced with a single pediment, whilst on the Naga-yon front this pediment was doubled at the juncture between porch and hall. The plinth has characteristic

No.50 upper: Abe-ya-dana front from north
No.51 lower: Abe-ya-dana window opening on south section of base with stone perforation work

Early Period mouldings with the rounded *kalasa* pot in profile and tightly banded line mouldings defined at right angles to each other whose full relief form contrasts with the temple base. The hall has side entrances instead of window openings, in this respect there is a similarity with the Pah-to-tha-mya. The square shrine base has three windows to each open side, as on the Nan-hpaya. There is, though, neither a dado nor a *kirtimukha* frieze. Though the exterior surfaces were originally stuccoed over, the Pagan craftsmen had yet to achieve the full glory of the exterior stucco ornamentation, found on the base walls of the Naga-yon and Ananda. Like the Nan-hpaya, the window openings are framed by cinquefoil pediments with spinodes, and appear fully arrayed above each of the temple base's window openings. These windows are perforated with stone, the designs for these perforations alternating from circular apertures to diamond ones, from window opening to window opening.

The terraces have crenelles. Copies of the central *sikhara* stupa motif are repeated at the lower terrace corners and the *kalasa* pot obelisk is placed in the upper two terrace corners. The superstructure follows the Pah-to-tha-mya type, only less ogival and based on a circle rather than a dodecahedron, with a thickly moulded indentation between the concavely-shaped *anda* and the *amalaka* sections. The positioning of a stupa on the superstructure rather than a *sikhara* is part of an architectural current met already at the Nat-hlaung-kyaung. It draws on a Pyu source which runs right through the Pagan Period and ultimately the stupa was to become the principal form of crown for *gu* in subsequent periods.[97] The Naga-yon and Ananda, built later in Kyanzittha's reign, return to the Nan-hpaya *sikhara* type with four flat faces tapering inwards and upwards, from a square, rather than circular or octagonal, base.

The ground plan, a play of squares, likewise must pre-date the longitudinally inclined Naga-yon and is closer in its arrangement to the Nan-hpaya. Like the Naga-yon, the orientation is a northern one. Once *dvarapala* would have stood guard on either side of the flat hall-shrine arch (restored), now only their pedestals remain. The hall was illustrated with a set of the 550 Jataka scenes, now in a lamentable condition.

The ambulatory with the lean-to or half-barrel vault of the Early Period temple has niches running about the inner wall. Most of these are now imageless. The two broad niches on either side of the shrine arch on the inner wall, surmounted by a *pyatthat* form in relief, contained Maya's Dream (east) and the *parinibbana* (west). These relief *pyatthat* pediments are an admixture of the *sikhara*-stupa already met, firstly at the Nan-hpaya, and then in the Pa-hto-tha-mya ambulatory, and also to be found, from the Myinkaba Kubyauk-gyi onwards, on temple exterior walls over the window openings.[98] Above these niches are painted scenes portraying the 'Conception of the Buddha', significantly arranged at the entrance to the shrine

after the 'past life' stories of the hall. The medial niches on each wall are also elaborated with the *pyatthat* pediment in relief, whilst the other niches have richly moulded cinquefoil pediments with the upwardly pointed spinodes. The niche lower corners have small guardian lions or *chinthe*, similar to those that carry the Myin-pya-gu trefoil pilasters, and first found at Pagan on the Nan-hpaya interior pediments. Between the outer wall window openings there are further niches. Both outer and inner ambulatory walls are covered in elaborate schemes of paintings, decorative and instructive.

The paintings on the inner ambulatory walls working upwards, through a spiritual hierarchy, from above the niches in tiers are:

1. Brahma, *deva*, heavenly beings and royal figures—in procession and paying homage.
2. Arahat in the *dhyanamudra*.
3. Buddhas in *bhumisparsa* alternating with *dharmacakra* buddhas with attendants.[99]
4. A broad floral band.
5. A band of buddhas.
6. A band of stupas.

In the spandrels between the niches are tondi containing Brahmanic deities riding their *vahana* or vehicles. There are no glosses and thus no clear textual source, though Luce has identified most of them.[100]

On the south wall, about the central niche, is painted the 'Attack and Defeat of Mara'. In this position, across the wall immediately behind the shrine and main image, the early painter placed this broad, vivid and phantasmic scene. This Abe-ya-dana version of the 'Attack and Defeat' may be the first surviving at Pagan, and is notably smaller in size than the Naga-yon or Myinkaba Kub-yauk ones. However, the sense of flux and movement and violence and horror instantly recall the Judgement scenes in the Sistine Chapel.

On the outer wall, starting from the lower tier above the dado:

1. Floral bands.
2. Seated *bodhisattvas*.
3. Seated *bodhisattvas*.
4. Cave scenes—featuring hermits, monks, buddhas, Taras, and Tantric deities, derived from a variety of textual sources.
5. Standing *bodhisattvas*.
6. Enlightened buddhas.

In style these are close to contemporary Nepalese miniature paintings: the line curvilinear and flowing; an art that worked on a single plane, yet revelled in the arabesque. At Pagan, at this time, there were two current painting idioms, one for the Theravada derived narratives, for example, Jataka painting that was based on a plastic idiom, two dimensional and utilising several spatial planes, in which form is modelled by the play of light and shade and is derived from the

Ajanta tradition of wall painting. The second idiom was more linear and florid in tendency and was usually employed for the depiction of decorative figures and motifs that are often spuriously described as Mahayana, or even Tantra, in origin. It is this second idiom that decorates the ambulatory walls here at the Abe-ya-dana. Possibly, the various *bodhisattva* may be individualised, extracted from an actual Mahayana text, their present much faded condition makes it difficult to distinguish the colourings, gestures and appurtenances that would assist in identifying such a text from the non-Theravada corpus of Buddhist literature. Alternatively, these figures do not represent a textually based programme, but, rather, 'art for art's sake': the picturesque rather than the instructive; something colourful to emblazon otherwise dull brickwork, the work of itinerant painters from one of the Himalayan kingdoms, possibly the Newars of Nepal. Just as the Tibetan *tanka* adorns many a Western salon without its esoteric language being readily comprehended, so, too, the Pagan Burman enjoyed these festive colours without closely enquiring into their exact significance.

To enter the shrine one must pass beneath an arch with bestial protectors painted on the insets and a vault covered with paintings of the stars. Symbolically, one passes from one world into another through the cosmic firmament. The sanctum is very dark and a torch is an essential piece of equipment for the earnest student. The main image of the Buddha, in *bhumisparsamudra*, is flanked by two devotee figures, likewise made of brick and stucco. Luce reckoned one of them to be Abeyadana herself, however, they seem more like monastics by their appearance, most likely the two disciples of the Buddha, Mogallana and Sariputta.[101]

No.52 above: Naga-yon east side
No.53 below: stucco work on
Naga-yon exterior
Fig.7: Naga-yon ground plan (EFEO)

At the Buddha's shoulder level are two *kinnaya*, the mythical man-bird met already at Kyauk-ku and here translated from the medium of stone to that of stucco upon brick. The shrine mural paintings are scarcely discernible beneath the centuries of grime that has collected upon these time worn walls.

No. 1192 NAGA-YON
နဂါးရုံ

Once, when Saw Lu was wrath with him and his prosperity and followers, Htihlaingshin slept alone in a grazing ground for horses; and while he slept a Naga watched over him. At that place when he became king, he built the Naga-yon pagoda.[102]

By its architectural style the Naga-yon must date after the Abe-ya-dana, and the reduction of heterodox iconographical elements, such as the inclusion of Tantra, Mahayana and Brahmanic deities employed in the painted wall decorations, may indicate that, by the Naga-yon's building, the great purification of Buddhism at Pagan, taken up by the early kings, had begun to exert an influence on the visual arts. However, North Indian currents of influence, that may be argued as Mahayanist in character, continue to appear in the paintings which, like those at the Abe-ya-dana, are picturesque rather than iconical in purpose. The influence of orthodoxy that Ceylon steadily exerted on Pagan-Burma brought about a revision of the *pitaka*, as part of Kyanzittha's purification programme, which manifested itself in the subjects and schemes chosen for the Naga-yon's paintings.

The temple's front, facing north in the direction of the palace, has a double pediment. The pediment's spinodes and *makara* fans have become more extenuated than on earlier temples and a stupa finial has been added to crest the inner pediment. The entrances, to the east and west sides of the hall, have single *torana*. The base has five window openings, their perforations mere crosses in brick, as at the Pa-hto-tha-mya, not the beautifully incised stone work of the Nan-hpaya. It seems that the virtuoso stone carvers who worked at Pagan in Anawrahta's time have either moved on or passed away.[103]

The medial projections of the Pa-hto-tha-mya temple base walls are dropped in favour of a longitudinal effect. However, side entrance openings (east and west) in the hall, which were employed at the Pa-hto-tha-mya, are here included. The window openings, five to each side, return to the cinquefoil pediments with *makara* at the capitals and spinodes, first seen in this role at the Nan-hpaya and developed further at the Abe-ya-dana. The window bases project out as if carried by the plinth mouldings. Stucco survives in fragments on the pediments and beneath the entablature, where the stone *kirtimukha* frieze of the Nan-hpaya and Kyauk-ku-ohn-min is translated into the both more abundant and pliable medium of stucco. This stucco frieze is among the earliest surviving at Pagan. The exterior surface is enlivened with the glowing greens of glazed tiles that were inset along the plinth and terrace lines. The brick-paved garth, enclosed by an inner and lower enclosure wall, was also glazed as was the interior flooring. The whole effect must have been magnificent—a glistening, gilded ornament floating on a cool jade sea.

This type of Kyanzittha temple has none of the tensions of possibly contemporary temples like the Pa-hto-tha-mya and Myin-pya-gu. There is no attempt to play base off with superstructure. The terraces are broad and the vaulting above the ambulatory is no longer masked by tall crennelles. The *sikhara* and its base offer a gradual climb upwards through the passage of terraces and is not set within a broad low-lying terrace as at the Nan-hpaya, or with the drama of the Pa-hto-tha-mya. The *sikhara*, in elevation, is tall and refined in shape, its vertical stroke equalising the horizontal base. On the terrace corners are free standing copies of the central *sikhara* motif.

The ground plan continues the distinction between hall and shrine generally found at the Early Period temple. However, the shrine is no longer square in plan. The emphasis is longitudinal, the base plan rectilinear. The inner walls of the hall, and both sides of the ambulatory, are lined with niches. The sculpture in those niches mark a further step in the development of the iconography and style of the Buddha image at Pagan and Pagan's growing knowledge of the Buddha legend or *bodawin*. The floor surfaces, like the garth about this temple, once gleamed with glazed flagstones.

In the hall are relief sculptures illustrating the *bodawin*. In style, these are the next logical development from the Buddha story reliefs at Kyauk-ku-ohn-min cave, which are the earliest at Pagan and the work of at least a decade earlier. However, in subject the scenes selected for depiction differ. The legend's pictorial possibilities increase, simultaneous to an improvement in the artist's sculptural dexterity. At Kyauk-ku, where the reliefs' crude simplicity contrast

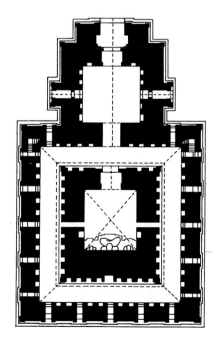

1st column:
No.54: retreat at Parileyyaka,
Gotama in pralambanasana
No.55: Kalangala and the golden
bowl (Ava period)
No.56: defeat of the heretics at
Savatthi - dharmacakramudra

2nd column:
No.57: the descent from Tavatimsa
No.58: the first sermon -
dharmacakramudra
No.59: dream of Maya

3rdcolumn:
No.60: the brahman Sahampati's
request
No.61 the enlightenment -
bhumisparsamudra
No.62: the parinibbana

with the excellence of the stone ornament work on the temple's front, the *bodawin* reliefs mark early attempts at portraying this theme by native artists, who at the same time were absorbing foreign artistic elements along with the purified teachings of the Buddha that were being disseminated at this time. Close in style to the reliefs at Kyauk-ku, the Naga-yon reliefs represent the next logical stylistic development in Pagan sculpture that lead to the ultimate expression of the *bodawin*, in stone, at the Ananda (c.1105). Contemporary to these sculptural portrayals of the *bodawin*, such scenes were being translated into the painted medium, for example, on the outer wall of the Pa-hto-tha-mya ambulatory. The scenes here in the hall are 'excerpts' from the *bodawin*, seemingly a random selection and randomly placed in the available niches, as if an afterthought.[104] Possibly they were rearranged at some later time for one clearly dates from the later Ava period.

On the south walls, each flanking the tall arch, are *bodhisattva* in a *dvarapala* role, made from brick and stucco, and not unlike the three standing Vishnu at the Nat-hlaung-kyaung. In the arching and wall corners, stone is used in the brickwork to reinforce these stress-loaded junctures.

The ambulatory walls are covered throughout with paintings, though now in tragic condition. In the Early Period the ambulatory vaults of longitudinally planned *gu* were never completely integrated with the base wall, which often resulted in a disastrous dampness seeping down through the soffits. Also, the temple's proximity to the dirt track that heads south from Myinkaba makes it suffer from clouds of dust raised by passing vehicles. The walls, inner and outer, are lined with cinquefoil arched niches, a change from the trefoils that abounded at the Myin-pya-gu. In total there are 56 niches, each filled with an image of a buddha. Like certain of the reliefs in the hall, the scene is relegated to the predella, the emphasis being on the image rather than the narrative. Down the line of buddhas the *mudra* alternates between the *bhumisparsa* and *dhyana*. The *dhyanamudra* images are the ones with a predella scene. U Bo Kay has identified the text as the *Buddhavamsa*, so that each of these relief figures represent one of the past 27 Buddhas and its predella scene depicts the 28th buddha—the latest buddha—Gotama, receiving the prophecy of future buddhahood in those of his past lives when he encountered the reigning buddha of the *kalpa* or time span (of which there have so far been twenty-seven buddhas). These images alternate with images of Gotama himself depicted at the moment of his enlightenment in the *bhumisparsamudra*.[105] As has been noted, 56 niches are utilised to illustrate this theme out of a total of 60, of the remaining 4, no doubt included by the architects for the sake of symmetry, other 'spare' images of the Buddha, or buddhas, in walking or standing postures were included. Of these, three standing figures were robbed from the temple in May 1988, again destined for an ever discreet international market place, where the thieved heritage of less fortunate nations is vended to the affluent with few questions asked.

In style, these images in the ambulatory seem more advanced than the ones in the hall, possibly the work of a later date or a different atelier. Typical of the early part of Kyanzittha's reign, moving and deeply spiritual, they are far more intense than his later images, found in the Ananda outer ambulatory niches. While being a marked development from the crude work of Kyauk-ku and those in the hall of the Naga-yon, the faces are less angular and accentuated than the Ananda type (c.1105). If the Ananda Buddha images are said to be Pala derived, then these must be derived from the Pyu tradition that took its sculpture from an earlier phase of Indian culture, the Guptan, yet astonishingly, only a decade separates them. Other Kyanzittha images may be found in the chronologically uncertain Pa-hto-tha-mya, which, in style, are close to these.

The ambulatory paintings, on outer and inner walls, are in poor condition and the darkness of the interior make them difficult to follow. They have glosses in Old Mon, and their inclusion at this time, as with other Early Period temples, reflects contemporary scholarly activities. The subjects depicted include: the Jataka and a selection of *sutta* from the *Sutta Pitaka*, each *sutta* portrayed by a standard *bhumisparsamudra* Buddha, with an identification gloss beneath. As with the *bodawin* reliefs in the hall, the arrangement of these illustrations are, as noted by Luce, haphazard, the panels exceptionally broad, the painting freehand—the artist had been given license to freely translate the texts, as expounded in the homilies of contemporary *thera*, into this expansive visual medium.[106] Beneath these broad upper panels on the outer wall are selections from the Jataka and on the inner wall similar smaller panels from the *Sutta Pitaka*.[107]

There are also a number of essentially decorative figures, painted in a style that differs from that employed on the portrayals of the texts—these may be of Mahayana or Vajrayana origin and depict various manifestations of the *bodhisattva* and the goddess Tara. These are subsidiary to the main Theravada subjects, being merely decorative embellishments. This work was probably the work of itinerant North Indian or Nepali artists who came to Pagan in search of employment, rather than to proselyitize the particular sect to which they belonged.[108]

On the south wall, inner panels, is the 'Attack and Defeat', with the attack on the left and rout to the right of the medial recess pediment. Like at the Abe-ya-dana, this too is a vivid and energetic piece of painting that confounds any suggestion that the Pagan painter was either stylised or unimaginative in his expression.

The arch between ambulatory and shrine also has an original wooden lintel with finely carved mouldings. Though Pagan architects had by this time perfected their knowledge of voussoir arching techniques, in his

temples Kyanzittha curiously preferred a flat arch or lintel between hall and ambulatory and a pointed one between ambulatory and shrine.

More light was admitted into the Naga-yon shrine than into its predecessor the Abe-ya-dana. This is not just because of the whitewashing the walls received, for on each side an opening passes through the thickness of the wall to the ambulatory, like at the Pahto-tha-mya.[109] The shrine contains three standing images of the Buddha. The central one in the *abhayamudra*, the others in the *dharmacakramudra.* The flanking Buddhas are less tall than the central image, the canopies and the painted *naga* covering of the central figure are later additions and the images themselves have been substantially regilded. These standing images are not unlike those at the Shwezigon that slightly pre-date this temple, which were also the work of Kyanzittha who particularly favoured standing images.[110] The walls of the shrine, as have been noted, have been whitewashed over—who knows what painted treasures lie beneath?

No.63 left: standing dvarapala in Ananda hall, restored in 18th century
No.64 right: Ananda outer ambulatory

No.2171 ANANDA

အာနန္ဒာ

One day, eight noble saints stood for alms at the king's palace. And the king took the bowl and fed them with food, and asked, 'Whence come ye?' And they said, 'From Mt. Gandhamadana.' Now king Htilaingshin was full of faith, and he built and offered the saints a monastery for the rainy season. He invited them from the palace and fed them continually with food during the three months of rain. Once he entreated them to call up the likeness of the Nandamula grotto, and called it Ananda.[111]

The Ananda too has inspired, later Burmese kings looked to the Ananda as the model for their own works of merit.[112] On this temple the whirlpool of styles and forms of the Early Period, with their varying derivations, come to rest. Pagan has developed her own architectural dialect from a combination of indigenous prototypes and the latest of North Indian artistic fashions.

There is no extant inscription that refers to the actual dedication of the Ananda.[113] The third Prome Shwehsan-daw Inscription set up by Kyanzittha in the Mon language, dates towards the end of the reign and records in a panegyrical style the main events of the reign, but curiously makes no reference to the Ananda, whilst talking of the *Nirbbanamulabajra* or Shwe-zigon.[114] Following on from the Shwe-zigon, it must date from around 1105.[115] In style the Ananda remains within the Early Period, with an exterior elevation that continues the balance between horizontal and vertical forces. The ambulatories remain dimly lit (and would have been more so before the application of white-wash in more recent times) and the shrines have the intense and moving atmosphere characteristic of the Early Period temple. The large scale is, though, innovative, here is the first 'great' Pagan temple. The fullness and confidence of the scheme heralds the proximity of the colossal Middle Period constructions.

The question of where the builders came from remains to be resolved. If the story of Kyanzittha's meeting with the Indian monks is true, and there is no reason to doubt that Indian monks did come to receive the patronage of Burmese Buddhist kings, they could well have sown the seeds of such a conception in the mind of Kyanzittha, possibly they may also have possessed some architectural knowledge. The style of the relief sculpture placed in the ambulatories and halls has been claimed as being distinctly Indian and the work of imported craftsmen.[116] Architectural proto-types exist: in Bengal, at Paharpur, according to Duroiselle,[117] and at the Lal Mai ridge, west of Comilla, again in Bengal, according to Luce.[118] However, archi-tectural developments at Pagan, based on Pyu proto-types and imbibed by innovations such as the square based *sikhara* crown from India, were leading up to the Ananda conception. For example, the 'Greek Cross' plan of the Ananda clearly originates from the Myin-pya-gu where the *lei-myet-hna* or 'four face' theme of the Pyu temple is redeveloped.[119] The Ananda represents the culmination of prevalent archi-tectural currents in Early Pagan and is not a direct imitation of a North Indian model. The vision of the Gandhamadana monks may well have served to inspire the king, gazing out from his palace across the moat to this site, to transcend past architectural boundaries and create a temple in keeping with his imperial Buddhist mission.

Prior to an examination of the temple itself, observe the enclosing wall and four gateways. The Naga-yon, possibly dating to around a decade before this work, was the first temple at Pagan to develop the enclosure wall and arched gateways into a visually spectacular feature in their own right. Here, at the Ananda, such seemingly extraneous peripherals are integrated fur-ther with the entire composition. From the distance, these outer constructions seem part of the overall effect and without them the Ananda would lack something. The wall itself is lined with stupa mould-ings. The gates are splendidly arched with a stupa finial above. Within the arch are *dvarapala* seated in *lalitasana*, as at the Naga-yon.

On the exterior, symmetry is the dominant force.

Each face is a balanced composition of pediments, ascending up through the terraces to meet the super-structure and *sikhara*. The hall projects outwards and has a triple pediment with *makara* motifs and a central deity in the central upper spinode. The effect of this symmetric tendency is best appreciated from the east side where the long arcades of shops, added in the early part of this century, that ruin the effect of the original facades on the other sides, have not been added. It should be noted, though, that the stucco work was substantially restored in 1783 in the current Middle Konbaung style as were many other parts and features of this temple.[120]

The plinth is short in height, no longer the grand play of mouldings of earlier temples, and there is no *kalasa* pot set in profile. A programme of illustrations, intended to instruct the faithful in the victory of their lord Buddha over the forces of evil has displaced the decorative richness of earlier temple plinths. A total of 554 indented panels containing glazed plaques, each depicting an animal, grotesque or deity proceed around the temple.[121] These depict, in narrative se-quence, the Attack and Defeat of the Army of Mara by the Buddha at the supreme moment of enlightenment, which has been met before in the wall paintings of certain of Kyanzittha's temples.[122] Between the north and south halls, to the west, is the procession of the routed army, and on the other half of the temple plinth is the march of the victorious *deva*, outward from the east porch.[123] Of interest are the paraphernalia and ceremonial objects of the 'Regents of the Quarters', these are similar to those used in depictions of the Buddha's footprints. In no place along the plinth is the Buddha anthropomorphically depicted, as in Early Buddhist art his presence is symbolised by a stupa. This may be because Burmese Buddhists believe it dis-respectful, and unlucky, to place an image of the Buddha at a level lower than one's own body and Early Period images of the Buddha are never barred to the elements.[124]

Emmanuel Guillon has recently published the most recent of a number of studies on these bas reliefs; in his monograph he presents a convincing thesis for a Mon-derived Sarvastivada textual and iconographic source for this story.[125] The Mon language was the *lingua franca* of Early Pagan and was used in all the inscriptions of Kyanzittha. Texts of Mon origin would certainly have been current at this time, though it would be a mistake to suggest that Mon culture in its entirety was supplanted into Pagan—as has been ade-quately demonstrated in architecture and iconogra-phy Pagan was heir to the Pyu, not the Mon. This Mon influence was brief in its duration, more authentic texts and scriptural recensions from Ceylon soon displaced any monopoly the Mons once held over Pagan's scholarly life. If the textual source for the 'Army of Mara' is Mon in iconographic origin, what re-mains to be asked is, what of the idiom in which it was depicted?

The didactic emphasis on the exterior continues

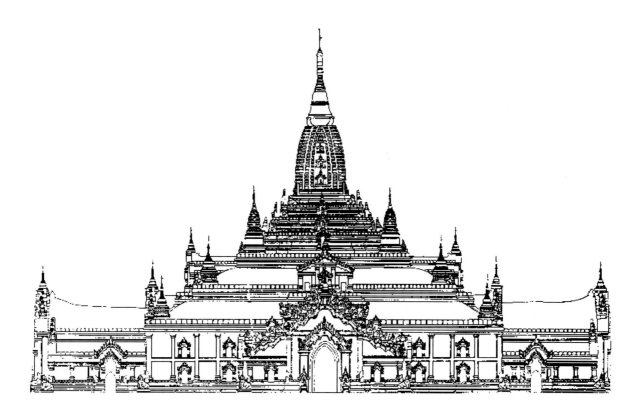

within the interior; in no other temple at Pagan is there so extensive a programme of Buddhist education. As Luce emphasises, Kyanzittha's conception was that the Ananda should be an instrument of instruction.[126]

Flanking each front doorway is a *bodhisattva* set in a niche and seated in *laitasana* with a pediment above the niche. Similar *bodhisattva* are enriched on each inner wall of the enclosure arches, and are repeated in the halls, only in this case standing. At the corners around the temple base are the *min-o-thila* or double-bodied lions, already met at the Shwe-zigon. *Chinthe* are poised, alternating with *bilu* at each corner of each of the three main lower terraces, and not alternating with the *bilu* on the three upper terraces, which mask the superstructure that carries the *sikhara*. These figures, like the pediments stucco ornament, were either reworked or added in Konbaung times.

The base walls have two rows of window openings that have no perforations, thus casting more light into the ambulatories than in previous temples. Kyanzittha was determined that the educational programme of relief sculptures running round the outer ambulatory outer wall were to be seen in a good light. He was interested in an impact art that would propagate the faith he had undertaken to reform. The inner ambulatory is darker than the outer. Closer to the *hpaya,* a reduction in light is conducive to intense spiritual experience. The wall between the two ambulatories has cross passages that repeat the outer wall openings. Thus the outer base wall is really a shell encasing an inner shell built about the central mass: the *hpaya.*

The terraces, superstructure and *sikhara* are a well balanced arrangement. The *torana* of the front is repeated on the lower terrace level, at the juncture

between hall and base wall, and is again repeated on the second terrace, where this pediment arrangement frames the medial sky-light opening from which a beam of light is diffused down onto the Buddha's face in the shrine beneath. The terraces are crenellated; the lower two have corner stupas, with the protective *bilu* and the *chinthe* ascending up the climbing terraces. The third and uppermost terrace has subsidiary *sikhara* obelisks, carried on a high base, and mirroring the central form. The heavily moulded superstructure, that carries the *sikhara* of previous Early Period temples, here receives a fuller treatment: it is heightened and broadened to carry a *sikhara* taller than ever attempted before at Pagan. To mask the necessary supportive mass a further three terraces were thus added, and there are bridging arches across the medial flights so as not to break the line of the terrace mouldings. These upper terraces also have crenelles with *chinthe* guarding the corners.[127] The *sikhara* has medial panel-niches, five to each face, each containing an image of the Buddha, this arrangement is an extension of the four Buddha theme to include the future buddha Mettaya.[128] Such a superstructure arrangement, with the inclusion of three further terraces, pre-empts the That-byin-nyu arrangement where an upper shrine is placed between lower and upper terraces.

The lower terraces house a complete set of Jataka plaques, 537 of them in all, named and numbered in Pali, and a further 375 plaques depicting the Maha-nipata or 'Last Ten Jatakas', this time in Mon, on the upper terraces. This is the only *gu* temple at Pagan which has a complete glazed set of Jataka plaques. Their recension is on the Ceylonese model and marks

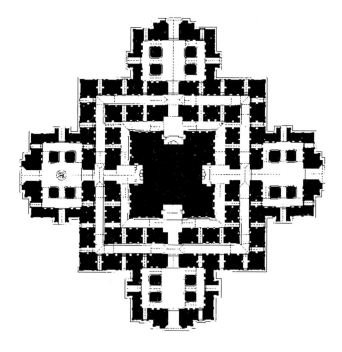

Fig.8 right: Ananda ground plan (EFEO)
Fig.9 left: Ananda elevation (RIT)
No.65 upper: stupa mouldings on the Ananda
enclosure wall
No.66 lower: scene from 'the army of Mara'
on the Ananda plinth

a development from the slightly confused Shwe-zigon numbering,[129] an indication of an advance in Pagan Buddhist studies under Ceylonese guidance, and the fact that the Ananda must date from after the Shwe-zigon's completion by Kyanzittha.[130] These glazed terracotta scenes are a vital and energetic yet curious art form. Stripped to the bare essentials, each scene is bold and pure like the faith they enhanced. The style of this terracotta estampage work evolves little over the next two centuries at Pagan, even in the later periods the forms and scenes vary little from the East and West Hpet-leik prototype. Interesting, though, is the exclusion of a stair passage, included by Kyanzittha in his other temples, thereby denying convenient access to these upper parts. This raises the whole question of whether the art of the Ananda was really a didactic one, or whether the inclusion of such material was 'token' rather than functional.

Entering the interior from the four, broad, spacious porches, one passes through the two ambulatories into the temple's core. The ambulatories have a half-barrel vault and here, for the first time at Pagan, diaphragm arches are required to pass the thrust of the greater mass of the superstructure out to earth. Noticeable also, though not for the first time, is the binding of stone masonry into the brick work to strengthen joins and other stress bearing points.

The outer ambulatory was conceived as a gallery for sculpture, devised to educate the people in the *bodawin*. There are 80 relief scenes in niches set on the outer wall at two levels, which would have been studied whilst the devotee made a double *pradaksina* before entering the shrines themselves. The Buddha story contents, or number of scenes included for portrayal, gradually expanded through the Early Pagan Period and here culminated in a full series derived from the *Nidanakatha*, the introductory section of the Jataka literature, that contains a life of the Buddha. There has also been a considerable advance in the quality of workmanship since the Naga-yon reliefs. The figures now are fuller in form, bodily and facial proportions perfected to new standards of aesthetic excellence, whilst subsidiary figures are generally reduced in size, with the all-encompassing, humane yet other worldly Buddha dominating each scene. In a number of instances, the actual scene is reduced to the predella, as at the Naga-yon, indicating Kyanzittha's emphasis on the Buddha rather than the narrative. Each scene is framed by a reredos, usually in the form of a tiered wooden *pyatthat*, these give some impression of now perished wooden architecture. Note, also, the depiction of trees and foliage. In each scene the details are reduced to a minimum, only the bare essentials are shown, yet the workmanship is highly polished, with the bejewelled raiments of the Bodhisattva beautifully elaborated. Throughout, Gotama as either the Buddha or the Bodhisattva, has a facial expression that is both spiritually intense and profoundly serene.

It is generally said that these reliefs must be the work

of immigrant Indians because the facial types are more Pala-style Indian in physiognomy than Burmese.[131] However, the hypothesis that this unprecedentedly fine work may be the culmination of indigenous developments should not be discounted. For from the cruder Kyauk-ku-ohn-min Buddha story reliefs to the Naga-yon ones, there is an evolution. The Ananda reliefs are the logical culmination of this indigenous stylistic and iconographic development. For example, the process by which the narrative was increasingly becoming subjugated to the predella was an indigenous one. The physiognomy of the figures is, though, startlingly reminiscent of the North Indian Pala statuary. Portable Pala images would have been brought to Pagan by travellers and returning pilgrims. Kyanzittha's inscriptions tell us that a mission had been sent to Bodh Gaya to restore the original Vajrasana temple; the Pagan artist would there have experienced something of current artistic developments in North-East India and would have returned to Pagan with a mind freshly invigorated with new aesthetic possibilities that he applied to his own native tradition that went back at least four hundred years to the original Buddhist penetration of Burma, when the current artistic movement in India was the art of the Gupta dynasty. To the native artist, such Pala images must have inspired imitation in the same way that the import of classical forms from Renaissance Italy in 17th century England led to a revolution in the arts without the suppression of the indigenous character. The Burmese artist, anxious to depict accurately events that once took place in India, that were enacted by Indians, naturally preferred a more current Indian model. However, it has been noted above that the Brahma reliefs in the Nan-hpaya are Mongoloid in physiognomy and not Indo-Aryan; comparing the facial features of these sculptures with those of Kyanzittha, there seems a natural technical and stylistic connection and it would seem an exaggeration to state that the Pagan artist actually copied from Indian prototypes.

The visitor to the Ananda, having made his *pradaksina* about the exterior, should enter from the east porch in order to avoid the 'shopping arcades' that undermine the original effect by blocking the fronts. Now it is necessary to make a further double *pradaksina* about the outer ambulatory to view these reliefs and learn something of the life of the Buddha. The scenes are on the outer wall and ranged in two tiers. Start with the lower tier on the west wall 1st north from the hall. These scenes have been identified by Luce and the original source for them, as has beeen noted, was the *Nidanakatha*.[132]

The outer ambulatory inner wall and the inner ambulatory niches contain reliefs of the Buddha mainly in *bhumisparsamudra* with devotee figures at worship in the predella. There are also a random selection of scenes from the life of the Buddha in the halls and shrines. In the cross passages between the two ambulatories are a number of other miscellaneous *bodawin* scenes. Luce reckoned them to have been rejects from the outer ambulatory for they differ slightly in style.[133]

Certain of the Ananda images display unusual *mudra*, seemingly indigenous departures from the established Indian traditions of portrayal and symbolism; either conceived at this artistically fertile moment in Burma's art history or originated from the iconographic schemes once nurtured by the Pyu, that had through their isolation departed from Indian iconographic norms. Perhaps the most striking example of these iconographic eccentricities are the four main standing images in the shrines, notably the east image that seems to be symbolising the concept of *dana* or giving, with both arms hanging down and outstretched before him, which has no known prototype in the Buddhist world. Less obvious iconographic curiosities may be found in the outer ambulatory inner wall, these *vajrasana* reliefs seem to portray the concept of *karunna* or compassion, with one hand placed across the chest and the other either in a half *dhyanamudra* or half *bhumisparsamudra*. This attempt to portray the fundamental Buddhist teaching of compassion may be seen in a number of Kyanzittha's standing images, particularly the four colossal standing images here in the Ananda, in which a hand is placed across the chest, palm turned inwards not outwards, as if making the sign of the *dharmacakra*.[134]

Recently the Archaeology Department removed some of the whitewash from the north hall to reveal original paintings. Possibly the ambulatories were also covered in mural paintings. If so, the Ananda would have been far darker and more mystical in atmosphere than it is today, with light being reflected off the now whitewashed walls.

The ground plan takes the form of a Greek Cross. As has been said, the immediate prototype for this is to be found at Pagan and not in India, though similar plans may be found in India. There is a double ambulatory around the central mass. The four shrines, medially placed, are opposite the halls and connect with them through tall pointed arches in the base and ambulatory walls. Within each of the four cella that recede into the great central mass is enshrined one of the last four buddhas of this time period. Not all of these are original; the east and west images were substantially repaired during the late 18th century restoration of this temple:

N -Kakusandha	*dharmacakramudra*	original
E Konagamanda	*varadamudra* (?)	18th Century
S - Kassapa	*dharmacakramudra*	original
W -Gotama	*abhayamudra*	repaired

These images are made of wood and approximately 9m high. Standing images were popular with Kyanzittha, he installed three at the Naga-yon and a further four at the Shwe-zigon. Despite regilding and other repairs, the original Ananda standing images (north and south) resemble earlier standing figures with broad hips, thin, striated waist, short upper body and a bunched edging to the broad and outwardly flowing robe, whilst standing upon a double lotus, as found at the Shwe-zigon and Naga-yon. Their heads have the *ushnisha*, long ear lobes and tightly curled hair that are the ostensible marks of a buddha. Kyanzittha's images from the later part of his reign are typified by long nose and chin, short rounded lips and long curving eyebrows. This style reaches a high point at the Ananda.

In the west shrine two rare portrait sculptures are to be seen, each of them flanking and at the feet of the main image; these depict a king, said to be Kyanzittha, and a *thera*, said to be Shin Arahan, the Mon monk who is believed to have led the Theravada crusade at Pagan and was Kyanzittha's preceptor. The traditional theme of having the two main disciples of the Buddha, Mogallana and Sariputta, as at the Abe-ya-dana, crouchant and flanking the Buddha, is here modified to include the two main supporters of the Buddha at Pagan. It has now been established that these are made of lacquer and, if original, as their style suggests, they are early examples of Pagan lacquerware.[135] Similar subsidiary figures may be found kneeling at the feet of the other three *hpaya*. The south Buddha is clearly flanked by Mogallana and Sariputta, though these by their style are Ava Period additions, but the north shrine exhibits an extraordinary pastiche of the church, state and Buddha triad of the west and the traditional and historical triad of the south. Here, the figure to the Buddha's left, that is east, is a standard monkish figure, whilst his counterpart on the west side of the Buddha has the shaven skull of a monk and the armlets and body jewellery of a prince. On closer examination it seems that the original head has been lost and a shorn monastic head was added to replace the original. It remains uncertain as to the material in which these images were made, they do not appear to be lacquer, but then neither do the west ones, and on inspection, when tapped gently, they give off the resonance of stone or some dense material and not a hollow casing.

Also of interest in the shrines are the pedestals used to carry the tall buddhas. These are composed of horizontal bands of mouldings, projecting out on each side to meet at a central projection in the middle. The bands of mouldings contain panels with figurative motifs set into them, for example, the *chinthe* Brahma and other supporters of the faith. These herald the splendid pedestal work at Mye-bon-tha.[136] The wooden railings are clearly Konbaung in period, so like those found in the carved monasteries of around Mandalay.

Finally, note the great teak doors between the halls and cross passages, believed by Luce[137] to be original, though said by U Bo Kay to be the work of Bodawpaya in the late 18th century.[138] They are quite unlike the doors discovered by Duroiselle at the Shwe-zigon, which are made up of a series of panels and not lattice work as the Ananda ones are, though not dissimilar to the Shwe-gu-gyi ones which may also be later in date.

No. 67 upper right: seated dvarapala on upper terraces
No.68 middle right: the tonsure , a scene from the Ananda bodawin
No.69 lower right: east figure in north Ananda shrine with monks head and princes ornament

There are two types of design work on the Ananda doors: on the north and east doors, the designs are low in relief, rosettes set within beaded margins, whilst on the south and west, the relief is high, the designs more naturalistic, even florid. However, in form and overall construction each of these door types are the same, with a lattice arrangement set within an ornamented frame with arched upper part filled with a *hamsa* or *chinthe* and it is unlikely that they date from different times.

The Ananda remains perhaps Pagan's most beautiful temple, certainly the most moving and popular with both tourist and Burman. Other Pagan temples may be greater or grander, more daring in their conception, or structurally complex, but none can rival the Ananda as an experience that enriches.

No.1323 MYINKABA KUBYAUK-GYI
မြင်းကပါဂူပြောက်ကြီး

> ...the queen's son named Rajakumar enshrined the golden Buddha, (and) having made the golden spire of the cave-pagoda, pronounced the dedication of this cave-pagoda, (and) having assembled (the men of) Sakmunalon, one village, Rapay, one village, (and) Henbuiw, one village, these three villages of slaves, the queens son Rajakumar, having poured out water to this cave-pagoda and Buddha spake thus: "May this that I am doing be a cause for giving me omniscience (and) wisdom! As for these slaves, be it my son, be it my grandson, be it my kinsman, be it any other person, if he shall do violence to those that I have dedicated this Buddha, may he never be permitted to approach the presence of the lord Buddha Ariya Mettaya." [139]

The *kubyauk-gyi*, or 'great variegated temple', at the village of Myinkaba stands to the west of a much renovated stupa, the Mya-zeidi. In the Mya-zeidi enclosure a four faced inscription stands, now protected by a cage built about it. This, despite its present location in the Mya-zeidi, refers to the donation of the nearby *ku-byauk-gyi* built by Prince Rajakumar in 1113, and not to the Mya-zeidi itself, for it mentions the building of a *gu* and not a *zeidi*. This is the first definitely datable temple with extant inscription at Pagan. The inscription's significance goes further than this, for it is quadrilingual, with a different language and script to each of its four faces. The languages are those of the Pyu, Mon, Old Burman and of Pagan's religion, Pali. The importance of this inscription is great and has rightly been described by some as the 'Rosetta Stone of Burma'. For, firstly, it affirms the continued existence of the Pyu as a cultural force and indeed confirms the much emphasised thesis in this work that the Pyu were active participants in the establishing of Pagan as a dominant political and civilising force in the region. Though the Pyu capital of Sri Ksetra fell to a Nanchao invasion in the first half of the

9th century, their language and culture must have survived at Pagan up to this time. Secondly, the Mya-zeidi inscription also indicates that the Mon were culturally active at Early Pagan, particularly, as has been noted elsewhere, in the literary sphere. Thirdly, this is the first time the Burmese language is written: the language, under the tutelage of Mon, Pyu and Pali scholars, here becomes literature—a significant moment in the development of a civilisation. Finally, it should be noted that Pali, the *lingua franca* of Theravada Buddhism, is now firmly rooted as the sacred language of Pagan.

Rajakumar, the builder of the temple and author of the inscription quoted above, tells that, as the son of Kyanzittha by the queen Trilokavatamsakadevi, he wished to earn the merit necessary for the salvation of his ailing father by building a *gu* and enshrining in it a gold image and handing over to the temple three villages of slaves, the fief of his mother up till her death, and then passed on to Rajakumar by his father. Kyanzittha himself came and poured the waters of libation at the dedication ceremony and cried out "*thaddu, thaddu*" ("Well done, well done!") the exclamation still made by the recipients of and witnesses to a meritorious deed in Burma today.

Orientated towards the east, the porch extension now lacks a pediment, though its pilasters survive. The hall is near square in plan and there are projecting bays on north and south sides with openings that are perforated with stone. Dividing the arched space of these openings is a horizontal lintel at the capital level and above this a further perforated opening, framed within which are two *kirtimukha* and *jatamukuta* motifs. Over these side bays, too, there would have been a standard pediment. A similar arrangement was applied to the hall side openings at Wetkyi-in's Kubyauk-ngè at a date approximately contemporary to this *kubyauk*. The stucco that ornaments these pilasters and the other exterior decorative elements is very fine—the finest found to this date at Pagan. Around the base, just above the plinth, is a stucco band of jagged upturned **V** motifs—lotus petals reaching up from the rolling waters of the plinth moulding, towards the firmament. The shrine window openings, three to each side, have double pilasters, richly embossed with tapering down and up **V** motifs with the space between left clear. The pedimental motif of a *sikhara*-stupa rising from a pyramid of tiers, recalling the *pyatthat*, superimposed by cinquefoil with *makara* above the capitals has been met with before from the Nan-hpaya onwards in temple interiors but never previously on the exterior. Here, it is brought out into the open and greatly enriches the three windows on each side of the shrine's base. The single corner pilasters have the **V** motifs, extending down and up, meeting mid-way to form a diamond bud. Beneath the entablature is the *kirtimukha* frieze, its loops droop low, the *mukha* nearly touching. Stucco, that starts with the Abe-ya-dana and Naga-yon, here achieves a richness and splendour hitherto not found at Pagan.

This stucco work heralds the Middle and Late Periods. The Myinkaba Kubyauk-gyi is surely the culminating achievement of the Early Pagan builder's attempts to create a perfected temple.

Terrace crenellations are here excluded in favour of straight line mouldings softened with lotus petal mouldings. Tall, firmly based *sikhara* obelisks are positioned on the terrace corners and serve to strengthen the temple's elevation. Where hall meets shrine the Middle Period upper storey is born—a small shrine housing an image with a cinquefoil pediment frontage and miniature *sikhara* above. The next attempt at an upper-level shrine was on the Mye-bon-tha-hpaya-hla, which slightly post-dates the Myinkaba Kubyauk-gyi. The Ananda's upper terrace arrangement, with skylights masked by grand double pediments and placed against the upper superstructure, has here been extended to become a separate unit. This movement has been noted with other monuments believed to pre-date the Kubyauk-gyi, for example, the Pah-to-tha-mya and Alopyé. The actual skylight, required to illuminate the Kubyauk-gyi image, has been relegated to a mere unmarked recess in the moulded upper mass, hidden by the upper shrine to its fore, as at the Pa-hto-tha-mya. Thus, by the beginning of the 12th century, the Pagan builders had begun their quest into the possibilities of a temple's upper levels, that culminated in the soaring upwards mass of the That-byin-nyu, where the inclusion ground level shrine was completely eliminated. Luce believed the Mye-bon-tha-hpaya-hla to pre-date the Myinkaba Kubyauk-gyi, however, as discussed in Chapter Five, the Mye-bon-tha must date from after the Kub-yauk-gyi and is clearly the work of a later period.[140]

In the hall, the paintings are now in a fragmented state and are not easy to follow, though Luce and Ba Shin identified some of the glosses. Noteworthy are the monstrous *dvarapala* painted on the porch inside walls. However, it is in the ambulatory that the finest paintings are to be seen. Now nearly completely restored from the centuries of dirt and grime by the Archaeology Department with the assistance of U.N.D.P., every inch of the ambulatory wall space, from floor to vault, is covered with paintings whose lucky condition, combined with the benefits of modern restoration, offer a vision of an Early temple interior's original brilliance. Rajakumar, who never actually succeeded his father to the throne, seems to have devoted his life to scholarly pursuits, particularly the translation and study of Ceylonese manuscripts arriving at Pagan towards the end of the 11th century. The subjects chosen by him for the Kubyauk-gyi's walls reflect the great leap in Burmese scholarship that had occurred with the influx of the *pitaka* and other texts from Ceylon. The paintings adhere strictly to the fundamental texts of the Buddhist canon: the *Sutta,* or collection of discourses, the *Abhidhamma,* or book of metaphysical philosophy, and the *Vinaya,* rule for the order of the monks. Perhaps the culturally most significant find in the temple are certain painted

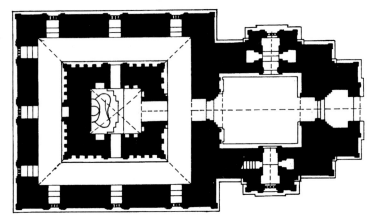

glosses that record the history of the religion and the history of Ceylon taken from the two Ceylonese chronicles, the *Mahavamsa* and *Culavamsa*. These historical jottings, though never actually mentioning Burma, go up to the time of Anawrahta and Kyanzittha's contemporary Vijayabahu of Ceylon (1055-1114). Burmese historiography thus starts from here. A historically aware civilisation is one that, having established suzerainty over territory, seeks to place itself as heir to a chronological process.

Though the painting schemes are Ceylonese in origin, and have glosses in Mon, they are, by their style, distinctly North Indian in character. As in earlier temples, for example the Abe-ya-dana, there are two current styles, the selection of which was determined by the subjects to be depicted. The Jataka scenes on the outer wall are painted in the 'monumental' idiom, with each scene reduced to the minimum of essentials, and the figures firmly modelled by the play of light and shade. This style derives from the art of Ajanta, and is used for depicting narratives based on mainstream texts; for purposes of classification it may be called the 'Narrative Style'. The 'Narrative Style' is thus a didactic idiom aiming to create a visual impact on the observer. In contrast, there is a linear, florid and more fanciful style that is derived from contemporary East

Bengali or even Nepali art and is decorative rather than didactic in intention—the 'Decorative Style'. Thus, two styles, employed beside each other, each representing a different geographical and sectarian origin, work together in harmony, one educating with its direct appeal and the other embellishing with delightful charm.

In the Narrative Style, the human figure is naturalistic in physique and less exaggerated and exotic than in the Decorative Style. This Narrative Style continues right through the Pagan period alongside the Decorative Style, though it undergoes some refinement. Characteristic of the decorative style figures are the long beak-like noses, exaggerated eyebrows and elegant, lissome bodies.

The two *bodhisattva* that flank the shrine arch are *dvarapala*, or guardians, and typical of the Decorative Style. Now cleaned, the richness of the original colouring has been rediscovered—once the whole temple must have blazed with these brilliant reds, indeed, the cave must have been 'Great and Variegated' as its name, *kubyauk-gyi*, suggests. These *bodhisattva*, ten armed with their *sakti* which guard the shrine as *dvarapala*, have been described as Mahayana, however, their presence here, surrounded by extensive portrayals of the Theravada canon, does

Myinkaba Kubyauk-gyi
Fig.10: plan and section (EFEO)
No.71: ambulatory passage

not necessarily imply that Rajakumar was a Mahayana follower. Above them, hierarchically arranged according to Rajakumar's religious beliefs, is the three-headed figure of Brahma, and above him is the Theravada *arahat*.[143] Thus the Mahayana *bodhisattva* are relegated to doorkeeper roles whilst the pinnacle of spiritual achievement to the Pagan Buddhist was being an *arahat*. The Mahayana and Brahmanic are subsidiary, religious supporters, and not actual icons in themselves.

On the ambulatory outer wall, from above the dado, to the upper part of the wall are Jataka scenes, each with a gloss in Mon naming it, and framed within an individual panel, ranged along six rows taking on a grid-like appearance.[144] The series starts from the east wall, south section, north end, row three from the top, and works around the temple, and then continues from the row beneath, and so on, down to the ninth row. Above the top Jataka row are two larger rows of panels. The upper contained the *bodawin*, sixteen scenes to each wall, sixty-four in all, few of them traceable today. The tier beneath has scenes depicting: the Four Maharajas, the Brahman Govinda legend and further episodes from the life of the Buddha.[145]

On the inner wall, upper tier: continuously running round the temple from the south section of the east wall is a series of scenes depicting the various cities where the Buddha taught the *Vinaya*.[146] The tier beneath relates to the *Abhidhamma*. It must have proved a hard task for the artist to translate the Buddhist system of metaphysical philosophy into an attractive pictorial presentation and he solves this problem by depicting the Buddha conceiving the philosophy and teaching it on earth and then to his mother in heaven; it goes on to follow the history of the *Abhidhamma* through the three great Buddhist Councils up to the time of the Asoka Maurya in the 3rd century B.C. The artist's source for this was the Ceylonese *Mahavamsa*.[147]

On the inner wall, west, above the grandly pedimented central niche that contains an image of the Buddha is a depiction of the 'Attack and Defeat of the Army of Mara'. Here, the artist's imagination runs wild; it is a fantasia of beasts and grotesques whirling in space, perhaps even more wild than those met earlier at the Abe-ya-dana and Naga-yon. Note the magnificent tiger leaping out from the wall. Other paintings of interest are the tondi on the outer wall window steps within which faintly erotic couples perform some exotic dance. The bands of naturalistic and geometric decoration along the dados, cornices, arches and vaults are similar to contemporary stucco ornamentation. In the art of Pagan, a design, motif or form is rarely confined to one particular medium.

No. 1476 PA-THA-DA

ပါထာၓ

Situated in line and a little to the south of the later Hsin-pya-group this temple is remarkable for its curious orientation, for the hall would have projected out to the west.[148] The neighbouring Hsin-pya-gu appears to have followed this earlier temple's unusual orientation. Like so many other temples from the Early Period, the Pa-tha-da ambulatory vaults have caved in because the half-barrel vault was preferred to the full one. The hall unit, which in the Early Period was never fully integrated with the shrine unit, has now vanished though the brick-strewn ground to the fore of the temple indicates its present whereabouts. The exterior wall running about the central block has five openings to each side, a larger number than other early *gu* temples. The windows are perforated with brick, as at the Pa-hto-tha-mya and Myin-pya-gu, and like the Pa-hto-tha-mya there are brick pilasters articulating the exterior surfaces, one placed between each of the window openings rising from plinth to cornice. This feature may indicate a date contemporary with these two temples in the reign of Kyanzittha. However, unlike the Pa-hto-tha-mya exterior there are *pyatthat* pediments over each window as at Rajakumar's *kubyauk-gyi*. Some vaulting survives on the north section and is a half barrel which on the other sections has not survived past earthquakes. There was no shrine receded into the central block and on each side there is a very broad yet shallow niche like those found at Gu Bizat (No.966).[149] The west-facing and principal recess is cut a little deeper into the block and here a much damaged image does survive. On the inner walls between these niches are rows of niches, six to each section, forty-eight in all. Forty-eight divided by two is twenty-four—the number of past buddhas with whom Gotama had an encounter according to the *Buddhavamsa*. These niches are now all empty though traces of brick and stucco bases for the images remain.

No.285 WETKYI-IN KUBYAUK-NGE

Lying low in the lush and shaded valley of the Shwe Chaung, upstream from the Wetkyi-in village and downstream from the new Nyaung U road, this lesser known early *kubyauk* well deserves a visit. The evolution of temple names can be curious, for this temple is known as the 'lesser' *kubyauk* whilst the later and far smaller *kubyauk* on the hill above is known as the *kubyauk-gyi*.[150]

With perforated window openings to darken the interior and a preference for the horizontal to the vertical in its elevation and lean-to vaults along the ambulatory, this is obviously a work belonging to the Early Period. With no lithic guidance on exact dating, which would greatly enhance an understanding of how the Pagan temple developed in the late 11th and early 12th centuries at Pagan, it is, though, possible to place the Kubyauk-ngè in a scheme of evolution according to its style and form. Most likely it is a work belonging to the latter part of Kyanzittha's reign, a little after the Naga-yon, for here an upper level has been added and contemporary to Rajakumar's work on the *kubyauk-gyi* at Myinkaba (1113), which has a similar type of upper shrine, detached from the *sikhara* mass. These two temples also have the same hall forepart type with a horizontal lintel dividing the arch. However, the *sikhara* mouldings here at Wetkyi-in, a scheme of rondos set within a grid framework, are far closer in style to the clearly Middle Period Mye-bon-tha-hpaya-hla that tradition, rightly, attributes to Sithu I. Thus this *kubyauk-ngè* may be said to be an intermediary work, when the Pagan builder began experimenting with the possibility of an upper shrine and testing out new designs for the *sikhara* ornament whilst retaining a characteristic Early Period base level and interior.

The base itself from the exterior has a *kalasa* plinth profile combined with panel mouldings and a double lotus band above (a compromise between two contemporary trends). There are four brick perforated apertures to each face, the perforations alternating between a circular and diamond design from opening to opening. A pediment surmounts each opening,

these too alternate in design, from a *pyatthat* crowned by a stupa to the same crowned with a *sikhara*. Between each opening a pilaster creates a division. The exterior corners are also defined by a pilaster arrangement; an examination of the stucco indicates that bonded onto the lower sections of these were some form of deity or *dvarapala* for the outline of a trefoil background remains intact.[151] Beneath the cornice hangs the garlanded loops of a stucco *kirtimukha* freize. As has been remarked, on the hall north and south sides are foreparts composed of a double pilaster and pediment arrangement with a lintel crossing the arch dividing the perforations as at the Myinkaba Kubyauk-gyi. The front, immediately suggestive of the Mye-bon-tha front, has an innovative style of pediment over the extending porch. Here, in high relief, a cinquefoil is set upon a tiered *pyatthat*, all imposed upon a framing pediment background. *Makara*, usually placed in the curved lobes of a pediment above the capitals, have been replaced by flower bearing figures standing on small elephants. Despite weathering and possible flood damage from the stream, the exterior stucco here is amongst the finest, certainly the most original, to be found in Early Pagan.

In the porch, between the two arches, are pedestals for *dvarapala* and decorative paintings remain on the porch vault. On the inner arch sides are painted figures in court attire advancing into the temple.

The hall is broad and spacious, the paintings that once earned this temple the name 'variegated' are now so darkened by centuries of grime that they are scarcely traceable, though the 550 Jataka can be made out. Here, like at the Pa-hto-tha-mya and other temples from the end of Kyanzittha's reign, the barrel vault springs, not from a soffit above a vertical wall, but from the floor curving up and in from that point. In this sense the wall is in fact the soffit. On the north and south walls of the hall are horizontally arched meditation niches and above these voussoired relieving arches which carry the stress down and around these breaks in the wall surface. The stair flight rises through the wall from the east niche on the south side. On either side of the arch that leads through to the ambulatory are *dvarapala* figures, each framed by an octofoil niche, their legs long, torsos short and gestures rhythmic.

The ambulatory outer wall contains niches filled with the broken rubble of what must have been the earliest portrayal of the 'Life' in brick and stucco at Pagan.[152] Again there is a logical connection with the subsequent Mye-bon-tha work, where in brick and stucco a 'potted life' of just four events were depicted about the *lei-myet-hna*. The arch between hall and ambulatory is a flat one, like at the Naga-yon and other Kyanzittha temples, whilst the arch between ambulatory and shrine is a pointed one surmounted by a splendid pediment arrangement. On the base of each pilaster is painted a *bodhisattva* in a guardian role, very similar in their style and attributes to the recently cleaned ones at the Myinkaba Kubyauk-gyi, a point that again confirms that this temple must be contemporary to Rajakumar's work of 1113.[153]

The shrine west wall, above the colossal Buddha, has been severely damaged by treasure hunters who have cut a hole through to the ambulatory. The central image of the Buddha is one of the largest surviving from the Early Period, rivalled only by the Manuha or possibly the Pa-hto-tha-mya. Squeezed into the gloomy space behind the Buddha's vast folded knees are the subsidiary, and consequently reduced in scale, figures of Mogallana and Sariputta. Around the other walls of the shrine are a variety of other stone relief figures placed in niches, including one fine *dharmacakra* version. In style these reliefs are close to the stone reliefs in the Myinkaba Kubyauk-gyi and more developed than those in the surely earlier Naga-yon.

The upper level has already been mentioned with reference to the inclusion of an upper level shrine. The difficult to date Pa-hto-tha-mya has four such upper shrine houses, whilst the Myinkaba Kubyauk-gyi attempted only the one to the east, following on from the Alopyé (No.228) where an upper block to the fore of the *sikhara* housed the stair flight exit onto the terraces. A little later the Mye-bon-tha builders attempted to integrate this feature with the actual superstructure, eliminating the skylight all together, thus forming the basis for subsequent two-storey types. Here, the Wetkyi-in Kubyauk-ngè upper shrine provides a vital link in the understanding of the evolution of the developed Pagan temple.

Luce connects the *sikhara*, with its tiered stucco panels filled with rondos, framed by myrobalan, with Kyanzittha's mission to restore the Vajrasana temple at Bodh Gaya which dates to c.1095.[154] This suggestion seems logical, for the design repercussions on temple superstructures of the 1225 mission by Nadaungmya may be seen in a variety of places about Pagan and at Salé.[155] This 1225 mission led to the introduction of what has been described throughout this work as the 'Bodh Gaya' type *sikhara*, with straight rather than curved receding planes. The Kyanzittha restoration mission resulted in the input of new ornament designs rather than architectural forms. However, what is interesting is that after 1225 the inclusion of the rondo form found here at Wetkyi-in and Mye-bon-tha comes back into vogue after a period of dormancy.

No. 315 (201) TAUNGBON LOKANTHA

Orientated towards the west, this rarely visited, uncertainly named and little known temple from the Early Period is, on account of its iconography, one of the most fascinating monuments to be found at Pagan. Though Luce included it in his monumental study of the Early Period, he insufficiently emphasised the significance of this work.[156] This monument is situated between the new Nyaung-U road and Minnanthu on the high ground, known in the inscriptions as Sarapuiy, and in the Early Period would have been the most distant temple from the palace city. Even with the prolific building activity of the Late Period the density of monuments here remained sparse. Outwardly, despite the unconventional orientation, the temple seems a regular enough early work, with a hall extending from shrine, three perforated openings on each of the shrine walls, each with its cinquefoil pediment and spinodes, and a further single opening on the hall north and south walls, all surmounted by a square based *sikhara* and terrace arrangement. Going in, the first unusual feature one notices is the replacement of *dvarapala* on either side of the shrine arch by meditation cells set within the broad mass of the hall shrine wall.

Next, on entering the shrine unit, there is no cella within the central block beneath the crowning *sikhara*. This is radical. It represents here, possibly for the first time at Pagan on a large scale, a departure from the Early Period ground plan type where an ambulatory surrounds the central core into which a cella was cut. At No.315 ambulatory merges with shrine—the *lei-myet-hna* of Pyu times, that was adapted for the Hindu community at Pagan in the form of the Nat-hlaung-kyaung, has been revived. An image is set in a shallow niche against each face of the central core. A similar arrangement was found in two other small Early temples, Alopyé (No.228) and No.1309, west of Taungbi village, which, with their circular-based stupa finials and solid central blocks, are also redolent of the Pyu *lei-myet-hna* temples of Sri Ksetra. Here, though, the *lei-myet-hna* is applied to a large temple most likely dating from the end of the reign of Kyanzittha. The obvious and immediate heir to this is the Mye-bon-tha temple which has been included below as a Middle Period work.

More surprises await the visitor to this nameless monument. On the north and south faces of the central block are colossal brick and stucco images of *bodhisattva*. These may represent Lokantha and Mettaya for the votive tablets of Anawrahta often included these figures as supporters or *dvarapala* to the Buddha, forming a triad that is not necessarily a Mahayana one, as handwritten on the converse sides of such tablets are statements of faith: "...King Anawrahta who conforms to the 'true doctrine' is the donor of this tablet."[157] Likewise, one finds painted versions of Lokantha and Mettaya, as *dvarapala*, on arch pilasters at the entrance to a shrine. So it is possible to argue that these colossal *bodhisattva* figures represent an extension of this contemporary iconographic movement when such figures were borrowed from the Mahayana to serve the Theravada. The figures themselves are now decapitated and disemboweled; seated in *lalitasana*, they swing out from the wall at a slight angle and are not dissimilar to bronze finds from this period.[158] Each is enriched by a marvellous stucco composition conceived to portray a grotto. This cave effect led Luce to say: "Surely there is here some East Bengal Mahayanist element, comparable to that in the Abeyadana," and he went on to quote from the chronicle the description of how the Bengali monks bestowed a vision of the Nandamula cave on Mt. Gandhamadana.[159] Whatever their symbolism, one can not help but marvel at the sumptuous texture of the stucco carving and the prodigious virtuosity of the craftsmen. Observe how the *kirtimukha* has been worked into the whirls emulative of a cave face. By the end of the 11th century the art of the stucco maker had reached a perfection unmatched by any subsequent period in Burma's art history.

Final notable points about this temple are: the three-quarter barrel vault, the painted figures of Mogallana and Sariputta about the east image and the inclusion of smaller niches for portable images beneath the cornice on the west wall. It was in this temple that the largest fragments of an original Pagan Period textile ever discovered were found here by Pierre Pichard in 1986. However, it has not been established whether it had really survived eight centuries lying folded on the floor, as it was found, or whether it had been hidden here more recently.[160]

No.369 HLAING-SHE-GU

လှိုင်ရှည်ဂူ

Presently under restoration, this monument, most likely dating to the early part of the 12th century, is a transitional work, in chronology placable somewhere between the Early and Middle periods, perhaps a little later than the Wetkyi-in Kubyauk-ngè (c.1110-15).[161] Hlaing-she-gu is easily reached from the new Nyaung-U Pagan road to the west of the Shwe *chaung* ford and not far to the east of Alopyé. Unlike the Kubyauk-ngè this monument has a central core with no cella receded into the block, in this sense Hlaing-she-gu may be placed alongside works such as No.315 and the later Mye-bon-tha-hpaya-hla dating from the Pagan temple's moment of transition from the Early to Middle Periods.

Not only does the exclusion of an inner cella indicate that this is a work of change, for here there is an upper level fully integrated with the base of the *sikhara*. In fact, the gradual development of an upper level takes a further leap forwards from the Mye-bon-tha experiment, for here the *sikhara* and terraces actually rise from a full upper level block, square in plan with a hall extending to the east. Though, unlike the That-byin-nyu, the three terraces between lower and upper blocks have been excluded. There is, though, at this temple a definite advance towards the That-byin-nyu's play of giant blocks. In other respects the Hlaing-she-gu retains a number of features from the Early Period, with a lean-to or half-barrel vault (which has not withstood past earthquakes) and perforated window openings. It is though, in elevation, of impressive height.

No.374 ALOPYE

အလိုပြည်

To the south of the new Nyaung U road, about halfway between the town and the Pagan village, a little to the west of the Shwe *chaung,* is this small *gu* with a stupa finial. Alopyé, along with No.1309 (south of Taungbi), represent an alternative movement in early Period *gu* design in which the Pyu prototype with a stupa placed on the superstructure is adhered to. The question is, are these Pyu type *gu,* along with the Nat-hlaung-kyaung, the earliest brick temples at Pagan, and was the inclusion of the *sikhara*, for the first time on the Nan-hpaya, the moment of departure from this old Burmese brick temple tradition? The answer is that this type of *gu*, with a rotund finial, marked a style that ran contemporary to the square-based *sikhara* type of finial. For the Abe-ya-dana and then a great number and variety of works from the Late Period continue this theme and by the Konbaung Period the square-based Pagan *sikhara* form was to revive after centuries of dormancy when a round-based type, emulative of the stupa, had reigned supreme. Further, the paintings within, which have Mon glosses, clearly belong by their style and iconography to a date contemporary with the Myin-pya-gu, in the early part of Kyanzittha's reign, when Mon literary influence was in the ascendent. Luce cites a date from an archaic Burmese ink inscription in the hall, B.E. 556 /1194 A.D., but he too believed that the temple was built "at least half a century earlier than this, indeed, a century earlier, if not more, would seem more probable." [162]

The exterior, in form, is simple enough: the hall extending to the east from a square-based shrine; window openings on the north and south sides of the hall, and the remains of a porch extending out to the east from the hall; there are three openings to each face of the shrine, each with a 'flame' pediment over it, there is no *kirtimukha* frieze, though the plinth is moulded into a pot profile. On the terraces there is a small stupa obelisk to the centre of the single crenellated hall terrace and corner stupa markers on the lower terrace of the shrine. The central stupa finial itself is concave and not dissimilar to those erected during the Early Period, for example, Anawrahta's ones at Myinkaba and Thiripyitsaya. To the fore of the shrine terraces is what appears at first sight to be an upper level shrine; it is actually an exit from the stair passage that passes up from the shrine north-east corner. This original device is the only example of such a combination at Pagan.[163] If an early dating for this temple is to be accepted, then the inclusion of this dormer marks the first attempt by the Pagan builders to add an upper level, which by the time of the remarkably articulated Pa-hto-tha-mya work was to be translated into an upper shrine.

Between hall and shrine the arch is flat, like on most of Kyanzittha's temples. The interior is far lighter than other early temples which led Luce to suggest that it must be a transitional work. There is, though, as Luce notes, still a half vault. The shrine has no inner cella. This returns us to the question of chronology: is this a Pyu derived work continuing the *lei-myet-hna* planning tradition of Sri Ksetra or is this another example of the central block revived, that is to say, part of the movement active at the end of the 11th century whose principal manifestations were No.315 and the Mye-bon-tha?

At the centre of each of the four faces of this block are tall yet shallow lancets with *makara* pediment above. No fragments of the original images once placed in these can now be seen and it may be surmised that they once contained portable images, perhaps of bronze or gilded wood and possibly standing. Other smaller niches run along the ambulatory outer wall; eight in all, they once bore the 'Eight Scenes'.

Alopyé should, though, be remembered for the mural paintings that cover the interior walls. Their unfaded condition combined with a more generous ration of light makes them readily viewable. Both inner and outer walls are filled with small panels each containing a figure of the Buddha seated and in *dharmacakramudra* flanked by a disciple on each side: this is the closest that the Pagan painter could get to portraying the *Suttas*, which were usually discourses on matters such as philosophy, morality or metaphysics, and thus not easily translated into a visual media. Beneath each excerpt is a gloss in Mon indicating the particular discourse.[164] Luce notes that the orthography of these writings suggest that they may date from after the Lokha-teik-pan, however, in style, the Lokha-teik-pan paintings, though representing a much broader number of texts, seem to be more elaborate in style, including both more detail and more movement, whilst the Alopyé paintings are closer to the identical panels repeated without variety in the inner walls of the Myin-pya-gu. Other than the *Sutta* there was no other text illustrated here. Fine though are the painted figures of *bodhisattva* that guard the shrine arch in the hall and again repeated on the inside of the arch.

No.72: W. Kubyauk-ngè
No.73: Temple No.315
No.74: Pa-tha-da

5
The Middle Period, c.1120-1170

BY THE END of the first decade of the 12th century, a transitional style is discernible in the temple architecture of Pagan. Most ostensibly with Rajakumar's Myinkaba Kubyauk-gyi, but also at Hlaing-she, and the Wetkyi-in Kubyauk-ngè. In each of these temples, the architects commenced an investigation into the possibilities of a temple's upper reaches. These experiments, though, at this stage, were not wholly satisfactory, and were to be continued through the Middle Period leading to the ultimate expression in upper level planning: the building of the That-byin-nyu between 1155 and 1160, where the ground level shrine, that would usually have been set within the base, is eliminated in favour of an upper level sanctum. The Myinkaba Kubyauk-gyi did perhaps represent the 'perfected' Early Period *gu* and it offered the contemporary architect a vision of possible innovations or elaborations on what had become a standard architectural arrangement. The Mye-bon-tha to a limited extent breaks from this norm: the distinction between hall and shrine is reduced, the ambulatory merges with the shrine and the *sikhara* elevation becomes more dramatically inclined. However, it is in 1131 with the building of the Shwe-gu-gyi that the style of a new period is clearly evident.

The Middle Pagan Period is possibly Pagan's most creative moment, certainly it is when Pagan art and architecture is at its most visually impressive. In contemporary literature Old Mon is used less frequently as the language of the inscriptions, though it was to continue being written on wall glosses, whilst Pyu was never to be written again. Old Burmese had become the official language. The inscriptions of this period are in language clear and highly poetic statements of faith, often in the form of a prayer from the heart crying out for salvation.[1] Likewise, the art and architecture of the Middle Period reflects this religious aspiration that is combined with a cultural process that may be termed 'Burmanisation'. This desire for escape from worldly shackles that is most perfectly expressed in an architecture that is a projection of structure into space, was a quest for a sublime solution to the aesthetic and spiritual hankerings of contemporary Pagan man.

This epoch is dominated by the towering imperial figure of Sithu I (1113-1170) or Alaungsithu as he was known in the chronicles. About this historically elusive figure little is known other than from quasi-historical skits in chronicles compiled long after the demise of the Pagan dynasty. Political events also are sketchy if not plain confusing. For example, the question of

whether the Ceylonese actually captured Pagan between c.1160-69 remains to be satisfactorily solved. Sithu I, judging by the longevity of his reign, must have been an astute king, consolidating the religious reforms of his father and their dynasty's political base.[2] The Pagan administrative and military machine must have become highly efficient and the revenues from the growing empire contributed towards the king and his circle's extensive temple building programmes. Buddhism having been re-established and purified under Sithu's predecessors, now blossomed, and monastic communities, with endowments of lands and villages attached to serve them, rapidly expanded to the scale of universities on the model of the great Indian ones such as Nalanda. Pagan had become an imperial civilisation in its own right.

This was a transitional, if not experimental moment, in Pagan's architectural history. Within a decade of each of other, two temples, diametrically opposite in their composition and effect, were put up less than a mile away from each other: the That-byin-nyu and the Dhamma-yan-gyi. If the That-byin-nyu is a triumph for the champions of verticality, then the Dhamma-yan-gyi with its depressed elevation marks a rejection of this success and a return to the forms of the Early Period embodied in the Ananda temple. The Middle Period was a short lived yet prodigious outburst of creative spirit that may be seen as the bridge between the naiscent forms of the Early Period and the prolific output of a matured and self confident temple type in the Late Period.

No.1512 MYE-BON-THA-HPAYA-HLA

မြဘုံသာဘုရားလှ

Sithu I is popularly said to have built a number of *hpaya-hla* or 'lovely pagodas' about the Pagan plain and there is no reason to doubt the assignment of the Mye-bon-tha one to a date within his reign. The Mye-bon-tha-hpaya-hla is a less well known, though highly significant, temple sited just off the cart track that leads from the main road to the Shwe-hsan-daw Pagoda. The Mye-bon-tha-hpaya-hla was, according to Luce, the precursor to the Myinkaba Kubyauk-gyi.[3] To Luce, the architect's attempt at adding a second storey, which he believed was here not entirely successful, was solved in the subsequent building of the Myinkaba Kubyauk-gyi.[4] The *hpaya-hla* has now been substantially restored following the collapse of the south shrine wall and the original stucco frieze was salvaged and is now stored in the temple's hall. The temple's name, Mye-bon-tha, means underground, for until the time of the repairs the soil level on the exterior and interior has risen to partly bury the monument. A slight distance to the north is a smaller version of this temple with a similar ground plan, tondo filled *sikhara* and frontal arrangement, this, along with the square based stupa to its north, may be taken by their style and location to be contemporary to the Mye-bon-tha-hpaya-hla, though their condition is less well preserved than their greater counterpart.

The Mye-bon-tha is a transitional work, half belonging to the Early Period and half belonging to the Middle Period. The base windows continue to be perforated and the mouldings and ornament follow on the Early Period type base formula. On the terraces and superstructure, radical innovations to the Early Period type are immediately apparent. Firstly, there is a centrally placed miniature version of the main *sikhara* over the porch, a device shared by the Wetkyi-in Kubyauk-ngè.[5] Though an obelisk in such a position, surmounting the pediment, was by no means unusual in the *gu* temples of this period, what is unusual here is the obelisk's prominence: it plays itself off against the main *sikhara*, a near frivolous gesture. Secondly, from the *sikhara* drum there extends outwards an upper shrine. This is a square unit, with openings on three sides, and houses an image. The middle terrace that encloses this unit extends out from the projecting shrine out over the hall, as if an upper *mandapa* for the shrine. The exterior distinction between hall and shrine is thus reduced by the inclusion of this extending upper unit. It is from this arrangement, even if slightly awkward here at its conception, that the great temples of Pagan follow.

The Myinkaba Kubyauk-gyi upper level shrine version must date from before this. There, the upper level shrine is a miniature temple in itself and is detached from the central mass like those found at the Pa-hto-tha-mya.[6] The Mye-bon-tha one is attached to the mass of the superstructure as on the Middle Period

Mye-bon-tha-hpaya-hla
No.75 left: from the south
No.76 above: front (east)
No.77:below: Brahma figures on the image pedestal within the shrine

temples. Likewise, the ground plan and interior bear more relation to later types. Within, there is no inner sanctum: the main east facing image is placed on a pedestal against the central block, not inside it. The interior is far lighter than earlier temples, again indicating a date after 1113 in the reign of Sithu I. Indeed, in ground plan the Loka-hteik-pan is far closer in this respect. The Mye-bon-tha-hpaya-hla is, however, a transitional work, the next architectural step following on from the Kubyauk-gyi, and only slightly precursing the Shwe-gu-gyi and Loka-hteik-pan. In plan, which corresponds to the *lei-myet-hna* iconography so favoured by the Pyu, it follows on from the large Early temple No.315.[7] A further indication of a dating within the first quarter of the 12th century is the technique used for vaulting, here a three-quarter barrel rather than a lean-to half-barrel used in other large Early temples.[8] In this respect, together with the greater height of the ambulatory vault, this temple bears comparison with the Hlaing-she Gu.[9]

The *sikhara* is far more elaborate than earlier *sikhara* types with hollowed tondos above the medial recesses to each side of its base. Tiers of panelled mouldings deeply incise the superstructure. This elaborate treatment, following from similar work at the Wetkyi-in Kubyauk-ngè, that may have been a by-product of Kyanzittha's mission to restore the Vajrasana Temple at Bodh Gaya, reflects contemporary developments in India where the possibilities of heightened temple elevations were also being explored.[10]

The stucco work here is similar to the Kubyauk-gyi and from this time onwards is to evolve little. The standard vocabulary of Pagan stucco—jagged edge dado above the plinth, tapering down and up V motifs on corner pilasters meeting mid way to form a diamond bud; window pediment reliefs with cinquefoil and *makara* superimposed upon a five (here, though sometimes three) horizontally-tiered *pyatthat* in relief that leads up to a stupa and *sikhara* composition—become the standard patterns for exterior ornamentation from the early part of the 12th century onwards.

As has been mentioned the Mye-bon-tha-hpaya-hla ground plan marks a radical change in Pagan temple design: the distinction between hall and shrine becomes lessened and the main image, the *hpaya*, is brought out from a shrine that in the Early Period was receded into the central mass, to be placed to the fore of it in a brighter and lighter environment. This is a return to the *lei-myet-hna* or four face type that was known to the Pyu which will be discussed below—a rejection of the Early Period 'cave' mentality. About this block, set in slight recesses about its four faces, is a compacted version of the *bodawin*. Here the 'life' has been reduced to its essentials with the Enlightenment (*bhumisparsamudra*) on the east face, the Nativity to the north, the Deer Park at Sarnath (*dharmacakramudra*) on the south and the Death (*parinibbana*) on the west (with head orientated towards the north). If the number of scenes for inclusion has been reduced here to the barest minimum, each has been increased in scale to a degree that may be described as monumental—monumental in idiom as well as scale. Here, brick based stucco carving at Pagan has surely reached its zenith—take the Nativity, despite damage and the loss of a number of subsidiary figures, there is a terrific energy and vibrancy hitherto not met in Pagan's stucco sculpture. At the Wetkyi-in Kubyauk-ngè a stucco *bodawin* series had been included but these figures by comparison are not just lesser in scale but also in drama entirely lacking the potent charge of energy possessed by those at Mye-bon-tha.

There are fragments of paintings in the Mye-bon-tha also, notably a painted *kirtimukha* frieze at the cornice level beneath the hall-shrine arch, an unusual feature on an interior. In the hall are narrative paintings close in style and colouring to the ones in the Loka-hteik-pan and less stylised than the ones in the Myinkaba Kubyauk-gyi, with a flux of activity passing from one scene on into another. Further paintings may be found in the shrine, devotees and *deva* about the Nativity and small triad panels, so characteristic of Early paintwork, on the outer walls.

The brick and stucco pedestal of the east Buddha image has a relief arcade of pilasters projecting outwards at graduated points towards its centre. Inserted between these miniature pilasters are sandstone Brahma figures.[11] The Brahma of the Nan-hpaya reliefs and of the shrine inset paintings at the Kubyauk-gyi here reappears, once again the supporter of the Buddha, hands clasped flat against each other in an attitude of pious respect. Their inclusion on an image pedestal has been met with earlier on the Ananda pedestals.[12] The pedestal is also remarkable for the fine floral and scroll work.

No.1589 SHWE-GU-GYI ‌ေ‍ရ‍ွ‍ဂ‍ူ‍ကြ‍ီ‍း

There was a king most wise, the lord of men,
Who loved the hearing of the good law; his name
Thibuvanadiccapavaradhammaraja.
This just and righteous ruler of the land
Bethought him: "Rarely, rarely in this world
are Buddhas born; and to be born a man
Is hard, and hard to bear the Buddha's Law!"
So truly wise with best intelligence
He ordered: "Make a pleasing lovely room,
A fragrant chamber for the mighty Seer,
Gotama Buddha. On a platform high
Exalt it, and adorn it with cetiyas
and images of the spirits." This great king,
Abode of Virtue, ordered to be made
(Most like the Noble Buddha where he lived)
An image glorious-wonderful and fair
Of the world's Lord, the Teacher, whose five eyes
Were without stain—so purely wise was He.[13]

The extant inscription by the Shwe-gu-gyi's donor Sithu I dates the building to 1131 and tells how the construction took only seven and a half months.[14] Sithu I became known by the title *Shwe-gu-gyi-taya-ga* or 'Donor of the Great Golden Cave', in recognition for this work of merit from the time of building onwards. The inscription itself is written mainly in Pali, though with the dates in Sanskrit, and is one of the finest and most poetic works in the literature of Burma.

The temple sits upon a tall platform (approximately 4m high) and is orientated in a northerly direction. A single flight of steps rises from the north-west corner to the open space before the front. The platform is a development from the early *gu* plinth, yet the sudden jump in height, with the exception of the Nat-hlaung-kyaung, is unprecedented and heralds the standard Late Period arrangement of setting a temple well within a raised platform. The platform's upper bands are moulded and some stucco figures of crowned *deva* were noted by Luce on the south section—these would once have run all the way around the plinth.[15] Glazed lobes of terracotta, still remaining in places, were set into the mouldings beneath the deva band.

The open space on the north side is similar in conception to the Nat-hlaung-kyaung *mandapa*, however, the Shwe-gu-gyi temple proper is set well within the platform unlike the Nat-hlaung-kyaung where the *mandapa* extends from the front. As the Shwe-gu-gyi was sited within the city-palace walls it may have been set close to the the now perished palace buildings whose ritual construction was meticulously detailed in one of Kyanzittha's inscriptions. It may be that, as religious architecture takes precedence over the secular in Burma, Sithu required his builders to raise the temple's base above the level of the surrounding palace pavilions by devising this novel *mandapa*-platform. The chronicles tell how Sithu on his death bed was taken to this, his work of merit:

> Now when he reached the age of one hundred and one he fell grievously sick. His son Narathu removed him from the throne and kept him within the Shwegu pagoda. And the king recovered consciousness awhile and said, "This is not my palace surely!" And the hand maiden spake into his ear saying, "Not thy palace, but thy work of merit!", "Whose trickery is this?" he cried. She answered, "Thy son Narathu decreed it."[17]

Whereupon Narathu smothered his father, fearing that "If the king arises I shall be utterly destroyed."

The original stucco, once brilliant in lustre, is now spoilt by the casual slapping of the restorer's cement trowel, though in places the gorgeously textured stucco mouldings survive, casting contempt upon the refurbishers efforts. On the plinth, though, there is still a hint of the pot moulding of the Early temple, the preference is for a composition of lotus petals above and below a central band of square panels that had been favoured on the Ananda. The lotus flower is a dominant decorative and iconographic motif in the art of Pagan as in all art throughout the Buddhist world and was used at Pagan without restraint in most visual media. Developing from the Myinkaba Kubyauk-gyi and Mye-bon-tha the lotus petal as a decorative element is here elaborated, creating an upwards movement that commences just above the temple plinth itself.

The 'Great Golden Cave' is in its elevation majestic. By no means a massive temple, the Shwe-gu-gyi stands proud and dominant on the Pagan skyline, holding its own against its towering neighbours. If the That-byin-nyu seems about to explode up into the stratosphere, the Shwe-gu-gyi seems quite happy with its place here on earth. On the terraces, tiered corner obelisks taper upwards, quite unlike stupa-*sikhara* obelisks met on Early temple terraces, and have passages cut through them—this is the precedent Late terrace corner obelisks follow. The terraces, which are crenellated, climb to meet the tall graceful *sikhara* with a replacement stupa finial rising above. The entire treatment of this upper section is one wholly directed towards an upwards movement: an aspiration for the sublime, not unlike the aspirations of the cathedral builders of Medieval Europe. In 1131 Pagan this upwards quest remains restrained, though it is a step towards the daring virtuosity of the soaring Gadaw-palin and marked a dramatic change from the vertical-horizontal equilibrium of the Early Period temple. The Shwe-gu-gyi's sense of poise and stately balance was in later times to be sacrificed for dramatic effect.

On the base, the window openings of the Early Period *gu* are expanded into entrances with exuberantly carved teak doors which, judging by the style of their carving, are late 18th century additions like those of the Ananda.[19] Like a blossoming lotus the temple has opened up on all sides. As at the Mye-bon-tha-hpaya-hla and No.315 there is no inner shrine cut out from the central mass, the Pyu *lei-myet-hna* has been reverted to in favour of an inner shrine contained beneath the *sikhara*. However, here the emphasis is on the north hall facing image, with a lesser recessed image to the south and two minor niches on the northern part of the east and west walls. The ambulatory thus combines with shrine and shrine with ambulatory, again the prototype for the Late Period temple. The dividing arch between the two units of hall and shrine has been broadened and it has now become possible to worship the image from the hall itself. The square planned ambulatory is plastered over and whitewashed and lacks the painted decorations so necessary for the enrichment of a temple interior. This plain treatment of the wall space is responsible for the lack of an atmosphere. As Luce noted: "What astounds me about the Shwegu-gyi is, on the one hand, the supreme competence and originality of the exterior; and on the other, his plain incompetence in the planning of the interior."[20] Had the ambulatory been painted, as was no doubt originally intended, the temple interior would be both architecturally more unified and more spiritually charged in atmosphere.

No.1580 LOKA-HTEIK-PAN

လောကထိပ်ပန်

This small and simply composed *gu*, set just west from the cart track that leads to the Shwe-hsan-daw, may easily be passed unnoticed by the visitor to Pagan. Built in the reign of Kyanzittha's successor Sithu I, Loka-hteik-pan means 'Adorning the Top of the World'. If Pagan's attraction lies in the splendour and magnificence of her greater temples it must also lie in the fact that little gems like this are able to hold their own alongside the colossal. 'Discovered' only in 1958, the Burmese archaeologist *Bohmu* Ba Shin devoted a whole monograph to the study of this temple: no other Pagan temple can boast this distinction.[21] The writings, or glosses, are in Mon and Old Burmese, and similar in spelling and calligraphy to those in the Myinkaba Kubyauk-gyi inscription though closer in orthography to Ajawlat's inscription in Old Burmese at the Dhamma-yan-gyi of 1165.[22] Thus, the Loka-hteik-pan must date somewhere between these two. Ceylonese, Pali and Old Mon texts had been translated into the vernacular by this stage in the rapid progress of Burma's developing civilisation. The Loka-hteik-pan and its contemporaries all mark a 'Burmanising' tendency in art and architecture that reflected such contemporary literary movements. The paintings, depicted in the 'Narrative Style', in idiom mark a distinct stylistic advance from those at the Myinkaba Kubyauk-gyi as well as a different treatment of colour. The spatial arrangements of this temple, as determined by its ground plan, belong by their architectural conception to the Middle Period. With the complete elimination of a distinction between hall and shrine, there is an increase in the quantity of light permitted to enter the interior. The Middle Period temple has found a form that is both functional and aesthetically satisfying.

Despite the Loka-hteik-pan's size there is a strength and majesty in its elevation and the proportions are balanced to a perfection. All the elements of the Early Period *gu* are here refined so as not to 'overdo' or deplete the exterior of its poise through excessive embellishment. There is no *kirtimukha* frieze; set in the midst of a plain plaster wall surface a single window opening to each face of the base wall has an elaborately stuccoed double octofoil pediment, with the *makara* and heightened spinodes that are characteristic of Middle Period exterior ornament. The heightened plinth has indented panels rather than roll mouldings.

Entering the interior one realises that the brilliance of this temple lies in the unity held between the paintings and architecture. For the first time at Pagan the painters seem to have got together with the architects and devised a scheme whereby each art will work to the others advantage. As has been remarked, there is no distinction between hall and shrine, the two units of the Early temple are now one. The windows let in more light and the absence of a dividing wall and arch between hall and shrine allows further light to

No.78 *Shwe-gu-gyi front from north*
No.79 *Loka-hteik-pan front from north*
Fig.11 *Loka-hteik-pan ground plan (EFEO)*

flood in from the porch. The hall unit has no openings on its sides, the architect has given the painter large areas of uninterrupted wall space for him to set his brush to. Nor is there a central block or *lei-myet-hna* as in the earlier Mye-bon-tha, the main image is placed against a freestanding reredos set to the fore of the south wall with the south window concealed behind.

The scenes portray events from the *bodawin* and Jataka. In them the individual figure's size has been increased to one that may be described as 'monumental' in effect. This enlarged vision of scenes and figures was conceived to create an impressive visual impact on the beholder. The 'Narrative Style' develops to a further state of boldness whilst the 'Decorative Style', of Northern Buddhist origins, in this temple is rejected in favour of a direct means of presenting such fundamental texts.[23] The emphasis of the paintings in the Loka-hteik-pan is thus didactic rather than decorative and the aesthetic is a tactile one, the figures being firmly modelled with light and shade played to an almost dramatic effect and they are isolated within each scene, uncluttered by extraneous paraphernalia, to boldly present the essentials of the Buddhist faith. Art, like Buddhism, had become purified by the time of Sithu I. There is little of the 'art for art's sake' mentality of the 'Decorative Style' of the Abe-ya-dana found here. Of interest are the costumes of the audiences in the Buddha's life scenes, these reflect contemporary textile designs, the crowns and regalia of the royal figures depicted likewise are of the type used by contemporary Pagan kings. Also note the pavilions depicted, they have tall *pyatthat* and give an impression of what 'lost' Pagan must have looked like.

Beginning from the east wall and working about the temple clockwise:

SHRINE EAST WALL
Top right - Dussa Cetiya in Brahmaloka—the stupa reliquary in which the Buddha's discarded royal robes were

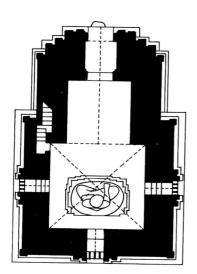

enshrined. **Top left** - Sulamani Cetiya in Tavatimsa—here the Buddha's hair was enshrined by Sakka. **Above window** - Vejayanta: the Palace of Indra with Buddha enthroned preaching the *Abhidhamma* to his mother with the cosmos about him; the ascent to the right and the descent to the left. **Lower left** - Dipankara Buddha's prophecy about Sumedha who is prostrate before him. **Lower right** - Bimbisara's request when the Buddha makes his way to Vesali to preach the *Ratana Sutta*.

SHRINE SOUTH WALL
Flanking the window - Sariputta and Mogallana, with elaborate halo border above flanked by two *kinnaya* (acted as back drop to the freestanding reredos and image which shields a small window opening to centre of this composition). **Upper centre** - the *Parinibbana*. **Upper left** - Dona's Intervention. **Upper right** - Distribution of Relics. **No.2 tier** - Mara's Army (attacking on left and retreating to the right). **No.3 tier, left** - the Four Tooth Relic Stupas.
SHRINE WEST WALL - the *Mahanipata*.
HALL EAST AND WEST WALLS - the Jataka.
HALL NORTH WALL - about and above the arch the *Buddhavamsa* (or 28 buddhas, each beneath his respective species of *bodhi* tree).

No.1597 THAT-BYIN-NYU သဗ္ဗညု

The That-byin-nyu or 'the Omniscient', along with the Dhamma-yan-gyi, was probably one of Sithu I's last great works of merit built towards the end of his reign.[24] The That-byin-nyu has no original inscription though there is one relating to the dedication of a new main image in the 14th century.[25] The chronicles attribute the temple's building to Sithu I and there is no reason to doubt this assignation, for in form, style and feeling the That-byin-nyu is the logical successor to Sithu I's earlier Shwe-gu-gyi. However, it seems strange that Sithu I, who became popularly known as 'The Donor of the Shwe-gu-gyi', did not take his title from this greater, at least in scale, work of merit.[26] The answer to this may be that the temple was never fully completed, for the intended Jataka set was never added and one wonders if there ever was a main image preceding this 14th century dedication.

The That-byin-nyu marks the full blossoming, or rather outburst, of the Middle Period temple when Pagan was at one of its most creative moments. The achievement of a strong and stable empire and administration, with a flourishing young literature and a strongly-felt commitment to Theravada Buddhism that had become purified and rarified to new heights of scholarly activity by the advent of the Middle Period, was reflected in the construction of so ambitious a temple. The That-byin-nyu is truly a monument to this phase in Burma's history when a spirit of innovation and experiment led to great climaxes of creative energy that were an expression of the self-confident Burmese spirit of nationhood.

In its exterior form the That-byin-nyu is a great play of cubes. The original *gu* or 'cave' conception has been left behind and the upper storey experiments of, first, the Kubyauk-gyi at Myinkaba, and then, the Mye-bon-tha-hpaya-hla near the Shwe-hsan-daw, culminate in the lifting of the main image and its sanctum from the ground level to an upper level. *Hpaya*, a non terrestrial concept, is thus raised to more elevated realms. The plan is square based, with the hall extending towards the east from the base block. The front has a triple arch pediment with tall spinodes and *makara*. There are further entrance openings at the cardinal points, slightly projecting outwards, breaking the flat surface of the base wall, yet in no way detracting attention from the focus of the mass above. They, like the front, are capped by a squat central bell-shaped stupa that centres the beholder's eye on the main mass, like the sights of a gun on a target. The ground level ambulatory is lit by windows, with the by now standard Middle Period spinode pediment super-imposed upon a five-tiered *pyatthat*. The next level, equivalent to a mezzanine or entresol, has a pediment without the *pyatthat* backing. Stucco ornamentation is here limited, for example, there is no *kirtimukha* frieze, though stucco is used to highlight the pediments. Possibly such ornament was intended though never added as Sithu's workmen turned their attention to

more pressing projects, perhaps the Dhamma-yan-gyi. The base is, as the term might suggest, merely a base, a platform from which greater things must rise. The architects realised this effect and created a scheme which, without monotony, will, whilst enhancing the whole, lead the pilgrim to climb up into the sanctum and stare out from it at what remains one of the sure glories of the world: Pagan.

Above are three terraces, at their corners stupa obelisks rise from square based blocks with passages passing through them, as at the Shwe-gu-gyi. The terraces have indented panels, 539 of them in all, that would have been intended to hold a Jataka plaque series, up to, but not including, the *Mahanipata*, or last ten, though none of these were ever added. The massive upper cube contrasts the close detailing of the terraces with its sheer blankness: openings are reduced to a minimum and there is scarcely any ornamentation other than the double pediments over the arched entrance openings. Above are three further terraces, with corner stupa obelisks and medial recesses. All this is surmounted by the extraordinary *sikhara*, a squat broad form that acts on the great play of masses beneath, like a pressure valve holding down some powerful and energetic force.

This dramatic play of forces and volumes, this comprehension of the energies inherent in the jux-

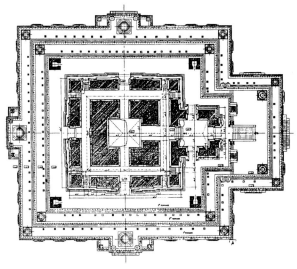

taposition of architectural forms, seems unprecedented at Pagan. Certainly it is on this scale, however, what the architects attempted was a continuance of the longitudinally planned *gu* type of plan combining with the crescendo effect of the Ananda's elevation. What is surprising, though, is the great leap in a mere two decades from the Shwe-gu-gyi to this. The emphasis is in aspiration, yet Sithu's builders did not go to the full extreme, suddenly halting the upwards soar with the counter stroke of a short *sikhara*. By the building of the Gadaw-palin the Pagan architect had lost any such restraint in his upwards quest.

The That-byin-nyu's interior planning makes it one of the most unique and innovative of Pagan Temples. In other temples, past and future, the stairway is usually relegated to a duct-like passage passing through the thickness of exterior walls. At the That-byin-nyu the stair passage becomes a significant architectural feature in itself. Facing the main opening, in place of the usual sanctum and image, the stairs rise from the arch up to the 1st level or entresol. The purpose of the entresols was to reduce the mass of the main blocks, they contain neither paintings nor images and thus had no didactic intention; if monks resided here it was coincidental. These long broad ambulatory passages are akin to the clerestory found at the earlier Myin-pya-gu which was again strictly structural and functional. In the upper entresol the original guttering systems are still in use. It has been suggested that the area within the central block was hollow or rubble filled, however, our recent investigation of the contemporary Dhamma-yan-gyi reveals that in fact temple cores were solid masses of brickwork and not hollow. The lower ambulatory contains some fragments of paintings; perhaps more survive beneath the centuries of encrusted lime wash.

To reach the first storey, one thus passes above the 1st entresol onto the ground level hall terrace and up the broad exterior stair-bridge linking the ground floor hall with the 1st floor hall. Here the image, a 14th century addition, is placed in a giant niche on the east

That-byin-nyu
Fig.12 above: plan of main shrine level (RIT)
Fig.13 right: elevation (RIT)
No.80 above left: east front
No.81 above right: pralambanasana buddha in
ground level ambulatory

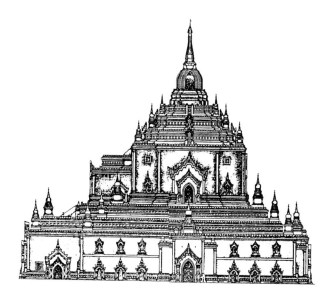

face of the central block, looking out to the shrine-hall. In the shrine, light is unlimited and the atmosphere cool and airy beneath the tall vaults. The pointed arch, known in Burma from earliest times, is now used for effect. At this level is the ambulatory proper, running about the *lei-myet-hna-hpaya* or 'Four Faces of the Lord'. Each image faces a tall and broad opening, there is no attempt, as in the Early Period, to enshrine the Buddha within an inner sanctum though the east image and its recess is naturally larger than the others. The second entresol is directly above the shrine level ambulatory and is again no more than a mass reducing device. From here, further passages of steps climb up through the outer wall to the upper terraces. It seems unlikely that Sithu's builders saw the ultimate goal of a pilgrimage to the That-byin-nyu as a mountaineering expedition to the peak of this cosmic mountain. Luce expressed the effect of the That-byin-nyu perfectly: "This is no lifeless pile of brick and plaster. It is the *Purha*, the Buddha, exhibiting the great miracle. See the deluge descending from his shoulders! See the holocaust ascending from his feet."[27]

Within the ambulatories are a number of Buddha monoliths including one rare piece in which the Buddha sits in *pralambanasana*. Finally, before leaving the That-byin-nyu, note the two bell pillars in the grounds of the monastery sited to the south-east of the front. The bell has now disappeared, its weight of bronze must have been a lucrative prize to some marauding war lord of later, less passive, times. The pillars are made from stone and recall memories of the stone-work on the Nan-hpaya and Kyauk-ku-ohn-min, as do the fine carvings of the downwards tapering **V** motif on each face of each pillar.

No.771 DHAMMA-YAN-GYI   ဓမ္မရံကြီး

Mystery emanates from the Dhamma-yan-gyi: from the temple's history as well as its architecture. With a ground plan based on the Ananda's Greek Cross type of plan, there would usually have been a double ambulatory with four medial recesses into the central block acting as shrines for the four buddhas. For some reason the arches and window openings between the two ambulatories have been bricked up and the inner ambulatory filled to the level of its vaults with rubble. The structure itself, as our recent exploration of the interior has shown, is strong enough, so this was no attempt to increase the base's support for the super-structure, this was a deliberate attempt to seal off the inner ambulatory and the north, south and west shrines. This denial of access to the inner part of the temple at a time, judging by the brick work, shortly after the termination of the temple builders activity is not easily explained. It is one of those great architectural mysteries.

Luce explains the mystery: according to the Ceylonese chronicles and a rock inscription at Devangala, the Ceylonese king, Parakramabahu I, in 1165, sent an armada to Burma to solve a dispute over trading rights and allegedly assassinated the king and sacked the capital.[28] Luce, following the chronicle tradition, believed this king to be Narathu who was also known as Kala-kya, or 'Fallen by Indians'.[29] The Dhamma-yan-gyi, according to Luce, was Narathu's work, and the Ceylonese, in an act of retribution that seems strange for a fellow Buddhist nation who up till now had enjoyed such close contact with Burma, denied Narathu the merit gained from such a dedication by sealing off his temple interior, though leaving the east and most important shrine open. Luce's explanation is brilliant, yet controversial, for he paints a picture of Ceylonese warriors roaming the streets of Pagan. It seems unlikely that, if they did reach Pagan, they could have safely resided there without fear of some retaliation. Pagan was after all the 'hub' of a great military state.

Wickramasinghe, the Ceylonese scholar, suggests that it is unlikely that a Ceylonese task force actually reached Pagan; their raid, arising from an elephant trading dispute and role of Burma as a buffer to Cambodia and other South-East Asian empires, seems to have been confined to the delta ports, possibly Bassein.[30] Neither the Devangala Inscription nor the Ceylonese chronicles make reference to an actual conquest of Pagan, the capital, itself and it seems extraordinary that a naval force should be able to penetrate so far inland, unhindered by the Burmese garrisons stationed on the route to Pagan. However, the Ceylonese sources do make mention of the assassination of the Burmese king, so possibly the Ceylonese executed a provincial governor and exaggerated their victory by claiming a slain king. What is significant though, is that from this date onwards, a new wave of Ceylonese influence is discernible in Pagan architecture, which must be a repercussion to renewed political and cultural ties with Ceylon following a solution to this dispute.

An inscription that Michael Aung Thwin has brought to light dates the death of Sithu I to 1169/70 and not to c.1155/60 as Luce had believed.[31] Therefore, Sithu must still have been king at the time of the Ceylonese raid, which the Devangala inscription dates to 1165. In the light of this the Dhamma-yan-gyi was begun in the reign of Sithu I himself and not by Narathu, who, according to this revised dating, must have begun his reign around 1169/70 and ended it in 1174 when Sithu II is definitely recorded to have succeeded.

The one contemporary inscription that records the dedication of the Dhamma-yan-gyi is found in the north hall of the temple and dates to 1165.[32] Its author was the Middle Princess Ajawlat, perhaps a daughter of Sithu I. Though recording the dedication, it makes no mention of who the builder was nor provides a clue towards an understanding of the strange events that must have occured at Pagan around this time.[33] What Ajawlat's inscription does is date the temple's construction to before 1165 which means that, according to the revised dating for Sithu I's death, it must have been begun in his reign.

The Dhamma-yan-gyi itself was never completed, possibly after Sithu's death interest in the building of so great a temple dwindled. The chronicles tell how his son Narathu smothered him as he lay on his death bed in his Shwe-gu-gyi; possibly this perpetrator of parricide had no inclination to complete his father's last great work of merit and ordered the brick layers to seal off the three shrines and their connecting ambulatory.[34] The That-byin-nyu, which was also one of Sithu's works, was likewise unfinished.[35] Pagan temples were put up with a startling speed as a personal act of merit for the donor, were he to die before his work's completion then a member of his family would often continue it. In the face of popular complaint, Narathu may have lacked the inclination to complete these two colossal projects of his father. Sithu's thirst for the ultimate temple, with the near simultaneous construction of two major works, may have drained Pagan of resources and her workers of energy. Perhaps Narathu, in a bid for popularity, terminated the work, choosing to seal off the Dhamma-yan-gyi rather than continue on the interior. However, our recent investigation of the interior shows that the inner ambulatory was in a complete enough state with stucco and some painted decoration on the vaulting.

As has been noted, in ground plan the Dhamma-yan-gyi takes the form of a Greek Cross. Though built well within the Middle Period, the Dhamma-yan-gyi in plan, but not in its elevation, marks a return to the Ananda type that dates from the Early Period. The spiritually charged and intense atmosphere of the Early Pagan temple is here reverted to after various experiments with different effects in atmosphere, achieved through play of plan and elevation, firstly at the Shwe-gu-gyi and then at That-byin-nyu. Indeed, Luce believed it to be the last of his 'Mon' temples. However, the Dhamma-yan-gyi marks a revival and not the end of a continuum, for six decades have passed between the Ananda and the Dhamma-yan-gyi and an architectural revolution at Pagan had taken place.

In elevation, any comparison between the Dhamma-yan-gyi and the Ananda must cease. The steeply climbing, horizontal bands of the terraces are dominant lines, rising in a crescendo, like the last movement of a thunderous symphony. These are far more monumental in effect than the equilibrious play of Kyanzittha's Ananda terraces. The Ananda initiated the doubled terrace type at Pagan, the That-byin-nyu developed the concept, breaking the two terrace sections with the shrine block, but here there is no upper sanctum: the architects have reverted to a ground level arrangement with all six terraces run continuously together with no break. The gap between each ascending terrace is shortened as height is gained, the broadest being the lowest. Thus, there is a steepening ascent: the graduated terraces climb with the effect of a crescendo that would have climaxed in the brilliant stroke of the now broken

Dhamma-yan-gyi
No.82 top: the twin buddhas, west shrine
No.83 above: inner ambulatory filled with rubble
Fig.14 below: ground plan (EFEO)

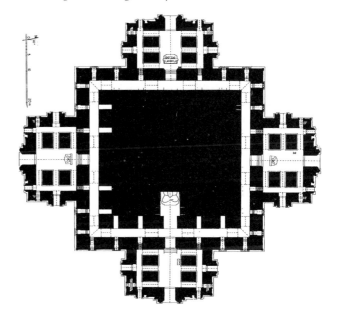

crowning *sikhara*. Horizontality is the maxim and the near-contemporary experiment in verticality at the That-byin-nyu has either been forgotten or rejected. One may conjecture whether there were two schools of architectural thought at Sithu's court, one championing verticality and the other horizontality, and wonder whether Sithu decided to give each a chance! If there is a precursor to the Dhamma-yan-gyi at Pagan, it must be the much earlier Myin-pya-gu which is akin in the overall effect of monumentality through the powerful downward strokes of horizontally arranged features. The original *sikhara* is now damaged, with it the exterior effect may have been lightened.

The halls have triple pediments over their fronts. The pilasters on either side of the entrance arches rise from elaborately pedimented niches that would once have contained seated *dvarapala* figures. The hall fronts are far broader than the Ananda ones and have tall, arched and pedimented window openings to each side of the porch. The porch arches themselves are narrower and taller than the Ananda ones, their tightness contrasting the front's overall broadness. Good examples of Middle Period stucco ornament survive on some of the side entrance openings with the deity figure in the apex. The window openings on the hall sides have straight brick lintels which were marvelled at by Yule in 1855.[36]

On each corner of the base there are two windows to two tiers that are divided by a continuous band. The stucco remaining on some of the window pediments is of breathtaking quality. Splendid *makara*, floral ornament and *kirtimukha* of great vitality and rich texture lavishly coats the octofoil pediments with their flame-like spinodes bringing to life the bare surfaces of the base walls.

The hall facade triple *torana* are repeated on the first terrace projecting outwards and upwards. The presence of these imposing frontages suggest the inclusion of an upper level shrine but in fact the arch leads to empty attics through which light would have been intended to pass into the now sealed-off shrines. Only on the east where the shrine is 'free' or open does this actually happen. Above rise the terraces, well worth scaling to admire the perfection of the brick work, for at the Dhamma-yan-gyi the craftsmen shunned the use of mortar, the bricks tightly interlock such that, in the words of many a local, "a pin could not pass between them." Indented panels running around each terrace were left for a Jataka series that, like at the That-byin-nyu, was never added. Medial passages cut through the terraces starting from behind the attic *torana* to meet the *sikhara*. On the east side only, the passages pass beneath short arches that link the terrace lines, an arrangement that was probably intended for the other sides but never completed. Note the dramatic use of mouldings: the bold indentations and projections of the bands as they build up, drawing closer together at each level as the temple climbs higher and higher. The whole elevation is strengthened by solid, square-based corner stupas on the

lower four terraces. Gone are the *chinthé* and *bilu* figures of the Ananda terraces in favour of a power and strength based on boldness and simplicity.[37]

On the interior, the hall vaults are carried by four monolithic piers that create aisles to the sides where there are further entrance openings. Steps rise up through the thickness of the four hall outer walls to a gallery passage that apparently leads nowhere. Local tradition has it that these reached a gallery-like wooden construction that ran at the jutting cornice level about the outer wall of the ambulatory. The presence of iron rungs set at intervals along the wall above the cornice further suggests the inclusion of some form of upper gallery, with the rungs holding a rail of some sort. Fragments of mural paintings remain on the inner sides of the main arches, added in the Ava period they depict the, by then evolved Burmese *dvarapala* or *bilu*. The halls are on a lower level than the ambulatories; at the steps leading into the temple's base are the main Buddha images set against a reredos on all sides but the east, where access to the shrine is permitted. These images too are Ava Period additions, the original shrine images, if they were ever made, remain imprisoned within.

Luce ended his magnificent work on the Early Period with these words on the Dhamma-yan-gyi enigma:

> Perhaps, with modern appliances, there is no need to wait till then. When peace at last returns to Burma, before swords are bent into pruning hooks, could they not first be flattened into spades, and join in opening, as a symbol of a new Burma, this old and priceless temple?[38]

Possibly in response to this clarion call from the doyen of Pagan studies, the Archaeology Department attempted to cut through the dense mass of brick that has filled the cross passage and shrine arches. Their attempt ended in failure, for the brick work is very fine on the Dhamma-yan-gyi, with the broad thin bricks tightly interlocking with each other and mortar used sparingly, so in the end the Department's labourers were compelled to hack at the brick work as if mining a coal-face and when they had failed to reach the inner ambulatory gave up.[39] It thus seemed that entry into the forbidden interior, without undertaking a major archaeological operation involving engineers and teams of labourers, was impossible until my friend Ko Kim Aung Way pointed out that villagers often go bat hunting in the inner ambulatory, entering from one of several unsealed upper cross passage openings that I had not previously noticed. Together with Pierre Pichard and Ko Kim Aung Way, aided by ladders donated to the department by UNDP and a tow rope from Pierre's jeep, and ground support from Ko Aye Hlaing, we managed, through a series of acrobatic manœvers, to reach the ledge of such an opening, high up on the wall just beneath the ambulatory vaults. On entering we found that the inner ambulatory had been completely filled to the level of the upper cross openings and vaults with rubbled brick. We were able to pass around the temple, crawling beneath the lower diaphragm arches as far as the east shrine which remains open. Thus, the ground level openings having been sealed, the entire interior had been filled in but for the east shrine. From this vantage point within, we were able to examine the vaults and upper walls to see if there were any cracks or other structural defects that might have required such an infilling but could see no evidence of any such weakness (nor recent earthquake damage). Of particular interest is that the vaults had been stuccoed and in some places there are fragments of painted ornament. This indicates that the inner ambulatory was in a complete state before its closure. From this upper passage, though, there was no access to the three shrines, for, as with the east one, the shrine arch is beneath the level of the ambulatory vault. If, by chance, these shrines had not been filled up with rubble the only possible access would be to cut down through the now sealed skylight opening from the terraces.

Treasure hunters had been in here before us: from above the top of one of the bridge-like diaphragm arches we followed a chiselled out passage deep into the solid core of the temple to a dead end filled with the pandemonium of countless bats dazzled by our flash-lights. We could sense the centuries old disappointment of these determined *tabena-sha* who, like the Department of recent times, have been foiled by this great mass of compressed brick.

Of the halls, the west one is of great interest. Here, set against a two panel reredos that is topped by three stupa finials, are two identical Buddha images seated in the *bhumisparsamudra* beside each other. The symbolism of this unusual double Buddha treatment is explained by Luce who cites the *Lotus Sutta*:

> The greatest moment known to the pious Theravadin is when Buddha meets future Buddha and Prophecy is made. To the Mahayanist, a greater moment is when two Buddhas, the old and new, sit for one brief moment together on one throne: symbol, at once of the change and the Continuity of the Dharma. Therein lies the strength of Buddhism as a world-religion.[40]

There is an inscription dating to 1205 in the hall that refers to the building of a *gu* and enshrining of a *hpaya* or image on the west face of the Dhamma-yan-gyi. If this refers to our double image, as Luce and U Bo Kay suggest, then the implication is that the hall was added or at least completed much later than the temple itself. This seems unlikely as the present hall, judging by the brickwork, would appear to be contemporary and is a fully integrated part of the temple itself.

The double Buddha as a symbolic arrangement was known in Pyu times, yet in Pyu arrangements Mettaya Buddha is always depicted crowned and it is extraordinary that after the passing of several centuries this type should suddenly revive and that Mettaya should have no crown.[41] On the reverse side of the reredos is a *parinibbana* scene, this too is Early Ava in style, and it was in this period that the *parinibbana* scene was usually enriched in the wall directly behind the main image.

The east shrine, as noted, has been left open. Here, the image also dates from the Ava period and the painted reredos is later still. One monolith of a seated Buddha in *dhyanamudra* placed in the east hall set against the inner pillar, has a painted inscription, now half destroyed since Luce read it, on the wall above: "dated 705s./1343 A.D., (it) tells how a pious person called *Mantham* ('royal officer') 'not being able to bear the sight of the ruin done by the heretics to the noble pagoda (or Buddha) called Dhammaram the ancestral site of king *Cañsu*' spent all his life savings, 'won by painful endeavour', in setting up (it seems) this *dhyana* monolith."[42] Others of this type, with taut serious faces, short necks and broad bodies, so unlike the usual cheerful and benign Early Ava Buddhas, have been found at Pagan and date from Anawrahta's time; what Mantham appears to have done was to rededicate an ancient image and not commission a new one.[43]

The Dhamma-yan-gyi remains enigmatic and mysterious. Its powerful shape dominates any Pagan vista. Like a great magnet, it draws believer and non-believer alike towards its stalwart mass. Once there, real access to the *hpaya* itself is denied. Local people fear the Dhamma-yan-gyi's wrath, they tell tales of great ghosts patrolling the ambulatories after each day's quick, tropical dusk. The Middle Period was a time of architectural transition and experimentation, after the Dhamma-yan-gyi's construction Pagan builders were never to attempt a monumental 'depressed' type on a Greek Cross plan again. In the Late Period, the royal patron, in his large two-storey temples, sought the majestic and the sublime and the rival claims of the Dhamma-yan-gyi and That-byin-nyu were to be harmonised into a classic architectural compromise, the most striking embodiments of which were the Hti-lo-min-lo and Sula-mani.[44]

No.394 BU-LE-THI ဘူးလယ်သီး

South of the new Nyaung-U Pagan road and west of the Shwe *chaung* is situated this middle sized stupa, so named after a gourd-like fruit on account of the bulbous shape of its crowning finial. This form, here adapted for an *anda*, has been met with before at Pagan, at the Pa-hto-tha-mya (c.1084-1113) temple, where the dodecahedron form was applied to the *sikhara*.[45] This is the only other surviving example of this form at Pagan and though this stupa cannot be exactly dated, it must follow the Pa-hto-tha-mya's lead and for this reason has been here included with the monuments dating from the Middle Period. The stupa itself resembles the Shwe-hsan-daw prototype, with medial stair flights, cutting up through the terraces. Most stupas built in the late 12th and 13th centuries had steepened terraces with no medial flights, the Bu-le-thi arrangement seems to be closer to the 11th century stupas at Pagan, so it may be not distant in chronology from the Pa-hto-tha-mya.

No.1085-6 SEIN-NYET AMA / NYI-MA
စိမ်းညက်ညီအစ်မ

The Sein-nyet *ama* or 'Elder Sister', which is a *gu*, and *nyima* or 'Younger Sister', which is a *zeidi*, as a group is an eloquent statement of the Middle Period architect's success in creating a sumptuous grandeur on a restrained and unpretentious scale. Sited close by to another brilliant foundation, the Somin-gyi Monastery, the Sein-nyet sisters glow from their location on a slight hillock, just south of the Naga-yon. These two architectural gems are close in their arrangement to the Hpyatsa-shwe-gu temple and stupa at Myinkaba, also believed to date from the reign of Sithu I.[46]

The *ama* temple is the standard Late Pagan type, with the shrine on the ground level: forthright terraces are carried on a tall, bold block-like base with triple pediments about the tall, arched, openings on each face and with an airy hall, opening out into a well-lit and lofty ambulatory. The hall extends out to the east towards the *nyima* and has a pair of perforated window openings on its north and south walls. This essentially Early feature of tight and compressed perforated window openings is contrasted by the inclusion of entrance or porch openings on the other three sides of the shrine base. Thus, this is very much a work of transition, the hall still in the 11th century, the shrine in the 12th. Within, the arrangement of images about the central block is distinctly reminiscent of the Shwe-gu-gyi arrangement, though here taken one logical step further: an **H** plan, with an image set on the east and west faces of the block, but not on the north and south sides.

The majesty of the *ama* is countered by the sumptuous tendencies displayed by the *nyima*. The stupa

base is squarely planned and there are no medial stairways: this is a pagoda to be seen—not scaled. The ornament remains crisp, tarnished neither by human nor element. Each of the three terraces is packed with banded horizontal mouldings and topped with a demarcating crennellated line. On the corners are obelisks of Hawksmoorian eccentricity. These vary in form, each carried on a tall and narrow circular base, they expand in bulbousness and girth as they make their ascent. In essence, these peculiar and unprecedented, yet highly satisfying forms, are a combination of the *kalasa* pot and subsidiary stupa usually employed in this position. The *kalasa* was to become an increasingly popular addition to Late Period stupa terraces, their ultimate manifestation being on the terraces of the Mingala-zeidi (1268).[47] What is notable is that here, in the first half of the 12th century, there has been a radical break with the set tradition of stupa building evolved and established at Pagan. For example, compare this sumptuous little ornament to the Pagan landscape with the circular based, bottle shaped, stupas of Anawrahta, like his one at Myinkaba, dating to only a couple of generations earlier. At Sein-nyet, though, the *kalasa* form, as an obelisk, is still used in an experimental manner.

On the terrace corners, original *chinthé* remain. Fragments of these leogryphs have been met already at Pagan, but here survive in excellent condition and in a form far closer to the characteristic *chinthé* of later times.

A polygonally banded section filters the eye from the steep horizontals of the terraces through to the comely curve of the *anda* which commences with a jagged band of lotus petals. The stucco ornament on the *anda* is in an exceptionally unblemished condition. The surface is bisected at the cardinal points with four niches for images of the four buddhas, all in *dharmacakramudra*. These niches are connected by a garlanded *kirtimukha* frieze. Above, what is perhaps most impressive is the *harmika,* which dramatically inverts with a serrated and multiple banded edge and then blossoms out—again a polygonal arrangement, repeating the arrangement between terraces and *anda*. From here there is a further inversion and then the now restored *chattrâvali* rises.

The *harmika* itself must predate the Ceylonese type, which was to become so popular after 1174 at Pagan, here the form is merely suggested, and is not the box-like feature of the Ceylonese type.

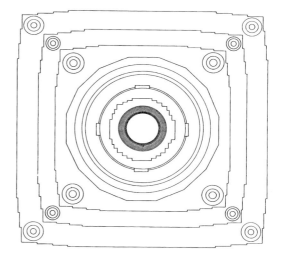

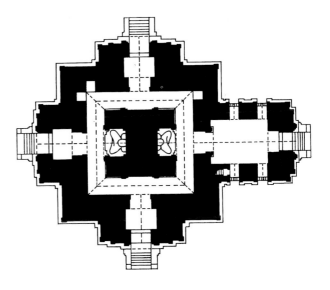

No.84 *upper left: Sein-nyet Ama from north-east*
No.85 *middle left: Sein-nyet Nyi-ma finial (restored)*
No.86 *lower left: Sein-nyet Nyi-ma anda*
No.87 *above: Bu-le-thi*
Fig.15 *upper right: Sein-nyet Nyi-ma, plan (EFEO)*
Fig.16 *lower right: Sein-nyet Ama (EFEO)*

6

The Late Period 1170-1300
(I) Inner Circle Monuments

THE MIDDLE PERIOD was a transitional and experimental phase in the architectural history of Pagan. For contemporary to each other two buildings as diverse the That-byin-nyu and the Dhamma-yan-gyi underwent simultaneous construction. In the Late Period the spirit of experimentation and innovation did not cease. The novel and highly original five-faced ground plan type was introduced onto the Pagan plain with neither precedent nor scriptural sanction.[1] The advent of this type of scheme represented a radical departure from all Buddhist architectural traditions and exemplifies the fact that the Pagan creative genius was in no way on the wane.

In this period Pagan remained open to North Indian influences; contact with Bodh Gaya led in a number of instances to the introduction of a new and novel *sikhara* type based on the Vajrasana temple at Bodh Gaya.[2] With the accession of Sithu II in 1174, a new era of relations with Ceylon were entered into, the most visual memorial of which was the addition of the *harmika* to stupas built during this phase of Pagan architecture. In spite of these innovations to the builders' repertoire Pagan temples and stupas, donated in ever increasing numbers, had evolved through the preceding phases to culminate in a standard scheme that satisfied the Burmese aesthetic temperament. The ultimate and most imitated embodiment of the temple ideal being the Sula-mani of 1183, in which a satisfying equilibrium between the horizontal trend displayed by the Dhamma-yan-gyi, with an overall effect of stately grandeur, and the verticalist trend, typified by the That-byin-nyu, which creates an overall effect of aspiration, had been achieved. This balance between the vertical and horizontal that had been a feature of the Early Period 'cave' temple exterior, was to be repeated without monotony to form a myriad of types and designs through this period. With this compromise, first apparent at the Sula-mani of 1183, between the two opposing architectural schools of thought that had existed contemporary to each other at Sithu I's court, Pagan builders no longer felt the urge to attempt daring new forms in their 'greater' two-storey temple elevations, preferring to vary and diversify, to the point of intricate nuance, the 'standard scheme' that had been achieved by the building of the Sula-mani.

Surprisingly, only one three-level temple was built, the Thisa-wadi at East Pwasaw, and according to an in situ inscription this colossal temple was built outside

our period.[3] In view of the multiplicity of forms that were attempted during this phase, when architects were seemingly unrestrained by set traditions and the design parameters usually imposed by an artistically conservative class of donors, and in view of the Pagan builders' quest for height and imposing elevation, it would seem logical for them to include a third-storey shrine and, moreover, numerologically symbolic (the *hpaya-thon-zu* only working upwards). However, whilst 'the original' was the claim of each temple and no doubt its donors and their builders, architectural extravagance seems always to have been avoided.

Likewise, decoration, whether stucco on the exterior or paint work on the interior, remained restrained and whilst architectural virtuosity was admired in the late 12th and early 13th centuries, exhibitionism was avoided by a court that had become increasingly cultivated and refined through the stability offered by the now well-established dynasty and its equally well-established faith. Yet, so startling is the restrained diversity of the thousand-plus monuments dating from the Late Period, one may wonder whether each donor insisted that his architect build for him 'something different'.

Though the great temples like the Sula-mani and the Hti-lo-min-lo had their main shrine on the upper level, single ground-level shrines on both a lesser and greater scale continued to be built in ever increasing numbers. The tendency, met in the Middle Period Shwe-gu-gyi, where the distinction between shrine and hall was gradually becoming eliminated, becomes more apparent in the Late Period, for example at the Wetkyi-in Kubyauk-gyi. This 'open plan' was, though, not always the rule and in a number of significant monuments the architects chose to differentiate between the two units. Likewise, following the Shwe-gu-gyi's precedent, temples tend to be carried on a raised and artificial platform. The window openings of the Early Period shrine base are expanded into entrances often with a slight porch and a grand arrangement of pilasters and pediments about it forming a forepart. Light is less inhibited in its penetration of the interior and the shrine images are usually set to the fore of the central mass rather than being receded within it.[4] There are numerous variants to this norm but these features are at least the standard forms followed by the Late Period architects and from which they joyfully seemed to have diverged from.

The Late Period was also a time of expanding

monastic establishments; great complexes grew up in the outlying areas, particularly around the villages of Minnanthu and Pwasaw. These reflect the increasing power, prestige and wealth of the *sangha*. A fire in 1225 had destroyed much of the city, so from this time onwards, donors tended to include a second enclosure wall about their dedications to act as a fire break and also, conveniently, to act as a residential area for junior monks and their servants and slaves.[5] It is to this phase in Pagan's history that the bulk of lithic inscriptions remain, relating to dedications and other meritorious acts. Religious life would also appear to have undergone some transformation in the 13th century with the rise of a powerful land owning, politicised and alcohol drinking sect under the leadership of Mahakassapa based in the Minnanthu area.[6] This sect has been connected with the Ari, the decayed monks cleansed by the Early Pagan kings, as told in the chronicles,[7] and Duroiselle suggested that certain temples in the Minnanthu area, whose painted wall decorations seemed to indicate the influence of Northern Buddhism, were the product of a connection between the Mahakassapa sect, based in Minnanthu, and Northern Buddhist practitioners.[8] These temples date from a time when Buddhists in India were being persecuted by the invading Moslems and may have come to Pagan to take refuge, assisting in the development of the Mahakassapa sect. However, as Dr Than Tun has explained, the 'Ari', or rather Arannavasi, were degenerate Theravada monks rather than converts to the Mahayana or Vajrayana, and rose to political and economic prominence from jungle-based practices in the Monywa areas in the late 12th century.[9] It must be noted that contemporary Tantra texts explicitly forbid a Tantrika from stopping in a Theravada monastery for more than seven days.[10]

The mural paintings in the Minnanthu temples in reality mark a return to the 'Decorative Style' of the Early Period and are not evidence of active Northern Buddhist cults. As with the Early Period examples, such as the Abe-ya-dana, the paintings are subsidiary to the fundamental Theravada icons and illustrate no known Mahayana or Tantra text. Thus, such works are more like a colourful and flamboyant 'wallpaper' than a devotional or didactic iconographic programme. The old question naturally arises, who were the artists? Were they local men or foreigners? The style of portrayal of these decorative works from the Late Period, which revelled in the architectonic, subjugating all figures and narrative to within a grandiose play of architectural decorations as at Paya-thon-zu or Penan-tha, may be derived from Nepal. For the human and divine figures' physiognomy resembles those of contemporary Nepali miniature painting.[11] Possibly itinerant Himalayan artists came to work at Pagan from time to time. What should be noted, though, is that these fantastic dummy architectural schemes, full of *trompe l'oeil* effects that combine the naturalistic delicacy of Etruscan art with rococo rhetoric, were conceived in the spirit of the Late Period and bear no direct relationship to contemporary schemes in North India or Nepal.

If the Arannavasi represented a degenerate aspect to the Buddhism of the period, then increased contact with Ceylon maintained a purifying current in the religious life of Late Pagan. The mission of the monk Sapada to Ceylon, as described in the chronicles, for reordination so as to strengthen the lineage connections between Burma and the heartland of Pali Buddhism was commemorated with the construction of the Sapada stupa, so named after him, which manifests this strong Ceylonese connection, with a Ceylonese type of finial and *harmika*, a feature that was to be repeated on numerous stupas built from this time onwards across the plain.[12]

Michael Aung Thwin has convincingly suggested that Pagan suffered a decline in the 13th century as a result of the transfer of wealth from the state to the *sangha* which led to a weakening of the state's authority.[13] As a glance at the selected Late Period monuments described beneath will show, this was hardly a period of decline. Normally, when a civilisation politically declines such instability is reflected in a decay in the quality of craftsmanship. No such degeneracy is evident in the arts of Late Pagan. If anything, temple construction and decoration become finer and finer, ever increasing in excellence. Even after the supposed Mongol 'sack', temples continued to be built—carefully following the three century old Pagan tradition of excellent workmanship.[14]

Finally, it is questionable whether Pagan actually fell to the Mongols, for Pagan was to remain a religious and cultural centre well into the fourteenth century with dedications of temples and lands continuing.[15] It is known from contemporary inscriptions that the Mongols did actually reach Pagan, indeed Pagan painters recorded their visit in the murals of the Kyanzittha Umin (that date from after 1287).[16] The amount of destruction caused by them, though, was limited and there is no evidence of the city having being put to the torch.[17] Pagan declined in the 14th century as it was no longer the political nerve centre or 'hub'. Vandalism and destruction were wrought, either by marauding Shan tribesmen coming down from the hills in search of booty, or during the centuries of warfare between Mons and Burmans whose armies periodically passed Pagan, either on their way up or down.[18] Yet, even in the Early Ava Period, new dedications were added to the old.[19] Pagan donors carefully provisioned for the maintenance of their endowment, and the most dreadful of curses awaited those *hpaya kywan* who broke their hereditary bonds. These service groups, on whom the preservation of a monument depended, do not appear to have been scattered by the Mongol incursions for later dynasties constantly sought to check these ancient endowments. Shin Disapramuk, who persuaded the Mongol emperor to accept levies of food in place of reaping destruction, recorded his words in an inscription: "A man who plants a garden pours water and makes the trees grow; he does not pinch the tips; when the trees have fruit, he eats the fruit."[20]

In the early 19th century, an artistic movement grew up in Burma that marked a conscious attempt to revive the styles and forms that were current during the Pagan periods. Numerous Pagan type *gu* in the Mandalay area, with a square base and flat-paneled *sikhara*, testify to this.[21] Imperial Burma, as she sought to territorially expand under the Konbaung kings on the model of the Pagan Dynasty, thus emulated the art of that period. In addition to this, the Konbaung kings not only took from Pagan but gave back to Pagan: new dedications were put up, old ones 'made new again', mural paintings in the latest styles were added and images replaced, as Pagan continued as an active religious centre. Even today, Pagan inspires imitation amongst the architects of modern Burma, though often tasteless ones, and Pagan as a place of pilgrimage invites new donations to be heaped upon the old. Tourism has brought the Pagan villagers a new prosperity, giving them, too, the opportunity to continue, albeit sometimes crudely, the great traditions of their ancestors.

For reasons of convenience to the reader, who may be using this work as a guide about the monuments at Pagan and because of the confusing number of Late Period monuments that cannot be logically nursed into a chronological framework, as with the past two periods, it has been necessary to divide the Late Period into two chapters. This one deals with the monuments in the vicinity of the Myinkaba, Pagan and Wetkyi-in villages and the monuments to the west of the Nyaung-U town: 'the Inner Circle Monuments'. The final one, Chapter Seven, dealing with the more distant monuments at Thiriyapyitsaya, Thategan, the two Pwasaw villages, Minnanthu and the monuments to the east of Nyaung-U: 'the Outer Circle Monuments'. This division is purely geographical, being neither according to chronology nor type.

No. 748 SULA-MANI   စူဠာမဏ်

> When king Narapatisithu returned from climbing Mt.Tuywin he saw a ruby radiant and shining in a hollow, the site of Sulamani; and he said, "It is a sign for me to make a work of merit here." [22]

The Sula-mani was perhaps Pagan's ultimate temple and the work of Pagan's tireless temple builder, Sithu II (1174-1211). Sithu II here found an architectural type that aesthetically pleased, whilst satisfing his spiritual and temporal requirements. In the Sula-mani, and its imitator the Hti-lo-min-lo (1211), the massive block arrangement of the That-byin-nyu type is combined with the monumentally of the Dhamma-yan-gyi. A compromise between the rival champions of verticality and horizontalism had been achieved. The Sula-mani is, in effect, the grandiloquent gesture

of an empire at its meridian.

The Sula-mani, or 'Crowning Jewel', as with the later Hti-lo-min-lo, has a square-based plan with a hall projecting to the east that is repeated on the upper level. Though the east hall on the ground level is recessed into the central block, the other three cardinal images are simply placed against the inner ambulatory wall. In elevation, it is pyramidal in effect with the strong lines of the terraces running horizontally about the temple between base and shrine and shrine and *sikhara*. The vast volume of the That-byin-nyu upper block-shrine has been reduced, whilst the wall surfaces are elaborated and enlivened, unlike the bare surfaces of the That-byin-nyu, with stucco ornamented forepart pediments, pilasters and mouldings. As at the Dhamma-yan-gyi, the entrance arches are tall and narrow, dramatically far more effective than the broader ones in the That-byin-nyu. In its overall unity of composition, the Sula-mani draws from the Dhamma-yan-gyi, rather than That-byin-nyu, whilst, in the exterior effect of giant piled cubes, it follows the That-byin-nyu.

The Sula-mani's stucco is very fine and in excellent condition. The *makara*, grotesques and other ornamental creatures are lively and energetic, their carving exquisitely delicate. Note on the upper level exterior corner pilasters, the innovation of a continuous wave of flame-like mouldings working up the pilaster's surface, in place of the tapering **V** and diamond bud that in the past was used on corner pilasters. What is perhaps the finest feature of the Sula-mani's ornament is the insertion of glazed plaques along the plinth and terrace mouldings. Still in good condition, these roundels, lobes and panels, filled with simple geometric motifs, gleam brightly, just as the ruby in Sithu's vision once did.

The paintings on the base ambulatory are from the Konbaung period—yet another indication that Pagan continued as centre for dedications after the supposed fall in 1287. There are two stair passages leading from the ambulatory to the upper shrine. Sithu II has rejected the That-byin-nyu concept of a central stair feature, preferring the more traditional hidden stair passage passing up through the walls. He did, though, allow the lower flights of steps to be open within the ambulatory with a handsome brick balustrade; the in-wall passages themselves are both more spacious and better lit than earlier stair passages. Note the excellence of the brick work, continuing the high standards set by the Dhamma-yan-gyi, the bricks bonded through carefully calculated moulding rather than daubs of mortar. Stone is now being used more generously, not only at load bearing structural points, but also at vulnerable exterior points, for example at the corners and edges of plinth and terraces.

As the Sula-mani dates to before the 1225 fire there is only a single enclosure wall, though a very high one at that, with a dramatic cornice moulding and corners strengthened by pilasters. At the cardinal points are the remains of magnificent gates, flat linteled with a system of relieving arches above carrying the load of the surmounting stupa finial down to earth. To the north of the temple enclosure is a second enclosure of the same dimensions, also surrounded by a continuation of the same wall. This was, and remains to this day, the Sula-mani Kyaung-taik, or monastery. Later dedications tended to place the senior monk's quarters, library, ordination hall and preaching hall within the temple or stupa enclosure whilst the residences for the junior monks and support groups would have been placed within the outer enclosure. Here, at the Sula-mani, the residential, and possibly other structures, like the preaching hall, were included in this northern enclosure. Unique to monastery planning at Pagan was the inclusion of one hundred cells, either for accommodation or meditation, probably both, about the inside of the enclosing wall.[23] There is also a water tank here, possibly the only original Pagan Period tank still in daily use. The system of draining the fields to the east to fill this tank would appear to be original too, for, as the chronicle mentioned, Sithu II had decided to fill this hollow with a temple and in so doing gave it a water supply.[24]

From this time onwards, most large scale two-storey temples imitate the form of the Sula-mani, the most obvious example of which being the Hti-lo-min-lo, for the Pagan king had found a temple form that ideally expressed all that a royal act of merit should: a demonstration of imperial prestige and stately grandeur and a glorious confirmation of faith in the world religion and of royal support for it.

No.187 SAPADA

၁၈၇

The Sapada stupa is a monument to Burma's good relations with Ceylon, the 'Island Jewel', that was the spiritual and scholarly heartland of Pali-based Theravada Buddhism. As told in chronicles and inscriptions, it was common practice for leading Burmese monks to visit the island and be reordained there, so as to ensure a pure lineage back to the first disciples of the Buddha. This religious contact had political and economic repercussions: trade flowed freely and intermarriage between the two dynastic houses must have strengthened an alliance already based upon a common religious faith. Hostilities between the two powers had ended with the accession of Sithu II in 1174 and the old alliance was revived, inaugurating a new era of Burma-Ceylon relations.

The Sapada stupa reflects this alliance. Sapada, a native of Bassein, was one of the monks to travel to Ceylon for reordination, and on his return to Pagan in 1181 erected this stupa to commemorate the visit.[25] The Sapada thus embodies the cultural affinities that existed between the two countries. Ceylonese influence is clearly evident for this temple has a *harmika*, the square box placed between the convexly-shaped *anda* and the indented *chattrâval* finial that had origi-

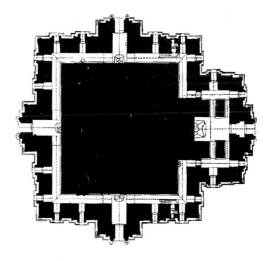

No.88: window opening and pediment on Sulamani temple
Fig.17: Sula-mani ground plan (EFEO)

nally contained the relics. In Early Buddhist stupas, and on Ceylonese *dagaba*, the *harmika* was generally included, and though as a form it was known to the Pyu, it had fallen into disuse in Burma up to this time.[26]

Raised on a platform, the panelled base of which doubles as an enclosure wall, the Sapada has a restored flight of steps, balustrades and pedimented arched gateway. The stupa itself has a high circular base with indented panels and close set, strongly emphasised bands of mouldings, from which the plain surface of the convex *anda* rises to bear the contrasting shape of the *harmika*. The *chattrâvali* that dramatically inverts on its lower portion to splendidly taper out and then in and up in seven bands, is a very pleasing arrangement. The architect has carefully calculated the widths and gaps between the various bands to gain the maximum effect. The Sapada is representative of this type of stupa that became a popular form of dedication in Late Pagan and was from the 1180s onwards to proliferate itself rapidly across the plain, though, with the exception of the Seddana-gyi, it was usually built on a small scale. This Ceylonese innovation of *harmika* and convexly-shaped *anda* was generally confined to the stupa, though it was applied to a number of the *nga-myet-hna* type temples.[27]

No.1622 GADAW-PALIN
ဂေါ်တော်ပလ္လင်

The most refined of Pagan's temples, the gleaming white Gadaw-palin rises with breathtaking grace and beauty, close to the river bank, within the enclosure of the old city wall. Luce, in comparing the That-byin-nyu with the Gadaw-palin, described their differences as the difference between the classical and the romantic,[28] whilst Quaritch Wales described it as the ultimate Burmese attempt at what he termed as 'aspiration'.[29] If the That-byin-nyu is 'classical' then it is also heavy and awesome. If the Gadaw-palin is 'romantic' it is at the same time sublime. The That-byin-nyu seems about to explode: the squat-shaped, crowning *sikhara* acts as if it were a pressure valve holding the great mass of brick down, preventing it all from to bursting out into the cosmos. At the Gadaw-palin the play of mass is streamlined, there are no tensions. All is a rational, upwardly directed movement; scientific exactness governs the proportions. It is like a slick rocket lifting off.

Begun in the reign of Sithu II (1174-1211), the Gadaw-palin was completed by Nadaungmya (1211-34).[30] Various traditions assert that the Gadaw-palin was constructed to commemorate the ceremony of paying homage to the king's ancestors, for *gadaw-palin* means throne or platform to which respect or homage is paid.[31] Another tradition asserts that the Gadaw-palin was so named because, when Sithu II built the Sula-mani, he caused such hardship that the

Venerable Panthagu fled Pagan in reproach and when eventually persuaded to return, the king paid obeisance (*gadaw*) to him on this site.[32] However, the ritual paying of respect to royal ancestors was an active ingredient of the kingship cult, and in the palace there may have been a hall in which statues of former kings were enshrined, as there were in later palaces. However, the Gadaw-palin is primarily a monument to the Buddha and, as there is no surviving dedicatory inscription, such semi-mythological traditions cannot be truly substantiated.

Like the That-byin-nyu and most large-scale Late Pagan temples, the main shrine is on the upper level, and, again like the That-byin-nyu, three terraces interpose between the base and the central block of the shrine, and a further three between the upper block and the crowning *sikhara*. The base is a square in plan, with a hall extending out from the east face. The upper block is likewise square in plan. The hall front is far less dramatic than the That-byin-nyu's, for here the emphasis is on the upper portions. The north, south and west entrances have projecting foreparts, each with an arrangement of tripled pediments and a medial stupa on the terrace projection above. The base wall space receives a fuller treatment here than on the That-byin-nyu, where unadorned wall space contrasts the crenellated terraces; here at the Gadaw-palin there are complete pediments over the window openings, arranged along a single tier that enliven, without over embellishing, the steep sides of this glistening diadem.

The Gadaw-palin is a *lei-myet-hna* type temple. There are four shrines on the ground level slightly receded into the central block, each containing monumental images of the Buddha. Fragments of paintings remain on the vaults and some walls in the lower ambulatory, though they may have been added later. Unlike the That-byin-nyu, the stair flight is not the central feature of the hall. This feature was never to be tried at Pagan again and one rises to the upper shrines through a stair passage that passes up through the walls. The upper block is set within a broad and spacious terrace. Unfortunately much of the original stucco has been restored, with great loss to lustre and detail, following the severe damage this temple underwent in the 1975 earthquake. Original ornament does, though, survive in places, for example, note the lotus petal bands of the stupa's bases on the terraces, with a large petal alternating with smaller ones. There are three types of subsidiary stupas to be found on the terraces: a medial one set on a plinth, to the fore of the front arched opening, corner ones raised high on blocks with passages cut through them, enabling the ritual circumambulation about the terraces, the uppermost of which is far larger, and, finally, the third type surmounts the entrance projections on all sides other than the front. A Jataka set was probably intended for the terraces but, as at the That-byin-nyu, was never added. The upper block's surface is royally enriched about the openings with triple *torana* pediments

No.89: medial stupa on Gadaw-palin terrace

whose *makara* filled cusps make a wave-like crescendo. The upper block's wall surface is textured and enlivened with base mouldings and pilasters and a harmonious effect has been achieved through the balanced disposition of the ornament. The upper shrine front projects slightly further outwards than on the other three faces. The hall-shrine within is a well lit, clear and open space. There are shrines at the other cardinal points, facing the arch and open to the magnificent view. The mass of the block or core, though conceptually solid, is said to be hollow in order to reduce the mass and save on the expense of filling the interior.[33]

The temple may be scaled further to the upper terraces. The *sikhara*, now rebuilt after the 1975 earthquake damage, is the Gadaw-palin's crowning glory: tall, graceful, it soars upwards, the *amalaka* rising from the four cusps of the lower section with poise and grace. The Gadaw-palin's beauty lies in its exterior effect, and the ambulatories and shrines can only be a disappointment to those not schooled in Buddhist conceptions of architecture.

The Gadaw-palin type, tall, refined and quite elegant, was never to be attempted again at Pagan. Generally the Late Period kings preferred a dignified self-restraint and control, projecting an impression of stateliness and composure in their large temples. The sublime was sacrificed for the stalwart and aspiration for splendour.

No.1812 HTI-LO-MIN-LO
ထီးလိုမင်းလို

When the king's father made a solemn vow and set the white umbrella in the midst of his five sons, it inclined according to the father's wish; at that place where the *hti* inclined the king built a pagoda after the likeness of Sulamani; it was called Htilominlo (after this event).[34]

The Hti-lo-min-lo majestically commands the road between Pagan village and Nyaung-U and as the quotation from the chronicles above states, Nadaungmya (1211-30), who has also been known as Htilominlo, modelled it on his father's great work, the Sula-mani.[35] Thus, this work may be dated to shortly after 1211.

In design, the Hti-lo-min-lo is indeed built in the likeness of the earlier Sula-mani, though it is even larger, and with minor differences in ornament. In the Late Period, the royal donor, when building his colossal temples, was less concerned with an explorative and experimental architecture.[36] By Sithu II's Sula-mani of 1183, a type had developed that satisfied the Burman aesthetically and doctrinally, when the That-bin-nyu's play of mass and verticalist tendencies were combined with the Dhamma-yan-gyi's awe-inspiring monumentality to create, in effect, a grandiloquent statement of the empire's self-confidence and magnificence.

Like the Sula-mani, the temple is orientated with the main shrine facing towards the east (for a correct appraisal of the temple, it had best be approached from the east). On the east side a hall projects outwards and above this, approached by a fine broad flight of steps, the upper shrine may be entered. Within the base is an ambulatory which is repeated on the level above. The base level ambulatory is tall, the soffits here rise more sharply than in the arched vaults of earlier temples. A comparison between the ground plan of this temple and that of its prototype, the Sula-mani, will show minor variations in the planning. At the Hti-lo-min-lo, the ambulatory opens out to face the projecting throne of the east shrine, whereas at the Sula-mani colossal piers break out into the ambulatory to form a recess for the image. The terraces, intermediary between base and upper section, and upper section and *sikhara*, ascend steeply, their horizontal lines holding down the base and letting the upper sections elevate with an imposing majesty. Each of the terrace crenelles is highlighted with a green-glazed terracotta plaque: these would have gleamed, set off against the original white of the Hti-lo-min-lo's exterior. Finally, note the perfection of the stucco: richly textured, animated and often naturalistic, it never attempts to over-embellish, rather it serves at all times to highlight those architectural subtleties that might so easily be overlooked.

No. 1670 MAHA-BODHI

မဟာဗေါဓိ

If a historian of Indian architecture wished to discover the form of the original Vajrsana temple at Bodh Gaya, as it stood in the early 13th century, he had best visit Pagan. For the Pagan Maha-bodhi temple is a direct imitation of the original Vajrasana and may well be the outcome of a second visit to Bodh Gaya sent by the Pagan *dhammaraja* kings to maintain so fundamental a Buddhist monument at a time when North India was being absorbed by the forces of Islam. Built after 1211, in the reign of Nadaungmya, the introduction of this type of *sikhara*, perhaps initially here at the Maha-bodhi, which, with its pyramidal shape, straight edges and flat planes, is a direct copy of the Bodh Gaya type, was to lead to this form's proliferation across the Pagan area and at Salé, where it enjoyed an even greater measure of popularity. An earlier mission to the Vajrasana temple at Bodh Gaya was documented by Kyanzittha in one of his inscriptions, and following that a number of innovations in temple ornament appeared at Pagan, notably on the Wetkyi-in Kubyauk-ngè and Mye-bon-tha temples.[37] Now, in the early 13th century, a second wave of North Indian influence appears at Pagan, this time not confined to the introduction of architectural ornament, but also full forms. From this time onwards must date the Kubyauk-gyi at Wetkyi-in, the Bogyoke-mi and the numerous, though smaller, Salé ones.

The Maha-bodhi double enclosure walls are low with a pair of *chinthé* flanking the outer gate, though this peripheral work is most likely later. The temple's elevation, with its tall, straight-lined form, is distinctly alien to Pagan, being a direct imitation of the Vajras-ana. The other products of this contact, such as the Wetkyi-in Kubyauk-gyi, borrowed the superstructure form, applying it to a locally evolved ground plan and base elevation. In fact, the Maha-bodhi is a 'one-off', of greater historical than architectural significance.

The base is tall and narrow, its height emphasised by the four receding planes of the monumental pilasters, each topped by a stupa finial. These stupa finials have boldly banded necks and short, squat *anda,* perhaps a Mahayana tendency in stupa design picked up in North India during the architect's visit there. The inner-most front stupa obelisks are shortened versions of the main *sikhara.* The *sikhara* itself rests on an upper shrine, reached by stairs that pass up through the lower hall walls. This upper shrine's exterior is indented with panels, each bearing a figure of a buddha. The multiplication of buddha image, seated and touching the earth, in stucco, throughout and at all levels of the exterior is a highly novel feature for Pagan temple exteriors.

Previously Pagan donors had been conservative when it came to multiplying the image of the Buddha on the exterior and placing them in a position that is open to the elements. Rows of buddha images were

No.90: detail of stucco on exterior of Hti-lo-min-lo

usually painted high on a temple's interior walls and rarely placed in open niches on the exterior (other than in indented panels set high within the *sikhara*) and rarely at the base level. The multiplication of buddha images recalls the text when the Buddha multiplied himself into one thousand Buddhas and was a popular illustrative theme in Pagan votive tablets.[38] In the Middle Period, buddha images were gradually becoming released from the temple's central core. For example, at the Wetkyi-in Kubyauk-gyi, buddhas are placed against the block and face out through the entrance openings. Thus the buddha makes his way outside—to pervade the universe. Exterior facings of multiple buddha images were common at this time in Mahayana and Vajrayana temple exteriors, there the buddha conception was seen to be an all-pervasive force. This belief may have been carried back to Pagan by the returning restorers.

These exterior images are crude: judging by the topknots the present ones are the work of a later restoration. The base *kirtimukha* frieze is emblazoned with a row of dancing figures not dissimilar to the stucco work on the five *gu* of the Dhamma-yazika. The mushroom capitals of the depressed lower arcade pilasters again appear to be direct copies of North Indian types. The main image on the ground level would seem to be original though. On the west side is a curious circular shaft, resembling a well that passes down from a lower terrace through the back of the base to the ground level, the purpose for which has yet to be satisfactorily explained. Yule, in 1855, noted that the Maha-bodhi hall was being used for the storage of inscriptions.[39]

No.298 WETKYI-IN KUBYAUK-GYI

ဝက်ကြီးအင်းဂူပြောက်ကြီး

There is no date for the 'Great Colourful Cave' at Wet-kyi-in. The *sikhara* shape does, though, suggest that the temple may be contemporary to the Maha-bodhi which dates to the reign of Nadaungmya.[40] It has been surmised that possibly a second mission, after Kyanzittha's one, had been sent to Bodh Gaya to restore or maintain the Vajrasana monument there, and that the Maha-bodhi temple at Pagan village and numerous other more conventionally designed monuments which are crowned with a *sikhara* modelled on the type found around Bodh Gaya, were the offspring of this connection. The Wetkyi-in Kubyauk-gyi is an example of this type, in ground plan the product of an indigenous evolution, whilst the superstructure betrays an alien influence.

The Ku-byauk-gyi is sited on a rise on the Pagan plain and orientated towards the east with the Shwe *chaung*, or stream, and the earlier Ku-byauk-ngè temple in the valley to the west. In Pagan times the planting of trees in the enclosure could be an integral part of any dedication and here the heirs of the original

Maha-bodhi
No.91 upper: from south-east
No.92 lower: exterior ornament

palms rise high, naturalistically framing the temple.[41] In this work the smaller, single level *gu* takes the next logical step from the Loka-hteik-pan, with the distinction between hall and shrine now virtually eliminated. The porch with a triple pediment arrangement, now in a fragmentary state, extends outwards as if a subsidiary hall in itself. The actual hall proper has been fully integrated with an east-facing shrine, with the join between the two units on the base's exterior wall hinted at by a single pilaster and not indicated at all on the terrace level.

As at the Loka-hteik-pan, there are no window openings in the hall, for the architectural scheme here has been determined by the programme of paintings intended for the interior's walls. There is thus an integration between the two artistic mediums that is lacking in the Early Temple. The shrine base wall does, though, have further entrance openings, framed by foreparts, that have now been claustured in brick by the Department to protect the temple's interior from goats, cattle and the heirs of Thomann. This tendency to open up the shrine to admit, not only more light, but the free access of devotees directly into the shrine on all sides had become the mark of the Late temple, possibly reflecting a new rationale in Pagan Buddhism which had become, with its firm establishment, less inclined towards mystical experience, preferring lighter and more rational environments in their temple architecture.

A double terrace runs around the shrine and hall, and the *sikhara* is set well within the upper terrace. The tall obelisk blocks on the corners would have originally carried copies of the central *sikhara*. The *sikhara*, as has been noted, is modelled on the Bodh Gaya Vajrasana temple *sikhara*. Its straight, tapering inward sides seem a little alien, surrounded by countless temples crowned by the more customary Pagan *sikhara* with curvilinear edges. Above each of the medial recesses, which no longer act as skylights like in Early *gu* temples, on the lower part of each plane, a triangular panel, filled with stucco work, emphasise the pyramidal effect of the *sikhara*, which contrasts with the block-like horizontal stability of the base. Above all this, the flat, circular, indented band that looks like a button or cap acted as base to the once circularly banded finial.

This *ku-byauk* is a *lei-myet-hna*, or four face type, here evolved to the stage where the distinction between shrine and hall has been, on the interior, eliminated. The east-facing image, the buddha Gotama, is placed on a throne that extends out from the central block into the hall-shrine and is not, as in the Early Period, placed in a niche within the block. This east buddha is considerably larger than the other three, for it represents 'the Buddha' himself. Open to mankind for all to admire and benefit from, the buddhas are no longer enclosed within an esoteric environment.

The hall-shrine is squarely planned, broad and well-lit, for the paintings are intended to be seen and their glosses read. This temple was conceived to be an educational experience, not a mystical one. The artist has laid out a clear programme, illustrating the doctrine and history of the religion across the open wall space. The paintings are in the hall whilst the other shrines, which contain no narrative paintings, are reduced to mere apses. All is concentrated on the hall-shrine.

Those paintings which escaped robbery are in excellent condition. The cycle was intact up to 1899 when the German adventurer, Thomann, desecrated the temple by systematically removing sections of the paintings with their plaster base, intending to launch them on the international art market.[42] In some places, high on the walls, contemporary newspapers are visible stuck on to the plaster's surface: Thomann and his team must have used the newspapers, pasted onto sections of the plaster, as a means of lifting the paintings from the wall's surface. It was until recently believed that the missing sections were in the possession of the Hamburg Museum; however Professor Whitbread, who carried out a piece of brilliant investigative research at Hamburg,[43] matching up Thomann's photographs with the panels in the museum's possession, has proved that the paintings in the Hamburg collections were from the Thein-ma-zi temple, also ravaged by Thomann, and not from the Wetkyi-in Kubyauk-gyi as had been supposed.[44] Thomann seems to have been a colourful figure not unlike Sir Aurel Stein or Albert von le Coq; he robbed Pagan temples with an academic thoroughness and no doubt described himself as an archaeologist.[45] Pagan has its own way of dealing with desecrators; as Professor Whitbread wrote:

> Buddhists may perhaps find some solace in the knowledge that Thomann died in somewhat unexplained tragic circumstances in 1924 and feel that he reaped his just reward. Perhaps it is fitting that a queen of Pagan should have the last word:
> "May all who destroy or rob any of these my works of merit be stricken with many ailments...When they die, in due course, may they be cooked in Avici hell within the earth for as many times as there are particles of earth from Nyaung-U to Thiriyapitsaya."[46]

The subject matters for the paintings, or rather the textual sources used, are the customary ones portrayed in the Late temple and follow, with some variation, from the pattern laid down at the Loka-hteik-pan in the Middle Period. The vault is decorated with the 'lotus pool', radiating patterns of curves from a central tondo that are symbolic of the act of creation. This is a cosmic diagram, representing the moment of genesis when the lotus rises out of the waters to carry the universe, an *imago mundi*. The vaults also have the *buddhapada* or double footprints of the Buddha, which by the Late Period were commonly painted in this position, and multiple sun-god motifs that radiate out in each direction from the central lotus pool.

Delicately rendered and highly naturalistic freezes of foliate and vegetal work run around the hall at the dado, between the panels and along the cornices.

On the north and south walls, upper tier, the 28 Buddhas are painted, 14 to each wall, each within their particular pavilion and backed by the particular botanical variety of tree under which that buddha was enlightened.[47] A descriptive gloss runs beneath.[48] The painting's clarity is remarkable: line is clear and sharp, defining each figure or form with a graphic accuracy, whilst each tree is so finely painted that the species are today still identifiable to the botanist. The various architectural structures sheltering each respective buddha reflect now perished contemporary structures.

At the east end of the north and south walls are two tiers, each filled with two tall panels. This arrangement continues round on to the east wall: thus there are four panels to each wall, or eight at each corner, making a total of sixteen panels or scenes. These depict the main events from the life of the buddha Gotama. Only two remain on the south wall: Drona's division of the relics and Dhanapala elephant scene.

The centre portions of the north and south walls are filled with far smaller panels containing the Jatakas— 544 small squares, each depicting a scene from each of the 547 former rebirths. The last ten Jatakas, or Mahanipata, required a more extensive treatment and were thus not included in this scheme, though the painter included some additional scenes from the life of the Buddha to fill the remaining space. The Jataka's treatment contrasts with that of the large panels, less linear and more plastic, the artist is governed by the smallness of each panel (just over 12cm square). Continuing in the 'Narrative Style' from earlier series at the Myinkaba Kubyauk-gyi, where the panels are quite large by comparison, the artist's brush has now become far defter when defining detail on so small a scale. The quality and condition of these paintings is very fine: the outlines sharp and the planes of colour distinct from each other. In idiom, these are in effect less monumental, or rather tactile, than the Myinkaba ones and highly polished in their execution. On each of these walls there is a larger central panel set in the midst of the smaller panels: here the Buddha sits, recounting the stories of his former rebirths to his disciples.

The main hall-facing buddha image is surrounded by a portrayal of the attack and defeat of the Army of Mara. The paintwork here is energetic, there is a holocaustic frenzy to the struggle taking place about the serene Late Period image. This outburst of imagination, a riot and rout of quasi-zoological beasts, birds and grotesques, contrasts the mildness of the paintings of the other walls.

The linear or 'Decorative' style used to depict the Mara scene may be derived from contemporary Nepal. The 'Narrative Style', used in the depiction of the Jatakas and primary texts, is an evolved form of the Ajanta style, as has been noted with early works such as those at the Myinkaba Kubyauk-gyi.[49] The linear or 'Decorative style', has been met with already in Early Period temples such as the Abe-ya-dana, but here, over a century later, it has become the work of a more refined hand. Further, there is less of a contrast between the two styles now, for figures are required to be painted on a far smaller scale than in the deliberately expressive work of Early Pagan, when a monumental idiom was required to have an effect, or rather impact, on the onlooker. Intermediary between the bold 'Narrative' and elaborate 'Decorative' styles found side by side in the Early temple and the work here at Wetkyi-in are the Loka-hteik-pan ones which begin the process of fusing the two idioms. The finest expressions of this florid, often fanciful, hand are to be found in certain of the Minnanthu temples and at Salé, where the scriptural scenes and textually-derived subject matter, are subjugated to flamboyant decorative schemes.[50] However, glancing back from the Mara's army to the other paintings in the hall, the Jataka, Buddhavamsa and *bodawin* still receive a prominent enough treatment.

No.1439 MINGALA-ZEIDI
မင်္ဂလာစေတီ

The Mingala-zeidi was the last great Pagan monument to be built on a large scale. The meritorious work of Tayok-pye-min ('the King who fled from the Chinese'), otherwise known as Narathihapati (1255/6-1287), the Mingala-zeidi was completed only a decade before the Mongol invasion of 1287. Taw Sein Ko described the Mingala-zeidi as marking "the zenith of Burmese religious architecture",[51] and one guide book describes the Mingala-zeidi as "the high water mark of Burmese religious architecture, because it was constructed only a few years before the subversion of the Pagan Empire by the Mongols".[52] What is curious about the Mingala-zeidi is its completeness; there is a full set of glazed Jataka plaques, extant and in good condition. The last full set of glazed Jataka plaques incorporated into a pagoda at Pagan was the Dhammayazika, three-quarters of a century earlier in 1196. However, glazing as an art never died and glazed lobes decoratively stud many a temple exterior, for example on the Sula-mani and Hti-lo-min-lo temples. Often glazed plaques were intended for a temple but were never added, the inclusion of a Jataka plaque cycle was presumably a costly undertaking. At the Mingala-zeidi, a mere decade before Pagan's 'fall', the king and his administration still possessed the organisational capabilities required to successfully build a large stupa and include a complete Jataka series. The Mingala-zeidi is thus hardly the work of a decaying empire, it is a self-confident symbol of Pagan's unruffled greatness. The language of the stupa's donor, Tayok-pye-min, expresses this self-confidence:

On Sunday the 6th, waxing of Tabaung 630 Sakkaraj

(1268) King Narathihapade whose reignal title is Siri Tribhuvanaditayapavara-dhammaraja, who is the supreme commander of 36 million soldiers and who is the consumer of 300 dishes of curry daily, being desirous of attaining the bliss of Nirvana erected a pagoda. Having done so the king enshrined within it 51 gold and silver statuettes of kings, queens, ministers and maids of honour, and over these an image of Gotama Buddha in solid silver, one cubit high, on Thursday the full moon of Kason 636 Sakkaraj (1274). On that occasion a covered way was erected from the palace to the pagoda. Bamboo mats were laid along this. Over these rush mats were spread and over these again pieces of cloth were laid, and at each cubit's distance along the way banners were placed. During the ceremony the princes, princesses and nobles threw a number of pearls among the statuettes and the Paya was formally named the Minga-lazedi.[53]

The chronicles offer a bleaker version of events and describe the gluttony and decadence of the king, their assumptions possibly based only on the reference in the inscription cited above to the 300 bowls of curry daily consumed. This inscription is a royal boast, part of a panegyric, and thus naturally exaggerated the king's capacity to eat curry in the name of 'greatness'. What is of interest, though, is that in this late inscription the pious ring of an earlier inscription, like that at the Shwe-gu-gyi, has been displaced by a bombastic grandiloquence.[54] The Glass Palace Chronicle goes on to discuss the building of the Mingala-zeidi:

> Now in those dark days a prophecy arose: "The Pagoda is finished and the great country is ruined!" Soothsayers, therefore, and masters of magic said: "When the zeidi is finished the kingdom of Pagan will be shattered into dust!" Hearing that word the king tarried and built no more for full six years.[55]

Pagan, judging by details on social preoccupations mentioned in the inscriptions, was a city in which the population, if not serving the king, was involved in propagating Buddhism through the construction and maintenance of religious dedications.[56] Thus the construction of a temple created employment and hence prosperity and it is unlikely that the building of the Mingala-zeidi economically ruined Pagan. However, there are limits to pagoda building activity and overambitious schemes could be destined to failure, for example, the Mingun-haya by Bodaw in the 18th century and possibly even the the mysterious Dhamma-yan-gyi.[57] The Mingala-zeidi, the last large stupa to built at Pagan, was actually completed and only a strong charismatic king, a man of *hpon,* could be capable of such a feat, for a meritorious construction undertaken by a person with insufficient accumulation of merit or *hpon* was destined to failure. Tayok-pye-min went on to build other equally impressive works, one two-level, large *gu* temple a little to the north west of Minnanthu village, named Tayok-pye

after him.

In its design, the Mingala-zeidi exhibits a number of novel features. Built on a square plan and set within a raised platform, the lower four terraces have *kalasa* obelisks rather than the standard subsidiary stupa or *sikhara* motif on the corners. This arrangement follows from the work found at Sein-nyet Nyima.[58] The finial has now been restored, as have the stucco mouldings of the *anda.* There is a set, originally complete, of glazed Jataka plaques in reasonable condition though some have been pilfered. In all other respects, though, the Mingala-zeidi is composed of the by now standard arrangement of terraces and medial stairways. In the Mingala-zeidi enclosure, the brick monastery or *kala-kyaung* of the presiding monk remains and attached to this would have been wooden structures as at the Lei-myet-hna complex at Minnanthu (1222).[59]

No.93: Jataka plaque on Mingala-zeidi terrace
No.94: terrace with Jataka plaques on Mingala-zeidi

No.1147 SOMIN-GYI OK-KYAUNG
စိုးမင်းကြီးအုတ်ကျောင်း

The Late Period was a period of ever-increasing endowments; monastic establishments expanded to the scale of universities in their own right and were constructed and embellished with grandeur and sumptuousness. Though there is no definite inscription relating to the Somin-gyi monastic foundation, an inscription found at the Maha-bodhi temple, and now in the Ananda Museum, mentions a lady called Somin, which Luce suggested might be associated with the Somin-gyi stupa that stands a short distance to the *kyaung's* north. Possibly, as Luce himself believed the stupa to be an Early one, the inscription, dated 1204/5, may refer to the monastery.[60] There is also one small Late *gu* to the south of the monastery, popularly known as the Somin-gyi Gu, which has some fine mural paintings, though, like the stupa, it is unclear whether this monument was connected with the monastic dedication.

In Pagan times, brick monasteries were referred to as a *kala kyaung,* or 'Indian Monastery', presumably because either the original builders of brickwork or their occupants were *kala* or Indians. *Kala-kyaung,* or *ok-kyaung* as they are known in modern Burmese, vary in type from a small block-like house set in the enclosure of a stupa or temple, to house an individual monk, with maybe a couple of novices, to a large complex consisting of a variety of structures to house a hierarchy of clerics and their servants and slaves. As has been noted above, Pagan was a city of wood and according to the inscriptions, the majority of monastic structures were made from timber. The immediate prototypes for establishments such as the Somin-gyi must have been of wood, though conceptually and in plan this monastery looks back to certain of the rock-cut caves at Ajanta in Northern India and other later monastic complexes in that region.

Sited on a rise, the *kyaung* is approached by a flight of steps that lead into a vestibule. The entry would once have been embellished with a *torana* pediment, and the pilasters that once carried this pediment remain visible. From the vestibule, one passes into the broad open space of the cortile. Opposite the vestibule, that is, in the western part facing east, is the main shrine enclosed within a cella and surmounted by a tower-like second level that rises above the courtyard, unifying the whole. Originally, this tower most probably had some form of brick *pyatthat* finial rising above it, like those found over the *ok-kyaung* in the Shwe-zigon area.[61] On the north and south sides are the cells, two to the centre and a further one at each corner. These would have been used for accommodation and meditation and recall the arrangement found in the north enclosure of the Sulamani where there are one hundred cells arranged about the walls, though here the community to be housed was obviously far smaller.[62] What is impressive about the Somin-gyi scheme is the compactness and sense of unity that still today reflects the ordered life of its former occupants.

Today the images, vaults and ornamentation are all gone. The imaginative visitor must recreate for himself the sumptuous interior decorations of gold leaf laid upon richly lacquered surfaces, resounding with the time-worn chants of the novices reciting their lessons, as the mellow resonant bells reverberated to herald the gain each meritorious deed brought for mankind.

The Somin-gyi is representative of one of a variety of types of monastery plan commonly used at Pagan. It is similar to the one north of the Myinkaba Kubyauk-gyi and also bears some resemblance to the two located at Tamani.[63] This type, with cells ranged about and enclosing a courtyard, was less common than the squarely-planned block-house, of which numerous examples may still be seen almost everywhere about Pagan. The Somin-gyi does, though, bear greater relation to the original Buddhist *vihara* found in India.

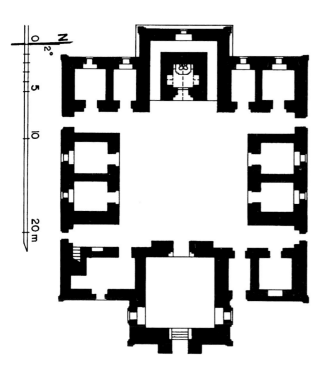

Fig.18 Somin-gyi Ok-kyaung ground plan (EFEO)
No.95: Somin-gyi courtyard

No. 264 SHWE-LEIK-KAN

ရွှေလိပ်ကန်

This small temple set a little to the west of the Shwe *chaung* and south of the old Pagan Nyaung-U road is architecturally highly curious. Raised on a high base, the east-facing recess or shrine is reached by a flight of steps. This recess is flanked by single pilasters, each semi-circular in profile. This is unusual and the only example of this type of pilastering featured on a Pagan temple, where usually the pilasters are rectangular in profile. The second remarkable feature here is the inclusion of the Bodh Gaya type of *sikhara* above, recalling the not distantly situated Wetkyi-in Kubyauk-gyi. The image is now lost, though there are some fragments of multiple buddha paintings. On the exterior, the stucco is still good in places and fragments of a figure, perhaps an *arhat*, remain on the *sikhara*. Likewise, in the blank shallow recesses on the north, south and west sides fragments of stucco figures remain. Though slight in scale, this little temple seems prominent through its poise and picturesque setting.

No. 232 OK-KYAUNG

အုတ်ကျောင်း

Set between the old Nyaung U-Pagan road and the river this *ok-kyaung* was restored in 1983. To the east projects the platform of what was either the *dhamma-yon* or *thein*. Interesting here is the inclusion of a double platform floored with stone, and onto the upper part *thein* marker stones have recently been added. Whether this upper plinth was originally an ordination hall is debatable, for in other places (such as at Minnanthu, Hsin-byu-shin and Hsu-taung-pyit) the *thein* was usually set aside from a residential structure and it would seem that the inclusion of an ordination hall here occurred more recently. The post holes of the columns that would have carried the two-tiered roofing may be found amongst the weeds. Stone was also used at the edges of the platform and for the steps. On the east edge rests a stone gutter carved in the shape of a *naga*, this has been removed from the *taik*. Also, in the middle of the upper platform, an upturned stone reredos lies flat on the ground, too heavy to turn over to see what was carved on the other side.

The *taik* itself is square in plan and built on two levels, with an access stair passage to the roof which is flat. There is a central hollow core which would have had a timber floor across it at the upper level carried by the intact protruding cornice. Our knowledge of the function of such structures remains vague and it is unclear whether the central compartments were used for accommodating the senior monk, an image, or perhaps the precious palm leaf manuscripts of Pagan's sacred literature. Possibly the ground level

compartment was used for accommodation whilst the upper one was a shrine. In the lower corridor, slots in the brick-work may be seen, wooden panels, which would have been gilded or lacquered, would have been fastened into these. The small niches set into the corridor walls are surmounted by an ogive type of arch pediment. Stone is used profusely on the floors and to strengthen the brickwork at stress-loaded junctures. In the upper corridor slots for cross-beams run along the soffits, there would thus have been a third level and the wooden ceiling would have been embellished in a similar manner to the panelled walls. On the west side, from the roof level, *naga* style stone drainage outlets, similar to the one to be seen lying outside on the plinth, remain in situ.

No.1391 MYINKABA KUBYAUK-NGE

မြင်းကပါ ဂူပြောက်ငယ်

In its exterior form, the Kubyauk-ngè at Myinkaba is representative of numerous other middle-sized single-storey *gu* temples dating from the Late Period and, like all its contemporaries, possessing its own individual quirks and nuances. On the remaining sections of the enclosure walls the heightened corner posts are noteworthy, also note the absence of gateway openings in north and south sections of the enclosing wall. Orientated towards the east, the hall extends out from the base and there is an imposing double pediment over the front, the lower of which retains its stucco covering. There are lateral porches, each surmounted by the customary foreparts with imposing pediment arrangements. Likewise, there are foreparts on the three exterior surfaces of the shrine base, the west of which projects further outwards than those on the north and south. Each of these grandly pedimented foreparts housed an entrance opening now claustured by the Department to exclude marauding cattle and art dealers.

The hall is square in plan with the medial openings in the lateral walls. An arch divides this unit from the shrine-ambulatory and this is elaborately pedimented with a stucco octofoil and *pyatthat* with splendid *makara* in the lower cusps. Though there are no paintings here, there are some ink glosses and sketches of the Buddha's horoscope on the inside of the hall-shrine arch. Perhaps the most remarkable feature of this otherwise unremarkable hall are the two short pedestals that flank the shrine arch pilasters on their outside. These blocks are carved with a *kirtimukha* feature unlike the *kirtimukha* that are usually to be found on temple exteriors; these beasts have arms with hands clasped before them like those found throughout India and in other parts of South-East Asia. These would have carried now lost *dvarapala* figures, possibly freestanding to require so stalwart a base.

The ambulatory surrounds the central block. The vault is a full barrel one, painted with circular geometric motifs. The east image, larger than the others, has been repaired though the head remains original. On this, fragments of an original resin-based, perhaps early lacquer, coating, are peeling off the brick and stucco undersurface. The south image is of the Buddha in *dharmacakramudra;* the arms are now broken off. The west image has been totally destroyed, though it most likely represented the *parinibbana.* The north image is of the Buddha seated and is flanked by a figure on each side seated in *pralambanasana.* This arrangement is similar to the ones found at Kyasin and temple No.359 Wu-tha-na-daw (north side of central pier) where a central image of the Buddha in *bhumisparsamudra* is flanked by buddhas in *dharmacakramudra* seated in *pralambanasana.*[64] Though here at the Kubyauk-ngè the north Buddha's arms are now broken off and only the lower parts of the flanking buddhas' bodies survive, it may be taken that this triad is iconographically similar to those found at Kyasin and No. 359 Wu-tha-na-daw. Luce explains the Kyasin version as being a portrayal of the moment when the Buddha created two *nirmana* buddhas: 'the Miracle of Savatthi'.[65] Thus, around the Kubyauk-ngè's core, an encapsulated narrative depicting four events from the life of the Buddha are to be found. This 'potted life' had also been tried at the Middle Period Mye-bon-tha-hpaya-hla, though there the choice of scenes differed.[66] Finally, note the lotus dado that runs continuously about the block linking the four image pedestals.

About the outer wall was a further series of twelve portrayals of events from the life of the Buddha in stone relief. What makes this series both interesting and important is that the medium used is stone, rather than stucco and brick which had become more popular by the Late Period. After the completion of the Ananda in the early 12th century, narrative sequences depicting events from the life of the Buddha had not been attempted, though isolated monoliths and reliefs were sporadically produced. The scenes here are carved in sandstone in a style typical of the Late Period, so different from those of Kyanzittha, with shorter, more rounded physiques and benign facial expressions. Starting from the niche on the outer wall

No.96 upper: Shwe-leik-kan
No.97 middle: Myinkaba
Kubyauk-ngè
No.98 lower right: stucco work
on Myinkaba Kubyauk-ngè
makara pediment
No.99 lower left: obival frieze
on Myinkaba Kubyauk-ngè
exterior

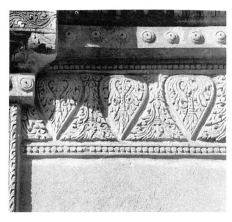

Myinkaba-Kubyauk-ngè
No.100-107: bodawin relief series (details opposite)
No.108 lower right: main image in bhumisparsamudra
Fig.19 right: ground plan (EFEO)

to the immediate south of the hall-shrine arch:

1. (No.100, top left) 'Sujata's Offering', the Buddha is in *dhyanamudra*. Punna is the central figure holding the goat's tether and a stick, whilst Sujata kneels on the right in prayer. Here, following the Ananda tradition, the alms bowl has been included, at Kyauk-ku it was excluded.
2. Empty.
3. Empty.
4. 'The Parileyyaka Monkey', (No.101, top centre) the Buddha is seated in *pralambanasana*, flanked by Mogallana and Sariputta and on his right is the Nalagiri elephant and on his left the monkey. This scene follows the conventions established at the Ananda with the Buddha's robe striated on his right side and smooth on his left.
5. Empty.
6. 'The Buddha Reclining', (No.102, top right) portraying the supreme moment of *parinibbana*. This is a tentative assignment, for the Buddha's head points to the south, whereas usually the head is directed to the north in a death scene (like at Manuha and Mye-bon-tha). A south-pointed recumbent figure usually depicts the Buddha resting in a garden (like at the Shin-bin-thaly-aung, where bamboo groves were painted on the walls about the image). However, here at Myinkaba, the setting of the reclining figure within a niche and halo-like reredos, with tiers of figures above and below adoring the relics, follows the convention of depicting a *parinibbana* and one may attribute such an unconventional orientation to artistic licence.
7. 'The Buddha', in *dhyanamudra* (No.103, middle left), in this scene the figure is sheltered by a *pyatthat*.
8. 'The Descent from Tavatimsa' (No.104, middle centre), Indra is on the right and Brahma on the left carrying the parasol.
9. Empty.
10. 'The Nativity', (No.105, middle right), close in style to the Mye-bon-tha verion: energetic, tactile and carved in high relief.
11. 'The Buddha' (No.106, lower left), standing in *varadamudra*.
12. 'The Buddha' (No.107, lower centre), standing in *dharmacakramudra*.

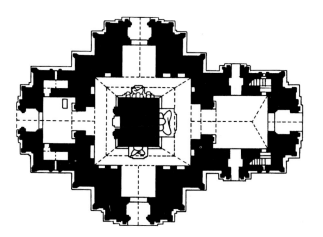

No.1790

By the Late Period, a popular small size temple was the type with a stupa superstructure set over a symmetrically-planned base that contained either four or five shrines. As with most temples with a circular-based stupa above, rather than with terraces leading to a square-based *sikhara*, No.1790 (old no.1091), which is sited in the field a short distance to the south west of the Ywa-haung-gyi temple, is built on a symmetrical plan with no projecting hall.[67] In later periods such as the Nyaung-yan and Konbaung the stupa superstructure was generally preferred to the *sikhara* and in examples from these periods a hall does usually extend out. The base is carried on a broad, square platform with short stone flights at the medial points corresponding to the four openings. The *anda* is of the Ceylonese type: convex to the point of hemisphericality, rising direct from the base, without the intermediary of terraces and there is a *harmika* fixed between the *anda* and finial. The circularly-planned plinth is encompassed by a line of outwardly-facing elephants made from brick and stucco, like at Seddana-gyi and one Ceylonese-type stupa a short distance to the south of the Paya-thon-zu at Minnanthu. Within, the ambulatory encircles the four images which are set against the core and face each opening. From the core, the full barrel of the vault springs out like a parasol from its handle. This type, though usually without the elephant mouldings, was a popular form of dedication, perhaps because it combined the qualities of the temple and stupa, an architectural compromise between two opposite forms: the one accessible and thus functional, the other interiorless and thereby purely symbolic.

No.1791 YWA-HAUNG-GYI/ LAW-KA-HMAN-KIN

ရွာဟောင်းကြီ လောကမှန်ကင်

The Ywa-haung-gyi is a well known large size temple, set a little off the new road to Nyaung-U, to the east of the Ananda turn off. The main image, which is featured on the cover of a popular travellers guide to Burma, has been restored at the expense of a German, perhaps in recompense for the damage done by certain of his countrymen in bygone days.[68] The temple too has been well restored, and is an excellent example of a late two-level temple. Here, the great spread of bastion-like temples, such as the Sula-mani and Hti-lo-min-lo has been thinned down, the terracing less expansive, the upper shrine and projecting hall rendered more streamlined. On the ground level access is permitted not only from the east front but also on the north and south sides of the hall and on all three exterior faces of the shrine. Each of these openings has been projected out to form a forepart and each is grandly superimposed by a dominant scheme of pediments and pilasters. This arrangement is repeated on the upper level where again the foreparts dominate the structure from which they extend. Indeed, the block-like units of base and upper storey are near masked by the foreparts. The lines of the upper terraces are deeply moulded with medial flights rising to the *sikhara* arched over by the continuous terrace mouldings, giving the impression, from a distance, of dummy niches.

The ground plan is noteworthy on account of the original treatment of the shrine's relationship to the hall. The units are separate, not united as in certain of the smaller late temples such as the Wetkyi-in Kubyauk-gyi. The Ywa-haung-gyi ground level and main shrine unit projects out from the central block across the ambulatory and into the hall. This arrangement is not dissimilar to the ground plan used at Bogyoke-Mi.[69] The ambulatory may be accessed from the hall, through side arches—to the north and south of the central shrine arch beneath broad diaphragm arches, or from within the shrine itself which has narrower arched openings on its north and south lateral sides passing into the ambulatory. The shrine is one step higher in level than the remaining floor space and all the floors have been surfaced with stone flags, whilst on the upper level brick was used. In the hall, there are some paintings: the 28 buddhas run about the upper walls beneath the painted cornice. Dummy pilasters and pediments frame the wall's surface areas and in these spaces are faded panels containing scenes from the life of the Buddha. There are no images on the north, south and west faces of the central block, the emphasis being on the east. Light shafts have been included in the stair passages, their openings forming neat squares on either side of the front porch. The upper level shrine is unremarkable, though the views at dusk are. Further steps pass through the upper shrine's walls to the steep, upper terraces.

No.1478 HSIN-PYA-GU

ဆင်ပြာဂူ

This middle sized temple is flanked on either side by stupas, an arrangement that would appear, on the basis of the ornament's design, to be contemporary with the building of the *gu*. Immediately to the south of the group is the Pa-tha-da temple that dates from the Early Period.[70] The Hsin-pya-gu's orientation follows that of its now declined neighbour, facing towards the west. There are a surprising number of eccentrically orientated temples at Pagan which can only be put down to local licence.

There is an arch between hall and shrine and in the shrine there are images only on the east and west sides, whilst there are openings on each of the transepts facing the blank north and south walls. About the west buddha are Ava period paintings of

Mogallana and Sariputta holding lotus flowers by their long stems. In the hall are some curious monochrome sketches with glosses possibly also later in dating. On the upper level there is an unimposing recess cut into the *sikhara* terraces housing the upper shrine.

The two stupas, to the north and south and in line with the shrine unit, are perhaps more interesting than the temple itself, for here survives the remnants of once lavishly glazed ornament. On the upper terraces of the north stupa are small plaques with a diamond moulding indented in the centre of each. The now missing lower terrace plaques are larger in their dimensions and may well have once held pictorial representations, possibly the *Mahanipata* for there are insufficient panels to house a Jataka set. The stupas have the high, steeply terraced square base that came into vogue in the Late Period. On each face is set an elaborately pedimented and stuccoed niche. The finest stucco is to be found on the south pediment of the north stupa with delicate *kinnaya* carried by sinuous lotus stems. On the north stupa, treasure hunters have cut passages through and down below the ground level in search for the *tabena*. Curiously, the south stupa's recesses have been bricked up, and this brickwork is contemporary to our period. Behind the bricked-up part of the south arch the recess is filled with rubble. This south stupa is in much poorer condition than its northern counterpart.

No.357 WU-THA-NA-DAW ဝုသနာတော့

This small temple, situated due south of the ford where the Shwe *chaung* crosses the new Nyaung-U road and a few paces to the west of Wu-tha-na-daw temple No.359, is highly interesting on account of its

unconventional exterior composition. The square planned base has four openings, the east of which has been left open whilst the other three have been claustured by the Archaeology Department, who have also restored the superstructure. Each of the foreparts about the openings reveals a conventional arrangement with a doubled pediment. In the tympanum of each superimposing pediment, though, are fragments of an expansive stucco scene. Beneath this stucco work are the arch openings; these are semi-circular, rather than pointed, as was usual at Pagan; further, there is a hint of an ogive about the octofoil. What is most remarkable, though, about this small temple is the placing of an upper level over a square planned base, an unprecedented device, though something similar was being done to *ok-kyaung* designs at around this time in the Late Period.[71] This upper shrine is surmounted by a stupa not a *sikhara*. It was not uncommon for a stupa to be placed upon a square based temple in Late Pagan, and indeed in the Early Period a number of *gu*, with a hall extension, were favoured with a stupa form in place of a *sikhara*. What is innovative here is the inclusion of an upper level.[72] Such experiment on the part of the Late Pagan architect, here at No.357, has proved successful for it is not an unhappy arrangement and once again the student of Pagan may be astonished by the diversity of architectural forms to be found across the plain.

The interior of Wu-tha-na-daw No.357 is also not without interest. There is no central block and the image, now half lost on its pedestal, is freestanding to the centre of the Greek Cross plan. The transepts contain deep lanceted niches that once served as meditation cells. Dummy painted architecture emphasises the architectural elements throughout the interior. Note that before three of the openings were claustured far more light would have been admitted.

No.109 upper left: Wu-tha-na-daw, no. 357
No. 110 upper right: Mi-nyein-gon from east
No.111 middle: Hsin-pya-gu with flanking stupas
No.112 lower : Wut-tha-na-daw no. 359 interior with central pier arrangement

No. 359 WU-THA-NA-DAW
ဝုသနာတော်

Like its neighbour Wu-tha-na-daw No.357, this is another highly curious small temple which is orientated towards the north. Over the north porch pediment, on the exterior, is a well preserved stucco figure on the apex of the octofoil—crowned and jewelled, he carries flowing lotus stems in each hand. Within, what is most interesting is the inclusion of a central block of unprecedented narrowness, in fact more like a square column than the central block of the *lei-myet-hna*. Pierre Pichard explains that possibly the builders, having attempted an open planned shrine as with this temple's neighbour No.357, they then encountered problems with so lofty a quadripartite vault, unsupported from the centre and thus were compelled to insert this column for support. Conveniently, such a column accorded with the *lei-myet-hna* concept. At the base of this dramatically rising shaft, along the four sides, are brick and stucco images. On the north is a triad of figures, with Gotama seated in *bhumisparsamudra* flanked on either side by now broken images of a buddha seated in *pralambanasana* with hands placed across chest in the gesture of *dharmacakra*. This triad is an illustration of the 'Great Miracle at Savatthi' when Gotama created two other buddhas.[73] The interior walls of this temple are covered in miniature panel paintings of the buddhas.

No.1499 MI-NYEIN-GON
မိုင်းမ်ကုန်း

This massive single storey *gu* dating to the 13th century is sited in a field to the east of the Pagan-Myinkaba road between the Pagan village and the hotel turn off. Here, the Late Pagan architect seems to have rejected past and contemporary tendencies of 'aspiration' or 'verticality', and returned to the horizontally emphasised single level type of the Early Period, last attempted on the Dhamma-yan-gyi (c.1160), albeit here on a less massive scale.

Restored in 1964, Mi-nyein-gon, from the exterior, offers a striking arrangement of boldly emphasised terraces raised upon the elevated, yet plain base of the shrine and hall. Orientated towards the east, the hall extends out in that direction with three openings on the north and south sides that lead through to side aisles in the hall. There are, thus, with a tripartite division of the hall ground space, three arched openings from the hall into the shrine. What is impressive about the interior of this temple is the sensation of loftiness and effect of monumentality present in the interior. As there is no upper level the architects were able to raise the ground level vaults to new heights, thereby creating an awe-inspiring atmosphere. There is a single image on the east face of the central block.

No.1467 LOKA-OK-SHAUNG
လောကဥသျောင်

West of the Shwe-hsan-daw lies this east-orientated temple now lacking a *sikhara*. Though perhaps not the most attractive of Pagan temples from the exterior, it contains a number of features worthy of remark. The design is the standard Late arrangement of hall extending from shrine with now claustured openings on the lateral walls of the hall and on the three exterior sides of the shrine. The treatment of these foreparts is curious, the habitual arrangement of doubled or tripled pilasters and pediments is here rejected in favour of broad, near ogive arches, framed simply by a doubled short pilaster. Also curious is the use of horizontal lintels on each of the window openings that flank the foreparts. The perforation of these is in fact original, rare for the Late Period.[75] On the north shrine forepart the stucco is in good condition, here there is the *deva* figure placed in the tympanum between pediments, bearing a lotus, held by its long stem in each outstretched hand as at No.357.[76]

The interior of the Loka-ok-shaung also contains a number of remarkable features. In the hall are two *dvarapala* on either side of the shrine arch, these stucco figures have long, narrow and rhythmic bodies, startlingly reminiscent of Khmer work, though to draw a connection would be tenuous. In the shrine there is one image, naturally set against the east face of the *lei-myet-hna*. The pedestal of this image is close in design to that found at Mye-bon-tha-hpaya-hla, with panels containing, alternatively, a leogryph and a figure of Brahma. About the colossal image itself are paintings of the *deva* and other heavenly bodies scaling up towards the elaborate stucco octofoil that acts as a reredos to the image. The other three faces of the central block are covered with now faint paintings.

No.291 SHIN-BO-ME-KYAUNG
ရှင်ဘိုမယ်အုတ်ကျောင်း

One of the largest *ok-taik* surviving from the period, the Shin-bo-me is to be found in the lush and shaded valley of the Shwe *chaung*, between the two metalled roads that run between Pagan and Nyaung U, a short distance to the south of the Wetkyi-in Kubyauk-ngè. Though it has been well restored, there are a number of original features worthy of study.

The dedication's enclosing wall follows the north, south and west sides of the square-based *taik*, but not on the east. What appears to have been the layout is that this wall cut in to meet the projecting platform of the wooden hall, to the fore of the *taik*'s front, thus forming a terrace, floored in stone, which is raised slightly above the level of the raised platform that extends out from this point towards the east. This terrace continued around the sides of the main *taik*

No.113 left: Thein-mazi from east
No.114 above: Thein-mazi terraces

and would have been covered over on the north and south sides of the house by a lean-to structure, something like a cloister facing out into the walled enclosure about the *taik*. Evidence of this now lost structure may be seen along the lower part of the exterior wall, on the north and south sides, where slot holes for beams and an overhanging lower cornice indicate the dimensions of this now perished wooden extension.[77] It does not seem, though, to have continued round to the back or west side of the block house. Though the outer wall is now in a state of disrepair one may speculate whether a similar lean-to cloister, or even compartments, as at the Sula-mani Kyaung-taik, formed a courtyard about the main house.[78] On the house's plinth is a *kalasa* pot profile, rare for a monastery and even rarer for a Late work.

Running around the upper part of the wall beneath the dramatic overhang of the cornice is a stucco frieze, each pendant filled with a devotee figure. Note also the stone perforated tablets set into the square, flat, arched openings, heirs to the Pitaka-taik ones.[79]

In the interior, some of the original wooden beams that crossed above the lower ambulatory, forming an entresol level, are still in place. The lower ambulatory itself has a full barrel vault. Like at monastery No.232, there may have been painted or lacquered wooden panels fixed to these walls. As with all of these *ok-taik*, there is a cella in the centre surrounded by the ambulatory, in this case the arrangement was repeated

on an upper level. One may speculate as to the function of such structures, in design so impractical for residence. Possibly they were intended as symbolic residences and the incumbents resided in an ancillary building. Alternatively, a structure such as this, attached to a *dhamma-yon*, may well have functioned as a *pitaka-taik*, for, after Anawrahta's Pitaka-taik (c.1060-70), the absence of structures named as such, despite their continued inclusion in dedicatory inscriptions, is striking. Possibly the scriptures were housed in the lower cella whilst the upper acted as a shrine chamber.

Going up by the stair flight, that passes through the south-west wall section, past the upper level corridor, onto the flat, brick-paved roof, there is a further unique feature. From here, a second stair descends to the level of the upper cella's soffits through the brick work of the upper ambulatory inner wall. This leads one to a clerestory running above and around the upper cella and there are two small lancet openings offering a view down into the cella. The purpose of so unique an architectural feature is a mystery. Such a clerestory doubtless acted as a mass saving device, as was common on a number of temples from this period, and there was a tendency at this time to permit access into clerestories or dummy passages, which had been sealed and inaccessible in earlier periods at Pagan.[80]

No.1219 KYASIN

ကျဆင်း

South of Myinkaba, east of the Thiriyapyitsaya road
and a little north of the Naga-yon, Kyasin temple may
be found without too much difficulty. Luce includes it
in his work on the Early Period on account of the fact
that Mon writings are found on the walls here and an
early date is given in one of the ink inscriptions.[81] Mon
glosses in a temple do not necessarily imply an early
date. Though by the mid-12th century Mon literary
influence at the court and in the sanctuaries was on the
wane, it was by no means extinct. Kyasin temple, in
architectural style, is clearly a work dating from the
end of the 12th or 13th centuries. The Mon writings
themselves narrate the *Buddhavamsa* text that details
the 28 buddhas. Luce also suggests that this temple
may be of mixed origin: the older part to the east,
which may well account for the curious ground plan.
His translation of the ink inscription confirms this
assumption for: "In 487s. (1125 A.D.) on the New
Moon of Kason (April-May) the donor of this pagoda
(Buddha?) called Baruci died. In 585 s. (1223 A.D.) San
Tra Uil gave the following name to this pagoda: Trai-
lok-luboh-buil, 'Strong Comfort of the Three Worlds'."[83]
There was thus a gap of a century between the death
of the donor and the naming, presumably upon
completion, of the temple. Possibly Shin Tra Uil, a
monk judging by his title, began the temple in memory
of Baruci who may have been his ancestor. There is
thus no firm evidence, epigraphically or architecturally, to suggest that Kyasin had actually been begun in
1125.

The temple's exterior marks a near radical departure
from the Pagan temple norm (though in fact there is
no such thing as a temple norm, other than the
generalised vision of the bewildered visitor to the
site). For though the base seems regular enough, with
medial foreparts about the shrine openings (now
claustured) and the hall extending out to the east, also
with foreparts, the superstructure is remarkable for its
elevation: the terraces rise high, and steeply, to a
narrow upper shrine. The steepness, or dramatic
ascent, of this arrangement is emphasised by the steps
that lead from the hall terraces up to the upper shrine,
these take the form of a dramatically arched bridge
and add to the effect of 'climb'. However, the overall
impression of all this is not one of 'aspiration' as on the
soaring Gadaw-palin, it is rather one of early baroque
majesty.

Inside, the hall opens uninterrupted out into the
shrine, forming a **T** plan. A much narrower central
core is used, for the thrust of the superstructure is
carried directly down through the outer walls. Thus
the central core of a number of Late Period temples is
reduced at Kyasin to a screen-like wall against which
the colossal images are placed, seated upon a continuous throne that extends out from the wall towards the
open space of the hall. The shrine space to the fore of

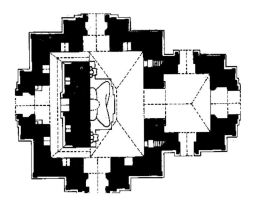

this dividing wall is covered with a quadripartite vault which springs from this wall. This general arrangement resembles the much smaller in scale scheme at the Loka-hteik-pan. The images themselves represent a buddha triad: the Buddha seated in the centre in *bhumisparsamudra*, with a buddha on either side, set at a right angle to the central figure, each in *pralambanasana*, whilst their hands are in the *dharmacakramudra*. According to Luce, this triad, found also at the Myinkaba Kubyauk-ngè and Wu-tha-na-daw No.359, represents the 'Great Miracle at Savatthi' when the Buddha created two *nirmana* buddhas.[83] Here, the scene is treated on a colossal scale, the images made from brick and stucco, the hands of the *nirmana* buddhas now broken, though the *mudra is* discernible. On the west side of the rectangular block, placed in the niches, would have been a further three images, this time standing, and now destroyed. There is no scheme of narrative paintings here, though a dummy *kirtimukha* frieze runs about with a row of *deva* figures holding flowers.

Between the ground and upper shrines, there is an intermediary level, comparable with the entresols of the That-byin-nyu. In the Late Period architects were beginning to explore the possibility of these levels, which in the past had generally had been sealed up, for their function had been purely to reduce mass. Thus at the the Hti-lo-min-lo and Tha-bai-mauk (No.363) temples access was permitted, though, like at the That-byin-nyu, there seems to have been no ritual function to these intermediary corridors. At Kyasin, dark and low vaulted passages pass from the east, at the lower terrace level, through to a western gallery where the vault heightens and there are both images and mural paintings. The effect of all this, after passing through the cramped passageway, is something of a surprise.

The inclusion of a bridge-like flight of steps from the hall terraces, ascending up over the shrine terraces, to the upper shrine has been noted; what remains to be emphasised is the excellence of the voussoired arch work, which, despite its seemingly fragile design, has survived many an earthquake. The upper shrine is square in plan with openings on each side: the narrowness of this unit has also been noted above. Placed to the centre of the shrine is a circular image pedestal, now lacking an image. Deeply incised with mouldings, this form has not been met with elsewhere at Pagan. Possibly a seated image of bronze or wood was placed here, for there are no stucco remains of an image.

No.115 upper left: Kyasin front from south-east
Fig.21 middle left: Kyasin section (EFEO)
Fig.22 lower left: Kyasin ground plan (EFEO)
No.116 upper right: Shin-bo-me-kyaung
front from south east
No.117 pralambanasana buddha in Kyasin shrine

No.766 NORTH GU NI

မြောက်ဂူနီ

South of the Shwe-hsan-daw, past its monastery, and south-west of the Dhamma-yan-gyi, are the two Gu Ni temples, medium to large in size, each similar yet different to the other. Alongside temples such as Ywa-haung-gyi and Thisa-wadi, this splendid pair also seem emblematic of the mature Pagan style, grand yet never flamboyant, embellished with a restrained yet rich texture, with each unit working in harmony with the other to create a balance between horizontal and vertical elements: an effect that uplifts, but is never showy.

In the hall of North Gu Ni, there are stone pedestals for *dvarapala* figures that would have once protected the shrine. The shrine itself is arranged around an **H** plan, similar in conception to the Hsin-pya-gu[84] and Middle Period works such as the Shwe-gu-gyi or Sein-nyet Ama.[85] Though the east-facing image is now damaged, a lotus petal dado runs continuously about the block linking the two thrones. The west image, lesser in size than the east one has now disappeared. Paintwork, rondos set in geometric patterns, may still be seen on the vaults. Two stairs climb to the upper shrine which also contains a central block on account of the great mass of the restored *sikhara* above. Between the hall terraces and the upper shrine crosses a bridging flight of steps.

No. 769 SOUTH GU NI

တောင်ဂူနီ

South Gu Ni differs from its northern counterpart in a number of slight ways, none of which are particularly significant: for example, the pediment designs vary and South Gu Ni has a squarely-planned upper shrine whilst North Gu Ni's has an eastwards extension. At South Gu Ni, the enclosing wall is in a better state and an arched gateway stands on the south section, there is also a stupa in the south-west part of the enclosure. Within, about the hall to shrine arch, is a pediment and placed in the lower cusps, above the pilasters, are *kinnaya* figures rather than the more commonly found *makara*.

The shrine unit contains a single colossal brick and stucco image to the east, built in a slight recess set into the central block, depicting the Buddha at the moment of enlightenment. On the three remaining faces are smaller niches containing further scenes from the *bodawin* or life of the buddha Gotama—the eight scenes:

1.	North	the Nativity.
2.	North	*dhyanamudra*: meditation scene, or possibly Sujata's Offering.
3.	West	Descent from Tavatimsa.
4.	West	*parinibbana*: the image is now lost though the pedimented niche's

design clearly indicates the original contents as does the niche's position in the temple.

5.	West	The Parileyyaka Monkey.
6.	South	*varadamudra*: standing and dispensing gifts.
7.	South	*dharmacakramudra*: Deer Park at Sarnath.

This arrangement is close to the one found at Myinkaba Kubyauk-ngè, only there are a total of 12 scenes carved in the medium of stone at Myinkaba, whilst South Gu Ni is more conventional in the sense that the standard 8 scenes are presented in the more abundant medium of stucco. The condition of these scenes is now poor though this is not unremediable. Fragments of the original polychrome work are still visible and from circular indents in the stucco it would seem that some form of mosaic, glass or lithic, was studded into the damp plaster.

No.1471 THEIN-MAZI

သိမ္မစည်း

The Thein-mazi temple is significant, not just for the original subject matter and disposition of the paintings within, but also as a monument to western vandalism. Easily reached on foot from the Pagan village, this middle sized temple is situated due west of the Loka-hteik-pan, east of the Myinkaba-Pagan road and south of the new Pagan-Nyaung U road. The enclosing wall has now disintegrated though the boundary is trace-able across these terracotta-strewn fields. Examining the exterior, the Thein-mazi seems regular enough: eastwardly orientated hall extending from shrine, foreparts about entrance openings (now claustured)

on each face of the shrine base, no upper shrine, terraces with medial steps crossed by arches, tall, square-
based corner obelisks on the terraces, all of which is
surmounted by the standard Pagan *sikhara*. The interior is, though, of greater interest: here the hall and
ambulatory-shrine are separated by an arch, there are
four cardinal images, the eastern one being the most
colossal (now damaged), each set against the *lei-myet-
hna* and not receded into it.

To see the paintings, though, should be the purpose
of any visit to the Thein-mazi. Despite the vandalism
of Herr Thomman at the turn of the century, when
large sections of the plaster were cut out to eventually
be sold to Hamburg Ethnographical Museum, there
remain considerable sections of wall space that have
not suffered his party's handiwork.[86] Firstly, the paintings in the hall are striking, not so much for any
innovation in style, but for a highly original disposition
of conventional scenes and the inclusion of new
subjects for portrayal. Though no other temple at
Pagan includes such arrangements, certain of the
temples of Salé, a satellite city of Pagan's to the south
of Chauk, do. Thus in the hall one finds, on the south
side, a large panel running along the upper section of
the wall portraying the 'Attack of Mara' and on the
north side the 'Defeat of Mara'. Usually this requisite
scene is painted either on the west face of the *lei-myet-
hna*, behind the main image, or, as at Wetkyi-in
Kubyauk-gyi or Nanda-ma-nya, on either side of the
east or main image. Also in the hall, beneath this panel
on the south side, is a depiction of one of the seven
cosmic Himalayan lakes, Anotatta, from which the
great rivers of India are believed to flow.[87] This Hindu-
Buddhist *mapus supramundi* is depicted in a similar
manner in Salé temple No.101, the only other known
version from this period in Burma.[88] On the hall's
north wall, again beneath the phantamachia of Mara's

*No.118 upper left: Loka-ok-shaung
window opening
No.119 above: North and South Gu
Ni, from south
No.120 below: stucco relief of the
Nativity in South Gu Ni ambulatory*

destruction, this Hindu-Buddhist cosmic cartography continues: here, Mount Meru is depicted. Mount Meru has been met with before at Pagan when the Buddha has either been making the divine ascent or descent, but here at Thein-mazi the Buddhist Olympus is depicted in its own right, as a cosmic reminder perhaps. These paintings, for the first known instance in Burma, represent an interest in Hindu originated Buddhist cosmology, a theme that was to develop in the Buddhism and its art of later periods in Burma.[89]

The arch between hall and shrine has the standard relief pediment composition of octofoil and *pyatthat* over it, about this on either side rising to the pediment's apex are painted figures of *deva* set amidst a florid, paradise-like background. Within a framework of painted dummy architecture, a highly original scheme of paintings may still be found, despite the detachment of large sections by the Germans. Beneath the painted cornice a series of buddhas run continuously about the outer wall broken only by the four transept arches. This is a portrayal of the 28 buddhas from the *Buddhavamsa*. The narrow, continuous band that follows beneath this contains a procession of dancing figures, each with hands in an individualised gesture, each part of a rhythmic dance about the shrine. From inscriptions, it is known that music and dance were offered to the Pagan *hpaya*, perhaps re-enacting the divine dance of this mural. This procession is not dissimilar to the lissome processions of the Nanda-ma-nya paintings.[90] The wall space between this processional band, down to a lower processional band set just above the dado, is filled with small panels: the Jatakas, here found without obvious precedent, in the shrine part of the temple. On the south section large parts of these have been cut away. Between the Jataka that fill most of the outer wall space and the dado beneath, is a further procession band working around the temple. The textual origin for this, if there is one, is, as yet, unknown. This procession, best viewed along the west sections where it is in a better condition, presents a colourful spectacle of militaria, vehicles and mounts, courtiers and royalty, all depicted in the manner of contemporary pageants bearing ritual receptacles as offerings to the *hpaya*. This circumambulatory procession of royal donors about the *lei-myet-hna* is not dissimilar to the procession *parabaik* of the Konbaung period that illustrate the progress of the court towards a new dedication bearing similar offerings.

The south image is now broken and the *mudra* presented no longer visible, however it may be surmised that this was a *dharmacakra* gesture, for the four faces of the central block are here used to illustrate four events from the life of Gotama, rather than to convey the *lei-myet-hna* theme; this follows from the earlier 'potted life' series found on the four faces of the Mye-bon-tha.

On the west face of the *lei-myet-hna* is a reclining image of the Buddha, set in a niche; the now damaged brick and stucco lord's head is directed to the north

indicating that this is a death scene or *parinibbana*.

No.1481-3 PE-NAN-THA-GU ပဲနံ့သာဂူ

This complex, located not far to the south-east of the crossroads between Pagan, the hotel, Myinkaba and Nyaung U, now consists of three temples each with a stupa superstructure, easterly orientated and set on a high brick platform. According to U Bo Kay this work was begun in B.E. 621 (1259 A.D.) and completed in B.E. 622 (1260 A.D.).[91] There were, though, originally five temples here: the *hpaya-nga-zu*, that is to say the four buddhas of this *kalpa* extended to include Mettaya, the future buddha. Normally this theme was architecturally conveyed in the form of a pentagonally planned monument. However, here the 'five lords' were placed in a row like the 'three lords', or Paya-thon-zu, at Minnanthu.[92] On examination, the platform indicates that the five *gu* were not sited in a straight line, the northernmost two, now lost, seem to have been set back (west) from the three surviving. Of these three, the rich articulation of the exterior elements and warm texture of the surfaces instantly recall the Paya-thon-zu. However, the Paya-thon-zu is a more unified work, the units connected by passages and typed to each other. The Pe-nan-tha-gu units are less connected, though in effect as architecturally chromatic.

No.1481 North Temple—has a Greek Cross plan with a rounded open floor space between the arms; the east arm forms the porch; the west acts as a recess for the now lost image; the north and south act as transepts. Filled with paintings, the comparison with the Paya-thon-zu must continue, for by their style and content here too is an extravaganza of painted architecture, divine figures and bestial configuration. Once again the late artist's brushes have revelled in a world of architectonic *trompe l'oeil* and supramundane fantasy.

No.1482 Central Temple—has a squarely-planned central space, originally the north and south transepts contained accessible openings which have now been claustured. Possibly an image would have stood free in the centre of the floor space, as in the south temple. The paintings here are less delicately executed and expansive in treatment than in the north temple. The *Buddhavamsa* is illustrated beneath the painted cornice.

No.1483 South Temple—has a squarely-planned central space, there is a now imageless freestanding pedestal in the centre of the floor space. On the walls lancet niches contain small stucco representations of the eight scenes.

As has been remarked before, the Pe-nan-tha-gu

XIX, previous: That-byin-nyu from the south
XX, upper left: That-byin-nyu front from east
XXI, lower left: Sula-mani from south-west
XXII, right: detail from the paintings in the Loka-hteik-pan hall
XXIII, next: the Dhamma-yan-gyi from the west

XXIV, left: the Dhamma-yazika at Pwasaw
XXV, right: Tayok-pye and the west from Minnanthu
XXVI, next: detail from the 'attack and defeat of the
Army of Mara' paintings in the Wetkyi-in Kubyauk-gyi

complex rests on a high brick platform. From the west a basement area may be entered into. Half subterranean, these compartments appear to have served neither a ritual nor accommodation function, being, rather, mass saving devices.

No.1570 SHIN-BIN-THALY-AUNG

ရှင်ပင်သာလျောင်း

Incorporated into a section of the enclosure wall to the south-east side of the Shwe-hsan-daw pagoda is sited this approximately 18m. long image of the Buddha reclining. It is housed within a long, low-lying brick building with gables and brick vaults. This image has been said to portray the moment when the Buddha achieved the ultimate state of *parinibbana* at the moment of his death. The visitor will note though, that the Buddha's head is directed towards the south and that traditionally in Pagan iconograph, a *parinibbana* figure would point to the north, as at the Manuha or Mye-bon-tha-hpaya-hla. In this instance, according to U Aung Kyaing, it would seem that the scene depicts the Buddha resting in a garden, a hypothesis reinforced by the highly naturalistic though later paintings on the walls and vaults about the recumbent figure. Though Luce and Ba Shin believed that the reason for this orientation was so as to prevent the image having its back to the stupa, that problem surely could be remedied by the Buddha turning over and lying on his left side, rather than his right.

Luce also reckoned the image to be an afterthought by Anawrahta at sometime after the completion of the pagoda itself. Early Period recumbent images were rare and with the exception of votive tablets even rarer in Pyu times. As an iconographic item it has had an insufficient existence at Pagan to suddenly manifest itself on so great a scale. The other reclining image that has been attributed to the time of Anawrahta is the one to the rear of the Manuha temple, however, this attribution is likewise open to question.[93] Judging by the style in which the Buddha is depicted here at the Shin-bin-thaly-aung, it would seem that this is an image from the Middle Period, for the face lacks the sharp, gaunt look of Early Period images.

The building that houses the image is of some interest; there is nothing like it at Pagan, the closest comparable brick structures are the *ok-kyaung* or brick houses for monks which date from the Middle and Late Periods. Likewise, the exterior pediments with heightened spinodes would also appear to date from the Middle Period. The vault is a fine example of Pagan bricklaying: it is a barrel one whilst the exterior ends are gabled. The interior walls are decorated with mural paintings that are full of surprise and vigour. Cheeky owls poke their heads through the lush fauna whilst sprites play mocking the spectator from their vantage points high on the soffits. This is the work of

redecorators in a later period and may be compared with some of the late 18th century work at Hpo-win-daung.

No.121: Shin-bin-thaly-aung

7
The Late Period 1170-1300
(II) Outer Circle Monuments

This chapter is a continuation of Chapter Six on the Late Period. The monuments included in the Outer Circle are arranged according to their geographical position rather than chronologically, or by their place in the story of the evolution of Pagan's architecture. For by the end of the 12th century, a single process of evolution and development fragments into a plethora of currents, sub-styles and forms. The Pagan temple and stupa, having reached their ultimate forms by around 1180-90, were to diversify into such a variety of forms, within a controlled framework, that a categorisation according to dating, style or form becomes impossible. The selection of monuments from the Outer Circle brought together here includes some of the most magnificent monuments in the Pagan area, though, in the past, they have been less favoured by visitors on account of their greater distance from the Pagan village. It was in the Late Period that these outlying areas, beyond the limits of the city, were developed as great monastic and university centres.

The selection of monuments described here begins from the west, at the Irrawaddy to the south of Myinkaba, and works round anti-clockwise, inland, and back to the Irrawaddy at the Kyauk-ku area, east of Nyaung-U. With motor transport, such a circle could be travelled in a day by the less discerning visitor, otherwise, each group of temples would be best visited singly, either in a morning or afternoon trip from the Pagan village.

No.995 BOGYOKE-MI KUBYAUK/
THIRI-YA-PYIT-SAYA KUBYAUK
ဗိုလ်ချုပ်မိီးဂူပြောက် /သိရိပစ္စယာဂူပြောက်

Bogyoke-mi is a popular name dating from the colonial period, for it was here that a leader of the patriotic resistance took cover from the Government forces.[1] Thiri-ya-pyit-saya Kubyauk as a name indicates this dedication's location a little to the south of the Thiriyapyitsaya village and not a great distance inland from the Loka-nanda stupa built by Anawrahta some two centuries earlier. Though an accurate dating cannot be readily assigned, this work can be placed somewhere between the middle of the 12th century and the demise of the dynasty at the end of the 13th. This distant site may have been beyond the city's southernmost limits, for the concentration of monu-

ments here is less dense with only one colossal monument in the area, the fortress-like Seddana-gyi not far to the south. The Bogyoke-mi itself is set a little off the local road from Pagan to Chauk and Salé. Salé itself was a prosperous satellite of the capital and there we find over a hundred monuments built in the style of Late Period and dating to the 13th century. What is curious is that at Salé the 'Bodh Gaya' sikhara arrangement was particularly favoured, a type that was introduced into the Pagan builder's repertoire following a possible mission of Burmese architects to the sacred site in the first quarter of the 13th century, the most notable examples of which at Pagan are the Maha-bodi and on the kubyauk-gyi at Wetkyi-in.[2] Though this feature was employed in a number of other dedications in the Pagan area, it never really caught on. However, the Salé dedicators seemed to have preferred this type, and here at the southernmost periphery of the capital, on the road to Salé, we find another version of this 'Bodh Gaya' type.

This middle sized gu temple's sanctuary is enclosed by a wall, now tumbled in places, with medial arches. Note the inner west arch retains some of its stucco, unusual to survive on an arch. The temple itself is orientated with the main image facing towards the east. The main shrine is on the ground level, though there is a minor shrine on the upper terrace set into the east face of the sikhara base. The front has a triple pediment over the porch arch. There are no openings on the north and south walls of the hall extension like at the Wetkyi-in Kubyauk-gyi; whilst on the three exterior walls of the shrine there are foreparts, each with a window aperture set high and without perforations, unlike those at Wetkyi-in which have entrances. The plinth is moulded in stucco with a continuous band of lotus petals. Above, the low-lying and undramatic terraces are gently crenellated, their corners marked with obelisks. The sikhara design has already been noted; what deserves further attention is the mastery of its treatment, for as one rises from the dark stair passage onto the terraces one is struck by the architect's device of dramatising the upward taper of the sikhara by downwardly tapering the base pilasters that carry it. Though, from a distance this device is not apparent, the effect certainly is. On the remaining three sides of the sikhara base are the dummy door panels found on this type of monument all over Salé. Above, on the sikhara itself, best seen on the east face, are a rising scheme of panels and tondos, like at

Wetkyi-in, only here more elaborate and better preserved. These ascending tiers are emblematic of Brahmaloka, for within each of the central panels is a figure of this three-headed deity; these rise up to six in number.

Entering into the hall, the connection with the Wetkyi-in Kubyauk-gyi is brought to mind once again, for as at Wet-kyi-in there are no openings on the lateral hall walls. This was indeed intended to be a *kubyauk*, or 'variegated' temple, with uninterrupted wall space for a full cycle of finely embellished wall paintings. These were never added, though, as with so many of this temple's contemporaries, dummy architectural elements such as cornices, pilasters and pediments were painted in.

The shrine is set in a recess, cut into the central core and is not, as was usual in the 12th and 13th centuries, projecting from the central block into the ambulatory facing the hall arch. Here, like on a number of other Late Period examples, the Early Period treatment of receding the shrine into the block to form a separate unit in itself, with its own special atmosphere, is revived in a similar manner to the Ywa-haung-gyi plan.[3] This treatment for the shrine is, though, quite different from that at Wetkyi-in, where the shrine and hall blend to form one clear unit. What these two *kubyauk* do have in common is that there are arches to the north and south of the main image leading to the ambulatory—in other words, the ambulatory in each of these temples does not directly open out into the shrine or hall, as the case may be. Within the Bogyoke-mi shrine unit there is an elaborate octofoil stucco pediment overhanging the image, in the deepest of reliefs with a surmounting *pyatthat*.

The ambulatory is crossed by double voussoired diaphragm arches which relieve the mass of the superstructure, with stone bonded in to strengthen the brick junctures. The vaults form a three-quarter barrel. A single passage of steps pass up through the south transept wall. There are no images on the north, south and west faces of the central block. The upper shrine has a stone threshold, there is architectonic painting and about the vandalised image is a stucco reredos.

No.987 SEDDANA-GYI

စေတနာကြီး

This colossal stupa is situated a short distance to the east of the rough road that runs between Thiriyapyitsaya and Chauk and is one of the most southerly of the Pagan area monuments dating from the dynastic periods and certainly one of the largest and most impressive of the more distant Outer Circle monuments, ranking alongside the Dhamma-yazika. According to the Glass Palace Chronicle, it was rebuilt by Nadaungmya (1211-30).[4] The addition of *harmika* indicates that this work must indeed date from after 1170 in the Late Period, when renewed contact with Ceylon

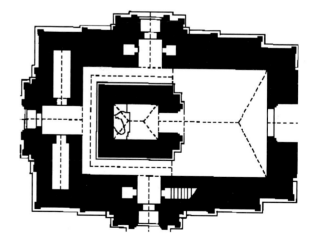

No.122 upper: Bogyoke-mi from south-east
No.123 middle: Bogyoke-mi sikhara from terraces
Fig.23 lower: Bogyoke-mi ground plan (EFEO)

120

led to an injection of this revived form into Pagan stupa design.[5]

Squarely planned, there are five terraces, which have no medial stairways—an unusual feature in so large a stupa, though in common with Late Period fashions.[6] The plinth is decorated with a row of elephants pointing outwards about the plinth of the lower terrace. The use of elephants in this position, partly decorative and partly protective, has been noted in only two other monuments at Pagan.[7] The elephant developed into a cult symbol in subsequent periods, yet at Pagan it is rarely portrayed other than in this role as a guardian and symbolic load bearer. The terrace corners are emphasised by the tall base blocks of now damaged subsidiary stupas. Within these corner blocks are enriched standing figures of the Buddha. The *harmika* seems an uncomfortable addition to the *anda*. Unlike the Sapada, or other Ceylonese-inspired stupas from this time, it is less well integrated into the overall design. In this respect its treatment is not dissimilar to the East Hpet-leik *harmika* that is believed to have been added at around this time.[8] On each of the four faces of the *harmika* box is a lotus petal design carved or moulded from the stucco, the only example of its kind, for it boldly stands out as a single motif, whereas usually such decorative motifs are far smaller and part of an overall exterior pattern of ornament. On the south plinth is an opening, now crudely closed by the Department, this leads deep into the interior of the stupa and the last party to attempt an entry and exploration suffered the loss of one life, so tell many a local, with a sense of satisfaction at the efficacy of their ancestors curses. However, it would seem, from discussion with those who have been 'inside', that the structural composition within, and beneath the ground level, is not dissimilar to that of the Shwe-hsan-daw and that either to economise on the mass of brick that would have been required to make the stupa 'solid', or to foil the so openly anticipated, judging by the epigraphy of the period, treasure hunter, or maybe both, the interior is made up of a labyrinth of compartments and connecting passageways.[9] Finally, note that like at the Shwe-hsan-daw the enclosure about the stupa is paved with stone.

No.947 DHAMMA-YAZIKA
ဓမ္မရာဇိက

The great king called Jeyyasura... having gone forth from his capital, Pukam, called Arimaddanapura, went looking and searching for a sight—with auspicious marks, to serve as a field of merit for the building of a royal *cetiya*. And verily he saw a column of vapour pure white issuing from the ground ascending, having the height and measure and girth of a palmyra tree.[10]

Isolated and reached only by reluctant horse cart or thickly-tyred bicycle, the Dhamma-yazika is worthy of a visit for it is an impressive statement of the religious beliefs prevalent in Late Pagan and an unsurpassed example of the Pagan architect's originality. As a cosmic metaphor and symbol of the five buddhas it is, in its proportions and geometrically guided lay-out, one of the finest expressions of the Pagan genius. The Dhamma-yazika was completed in 1196 by Sithu II when Pagan, as an empire and a civilisation, must have been at its peak. From contemporary inscriptions, of which there are a great many, we are told little of Sithu II, though he ruled for nearly three and a half decades. Judging by the endowments of property and manpower listed in these dedicatory inscriptions, Sithu II's Pagan was prosperous, with all surplus

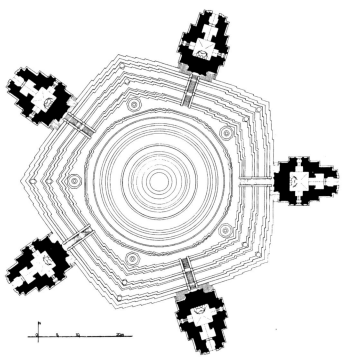

No.124 *left: Sedana-gyi harmika*
Fig.24: *above: Dhamma-yazika ground plan (EFEO)*
No.125 *above right: sikhara upon shrine at*
Dhamma-yazika
Fig.25 *right: Dhamma-yazika elevation (EFEO)*

wealth being converted into religious dedications and endowments. Sithu's empire was still expanding; from the Dhamma-yazika inscription itself we know that the Chindwin and Mu valleys were centres for Burmese settlement and colonisation, whilst territory as far south as Tenasserim was claimed for Burma.[11] Pagan was at peace; the elephant trading dispute with Ceylon had been settled and a second phase of cultural exchange with Ceylon resulted in an efflorescence of new forms appearing in Pagan architecture.

It is within this historical context that Dhamma-yazika must be viewed. This stupa is diverse in nature; it departs from the stupa norm in the conception behind the ground plan. As a departure from the Buddhist stupa norm, it is a supremely self-confident one. The doctrine that determined this pentagonal ground plan must have been a mainstream element in contemporary Pagan Buddhism. For Buddhist architecture is essentially conservative, and standard forms conceived in the earliest days of the religion are rarely departed from. The addition of a fifth side to temple and stupa ground plans in Burma is without precedent throughout the Buddhist world and the Burmese were possibly the first society throughout the world to attempt this pentagonal type of plan for a major architectural work. The origins of this movement lie in contemporary religious thought: the cult of Mettaya, the future buddha, and the present cycle of five buddhas.

The *lei-myet-hna* concept, that dated in Burma back

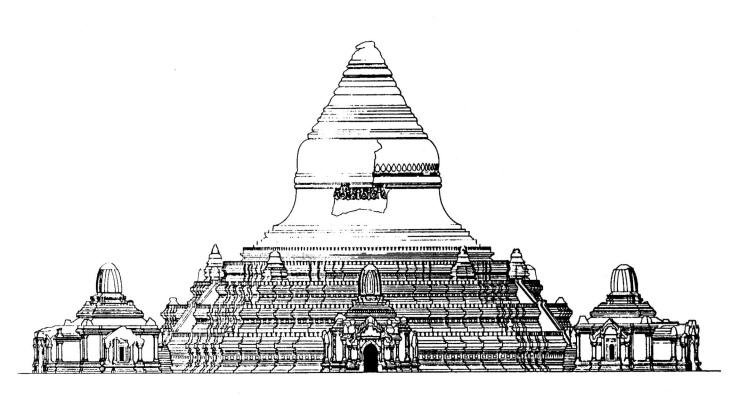

to Pyu times, was revived at Pagan towards the end of the Early Period in temple architecture. Likewise, it had been a predominant theme in stupa ground plans, for example the Shwe-zigon, which has a square base, with each side representing one of the last four buddhas of this time era. At the Dhamma-yazika, a fifth face is added, making it a *nga-myet-hna*, or five face type, the fifth face representing the buddha to come—Mettaya, the final buddha of this *bhadrakalpa*. Mettaya enjoyed a cult following at Pagan and from inscriptions it is evident that devotees hoped to be present when he is born on earth so as to enjoy the benefits of salvation at the hands of an actual buddha, who would offer mankind a dispensation.[12] As a cult it was an extensive one, patronised by the king and court and marked a messianic tendency in contemporary Pagan Buddhism. The 'Five Sacred Lords' or *hpaya-nga-zu* as an iconographic portrayal was known to the Pyu and two large stone reliefs found at Sri Ksetra depict five buddhas seated in niches beneath a stupa, each in the *bhumisparsamudra*.[13] It would thus appear that in the Late Period at Pagan this old Burmese iconographic item was translated into an architectural form—the *nga-myet-hna*. The *nga-myet-hna* or pentagonal type of plan was also used in Late Period *gu* temples, seventeen of which have been counted including one at Salé.[14] Non-pentagonal manifestations of the *hpaya-nga-zu* theme may be seen at the Pe-na-tha-gu group and at the Min-o-chantha, the former having lost two of its original units and the latter which has been restored in later times.[15]

The Dhamma-yazika, which was the largest stupa built at Pagan since the Shwe-zigon, is set within a broad enclosure. Today, no evidence of ancilliary buildings, monastic accomodation, subsidiary shrines and sacred structures, or even a tank, may be seen. However, the area about the enclosure walls is littered with the remains and rubble of numerous lesser dedications, including a large quantity of now destroyed *ok-taik* whose incumbents may well have served or been attached to this great dedication. The enclosing wall itself follows the geometric pattern laid down by the stupa base's pentagonal ground plan, only having fifteen sides, five of which have arched gateways, each

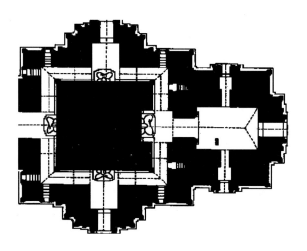

in line with the five shrines. The shrines and central stupa are set well within a broad and raised platform as the Mingala-zeidi was to be.[16] The question of orientating a five-sided monument has been conveniently solved by placing the easternmost shrine directly on a north-south axis

The Dhamma-yazika has three terraces containing a full series of Jataka plaques, some of which have been thieved, whilst others have been much battered by the elements. The *anda* or bell rises from a nine-sided band, customarily there would be an eight-sided band, but in this case the design of the upper sections has been determined by the ground plan. On the upper terrace corners are subsidiary stupas, though there are no corner obelisks on the lower terrace, and medial stair flights rise through them: the standard arrangement for a Pagan stupa. Weathered stone equestrian figures survive on the north-west terraces, flanking the stair flight.

What make the Dhamma-yazika so dynamic a structure are the five 'perfumed chambers' attached to the plinth, one to each face. These are standard, small scale, Late Pagan *gu* temples, well lit with full barrel vaults, with the hall opening into shrine to form a **T** plan. At Kyanzittha's Shwe-zigon, the shrines or 'perfumed chambers' are detached and set at the cardinal points well back from the base itself. Here they are unified into the whole scheme—arranged like satellites about the cosmic mountain. Their bold lines, a rectilinear emphasis, juxtaposes the circular tendencies of the concavely-shaped stupa centrepiece about which they seemingly revolve.

On their front and forepart pediments some of the finest stucco decoration to be seen at Pagan remains unmolested. Note how the *makara* has become a fantasia of lively detail, flowing from his jaws myriad grotesques vivaciously emanate whilst each of the pediment's spinodes is occupied by a *hamsa* or sacred duck. The *kirtimukha* friezes also have come to life; within each garland an *arhat* sits suppressing a devil.

No.126 upper right: Dhamma-yazika shrine terrace and sikhara
No.127 middle right: Thisa-wadi
Fig.26: Thisa-wadi ground plan
No.128 far left: Hsu-taung-pyit ok-taik pediment
No.129 near left: makara at Hsu-taung-pyit

Kinnaya, naga, Garuda and all the other members of the Pagan decorator's gallery animate these exteriors without overpowering through excessive embellishment. Finally, note the *sikhara* of each chamber—placed in the inner lobe of each face is a meditating buddha, with his *bodhi* tree rising above.

The shrine interiors are well-lit; the paintings and glosses are from the Konbaung Period whilst the images are contemporary. In the shrine facing east is a large, flat stone resting up against the wall, this is not a *yoni* as one might think. As U Bo Kay explains, this was most likely the base for a portable Buddha image and served to drain off the waters when the Buddha was ritually washed. Also to be found at the Dhamma-yazika, in the south-east *gu* is one of Anawrahta's ubiquitous *dhyana* monoliths.[17]

No.918 THISA-WADI
သစ္စာဝတီ

This late and large sized temple is one of the most unique structures on the Pagan plain for it is a three-level temple. The story of Pagan's architecture may be told in terms of the early Burmese striving against the forces of gravity to create structures that dynamically soar up without sacrifice to stolidity and splendour. Though it has been noted that by the end of the 12th century architects and their patrons had achieved a form based on the Sula-mani that satisfied their aesthetic and ritual requirements, this did not mean that innovation ceased. Here, some miles to the south of the old city centre (the Pagan village of today), was attempted a radical departure from conventional forms. However, given the Pagan builder's record, it seems surprising that so obvious an extension from existing forms and ideology as the addition of a third-level shrine was not attempted either earlier or in greater numbers. For example, as early as the That-byin-nyu (1155-60), stair passages ascended to the level of upper terrraces and *sikhara* and it would have seemed natural to include a small shrine recess at this point though this was not to occur till now, over a century and a half later.

An on-site inscription dates this large temple to 1334, three decades after the end of our period and half a century since the departure of the Mongols, yet not only was there still money in the Pagan treasuries, but there remained a determined spirit of innovation and the quest for novel and individualised architectural forms, with no slackening in the quality of craftmanship, as the survival, in good condition, of this major yet little-known monument attests.

With the exception of the unique inclusion of a third-level shrine, the Thisa-wadi retains the standard features of a large size Late temple. In the ambulatories, note the diaphragm arches that carry the thrust of all that mass above down to the earth.

No. 906-9 HSU-TAUNG-PYIT

ဆုတောင်းပြည့်

This monastic complex is situated a little to the east of the Thisa-wadi temple on the track between the villages of West Pwasaw and Thategan. It is a spacious, square planned enclosure, the outer wall of which has now disintegrated, though it remains traceable on the east side. Between the two enclosure walls on the east is a line of brick *taik*, similar, though less numerous, to those found at Hsin-byu-shin off the Minnanthu road.[18] These were the sub-houses of the main *taik* which is within the inner walls, and housed individual monks and their novices and servants. Possibly, like in many contemporary monastic complexes today in Burma, these lesser houses may have been often semi-autonomous, operating independantly, whilst paying the necessary obeisance to the senior *thera*.

The two enclosures are square in plan. On the inner wall, notable for its height and dramatic edgings, are arched gateways. Within, the arrangement is immediately reminiscent of Anantasura's Lei-myet-hna at Minnanthu, though here there is a stupa in the south-west corner rather than a temple. Possibly the close-by Thisa-wadi temple was served by this community.[19] The stupa is still maintained by the local people of this area and there is a modern *nat* shrine to the west of it, within the inner enclosure. In the north-east corner is another modern wooden structure housing some nuns who have selected this distant spot for its quietness. Like at the Minnanthu Lei-myet-hna, there are four original structures occupying the four quarters of the square, though here the donors have been more generous in their gift of ground and there are broader areas of open space between the structures. As has been noted, the stupa stands in the south-west corner; in the north-west is the remaining brick section of the *dhammasala* or *dhamma-yon*, as it would be known in modern Burmese. Here, above the lines of the now lost three tiers of wooden gables, remains some of the finest and most elaborated stucco to be found at Pagan. In each of the ascending straight lines of spinodes rests a *hamsa*, whilst the cusps are filled with a frenzied sub-aquatic duel between *makara* and demonic forces.

In the north-east quarter is the *taik-gyi* which would have housed the premier monk and his immediate followers. This structure is in grave disrepair with many of the vaults caved in, preventing access through the corridors. Were this *taik* to be surveyed and restored, our knowledge of monastic life might be considerably increased. At present, it is a bewildering mass of brick, a glance at which tells us nothing of the way in which the monks lived from day to day.

Finally, in the south-east quarter is the plinth upon which the *thein* would have been erected out of timber. The platform is edged with stone and the steps are likewise of stone.

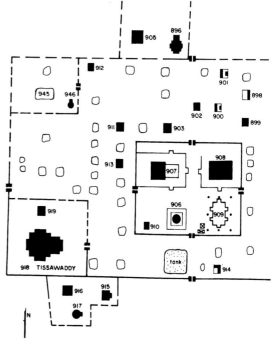

No.566 EAST ZANTHI NGA-MYET-HNA

အရှေ့ဇံသီးငါးမျက်နှာ

South-west of Minnanthu, and set beside the East Zanthi temple, this small *nga-myet-hna* temple-stupa is worthy of remark. It is unlike all other five-faced temples on the plain, not just on account of its size but also design. Raised on a square based platform, of about 1m high, with the surprising inclusion, at this late date, of a *kalasa* profile, there is only one access opening facing west towards the East Zanthi temple itself. The other four faces are blank panels. Above, there are three terraces surmounted by a Ceylonese stupa. Within, there is a simple cella. Once again, the Late Pagan architect has attempted and succeeded in achieving the original and in this case managed, by Pagan norms, the eccentric.

No.558 EAST ZANTHI

အရှေ့ဇံသီး

This temple in plan and overall design is not dissimilar to the neighbouring West Zanthi being a Greek Cross in plan, with a stupa superstructure above. Normally this type of arrangement at Pagan is completely symmetrical with no hall or porch extensions, however, here the east transept is very slighly expanded.[20] About the central block, that carries the stupa super-structure above, were the four images, the west now missing. There remain, though, some paintings: Mogallana and Sariputta flanking the east image, a panel depicting the 'Descent' on the east transept north wall, 'Decorative' in style, though not without impact and surprisingly large for the period, and the others of the eight scenes in less vivid condition. The inscription here dates this temple to B.E. 679 (1367 A.D.) nearly a century after the Mongol incursion and still in the style, and built according to the methods, of the Late Period.

No.803 PYA-THA-DA

ပြသဒါး

The word Pya-tha-da is the Burmese version of the Pali *prasada*, otherwise pronounced as *pyatthat*, a nor-mally seven-tiered pavilion made usually of wood that protects a sacred site such as a palace, image or ordination hall.[21] It is, though, in Pagan times rare for *gu* type of brick temple to be surmounted by this type of structure. Possibly, as the temple's superstructure was never added, a wooden *pyatthat* was at one time placed on the open space above. The Pya-tha-da's incompletion is explained in the chronicles, who tell of its pious builder Kyaswa:

> ...he laboured at the sacred writ of the religion, and built the Pyatthada pagoda, his work of merit, but did not finish it because the people were ill-paid and ill-directed. He bequeathed these words for history: "I care for naught save virtue." [22]

Kyaswa, despite the neglect of his workers, appears to have been the ideal Buddhist monarch, devoted to scholarship and promoting the *dhamma* with hu-manitarian policies. In 1249 he issued an edict that was to be put up, carved on stone, in every village of more than fifty houses in the empire:

> Kings of the past punished thieves by divers torture, starting with impaling. I desire no such destruction. I consider all beings as my own children and with compassion to all I speak these words...[23]

In its incomplete state the Pya-tha-da is an ideal site for those who wish to study Late Pagan Period building techniques. The burst open walls, particularly on the east side, reveal the mass-reducing structural tech-niques used by the Pagan builder in the construction of massive temples. Closed clerestories and flying buttresses reduce the amount of brick required, and thus building costs and time taken, whilst enabling the

*No.130 upper left: Thisa-wadi front, from east
No.131 middle left: Hsu-taung-pyit dhamma-yon
Fig.27: site plan for Hsu-taung-pyit and area including Thisa-wadi (EFEO)
No.132 far right: East Zanthi Nga-myet-hna
No.133 right: East Zanthi*

inclusion of taller and more dynamic superstructures. In this case, a superstructure was never added. As the chronicles frequently indicate, pagoda building could at times exhaust resources and even a 'good' king like Kyaswa might have lacked the organisational capabilities to complete it.

The Pya-tha-da was obviously conceived as a major temple, ranking alongside works such as the Sulamani or the nearby Tayok-pye and, if completed, would have been the last of the great Pagan temples dating to the dynastic period. In plan a now half-ruined hall extends to the east. Of particular interest here is the system of relieving vaults, with open compartments between them, visible where the vaults have collapsed. The Pya-tha-da is at present undergoing restoration, for not only was it left incomplete, but it suffered badly in the last earthquake.

No.447 MINNANTHU LEI-MYET-HNA

မင်းနန်သူလေးမျက်နှာ

The temple [447], situated in the south-west quarter of this complex, named after its plan, 'Four Faces', has been whitewashed by the villagers of Minnanthu, who use it as their local temple and therefore have maintained the dedication, periodically renewing the *hti* finial and regilding the main image over the centuries. For this reason, as traditional restoration necessitates alteration, this temple is of limited interest, whereas the other three structures in this sanctuary, alongside the Hsu-taung-pyit complex, offer one of the finest surviving examples of a complete sanctuary. There are, though, some mural paintings within the *gu* that have escaped the slap of the local's whitewash. The temple itself is a conventional Late Period type of single level *gu*, symbolically resting on a high artificial platform to raise it above the surrounding buildings, with tall, steeply rising crenellated terraces and elegantly profiled *sikhara*. Fortunately the dedicatory inscription survives to tell us of the foundation and its donors. Nadaungmya's minister, Anandasura, and his wife, completed their work on 17th December 1223:

Upon a fine platform we built our temple. To enshrine in that temple we encased the holy relics in a sandalwood casket, placed it in a crystal casket, then in a red sandalwood casket, then a gold casket, then a silver casket, and lastly into a miniature stone pagoda, the spire of which was made of gold, and the golden umbrella of which was hung with pearls and coral. In the chamber of the temple we made four images of the Lord placed back to back and facing the cardinal points, and made them shine wondrously with gems. Many more images were placed around the walls. On the walls were beautifully painted scenes from the 500 Jataka.[24]

Not content with so fine a temple Anandasura and his wife went on to describe their donation of a *pitaka-taik* (library), *thein* (ordination hall), *dhamma-yon* (preaching hall), *thera-kyaung* (chief monk's residence), various dormitories, an alms house and a rest house. In addition, both a well and tank were dug to the south-east outside the double enclosure. All this was enclosed by a magnificent double brick wall, the inner of which only remains today. Between the two walls, the lesser buildings, such as dormitories and alms houses, all built of wood, would have stood. The arrangement of the inner enclosure site was symmetrical, with the temple lodged in the north-west corner and the three other buildings filling each remaining quarter. The outer enclosure was less symmetrical, with a broader area to the south which still contains an active monastery supported by the local people.

Sited in the north-west corner is a brick *taik* [449], an

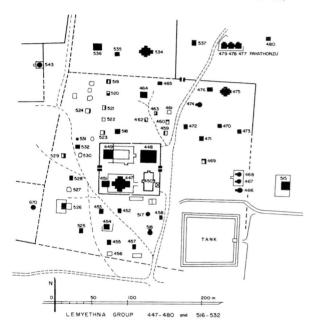

LEMYETHNA GROUP 447-480 and 516-532

impressive structure from which the *dhamma-yon* or preaching hall extended. Most likely this *taik* was the *pitaka-taik* mentioned in the inscription. The lines of this wooden structure's gable are still visible with fragments of the stucco spinodes that would have been aligned to match the gables of the roof tiers. From here the *thera* would have emerged to preach the *dhamma* beneath the shade of a tiered and finely-carved teak shelter. The post holes for the hall pillars are made of stone, as are the steps that lead up to its platform which is also edged with stone. Note the curved balustrades that recrudesce so flamboyantly in later Burmese art—another architectural feature that becomes common in the Late Period. The Pagan historian Minbu U Aung Kyaing, in his book on the architecture of Pagan, has recreated the wooden architecture of the original hall using his knowledge of Pagan woodcarving as depicted in contemporary paintings.[25]

Facing the *dhamma-yon* is the *thera-kyaung* [448] which has a central core with an ambulatory running around it. Within, there must have been two levels as the slots in the brick work indicate where the beams would have crossed from; some form of ladder must have connected the two levels. From epigraphy, it is known that donors paid particular attention to the lavish interior decoration of these residences, gilding and possibly lacquering them. Examples of this sumptuous interior work survive from later periods, when a learned cleric would likewise have been honoured as a living exponent of the *dhamma*.[26]

To the fore of the temple the remains of the *thein* [450] or *sima* may be seen, like with the *dhamma-yon* there are a series of post holes placed on a slightly elevated platform that is also edged with stone. This too would have been covered over with an elaborate carved wooden structure. Altogether, Anandasura and his wife presented the monks with a formidable donation.

No.134 above left: Pya-tha-da vault systems
No.135 below: Pya-tha-da from west
Fig.28: site plan of Minnanthu Lei-myet-hna complex (EFEO)
No.136: Lei-myet-hna enclosing wall, east

No.539 TAYOK-PYE
တရုပ်ပြေး

This large temple, situated a little to the west of the main Minnanthu groups, was built by Narathihapate (1256-87), otherwise known as Tayok-pye or 'Fleeing from the Chinese'. This unfortunate king's hasty withdrawal from Pagan, in the face of a Mongol-Chinese advance, may have been the cause of this temple's incompletion for there is no *sikhara*. Alternatively, the *sikhara* may have been lost in some past earthquake as with so many other temples at Pagan. Narathihapate had successfuly completed an earlier dedication, the Mingala-zeidi, in 1268, revealing little decline in either craftmanship or royal organisational capabilities.[27] Likewise, here at Minnanthu, this great temple, despite its absent superstructure, reveals no slackening of the craftsman's hand. Right down to stucco and glazing the work is polished and exquisite, and it would thus seem wrong to claim that this king, who boasted a daily meal of three hundred dishes of curry, administered a crumbling empire.

The *gu* is two-levelled, placed within a broad area, enclosed by a tall, fire-preventive wall and set above the now perished wooden peripheral buildings that sprang up like satellites about the *gu*, which was elevated upon a platform, setting it upon a higher level than the other less sacrosanct structures, as was conventional at Late Pagan. The exterior is richly articulated: with forepart pediments over the openings of the porches on each side and delineating pilasters. Indented into the plinth mouldings and those of the lower terraces are glazed rondos similar to those that enliven the Sula-mani with cool colour. The exterior stucco work here is also particularly fine, with the east pediment, over the front, in the best condition—here an array of figures, part decorative and part defensive, are presented in clear, yet minute detail.

What is of interest in the interior is the device of low, full-barrel vaults, running about the central block and opening out into lofty halls. In other large two-level temples where it was necessary to support a large mass above, the architects had spanned diaphragm arches across the ambulatory to relieve the thrust. Thus, at Tayok-pye, the diaphragm arch is taken to its next logical development and becomes the main ambulatory vault itself—an innovative feature that proved atmospherically effective.

On the upper level, where there was less mass above, there was no requirement for such a relieving vault. Here, there are a few broken stone images, decapitated for the souvenir trade. Some painted fragments are also evident.

No.477-9 PAYA-THON-ZU
ဘုရားသုံးဆူ

The 'Three Temples' of Minnanthu date, by their architectural style and iconographic content, from the second half of the 13th century, though there is no surviving epigraphy to validate this assumption. Only two of the three shrines have complete cycles of painted decorations which has lead some scholars to suppose that the temple's decoration was arrested by the advent of the Mongols in 1287. However, the Mongol incursion does not appear to have dramatically interrupted the life, artistic or otherwise, of Pagan.[28] This temple, together with its neighbour the Nanda-ma-nya, have been associated with the alleged Tantric practices of the Arranavasi sect, which has been said to have influenced the character of the mural paintings.[29]

The Paya-thon-zu, orientated to face the north, is carried on a low-lying and unadorned platform which extends out to the front in a similar way to a *mandapa*. There is a second and slighter step projecting from the plinth. The plinth also is unadorned and lacking in mouldings. In plan there are three units, each comprising of a shrine and hall and each linked by a connecting passage from shrine to shrine. On the exterior the effect of this is remarkably stimulating. This play of units, firmly articulated with a controlled undulation, is dramatic: visually impressive without stooping to flamboyance. Each of the units is in essence the standard, small scale, Late Period single-storey *gu* with the hall and shrine divided by a cross wall and arch. The base walls are framed by the crisp lines of plinth, pilaster and entablature. Double pediments frame the three fronts over the entrances. There are further entry openings on the east and west sides entering into the shrine and a small window opening on these sides for the halls, that may possibly be later additions. Above, the finely clustered horizontal lines of the terraces boldly rise to carry the warming shape of the finely indented, tapering *sikhara*. All this, when multiplied by three, with each unit connected by the counter-stroke of a low-lying depressed passage, creates an enriching impact on the beholder.

If the temple's overall design is unprecedented at Pagan, it is also a remarkably successful attempt at architectural innovation. A less unified version of this type of ground plan, in which individual architectural units are placed in a line to emulate the buddhas, is the Pe-nan-tha-gu group which dates to 1260 and must be approximately contemporary to the Paya-thon-zu, though the latter is a far more articulate work, suggesting that it followed from the earlier experiment.

Within, the interiors seem surprisingly dark for a Late Period temple, however, the closing of two of the entry openings, by the ever-prudent Archaeology Department with perforated bricking, has reduced the quantity of light admitted. In addition the central shrine through which one now enters is naturally

darker as it lacks the end openings of the other two. As has been said, each unit consists of a hall and shrine separated by a broad arch, a **T** plan. Only the west shrine now contains an image which has been restored. In the other two, the brick image pedestals remain, indicating by their broad forms that these too bore seated images.

The symbolism of the *lei-myet-hna* and *nga-myet-hna* have been discussed above, but what of the three image type? This is the first surviving *hpaya-thon-zu* monument in Burma. The 'three pagodas' became a common feature of the Burmese landscape in later times but at Pagan was rare, though more common at Salé. Modern Burmans, when asked to explain this symbolism, tell how it represents the three refuges, the three most fundamental aspects of a Burmese Buddhist's faith: the Buddha, the *dhamma* and the *sangha*. What is curious, though, is that so obvious a form, representing so crucial a formula, if this interpretation of the symbolism is to be followed, was not attempted at Pagan until the last decades of the dynasty, and that it was not until later centuries that it was to become a commonplace feature.

The contents of the mural paintings have aroused some scholarly interest and debate. Duroiselle in 1915 connected them with the Ari, a heterodox sect, made much of in the Post-Pagan literature of Burma, whom he believed to be associated with Northern Buddhism, as did Niharranjan Ray in his monograph *Sanskrit Buddhism in Burma*.[30] However, as Dr Than Tun in his elucidating doctoral thesis proves, the Ari were in fact misconstrued by the chroniclers of later times and

historians who used the chronicles as a prime source.[31] They were neither Mahayanists nor Tantrika. In fact this sect, the Arannavasi, represented an indigenous development in the Late Period. The Arannavasi were an expanded and institutionalised development of traditional *taw-kyaung* or jungle monasteries. This sect, as it became associated with the establishment, centred itself within easy reach of Pagan, at the village of Minnanthu under the leadership of the *thera* Mahakassapa. Anxious to increase the status of his sect, Mahakassapa set about expanding his estates through land purchases that were recorded in contemporary epigraphy. His sect's rule was more relaxed than his rival sect who looked to Ceylon for periodic purification through reordination. Indeed, Mahakassapa may be viewed as a Burmese phenomena opposed to foreign importation. There is no evidence that this sect was involved in Northern Buddhist practices, they were simply decayed Theravada monks interested in property, magical practices, politics and other worldly pursuits.

Though a connection between Mahakassapa and the Paya-thon-zu and its neighbour the Nanda-ma-nya cannot be ruled out—for the temple is sited at the centre of the Arannavasi locality—what may be ruled out is that the mural paintings were painted under the direction of Burmese Tantrika.[32] So far, it has not been possible to connect the supposedly Tantra elements with any text or similar scheme in Northern Buddhist countries. Indeed, as Niharranjan Ray noted, "I have not succeeded in tracing the *sadhanas*". This returns one to a similar problem presented in the case of two temples of the Early Period, the Abe-ya-dana and the Naga-yon. In these temples the art historian is faced with the dilemma of identifying the alleged Northern Buddhist elements and connecting them to a definitive text.[34] In addition, as has been underlined above, these works are subsidiary to the fundamental Theravada icon of the buddha Gotama, usually seated in the *bhumisparsamudra*, and the essential Theravada or Pali-based texts that were illuminated on the most prominant parts of a temple's wall space. The explanation reached for the Abe-ya-dana likewise applies to these controversial Minnanthu temples: such curious figures are simply decorative. Depicted in a florid, fanciful and highly delineated manner, these alleged Tantra figures fill awkward gaps in the wall space: in the sofitts, arch insets and at corners, always between or about the fundamental scenes depicting the main events in the life of the Buddha. In the Early Period, two currents of mural painting were discerned, the 'Narrative Style' and the 'Decorative Style', the former, tactile and didactic, was based on the art of Ajanta, and the latter, florid and ornamental, was derived from contemporary Northern Buddhist cultures. Here, at the end of the dynasty, the 'Decorative Style' would seem to be very much in the ascendant. However, the hypothesis that this was the work of immigrant artists, possibly taking refuge at Pagan from strife-ridden Northern India, should not be excluded for there are many similarities between them and contemporary Nepali manuscript illuminations.[35]

The paintings themselves, like at the Pe-na-tha group, revel in the architectonic and *trompe l'oeil*

effect. Only the east *gu* has a complete scheme, the central *gu* ones, though half finished, are in a better state of preservation, for this unit is far darker and thus the paintings less subject to fading. As a result of this, the colouring is much richer than in the east *gu*, with reds and dark blues dominant whilst next door the colouring is far fainter.

In the east hall, between the dominant painted architecture, *bodhisattva* and other exotica, certain popular texts were portrayed, though, quite significantly, subjugated to the decorative scheme. A brief selection from the *bodawin*, or 'Life', with panels set amidst the minutely painted Jataka, and on the sides of the east recess, included the following scenes: the 'Nalagiri Elephant', the 'Deer park at Sarnath', 'Sujata's Offering', the 'Descent' and the 'Nativity'. Beneath the lozenge filled cornice runs the *Buddhavamsa* or '28 buddhas'. The vault paintings are now nearly all lost; these would, like in the shrine, have been filled with minute panels each containing a buddha and set against a naturalistic background.

There are fewer narrative or textually-based paintings in the shrine, though the *Buddhavamsa* continues round beneath the cornice and like at the Nanda-ma-nya, the *Buddhavamsa* has been expanded to include the tonsure scene for each past buddha.[36] There are also a great proliferation of miniature buddhas in *dharmacakramudra* set in small panels on the vaults and squeezed between the decorative work. Indeed, the walls seem to have been entirely given over to architectural, zoological and supernatural fantasising—the divine world of the *deva*.

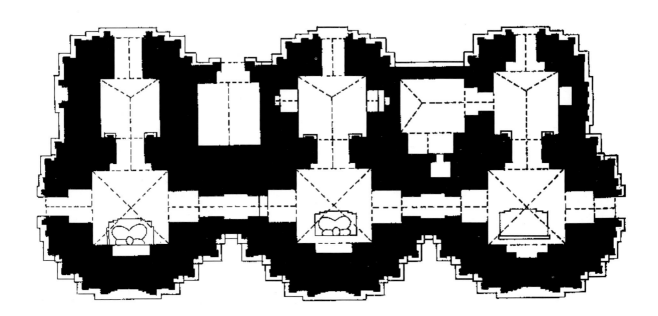

Fig.29 Paya-thon-zu ground plan (EFEO)
No.139: kinnaya painted on Paya-thon-zu
shrine wall

In the incomplete central shrine there seems to have been a greater degree of textually-derived painting and there are larger panels of the Buddha standing in various *mudra*. In the east shrine, the miniature and multiple buddhas were seated and in *dharmacakramudra,* whereas here the dominant *mudra* is the *bhumisparsa* one. At the centre of the vault is a rosette-like motif symbolising the lotus pool of creation. Fortunately these paintings have not been 'touched up' like those in the east *gu*. The central *gu* hall has no complete paintings though there are some highly interesting preparatory sketches marked out by the artists where the pigments were never added. These offer some insight into the Pagan painter's technique.

The westernmost unit remains undecorated; what is of interest, though, are the red ochre sketchings on the walls. These, noted by Braxton Sinclair in 1920, feature contemporary wooden structures, all of which have now perished.[37] This 'grafitti' offers a vision of how Pagan, originally a city of timber, must once have appeared. The *pyatthat* depicted are extravagantly carved with tall and sinuous spinodes, wave-like and rising on each tier. If Pagan monuments might seem controlled in their ornamentation, on their timber counterparts the carver's virtuosity was unleashed. The Pagan plain's suface must have once been densely filled with these elaborate structures, punctuated at intervals with the rising brick mass of a temple or stupa. All this, wood or brick, was polychromed and gilded with banners flowing and bells ringing: an emblazoned tableau of joyful colour and sound.

No.482 THAMBULA

သ၊ဗူ၊လ

The Thambula temple is so named after the queen of Uzana (1249-56) who dedicated this work in 1255, as told in the inscription found in the temple's hall. Though the queen and her temple are nowadays called Thambula, in old Burmese the name would have been Thonlula from the Pali Trilokcandadevi or 'Moon of Three Worlds'.[38]

Set in a spacious enclosure, with a tall though in places tumbled wall which has arched gateways at the cardinal points, the Thambula is orientated towards the east. Like most temples from the Late Period, whether large or small, the plinth rests on a broad, raised platform, in this case of brick. Though technically a large temple, the Thambula's architects rejected the option of an upper-level shrine, whilst the terraces are accessible from the interior by a flight of steps on the north-east corner of the ambulatory. The exterior profile seems conventional enough, with the usual arrangement of foreparts about the base over the arched openings, granting access to the shrine transepts from each side. Likewise on the superstructure there is the customary bold arrangement of crenellated terraces, corner obelisks, medial steps topped by a *sikhara* diadem. What needs to be emphasised with this work is that this is essentially a small temple expanded to a greater scale, extending to the onlooker a sensation of stately dignity, without taking the upper storey option.

On the hall front pediments the original stucco remains well preserved. Inside, the hall's north and south wall spaces are broken by further porched openings. The paintings here, though mainly in faded condition or uncompleted, remain vividly graphic. On either side of the shrine arch are *dvarapala* figures seated in *lalitasana*, their outlines clear though never coloured in, perhaps on account of the scarcity of colouring pigments at Pagan. About these *bodhisattva* ascend *deva* in *namakkaramudra*. On the other walls of the hall are broad scenes depicting the buddhas seated under their various pavilions and *bodhi* trees. On the east wall is a scene of the Buddha surrounded by fire.

Of the four shrines themselves, the eastern colossal buddha has a painted *bodhi* tree about it—the enlightenment. The south image has a painted architectural background with a *sikhara* above and at the Buddha's sides both *kinnaya* and *bodhisattva*. On the west is the attack and rout of the demonic forces of Mara. On the north there is a similar painted architectural arrangement to that found on the south. These scenes are all concerned with the great and heroic moments of the Gotama buddha's enlightenment and in each the buddhas are seated in *bhumisparsamudra*. Are these really the four buddhas of this *kalpa* or are they not all one, Gotama? At Mye-bon-tha, the *lei-myet-hna*, a cosmic scheme that theoretically symbolised the last four buddhas, was adapted to portray an encapsulated programme of scenes from the life of the buddha Gotama. Here too, it would seem that the iconographer's intention was less the illustration of the supreme teachers of the *bhadrakalpa* than the glorification of the buddha Gotama at his own supreme moment.

In the transepts about the south, west and north sides of the shrine are further painted scenes. The events selected for portrayal are the customary ones derived from the eight scenes portrayed on votive tablets from the earliest times at Pagan. The eight scenes lent themselves well, whether in the medium of sculpture or painting, to the architecture of a Late Pagan temple, which usually had eight available wall spaces about the central square block, either in the ambulatory or in the transepts. At the Thambula, the decision was to put the eight scenes on the walls of each transept whilst the theme of the 28 buddhas, or *Buddhavamsa*, was depicted in the ambulatory.

Paintings about the shrine:
South transept:

East	boat race
West	unclear

West transept:

South	*dharmacakramudra*, the Deer Park at Sarnath
North	standing Buddha and further scene of the Buddha in *dharmacakramudra*

North transept:

West	Descent from Tavatimsa.
East Upper	*parinibbana.*
East Lower	*dharmacakramudra*

Though eight scenes were to be depicted, the choice of which scenes and their placement on the wall surfaces appears to have often been a random matter. The style of these narrative scenes differs from that of the *dvarapala* and *deva* in the hall, these are less ornate and detailed, treated in planes of a single tone, they are more expansive, and the effect more tactile. This dichotomy in painting style has already been noted in the preceding descriptions of certain of the temples dating from the Early Period, and though generally less exaggerated in the Late Period than in the Early Period, when the 'Narrative' and 'Decorative' styles dramatically contrasted each other, there remains this variance in style conditioned by the nature of the subject matter.

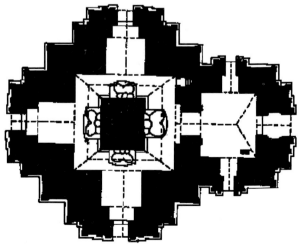

No.139 upper left: dvarapala figure painted at entrance to Thambula shrine
No.140 middle left: Thambula temple from east
Fig.30: Thambula ground plan (EFE0)

XXVII, previous: bodhisattva figure in the Paya-thon-zu east shrine
XXVIII, left: Pe-nan-tha-gu with Gadaw-palin in the background
XXIX, right: Paya-thon-zu from north

*XXX, previous: the plain from Minnanthu
with the Tayok-pye temple in foreground
XXXI, above: Pya-tha-da
XXXII, left: nativity scene from the
Nanda-ma-nya
XXXIII, opposite: bodhisattva with twin sakti
in the Paya-thon-zu east shrine
XXXIV, next: Ywa-haung-gyi temple*

No.141: Nanda-ma-nya from east

No.577 NANDA-MA-NYA

နန္ဒမည်ာ

The Nanda-ma-nya's present name is an evolved form of *anantapannya* or 'Endless Wisdom'.[39] Built on the order of King Kyazwa (1235-49), there is an inscription relating to the dedication that dates it to 1248. However, this inscription is vague and the chronology it mentions mistaken for it mentions Shin Arahan as still being alive. Possibly this inscription was added at a later date.[40]

The temple's exterior form is a combination of a symmetrical and stellately planned *gu* with a stupa form for the superstructure in place of the more common tapering, square-based *sikhara*. This combination was not uncommon in the Late Period when applied to single-level shrines that were lesser in size, though here at the Nanda-ma-nya the stupa rests on three horizontal terraces, whereas on stupa No.1790 there are no terraces, the difference being that here the *anda* is concave whilst No.1790, being a Ceylonese type, is convex.[41] The temple is set well within a broad, squarely-planned and unadorned platform. On the exterior, there are, in addition to the east porch opening, two small window openings leading through the wall to the apse bays, or transepts, on the north and south sides. Within, the now damaged image fills the west apse whilst the north and south ones are open and, of course, the east one acts as entrance and porch.

The Nanda-ma-nya is notable for its mural paintings, described by Duroiselle in 1916 as being "...of a character so vulgarly erotic and revolting, that they can neither be reproduced nor described".[42] This description does perhaps raise the licentious visitor's expectations, but on examination there is little that is overtly erotic to be viewed. The scenes that offended Duroiselle were most likely those in the south transept, filling a predella-like panel beneath large scenes of buddhas seated in their pavilions, that depict women in various stages of undress. This is a portrayal of the 'Temptation by the Daughters of Mara', the moment when the Buddha was tempted before defeating Mara and his army and becoming enlightened, an orthodox enough theme to be portrayed in a Theravada temple. Also on the Mara theme, the 'Attack and Defeat' is in its usual place about the Buddha, as vibrant and vigorous as ever and stylistically close to the one about the main Buddha in the Wetkyi-in Kubyauk-gyi. In fact, contrary to Duroiselle and others, iconographically the only possible Tantric elements are the *tribhanga bodhisattva* that flank the window recesses in the north and south transepts, and these, as has been thoroughly discussed earlier in this work, had long been integrated into the Theravada temple decorative scheme as *dvarapala*, rather than as objects of people's devotions. The principal text depicted in this temple is the *Buddhavamsa*, which is now more fully treated than at Wetkyi-in, for here each buddha's 'Tonsure' is included, running beneath the cornice of the central domidal vault. In addition to the 28 buddhas themselves, running beneath the cornice on the three open arms of this Greek Cross plan temple, larger panels fill the wall space with individual buddhas seated, touching the earth beneath their respective pavilions and trees. These are of interest for in each the architectural design varies, in some the buddha is crowned by a *sikhara* and in others a stupa. Also of interest are the water life panels beneath the window recesses, perhaps unique for Pagan, these animated and highly graphic seascapes cannot help but charm with their marine life and sea monsters. Also included amongst this curious mêlée of subjects for the Nanda-ma-nya paintings are selected scenes from the *bodawin* .

In style and content, the paintings are close to the ones in the Paya-thon-zu and probably the work of the same hand, though the pigments used for the colouring here tend towards greens and yellows rather than reds and blues of the Paya-thon-zu.[43] As with the Paya-thon-zu, certain decorative elements that are derived from the lands of Northern Buddhism, are subsidiary to the fundamental Theravada icons and scenes depicted. These paintings are surely of interest for their beauty and their capability to charm the onlooker through playful line and humorous expression and not through some obscure esoteric connection.

No.283 TAW-YA-KYAUNG

တောရကျောင်း

The aptly-named Taw-ya-kyaung or 'Wilderness Monastery' is possibly the last occupied original Pagan period monastery—by an incumbent seemingly as ancient as his shelter. Due north-east from Minnanthu, best reached across the fields from the Nanda-ma-nya, this *kyaung* is of interest for its pavilion type of superstructure. Other examples of this type may be found in the Shwe-zigon area and there is one temple in which a similar upper-level shrine-pavilion has been included.[44] Essentially this is the wooden *pyat-that* seen in the murals of so many temples, often sheltering the Buddha, or buddhas, transferred to the medium of wood. This seems a natural enough application, for monasteries were usually built of wood and from the east wall of this square *taik* would have extended a timber hall. Curiously in this *taik,* there is no access stair leading to the upper level: either the brick *pyatthat* superstructure was entirely ornamental, or there was once a wooden flight of steps going up from the exterior.

No.659 WINIDO

ဝိနည်းမိုရ်

The Winido group of temples are rarely visited by either locals or tourists, yet approached from Minnanthu or from Nyaung-U this group is not an inaccessible one and certain of its monuments contain a number of features of some interest.

No. 659 is outwardly a typical middle-sized, late temple on a single level and is most notable for the mural paintings in the interior. The hall and shrine are separate units with an arch separating them. The inscription in the hall dates this temple to B.E. 605/ 1243 A.D. and records the donors as Min Mainma, sister of the *taga-gyi* or 'great donor', and Thanmyin Thamantakuntham, an uncle of King Uzana.

The hall paintings are in the style of the Late Period: decorative in tendency, florid and sinuous, delicate whilst at the same time quite extravagant. In both style and content, they are not dissimilar to other paintings in the Minnanthu area as at Paya-thon-zu or Thambula:

East—about the door is Brahma and Indra, above them reaching up about the arch of the door are heavenly beings, *deva* and *devi*, four on each side of the door. At the apex of the arch is seated the Buddha in the *dharmacakramudra*.
North/South—the 550 Jataka, each scene in its own panel, identifiable by a gloss and number in Old Burmese.
West—about the shrine arch are paintings of *bodhisattva* in a *dvarapala* role, set amidst the deepest of painted foliage with *deva* set in this floral background, climbing up and about the arch.

Vault—on the western part are the *buddhapada* or Buddha's footprints and on the eastern part, the lotus pool of creation.

In the shrine, like at No.357, the image is freestanding to the centre of the square floor space.[45] The seated, earth-touching Buddha is backed by a reredos supported by original timber posts. There are no entrances into the shrine from the exterior though window openings were placed high on the exterior walls. This temple was intended as the preserve of the painter and the architects made as much wall surface available as possible for the painter's work.

Shrine Paintings:
Inside of outer arch—panels containing three-headed figures in attitudes of worship pointing into the shrine.
Inside of inner arch—larger scenes (unidentified).
West wall about the transept arch—Attack and Defeat of Mara.
North and south walls—the *bodawin*, in panelled scenes.
North and south transepts—the wall spaces of these units, about the meditation niches, are filled with paintings not dissimilar to those at Paya-thon-zu—a combination of architectural and naturalistic fantasia, with heavenly beings in worship.
West transept—here, there are two larger panels superimposed upon a background of smaller ones. Above the panel section, just beneath the obival cornice, is an ornithological frieze. The smaller panels depict buddhas under their trees seated in a pavilion. There are more than 28 of these, so it is possible that the textual source is not the *Buddhavamsa*. The larger panels, expanded versions of the small panels surrounded by framed rectangles of devotees, are likewise hard to identify.

No. 653 WINIDO
ဝိနည်းဓိုရ်

Situated to the north of No.659, this temple stands in the western part of the main cluster of Winido temples. With a stupa superstructure, it is raised on a square plan base. There are four openings, each facing one of the buddhas set about the central block of the *lei-myet-hna*. There is thus a Greek Cross type of plan arranged about a central core from which the vault springs out, with the four porches here reduced to broad yet shallow niches. Here too, there are mural paintings, though less polished in their execution than in the nearby Winido No.659. There are, though, some expansively treated paintings of the Buddha's terrestrial and celestial supporters. On the east and south porch arch are painted *bodhisattva*, whilst on the west and north porch walls are painted Mogallana and Sariputta.

No.142 upper left: Taw-ya-kyaung from south-east
No.143 upper right: Winido 659 from east
No.144 middle left: Winido group including monument 653 with stupa superstructure and 657 behind it
No.145 lower right: interior of shrine in Winido 653
No.1 46lower left: votive plaque in Winido 657

No.657 WINIDO

ဝိနည်းမိုရ်

Facing No.653, this temple is orientated with its single entrance opening facing towards the west, that is towards No.653. The inscription here dates this temple to B.E. 586/1224 A.D. and records the donation of land and slaves to the monastery of *thakhin* Winaya by the minister Athinkhayar. The other inscription here, dated to B.E. 597/1235 A.D., has been brought here from the Aleya-gu (No.632). From the west porch, one passes into a square planned shrine and there are transepts to each of the other cardinal points with the main image placed against the east wall. This temple is in a state of serious disrepair: the plaster base for the paintings is cracking and dropping off in great lumps, whilst the temple superstructure, in this case a stupa form, has been dislocated from its base and rests dangerously at an unnatural angle. About the inside walls are sixteen shallow arched niches; in five of these survive large (about 1m in height) terracotta plaques containing multiple buddha images, each in *bhumisparsamudra*. Though such estampages in clay were known at Pagan from the earliest of times, there are no other surviving treatments of this theme on so large a scale. There is one other of these plaques safely deposited in the Pagan Museum.[46]

No. 610 SA-THIN-GU

စာသင်္ဂူ

On the high and somewhat desolate ground between Nyaung-U and Minnanthu, to the east of the Shwe *chaung*, that according to Luce was called the Sarapuiy in Old Burmese, is sited this highly irregular structure. Seen at first from a distance, the Sa-thin-gu appears to be an *ok-kyaung*, with a brick pavilion-*pyatthat* type of superstructure placed well to the centre of the upper level, with no receding terraces. The base, from the exterior, adds to the illusion that this is a monastic structure with its plain and featureless surfaces of brick. However, this is, in fact, a *gu*, even if an eccentric one in its design. There are two shrine areas, one to the east and one to the west, with ambulatory passages connecting them running between the base wall and the central block. The west shrine would appear to be the more significant of the two, for here the image is receded into the core, whilst on the east, it is placed against the central block. The hall area to the fore of the west shrine is aisled with cloister arches and there are a number of empty niches set into the base wall. This wall on the north side has collapsed in places, though conservation work has halted further decline. Steps pass up on this side to the upper level which, as has been noted, lacks the customary arrangement of terraces. The upper shrine,

in form more like a brick pavilion, has an octagonal band above and therefore most likely carried a stupa finial which would certainly have added further to the eccentric appearance of this monument.

No.147 THET-KYA-MUNI

သကျမုနိ

Orientated toward the west, facing in towards the pleasantly shaded monastery grove, this small and late work contains a delicately rendered series of paintings surviving to this day in decipherable condition. The temple itself, despite its small size, presents a richly modulated piece of architecture when viewed from the exterior. Foreparts, terraces, *sikhara*, all work together to create an effect of sumptuous dignity enhanced by the beauty of the Thet-kya-muni's setting.

There are two inscriptions here recording the donations of slaves in B.E. 600 /1238 A.D. by Ngapaikthin, and his wife and in B.E. 625 /1263 A.D. by Apwar ('grandmother').

The paintings' subjects and layout follow the conventions that had been established at Pagan by the beginning of the 12th century. Running around the hall beneath the cornice are the 28 buddhas under their respective trees and pavilions. Beneath these is a further series of 20 larger Buddha panels, each figure surrounded by a naturalist background, whilst the cornice, painted onto the soffits, is composed of obival motifs. Between the north and south walls are divided the 550 Jataka panels, here, despite the minuteness of size, clear and easily followed. About the west arch of the entrance are a further 16 panels of the buddhas and inside them 6 larger scenes. There are inscriptions in the medial recesses of the hall. In the shrine fragments of the original wooden reredos remain visible. The shrine paintings are in less good condition though; it would appear that scenes from the life of the Buddha have been the choice once again here.

No.148 ZU-LAIN

ဇူလှိုင်

Set in parallel to the north of the Thet-kya-muni, one finds a Pagan temple in miniature. Indeed, with its low entrances (about 1m high) it would seem to be a 'wendy house' of a *gu* temple. This does not, though, imply that No.119 is any less complete as a dedication, for all the standard elements are here included with no slackening in the quality of their execution. Note the exquisite stucco on the exterior and full set of Jataka within: nothing has been omitted.

No.151 KON-DAW-GYI
ကုန်းတော်ကြီး

As the temple's name implies, the Kon-daw-gyi, or 'great royal mound', is sited on the steep, sloped hillock that overlooks the Thet-kya-muni. Orientated towards the east, and enclosed by a brick wall, this small temple is of interest because, though there is a stupa superstructure, there is also a hall extension. Stupa superstructures became a popular alternative to the *sikhara* in temple dedications in the Late Period (though this form was known in the Early Period) and were to become the norm in the Ava and Konbaung Periods.[47] At Pagan they were usually carried on a square base with a Greek Cross, that is, a completely symmetrical ground plan. However, exceptions may be found, for example East Zanthi (1367 A.D.) has a slight outwards extension to its eastern transept. But here, at the Kon-daw-gyi, which most likely dates from within our period, the full post-Pagan temple style is manifest. There is no porch projection from the shrine, the floor surfaces are paved in stone and there are later wooden gates between hall and shrine. There are paintings: Jatakas in the hall, on the shrine walls rondos are occupied by animals set against a naturalist background, on the vaults are small panels containing images of the Buddha (or buddhas). The main image has been restored, though fragments of original woodwork on the throne are visible.

No.147 above right: Thet-kya-muni
No.148 above: Zu-lain
No.149 right: Kon-daw-gyi

GLOSSARY

abhayamudra—fearless.

Abhidhamma—see 'Tipitaka'.

amalaka—lotus leaf clasp from which the finial rises on a monument.

anda—literally an egg, either the concave or convex part of a stupa.

Anantasayin—image of Vishnu reclining upon the serpent Sesha.

andagu—steatite or soapstone.

arhat—a monk who has attained *nibbana* [*q.v.*].

Arimaddanapura—'City of the Enemy Crusher', classical name of Pagan.

Arimetteyya—the future buddha: Mettaya or Maitreya [*q.v.*].

Arannavasi—a sect, originally of hermit monks residing in the jungle who rose to some degree of prominance during the Late Period.

asana—the sitting posture of a buddha, *bodhisattva* [*q.v.*] or deity.

athwat—Old Burmese name for the *chattrâvali* [*q.v.*].

atthatthana—the 'eight scenes' depicting the main events of the Buddha's life that incorporates the 'seven sites', each at which the Buddha spent one week in the first seven weeks after his enlightenment, the eighth scene portrays the *parinibbana* [*q.v.*]. These events are usually portrayed on votive tablets.

bhadrakalpa—the present of a series of time units (*kalpa*) [*q.v.*].

bhakti—'devotion'.

bhikkhu—a member of the *sangha* [*q.v.*].

bhumisparsamudra—gesture of touching the earth at the moment when the Buddha defeated Mara and attained the state of *nibbana* [*q.v.*].

bilu—an ogre; a Burmese version of the *dvarapala* [*q.v.*].

bodawin—the life story of the Buddha.

bodhisattva—may refer to Gotama in his past lives and up to the moment of enlightenment (*bodhi*) [*q.v.*] in the Theravada sense of the word, or it may refer to a being (*sattva*) who has renounced Buddhahood so as to help mankind towards salvation.

buddha, The Buddha—literally the 'enlightened one'; 'the Buddha' usually refers to Gotama, the Sakyamuni ('Light of the Sakya'), the third 'teaching Buddha' of the *bhadrakalpa* [*q.v.*], a historic figure who lived and taught in North India in the 5th century B.C. In Burma 28 teaching buddhas are recognised, of which Gotama is the second last, with Mettaya yet to come.

buddhapada—Gotama buddha's footprints.

byauk—'variegated', a term used to describe a temple with a colourfully painted interior.

cakka—the sacred wheel.

cakkavatti—literally a 'turner of the wheel', a world emperor who turns the wheel of temporal law.

caitya—a stupa form; in Burmese *zedi*.

chattrâvali—the seven-tiered finial section of a stupa that rises from either the *harmika* [*q.v.*], or, where there is no *harmika*, the *anda* [*q.v.*]..

chaung—a stream.

chinthe—a leogryph figure, usually in a guardian role placed about the base or terraces of a monument.

deva—a Hindu-derived god; in post-Pagan times such celestial figures become called *nat* [*q.v.*].

deva—female version of the above.

dhamma—the ideal truth, being the teaching of the Buddha, literally 'the Doctrine'.

dhamma-yon—a hall in which the *dhamma* [*q.v.*] is preached, or, in Pali, *dhammasala*.

dharmacakramudra—'the Turning of the Wheel of the Law', expressed by the clasping of the Buddha's hands together against his chest in a gesture that indicates a turning motion.

dhammaraja—'king of the *dhamma*' [*q.v.*], a contemporary conception of kingship in which a king protects and propogates the *sasana*.

dhyanamudra—the gesture and posture of meditation in which the Buddha sits in *vajrasana* [*q.v.*] with his hands folded in his lap.

Dhyani-buddha—or Jina, the five cosmic Buddhas of the Mahayana.

dvarapala—guardian deity, usually placed at the entrances to a temple or its enclosure.

gandhakuti—'perfumed chamber', a shrine, usually placed at points about a stupa, named so on account of the scents offered to the image.

Gavampati—an early follower of the Buddha, his image may have combined with Ganesa's; alternatively, the 'Fat Monk' images found throughout Burma may depict this figure who is referred to in the contemporary epigraphy.

Garuda—the 'king of the birds'; the *vahana* of Vishnu.

gu—literally a cave, derived from the Pali *guha*, at Pagan it becomes the generic term for a temple that may be entered and has an interior.

hamsa—a mythological duck of Indian origins.

harmika—the box-like component that acted as a reliquary casket and was placed between the *anda* and the *chattravali* [*q.v.*].

hpaya—'Lord', derived from the Pali *purha*, it may be applied to any part of the *triratana* [*q.v.*], and is the generic term for most Buddhist edifices; it was also applied to kings who were *hpaya-lon* or *bodhisattva* [*q.v.*], and nowadays may be used as a mark of respect when adressing not only members of the *sangha* [*q.v.*], but also laymen of a venerable age.

hpaya kywan—'pagoda slave', the lowest cast at Pagan, the members of which were hereditarily bonded to an endowment.

hpaya-nga-zu—'Five Sacred Lords', a portrayal of the five buddhas of this *bhadrakalpa* [*q.v.*].

hpaya-thon-zu—'Three Sacred Lords', a triad of three buddhas, usually Gotama in different mudra. In the Late Period this theme became manifest in architecture.

hpon—'charismatic glory', the essential quality of a leader.

hsaya-gyi—'great master'.

hti—sacred parasol fixed onto the upper portion of a finial.

Jambupati—an image of the buddha Gotama, crowned and regaled as a king, though still wearing the monk's robe and touching the earth. Though found at Pagan, these images became popular in later periods. The term Jambupati is not commonly used in Burma.

jatamukuta—the crown-like headress worn by *bodhisattva* [*q.v.*] and Hindu deities; this term may also refer to the loop-like ornaments that connect *kirtimukha* [*q.v.*] on stucco or painted friezes.

Jataka—the birth stories of the Buddha; normally numbering 547, though an additional 3 were added in Burma for reasons of symmetry in mural painting and sculpture.

Jayabhumi—'Land of Victory', the uncorrupted name for the Shwezigon.

kappiya—a layman who voluntarily chose to act as a monk's servant so as to earn merit.

kala-kyaung—'Indian Monastery', brick buildings either built by Indian immigrant craftsmen or housing Indian *bhikkhu* [*q.v.*].

kalasa—the sacred pot from which temple plinths at Pagan often take their profile; *kalasa* also appear in their pot form as obelisks on temple terraces and more rarely in relief as part of a temple's exterior ornament.

kalpa—a unit of time during which a number of teaching Buddhas may manifest themselves; such units are vast in length.

kamma—moral deeds that affect the course of one's present and future lives.

kharuin—'the hub', the political and administrative centre of an empire in Old Burma.

kinnaya—a bird man; the lower body being in the form of a bird, the upper body being human, with ornitho-human facial features. Derived from Pali *kinnara*.

kirtimukha—a motif usually found, at Pagan, on friezes placed between the *jatamukuta* [*q.v.*].

kyaung—monastery or school.

kyaung-taik—monastery house, usually of brick.

lalitasana—sitting posture of *bodhisattva* [*q.v.*], with one leg drawn up whilst the other dangles beneath, resting on a lotus pedestal.

lei-myet-hna—'four face', a monument built on a square ground plan.

lokottara—the supreme state of Buddhahood, a divine aloofness that was embodied in the Mahayana art of the Pala dynasty.

Mahanipata—the last ten of the Jatakas [*q.v.*].

Mahayana—'the Great Vehicle', in which b*odhisattva* [*q.v.*] assist the devotee towards salvation.

Mahavamsa—the main chronicle of Ceylon that records the history of Buddhism and the Ceylonese, not only does it refer to Pagan, but as a text was narrated on temple walls.

makara—sea monster, a common pictorial motif.

mandapa—the plinth that projects from the porch temple (there is only one *mandapa* proper at Pagan: the Nat-hlaung-kyaung).

Mettaya—the fifth and last buddha of this *bhadrakalpa* [*q.v.*] and the twenty eighth buddha of all times.

man-o-thi-ha—a double-bodied lion with the single upper body of a human.

Mi-lo-fo—Chinese version of Mettaya.

Mogallana—leading disciple of the Buddha together with Sariputta [*q.v.*].

Mucalinda—the *naga* [*q.v.*] king who protected the Buddha whilst in meditation from a storm. A scene visually portrayed from the *bodawin* [*q.v.*].

mudra—a hand gesture that indicates the activity of a buddha. In the case of Gotama it illustrates a historic moment in his life.

nga-myet-hna—'five faces': a temple built on a pentagonal plan.

naga—a serpent god.

nat—a Burmese spirit or god. In later times '37 Lords' evolved into a national pantheon; there is no evidence of the 37 Lords being followed during the Pagan Dynasty, though certain of these 'lords' were borrowed from Hindu deities known at Pagan.

nibbana—'extinction', the ultimate goal of Theravada Buddhists when the cycle of their rebirths will cease.

padmasana—the posture of a figure seated upon a lotus throne, pedestal or cushion.

pagoda—in Burma this Western term has evolved to describe a stupa or *zedi* in contrast to a temple or *gu* [*q.v.*].

Pali—the sacred language of Theravada Buddhism, originally an early Indian dialect of the Prakrit area in which the teachings of Gotama were spread first orally and then as a literature.

parinibbana—the final *nibbana* [*q.v.*], or decease of a buddha that in the case of the Buddha Gotama occured at Kusinagara. It is iconographically portrayed with the figure in a recumbent position and at Pagan generally with head pointed in a northerly direction.

pitaka—literally 'basket', of which there are three (*tipitaka*) [*q.v.*], each of the baskets containing a portion of the scriptures.

pitaka-taik—scripture house.

paritta—'protection'; a section from the scriptures that is recited at auspicious moments by assembled members of the *sangha* [*q.v.*], particularly the dedication of sacred structures.

pradaksina—the ritual circumambulation about a shrine or stupa by the devotee.

pralambanasana—the posture that has erroneously been described as sitting in 'the European manner', with legs hanging free before and beneath the figure.

sakti—the female partner of a *bodhisattva* [*q.v.*] or *deva* [*q.v.*].

sangha—'community': the Buddhist order of monks.

sangharaja—'king of the *sangha*' [*q.v.*], a contemporary conception of a king's role, in which using his temporal power he supports the *sangha*; alternatively, in later times, this term may refer to the primate of the *sangha*.

Sariputta—a leading disciple of the Buddha, usually associated with Mogallana [*q.v.*].

Sarvastivada—an early Buddhist school that was followed alongside the Theravada in pre-Pagan Burma.

sasana—'the religion', the Buddhist movement as a whole.

sima—ordination hall; in Burmese *thein* [*q.v.*].

stupa—the primary Buddhist monument, originally a tumulus or cairn and then the funeral monument of a *cakkavatti* [*q.v.*], the stupa may be seen in addition to being a giant reliquary as a cosmic symbol of buddhahood. In Burma the European term 'pagoda' describes this type of monument, in Burmese *zeidi* is more commonly used.

Surya—the sun god.

sutta—a dicourse given by the Buddha, collected together they form the first basket of the *tipikaka* [*q.v.*].

tabena—a sealed box containing a relic or other enshrined objects within the core of a monument.

taik—a building.

Tambadipa—'Land of Copper', an early name for Pagan.

Tantra—a religious discourse; this term is often applied as 'Tantric Buddhism', to describe the Vajrayana [*q.v.*].

Tattadesa—'parched land', Old Mon name for Pagan.

thera—a senior member of the *sangha* [*q.v.*].

Theravada—an early Buddhist school that spread to Sri Lanka in the 3rd Century B.C. where the scriptures were written down in Pali. From Sri Lanka this school spread to South East Asia.

thein—Burmese for a *sima* [*q.v.*] or ordination hall.

torana—an ornamented gateway to shrines, for Pagan architecture this term may be applied to the arrangement of pilasters and pediments that frame an arched opening to a monument's enclosure or interior.

tribhanga—'triply bent', the stance of *bodhisattva* [*q.v.*] or *deva* [*q.v.*] with neck, waist and one knee relaxed.

tipitaka—'Three Baskets', the collected Pali canon divided into three parts: the *sutta-pitaka* or discourses of the Buddha, the *inaya-pitaka* or rules of discipline for members of the *sangha* [*q.v.*], and the *abhidhammapitaka* or analysis of the *dhamma* [*q.v.*].

triratana—'Three Gems': buddha, *dhamma* [*q.v.*], *sangha* [*q.v.*].

usnisha—'wisdom bump', the cranial projection on a buddha's head that is the mark of a buddha.

vahana—'vehicle', a beast, mythical or real, upon which a *bodhisattva* [*q.v.*] or *deva* [*q.v.*] rides.

vajra—originally the thunderbolt of Indra, though also the attribute of other deities and *sattva*.

vajrasana—'adamantine seat of victory', the enlightenment, the Buddha sits cross-legged with soles of both the feet turned upwards.

Vajrayana—'the Way of the Vajra', often called Tantric Buddhism, practised in the Himalayas and extending to the Far East. In essence esoteric, the Vajrayana incorporates what may be known as 'white magic'.

varadamudra—gesture of giving, with hands outstretched.

vihara—monastery.

virasana—'heroic posture', one leg placed across the other with the sole of the right foot placed upwards while resting on the left leg folded beneath.

vitarkamudra—the gesture of elucidation, one or two hands are raised with the palm facing outwards.

zeidi—the Burmese term for a stupa [*q.v.*].

NOTES

INTRODUCTION

1. As stated by Pierre Pichard in *Pagan Newsletter*, No.1, 1982.
2. Ba Shin, *Lokhateikpan*.
3. Luce, "A century of progress in Burmese art and archaeology." pp.79-94.
4. Luce, *O.B.E.P.*, I, Preface, p.vii.
5. Tinker, "The place of Gordon Luce in research and education in Burma during the last decades of British rule." pp.174-90.
6. Marco Polo, *The travels*. Trans. R. Latham, pp.188-9.
7. *ibid.*, p.188.
8. Symes, *An account of an embassy to the kingdom of Ava...*
9. *ibid.*, p.265.
10. *ibid.*, p.383; for detail on this Konbaung restoration, see Than Tun, "Pagan restoration." pp.53-4.
11. Quoted in Henry Yule, *Mission to the court of Ava in 1855*, p.33.
12. Crawfurd, *Journal of an embassy...*, p.129.
13. *ibid.*, p.151.
14. Yule, *op.cit.* p.32.
15. *ibid.*; see Tinker's introduction to the 1968 reprint, p.xiv.
16. *ibid.*, p.33.
17. Luce, "A century of progress..." p.84.
18. Forchammer, *Pagan I. The Kyaukku Temple*. 1891. Reprinted 1919.
19. Luce, *op.cit.*, p.85.
20. The von Nöetling collection is catalogued by Grunwedel, *1. Glasuren on Pagan...*1897.
21. Whitbread, "Medieval Burmese wall paintings..." pp.89-92.
22. Bo Kay, ပုဂံသုတေသနလန်းညွှန်.
23. Whitbread, *op.cit.*, p.21.
24. Luce, op.cit., p.85.
25. Whitbread, *op.cit.*, p.21.
26. Duroiselle, *Guide to the Mandalay Palace*. pp.18-19.
27. I am grateful to U Aung Kyaing for telling me this story.
28. Taw Sein Ko, *Archeological notes on Pagan*. 1926.
29. Duroiselle, *The Ananda Temple*. 1937.
30. Below, Ch.5, pp.87.
31. Tinker, op.cit., p.175-6.
32. *ibid.*, p.181.
33. Luce, "A century of progress..." p.89.
34. Tinker, *op.cit.*, p.181.
35. Than Tun, "Review of old Burma-early Pagan." *Mandalay University Mimeograph*.
36. *Pagán and Velu*. Translated by U Khin Zaw from the Burmese of U Wun, and here quoted from *Essays Offered to G.H. Luce*, p.ix. Velu is a name given to Luce by the Taunggwin Thathanabaing.
37. The most outstanding Burmese contributions to Pagan studies being the work of U Bo Kay, ပုဂံသုတေသနလန်းညွှန်း and his disciple U Aung Kyaing, ပုဂံခေတ်ဗိသုကာလက်ရာမြို့
38. See: *Essays on the history and Buddhism of Burma by Professor Than Tun*.
39. In the case of the Bu-paya, reconstruction was carried out by the less archaeologically-inclined defrocked monk, formally titled Poppa U Parama Wunna Theidi. As Dr. Than Tun comments, "Nothing old could have survived this monk's generous work of restoration." In *Study and preservation...*, p.78.
40. Forthcoming: Pichard, *An inventory of Pagan monuments*, E.F.E.O., Pondicherry.

CHAPTER ONE

1. Than Tun, "Pagan Restoration..." p.49, details that at Pagan 2,217 red brick edifices have been counted, of which 378 are conserved by the Archaeology Department.
2. Than Tun, *The Buddhist Church...*, pp.1-2; Luce, "Old Kyaukse and the coming of the Burmans." pp.89-90, and *O.B.E.P.*, I, pp.5-6; Duroiselle, *A.S.I.-A.R.*, 1912-13, p.136.
3. Luce, "Notes on the peoples of Burma in 12th-13th centuries, A.D." pp.52-74.
4. Than Tun, *The Buddhist Church...* pp.7-8; Luce, *O.B.E.P.*, I, p.6.
5. Luce, *ibid.*, p.8.
6. Than Tun, *op.cit.*, p.8.
7. Many older local people at Pagan tell how, with shortages of firewood, there has been a drastic reduction in trees in recent times.
8. Aung Kyaing. Examples of these marked bricks are in the Pagan museum.
9. See map, p.viii.
10. Thin Kyi, " The old city of Pagan." pp.179-188.
11. *Epig.Birm.*, II, pt.I, Inscription No.IX.
12. Duroiselle, *A.S.I.-A.R.*, 1912-13, p.136; *G.P.C.*, p.28.
13. A stone pillar has been erected on this site and at another site near W.Pwasaw village, also said to have been the place of a former palace. There is no archaeological evidence to support this tradition, but, like all such traditions there may be an element of truth in it. For example, academics rejected the tradition that Tan-chi-taung stupa was built by Anawrahta until 1974, when the earthquake split the casing to reveal votive tablets signed by the king.
14. Original Pagan carving may be found on the Shwe-zigon doors, and on image pedestals at Salé.
15. Duroiselle, *Guide to the Mandalay Palace*.
16. Hall and Whitmore, *Maritime trade...* p.222-5.
17. Aung Thwin, *Pagan...*, p.101; Than Tun, "Social life in Burma, A.D. 1044-1287," pp.37-47.
18. Coedès, *The indianised states of Southeast Asia*. pp.15-16., "...the Indians were not confronted by uncultured 'savages', but on the contrary, by people endowed with a civilisation that had traits in common with the pre-Aryan India."
19. Aung Thwin, *op.cit.*, pp.23-4. A number of Pyu type images have been found at Pagan, see below, p.24.
20. Luce, "Old Kyaukse...," p.77; and *Phases of pre-Pagan Burma...*
21. *G.P.C.*, pp.77-9.
22. *ibid.*, p.78.
23. Aung Thwin, *Pagan...*, pp. 22-3.
24. Luce, "A Cambodian raid on Lower Burma." And reiterated in *O.B.E.P.*, pp.21-3.
25. Illustrated in Ray, *Brahmanical Gods...*, Pl.15-22, and Luce, *Phases...*, Vol.II, Pl.88-90.
26. Luce, the main promoter of the theory that the Early Period was dominated by Mon culture, and that the early temple was what he called a 'Mon type', and going as far as to call the Early Period the " 'Mon' period", does, though, admit, "The large Pagan *ku* temples naturally evolved from the vaulted chapels of Sri Ksetra...," *O.B.E.P.*, I, p. 243. Yet elsewhere Luce wrote, "The Burmans, learning from Mon mistakes, greatly improved the quality and drainage of roofs...," *ibid.*, p.245. There is some confusion here, if not contradiction. In any case, no prototypes exist, in the Mon country, for

the Early Pagan temple.

27. See Hall and Whitmore's references to Pagan's interest in the Kra Isthmus: "Southeast Asian trade and the Isthmian struggle," p.199 and Luce, *O.B.E.P.*, I, pp.91.

28. *G.P.C.*, p.65-6. Perhaps the source for Pagan bronze casting? Below, Ch.3, p.21.

29. Luce, *O.B.E.P.*, I, pp.19-20.

30. *G.P.C.*, pp. 86-9. The chronicle's statement seems to be substantiated by the discovery of Anawrahta's tablets here. Taw Sein Ko, *A.S.I.-A.R.*, 1908, pp.41-2.

31. *ibid.* pp.41-2.

32. The Myazedi Inscription; below, pp.71.

33. Curiously, surprisingly little jewellery has been found at Pagan, whilst finds from an ever-increasing number of Pyu sites, both legal and today, increasingly illegal, abound.

34. Luce, *O.B.E.P.*, I, p.230.

35. Wickremasinghe, "Ceylon's relations with South East Asia..." p.41. The event is recorded in the Ceylonese chronicle, the *Culavamsa*, "He sent to his friend Prince Anurrudha, in the Ramanna country, messengers with gifts and fetched thence *bhikkus* who had thoroughly studied the three Pitakas, who were a fount of moral discipline and other virtues, and acknowledged as *theras* after distinguishing them by costly gifts.

36. Landmarks in a foreign policy enacted by the *sangha* were Sapada's mission to Ceylon, in late 12th century, documented in *G.P.C.*, p.143-4, and discussed by Wickremasinghe, *op.cit.*, pp.52-3; though Sapada's mission was commemorated with the building of a stupa named after him at Nyaung-U, below, Ch.7, p.96, the first lithic reference to his mission was on the Mon Kalyani Thein Inscription of 1475 by King Dhammaceti, trans. in *Epig.Birm*, III. Another monk-mission of note was that of Shin Disapramuk to the court of Kublai Khan in 1278, discussed in Pe Maung Tin, "Buddhism in the Inscriptions..." pp.63-4, and Than Tun, "History of Burma, A.D.1000-1300." *B.B.H.C.*, I, pt.II, pp.56-7.

37. Below, Ch.4, p.49.

38. Below, Ch.3, pp.27-31.

39. Below, Ch.4, p.4, and p.54.

40. As clearly stated in contemporary epigraphy: "...Thereafter, the three holy Pitakas, which had become obscured, (he) proceeded to collect (and) purify." 3rd Shwehsandaw Inscription, *Epig.Birm.*, I, pt.II, p.163.

See Luce and Bohmu Ba Shin. "Pagan Myinkaba Kubyauk-gyi temple of Rajakumar (1113 A.D.) and the Old Mon writings on its walls." *B.B.H.C.*, Vol. II, 1961, pp.277-416.

41. Luce, *O.B.E.P.*, I, p.230.

42. Regarding this possible Mahayana connection, through the vehicle of a Bengali queen, Luce writes: "...Almost everywhere Buddhism was in retreat: before neo-Confucianism in China, before Brahmanic revival in Bengal; before the advance of Islam in Northern India; in Dvaravati (Siam) before the ambitions of the Saivite rulers of Angkor; in Ceylon, before the conquests of the Cola; in Malaya before Cola raids, Javanese revolts and commercialism.
The Mahayanists who came to Pagan were refugees rather than missionaries....If East Bengal had been able to provide Anirrudha with the texts he wanted, Burma, like Nepal and Tibet, might have been Mahayanist today. As it is Pagan was deeply indebted to Bengal for most of its iconography, and (I suspect) much of its architecture. The Abeyadana is the crowning point of Mahayanist influence here." *O.B.E.P.*, I, pp.201. For an analysis of this monuments iconographic content see below, Ch.4, pp.59-61.

43. Stargardt, "Burma's Economic and Diplomatic Relations..." expands, with little recourse to primary sources, this theme of Pagan as 'hub', not only to her own empire politically, but also, economically, further afield. For a broader picture see Hall, "Transitions in Southeast Asian commercial and political realms, A.D.1000-1400" in his *Maritime Trade...*

44. Mon Inscription No.IX, "An inscription found near Tharba Gate, Pagan."

45. Like the Shwe-hsan-daw, "Golden Hair Relic," or the Shwe-zigon, which houses the frontlet relic brought from Sri Ksetra.

46. Than Tun, "Religion in Burma..." p.51.

47. Tambiah, *World conqueror and world renouncer*, discusses the Asokan model, as applied to South East Asian kingship in some depth.

48. Popa Saw Rahan; *G.P.C.*, pp.52-3.

49. Pe Maung Tin, "Buddhism in the Inscriptions of Pagan." p.57.

50. A thesis presented in *Pagan, the Origins of Modern Burma.*

51. Notably the impressive Thisawadi at W.Pwasaw; below, Ch.7, p.124.

52. Trans. by Pe Maung Tin, *op.cit.*, p.64.

CHAPTER TWO

1. Than Tun, "Religious buildings in Burma," p.73.

2. Such a cosmology, as applied to a Buddhist monument, is common throughout South East Asia; see Coedès, *Angkor: an introduction.* pp.39-53.

3. Duroiselle, "Pictorial representations of the Jatakas in Burma."; Luce, "The 550 Jatakas in Burma."; Lu Pe Win, "The Jatakas in Old Burma."

4. Below, pp.121-4.

5. Below, p.102.

6. Below, p. 109.

7. See the description of our recent investigation of the Shwe-hsan-daw interior; below, Ch.4, pp. 43-44.

8. According to the chronicles Anawrahta's raids on Thaton and China were inspired by relic collecting motives; perhaps an attempt to establish legitimacy. *G.P.C.*, p.78-81.

9. One such glass image is now in the museum at Pagan. A fine bronze image, from Kyanzittha's time, was recently discovered in an upper *tabena* at one temple near Chauk. Also, after the last earthquake, according to U Aung Kyaing, a number of bronze images were revealed at the Shwe-zigon likewise encased in a sealed upper chamber; below, Ch.4, p. 57. For descriptions of enshrinement rituals see quotation from Mingala-zeidi inscription, below, Ch.6, pp. 102-3.

10. Like the Myaung-gan ones from Sri Ksetra, illustrated in Luce, *Phases...*, Pl.33-4. See Than Tun's lists of items for enshrinement: "Religious Buildings in Burma, 1000-1300." p.74.

11. At Kyasin the temple was completed by a later generation; below, Ch.6, p. 113.

12. In collection of Archaeology Department Museum at Hmawza.

13. Below, Ch.6, p. 94.

14. Below, Ch.5, p. 92.

15. Below, Ch.6, p. 102.

16. Than Tun, "Religious buildings..." p.72.

17. The temple is the Singu Naga-yon.

18. Mya, Pl.1.

19. Aung Thwin, *Pagan...*, pp.47-8.

20. For example, the Nga-kywe-na-daung; below, Ch.4, p. 38.

21. However, would-be Indian prototypes are stone built, not brick, and the local tradition, perhaps self-

evolved, was a brick one, mastered by the Pyu, who, recruited by the expanding Pagan kings, assimilated more current architectural styles then prevalent in North India.

22. The word *gu*, or *ku* in Old Burmese, is derived from the Pali *guha*, likewise meaning cave. Caves are traditional places of meditation and the earliest temples in India, like Ajanta, are cut from rock faces. On the flat plain of Pagan there was a lack of either natural caves or rock faces to carve out, other than on the high ground above Nyaung U, so the Pagan donors set about constructing artifical caves.

23. The Burmese facination with caves has continued to the present day with often remote cave complexes, such as Hpo-win-daung or Pindiya, attracting pilgrims from throughout the Union.

24. The term *bhakti* was not used in Old Burmese, nor in Modern Burmese, however, as a concept its use is certainly applicable in a description of Pagan's religious life.

25. "...the three holy Pitakas, which had become obscured, (he) proceeded to collect and purify." From the Prome Shwe-hsan-daw Inscription, *Epig. Birm.*, I, pt.II, p.163.

26. Bronze examples of Tantric figures were found in Scovell's Pawdawmu and at Paung-gu; illustrated in Luce, *O.B.E.P.*, III, Pl.446, 444.

27. See quotation from Mingala-zedi Inscription; below, Ch.6, pp. 102-3.

28. Than Tun, "Religious Buildings...," pp. 71-80.

29. Two exceptions being Kyauk-ku, below, pp 51-52, and Than-daw-gya, *Glimpses...*, p. 23.

30. For example the Bogyoke-mi, below, Ch.7, pp. 119-120; or Ywa-haung-gyi, below, Ch.6, pp.108-9.

31. No.547; in E.B.Cowell, *The Jataka...*, Vol.VI, pp.246-305.

32. In a small temple set close to the junction of the Museum and Pagan-Myinkaba roads.

33. Though the *sikhara* form was used on votive tablets by the Pyu; Luce, *O.B.E.P.*, III, Pl.70, a,b,c.

34. Pe Maung Tin, "Buddhism in the inscriptions of Pagan." *J.B.R.S.*, XXVI, pt.I, p.60. According to U Pe Maung Tin *naracana* was a type of musical performance with six instruments.

35. *ibid*. p.61.

36. *ibid*. p.61.

37. For example, the Maha-mya-muni in Mandalay, or at the less well known Shwe-nat-taung monastery south of Shwedaung.

38. Below, Ch.4, p. 39.

39. The Wetkyi-in Kubyauk-gyi is one of the few temples where the shrine forms the same unit as the hall. Generally on middle and large size temples there is some form of distinction between the components; on small temples, like the Loka-hteik-pan, the hall opens uninterrupted out into the shrine.

40. Sithu notes in his Shwe-gu-gyi Inscription of 1131, "As when a fisherman with subtil net/Encompasseth a water, all things found/ Within the water needs must enter in/ So divers heretics, ill-doers, who lept/Into the clutch of heresy, beguiled/By specious handling, were encompassed round/ With the pure Buddha-vision and clean eyes,..." Trans. Pe Maung Tin and Luce, revised version, Luce, *O.B.E.P.*, I, p.87.

41. Below, Ch.7, p. 121.

42. See Aung Thwin's discussion of the repercussions of this policy, in *Pagan: The Origins of Modern Burma*. Ch. 8, "The economic implications of the Merit-Path to salvation." pp.169-182.

43. Below, Ch.7, pp. 125, 127.

44. Than Tun, "Religious buildings...," p.77.

45. "My parents, grandparents, and great-grandparents have departed, abandoning their inherited property. And my beautiful beloved son has abandoned his inherited property and his own mother. Knowing that I too cannot take with me the inherited property left by him, I offer it as a gift to the end that it may be for my parents, my son and all my relatives, a means of attaining nirvana." Trans. Pe Maung Tin, "Buddhism in the Inscriptions of Pagan." p.54. The son may have become a monk.

CHAPTER THREE

1. The term *bhakti* must be used with some reservation, as a concept it may appropriately be applied to Early Pagan religious life; however, as a term, it does not seem to have been linguistically adopted in Burma.

2. Below, p. 84.

3. The central images at Kyauk-ku and Than-daw-gya are made of stone blocks.

4. The finest examples of such work being the gold repoussé plaques in the Pagan museum, Pyu in workmanship (compare them with the Khin Ba mound finds (*A.S.I.*, 1926-7, Pl. XL, a,b,c.), and the figures so like the Nan-paya reliefs in physique and facial type. Note Luce's comment, "the Pyu had expert stone carvers and metal workers: in these respects I should rank them above Pagan craftsmen." In: "The ancient Pyu," p.313.

5. Below, Ch.4, p. 46, and p. 49. For Pyu examples see the Hmawza museum collection, or the illustrations in Luce, *Phases...*

6. Notably the Shwe-zigon doors.

7. Luce, *O.B.E.P.*, III, Pl.419-22.

8. Salé Singu temple.

9. Fraser-Lu in her work, *Burmese Lacquerware*, states that lacquer making was practiced at Pagan, p.3, her source being an early reference by A.P.Morris, "Lacquerware industry in Burma," *J.B.R.S.*, X, 1919, p.4, which refers to discovery of a lacquer box there. However, as this piece is now lost it is impossible to accurately date it, and, like the Bayinnaung images found after the last earthquake in the Shwe-zigon, it may well have been a later addition. Arguers for Pagan knowing lacquer may look to the Ananda west shrine images of Kyanzittha and Shin Arahan that Griswold, in a note in Luce's *O.B.E.P.*,II, p.126, records as being made from lacquer, and which are clearly Early Pagan in physiognomy; see below, Ch.4, pp. 70-71. Fragments of some resinous coating may also be noted peeling from the faces of brick and stucco images, perhaps lacquer?

10. Below, Ch.4., p. 76.

11. I.B. Horner, *Minor Anthologies...*, discusses and presents a translation of the *Buddhavamsa*, the source for the Pagan artist's portrayal of this theme. See also Pierre Pichard, "Les monuments...," pp. 308-10.

12. Notably in one small temple at the junction of the museum and Pagan-Myinkaba roads.

13. Ray reaches these conclusions in his monographs *Sanskrit Buddhism...*, and *Brahmanical gods...*

14. Ray, *Brahmanical gods...*, pp.25-6.

15. Kyanzittha recorded his mission in his epigraphy; there is no epigraphic evidence to prove that Nadaungmya actually sent a second mission, though dating from his reign, a new wave of North Indian influence is evident at Pagan, and under his direction an actual copy of the Vajrasana temple, at Bodh Gaya, was constructed at Pagan, the Maha-bodhi Temple; below, Ch.6, p. 99.

16. Snellgrove, *Image of the Buddha*, p.135.

17. Luce, *O.B.E.P.*, I, PP.196-7.

18. Duroiselle, *Ari of Burma...*

19. Zimmer, *The art of Indian Asia...* p.190.*ibid...*p.191.
20. Luce, *O.B.E.P.*, I, p.421.
21. U Mya, *Votive tablets...*, Pl.62.
22. Below, Ch.6, p. 105.
23. Below, Ch.4, pp. 69-70.
24. Illustrated in Luce, *O.B.E.P.*, III, Pl. 442-3.
25. Though a history of Pyu art has yet to be written, a number of examples from this period are illustrated in Luce's *Phases of Pre-Pagan...*
26. Luce, *O.B.E.P.*, I, p. 151.
27. U Mya, *op.cit.*, p.1.
28. Below, p. 33.
29. Luce notes that one of this type has been found in Thailand, and that, "one needs evidence of their manufacture in Bihar or Bengal." *O.B.E.P.*, I, p.151.
30. An example of the black stone ones from Bengal was shown to me by the Sayadaw of one monastery near Ywathitgyi in Sagaing Division. This was clearly Bengali in origin, perhaps one of the prototypes for the Burmese *andagu* variety.
31. "Together with my lord (the Mahathera) I cleansed the religion of the Lord Buddha." *Epig.Birm.* I, Pt.II, Insc. No. I, 'Shwezigon', l.48, p.117.
32. Below, Ch 4, p. 39.
33. Below, Ch 4, pp. 46 and 49.
34. Luce, *O.B.E.P.*, I, pp.290 and III, Pl.135.
35. Verbal communication, 1987. This point is emphasised in the Nan-paya entry in the official guide, *Glimpses of glorious Pagan*, p.41.
36. Below, pp. 49-52.
37. *Report on the Kyauk-ku temple...*p. 9.
38. Below, Ch.4, p. 61.
39. Duroiselle, *Ananda temple at Pagan.*
40. Luce, *O.B.E.P.*, I, pp. 363-4.
41. *ibid.* p. 364.
42. Below, Ch.6, p. 105.
43. Below, Ch.6, pp. 80 and 115.
44. Below, Ch.4, pp. 52-54.
45. For example in the Paya-thon-zu or Nanda-ma-nya; below, Ch.7, pp. 129 and 134.
46. Luce illustrates a number of crowned wooden figures which he describes as "Bodhisattva kings" and makes reference to Forchammer (*op.cit.* p. 12-13) who mentioned the presence of 12 wooden standing figures at Kyauk-ku; *O.B.E.P.*, III, PL.421-2.
47. Gutman, "Crowned Images of Arakan," pp. 48-56.
48. Luce, *O.B.E.P.*, III, Pl.444, and, I, p.184. Also see: A.S.B., 1939, Appendix F, p.xii, no.79.
49. Gutman, *op.cit.* pp.50.
50. Luce, *O.B.E.P.*, I, p.186.

51. Luce, *O.B.E.P.*, III, Pl.444, and, I, p.184.
52. *Mahaparinirvana Sutta.*
53. Pierre Pichard notes the absence of crowned images of either Gotama or Mettaya in *hpaya-nga-zu* monuments, "Les Monuments sur plan pentagone..." p.314.
54. Than Tun, "Religious buildings In Burma." Such rituals continue in certain of Burma's shrines to this day, for example before dawn each day at the Maha-mya-muni Temple in Mandalay.
55. Snellgrove, *Image of the Buddha....*p. 85.
56. Pe Maung Tin and Luce, "The Shwegu-gyi inscription, Pagan." *B.B.H.C.*, I, pt.I, pp.1-28, and revised in Luce, *O.B.E.P,* I, 85-88.
57. Mya, p.11, Fig. 4-5. Translated by the late U Ko Ko of Mandalay University.
58. Than Tun, "Religion in the Pagan Period."*J.B.R.S*, XLII, pt.II, 1959, pp. 53 and 57.
59. Below, Ch.6, p. 121.
60. Snellgrove, *op.cit.*, p. 89, and pp.134-6.
61. Archaeology Department Collection, Rangoon.
62. Luce, *O.B.E.P.*, III, Pl.411b.
63. Below, Ch.5, p. 87.
64. Mya, *op.cit.*, fig. 7.
65. See Luce's discussion on this in his description of the Dhamma-yan-gyi; *O.B.E.P.*, I, p.421.
66. Mya, *op.cit.* p.9. Trans. by U Ko Ko.
67. Luce, *O.B.E.P.,* III, Pl.446 a,b; II, pp.206-7.
68. Gutman, *op.cit.*, fig.2 and pp.50-1, makes refence to a Sino-Tibetan image found in Arakan, such contacts must have extended to Pagan.
69. Luce, *O.B.E.P.*, III, Pl.447 a-d.
70. Luce, *O.B.E.P.*, III, Pl.55c illustrates such a Pyu Mettaya; Mya, *op.cit.*, fig. 6, 7.
71. Mya, *op.cit.*, fig.7. Trans. by U Ko Ko.
72. Illustrated in Toru Ono , *Mural Painting...* Pl.159.
73. Luce believed one of which to represent the queen herself; see discussion below, Ch.4, p. 59.
74. Luce, *O.B.E.P.,* III, Pl. 58,59,434.
75. *Epig.Birm.*, I, pt.II, 'Inscription No.I.', trans. Duroiselle, pp.112-5.
76. *ibid.*, III, pt.II, 'Inscription IX', trans. by Duroiselle, p.38.
77. Luce, *O.B.E.P.*, I, pp. 204-5.
78. Shorto, "The Gavamapati tradition in Burma."pp.15-30.
79. Luce, *O.B.E.P.*, I, pp. 207-8.
80. *ibid.* p.208.
81. In Burmese language press.

82. Below, Ch.4, p. 58.
83. Ray, *Brahmanical gods.*, p. 67.
84. Luce, *O.B.E.P.*, I, p. 208.
85. See Pl.37 of Thomann's book, *Pagan ein jahrtausend...*, which illustrates the Nat-hlaung-kyaung interior as it was in 1899.
86. *Epig.Birm.*, I, pt.II, 'Inscription No.I.', trans. Duroiselle, pp.112-5. Also see *G.P.C.*, pp.26-9.
87. *ibid.*
88. Ray, *op.cit.*, p.59.
89. *Epigraphica Indica*, VIII, No.27, pp.197-8.

CHAPTER FOUR

1. Luce, *O.B.E.P.*, I, pp. 299-302.
2. "The Myazedi inscriptions." *Epigraphica Birmanica*, I, pt.I.
3. Luce, "Old Kyaukse and the coming of the Burmans."
4. See Ch. 3, pp. 23-4; Ray, *Sanskrit Buddhism...*, p.16: "Some Gods of the Mahayana pantheon have been incorporated into the Hinayana mythology of Burma, but this curious fusion still remains unexplained."
5. E. Hpet-leik has a 3/4 barrel and Myin-pya-gu a full barrel.
6. The chronicle's date for Pagan's foundation, since followed by Duroiselle, *A.S.I.-A.R.*, 1913, p.136, and Luce *O.B.E.P.*, I, pp.6-7.
7. Taw Sein Ko, *A.S.B.-A.R,*1907, p.12.
8. Luce *O.B.E.P.*, I, p.259.
9. *ibid.* p.258
10. No.230.
11. Nat-*daw*-kyaung is used by U Kala in the *Mahayazawingyi*.
12. This image was taken to one of the Berlin museums, possibly by von Nöetling, though I have not established in which sector of the city it is, or even whether it survived the bombings of the last war. Luce in a footnote (*O.B.E.P.*, I, p.284) mentions the discovery of another Vishnu reclining, this is now in the Pagan Museum. Bo Kay, *Pagan...*, pp.282-3, discusses the name Nat-hlè-kyaung.
13. The most significant reference to the presence and role of the Brahmans at the Pagan court is the Tharba Gate Inscription (1101 A.D.), in *Epigraphica Birmanica*, Vol.III, Pt.I.
14. John Marr, S.O.A.S.
15. Pierre Pichard, E.F.E.O.
16. At Early Pagan temples with a stupa finial include: Abe-ya-dana (No.1202), above p. 59, Alopyé (No.230), above p. 77.
17. Luce, *O.B.E.P.*, I, pp. 221-2, lists these in detail.
18. Pierre Pichard.
19. See Phayre's note in Yule's *Mission*

to Ava.

20. Luce, *O.B.E.P.*, I, pp.217-8.
21. If they may be called this in a Sanskrit based temple.
22. W. Hpet-leik was excavated and restored by the A.S.I. in 1907 by Taw Sein Ko on the initiation of Sir John Marshall (*A.S.I.-A.R.*, 1907), whilst E.Hpet-leik was repaired under Duroiselle's supervision in 1912 (*A.S.B.-A.R.,* 1913).
23. Luce, *O.B.E.P.*, I, pp. 262-263.
24. Below, p. 52.
25. *A.S.I.-A.R.*, 1907. Taw Sein Ko also referred in the same report to a fragment of a stone lion that is now missing, this may be the earliest *chinthe,* or mythical lion, that has been found at Pagan, alongside the leogryph pairs high on the Nanpaya shrine pediments. Some broken stone images are, though, noticeable in the E. extending hall of the E. stupa, though I am not certain whether these are contemporary with the original structures.
26. Gu Bizat may be found in disrepair between the Maha Bodhi and Irra Inn.
27. Above, p. 38.
28. Below, p. 42.
29. Duroiselle, *Pictorial representations of the Jataka in old Burma.* Luce, *The 550 Jataka in old Burma,* and, *O.B.E.P.*, I, p. 263. Below, p. 67.
30. Luce, *O.B.E.P.*, I, pp.., 260-1; this assumption is based on a reference in the *G.P.C.* , p. 94, to the enshrinement of a hair relic presented by the king of Ussa (Pegu), naming the stupa Mahapeinne, and as images of Mahapeinne have been found at this site this therefore must be the same. What does, though , confirm Luce's attribution is the discovery of Anawrahta's votive tablets in the *tabena.*
31. Verbal communication from school teacher Daw Khin Shwe.
32. Above, pp. 3-4.
33. *O.B.E.P.*, I, pp. 261-2.
34. Namely: the east hall of the Dhamma-yan-gyi, the south and east *gandhakuti* of the Dhammayazika, and in a modern shrine to the east of the Lokanada. The image from the Shwe-hsan-daw unearthed by the A.S.I. is now in the Pagan museum. See above, Ch3, p. 25.
35. Below, p. 49.
36. Below, p. 118.
37. *G.P.C.*, pp. 78-79.
38. Than Tun, "Religious buildings..." p.77.
39. Pagan was razed by a fire in 1225.

40. An accessible example of this type of work from the Late Period is No. 195.
41. Symes, *An account of an embassy....*
42. *G.P.C.*, pp. 79-80.
43. *G.P.C.*, p. 80. *Glimpses of glorious Pagan* , p. 40.
44. Possibly with the exception of the Hpet-leik monuments that may be argued to be *gu* rather than stupa.
45. U Mya, *Note on the Nanpaya temple...*
46. A.S.I, 1907-8, p. 34.
47. Compare Plate 134 with 135 in *O.B.E.P.*, Vol. III. Though outwardly the forms are similar, the manner in which they have been carved differs and their effect by no means similar. I am grateful to U Bo Kay for pointing this out to me.
48. This is emphasised in the official guide, *Glimpses...* , p. 41.
49. U Mya, *Votive Tablets...*, Pl. 53, 54.
50. Taw Sein Ko, A.S.I., 1907-8, p. 34. Brahma continued throughout the period as a popular supporter of Buddha, along with Indra, he assisted the Buddha in his descent from Tavatimsa, as seen in so many Pagan murals. About a throne he was next to reappear at the Mye-bon-tha-payahla, below, pp. 80-81.
51. Alongside the Vaisnaivite ones in the Nat-hlaung-kyaung and those at Kyauk-ku.
52. Forchammer, *Report on the Kyauk-ku Temple...*, p. 2.
53. Alongside the Hpet-leik monuments which are also arguably temples.
54. Luce, *O.B.E.P.*, I, p. 289, discusses Taw Sein Ko's (*A.S.B.* 1904, p.27) discovery of an inscription dated 1188 found here but logically refutes Taw Sein Ko's assertion that this temple was Narapatsithu's retreat.
55. c.1080; below, p. 54.
56. For example those *bilu* housed to the south west of Shwe-zi-gon.
57. With the exception of Arakan, where stone carved jambs were deployed on certain of the temples at Mrauk-U.
58. *O.B.E.P.*, I, p. 290.
59. *Bodawin* is in fact a modern Burmese term, but more aptly describes the concept of a narrative portrayal of the life of the Buddha than any Old Burmese or Pali term.
60. The Pyu were familiar with the *Bodawin* which they portrayed in nine scenes on their votive tablets, U Mya, *Votive tablets...*
61. Forchammer, *ibid*, p.9. Luce, *O.B.E.P.*, I, p.291.
62. Above, p. 41
63. Thus there is an indigenous prototype for the Ananda, below, p. 65.
64. Above, Ch.3, p. 41.
65. Luce, *O.B.E.P.*, I, p. 293.

66. Luce, *O.B.E.P.*, I, p. 309.
67. Luce, *O.B.E.P.*, I, p. 303.
68. Gu Bizat may be found between the Maha Bodhi and Irra Inn.
69. Below, p. 77.
70. Below, p. 71.
71. Below, p. 84.
72. The only other dodecahedron finial at Pagan is on the Bu-le-thi; below, p. 91.
73. Above, p. 46.
74. Below, p. 71.
75. Luce, *O.B.E.P.*, I, p. 304.
76. The introductory section to the Jataka may be found in English translation in T.W. Rhys Davids, ed. C.A.F. Rhys Davids, *Buddhist birth stories.* London, 1925.
77. Luce, *O.B.E.P.*, I, pp. 304-5.
78. Luce suggests the 'Conception'; *O.B.E.P.*, I, p. 304.
79. *Buddhavamsa* has been translated into English by I.B.Horner.
80. The Naga-yon predellas contains cenes where the Bodhisattva Gotama encountered each of the 28 buddhas.
81. This arrangement of colossal images is similar to the Wetkyi-in Kubyaukngè, only there Mogallana and Sariputta take the place of *nirodha* buddhas, below, p. 75.
82. Below, pp. 67-9.
83. Below, pp. 62-4.
84. Luce, *O.B.E.P.*, I, p.275.
85. Verbal communication by U Aung Kyaing who told me that after the 1975 earthquake, a number of bronzes dating from Bayinnaung's reign were found enshrined in a *tabena* in the upper part of the stupa that was broken open by the seismic shock.
86. *G.P.C.*, p.87.
87. In none of his inscriptions does Kyanzittha refer to his great forerunner; Luce, *O.B.E.P.*, I, p.268.
88. Luce, *O.B.E.P.*, I, p.268. The chronicles also mention that Anawrahta dwelt in five *pyattthat* south of Shwe-zigon. *G.P.C.*, p.87.
89. *Epigraphica Birmanica.* I, pt.II, Insc. nos.II.
90. *Nirbbanamulabajra...*; Luce, *O.B.E.P.*, I, p. 268.
91. Below, p. 70.
92. *G.P.C.*, pp.109-110. Also see Luce's quotation on the Nats history, as told by the shrine's keeper, in *O.B.E.P.*, I, pp.275-6.
93. *G.P.C.*, p.108.
94. Luce, *O.B.E.P.*, I, pp.311-2.
95. It is important to understand that the Early Pagan kings purified the existing faith, a decayed Theravada or Sarvastivada Buddhism, they did not

introduce Buddhism into Burma nor was their purification necessarily an attack on non-Pali Buddhist practices.

96. Luce believed each of these works to date to the early part of Kyanzittha's reign, with the Naga-yon preceeding the Abe-ya-dana; *O.B.E.P.*, I, p.311.

97. That is, on Ava and Konbaung temples.

98. If an early date is to be accepted for the Pa-hto-tha-mya; below, pp. 54-6.

99. A theme met, possibly earlier, at the Pa-hto-tha-mya and found on the sculpture of the Naga-yon which has been identified as illustrating the Buddhavamsa text.

100. Luce, *O.B.E.P.*, II, pp. 109-110, I, pp.326. Also see U Mya's mono graph on the subject.

101. Luce, *O.B.E.P.*, I, p.321.

102. Kyanzittha was 'lord' of Htihlaing; *G.P.C.*, p.108.

103. Though stone peforated windows do not necessarily die out, they were retained in *ok-kyaung* structures, where dark interiors remained in vogue.
Below, p. 112.

104. Again the source may have been the *Nidanakatha*.

105. Verbal communication. Also noted in Luce, *O.B.E.P.*, I, pp. 313-314.

106. Luce, *O.B.E.P.*, I, p.315.

107. Luce, *O.B.E.P.*, I, p.317-20.

108. As with the Abe-ya-dana, above, p 59-60.

109. Above, p. 56.

110. Above, p. 57

111. *G.P.C.*, p.110.

112. E.g. the Taungthaman Kyauk-taw-gyi at Amarapura by Bagyidaw in 1847. The Konbaung monarchs of this period seem to have consciously set about reviving 'classical' Pagan architectural forms, which was tantamount to a 'renaissance'.

113. Luce calls the Ananda the Nanda, simply on the basis of the chronicle tradition of calling this temple the Ananda is followed in this work.

114. *Epig. Birman.* vol.I, pt.II.

115. Luce, *O.B.E.P.*, I, p.357.

116. Duroiselle, *The Ananda temple*.

117. *ibid.* pp.6-8.

118. Luce, *O.B.E.P.*, I, p.358.

119. Above, p. 52.

120. Than Tun, *Restoration at Pagan*.

121. The textual source being the *Nidanakatha*.

122. Abe-ya-dana, above, p.60, and Naga-yon, above, p.64. Guillon,

L'Armée de Mara, p.31, notes the fragment of a gloss on this subject in the Naga-yon. Guillon argues that a different recension was employed at the Ananda on a Singhalese model.

123. Shorto, *The Dewata plaques on the Ananda basement*.

124. By the Maha-bodhi (early 13th C.) images were being placed on a temple's exterior; below, pp. 99-100.

125. Guillon, *L'armée de Mara*. 1985.

126. Luce, *O.B.E.P.*, I, p.361.

127. It is unlikely, though, that Kyanzittha included this clutter of *chinthe* and *bilu*.

128. Above, Ch.3, p. 32.

129. Luce, *O.B.E.P.*, I , pp. 359. Duroiselle, 'Talaing Plaques on the Ananda', *Epigraphica Birmanica*.

130. Above, p. 57.

131. Duroiselle, *The Ananda temple.*.

132. Luce, *O.B.E.P.*, II, Pl.278-287; Also see I, p.367.

133. Luce, *O.B.E.P.*, I, pp.368-70.

134. For example see Luce, *O.B.E.P.*, III, Pl.409b, or the wooden 'kings', Pl.421-2, though whether these are contemporary is highly debatable.

135. Griswold's note in *O.B.E.P.*, II, Pl.276, where he tells how, during the war, thieves cut off the nose and a couple of fingers of the Kyanzittha image believing them to be of gold. U Lu Pe Win on investigating the damage discovered that the statue was made from lacquer and the interior filled with cloth that disintegrated when touched. On the basis of this it may be argued that the lacquer craft was known at Pagan, for in style this image certainly appears to be contemporary.

136. Below, p. 81.

137. Luce, *O.B.E.P.*,I, pp. 372-373.

138. Verbal communication, Pagan, 1987.

139. *Epig. Bir.* Vol. I, pt.I, p. 57.

140. Below, p. 80.

141. *B.B.H.C.*, Vol. II.

142. *ibid.* pp.280-1.

143. Brahma has been met before, guarding a shrine recess at the Nat-ha-lung-kyaung.

144. Said by Luce to be the fullest set with Mon glosses, there being 496 panels here, *O.B.E.P.*, I, p.376.

145. *B.B.H.C.*, II. Luce, *O.B.E.P.*, I, p.376.

146. *ibid.*.

147. *ibid.*.

148. Below, p.109.

149. Near the Maha-bohdi.

150. Luce calls it the Shwe Kyaung Kubyauk-nge, *O.B.E.P.*, I, pp.347-9.

151. Note that in Luce's time such figures were extant, *O.B.E.P.*, I, p.348.

152. Reconstructed by Luce, *O.B.E.P.*, I, p.349.

153. Above, p.71.

154. Luce, *O.B.E.P.*, I, p.347.

155. Most notably the Maha-bodhi (below, p. 99) and Wetkyi-in Kubyauk Gyi (below, p. 100)

156. Luce, *O.B.E.P.*, I, pp.355-6; Plate 256-7 in Vol.III show the monument before restoration,

157. U Mya, *Votive tablets...*Pl.6-7, p.12.

158. For example Pl.445-6, in Luce, *O.B.E.P.*, III.

159. *ibid.* p.356.

160. The textile at the time of writing is in Italy undergoing restoration.

161. See Luce, *O.B.E.P.*, III, Pl. 252, a-c, for pre-restoration appearance.

162. *ibid.*, vol.I, p.388.

163. Possibly with the exception of the That-byin-nyu.

164. Luce details these, *O.B.E.P.*, I, pp.389-391.

CHAPTER FIVE

1. Most notably the Shwe-gu-gyi inscription translated by Pe Maung Tin and Luce in *B.B.H.C.*, I, Pt.I, 1960, pp.1-28, also quoted below, p 81.

2. "What Aniruddha and Kalancacsa had struggled for—unification of human and intellectual forces—Aloncansu took for granted." Aung Thwin, *Pagan...*, pp.24-25

3. Luce, *O.B.E.P.*, I, p.374.

4. *ibid.*, p.374.

5. Above, Ch.4., pp. 75-76.

6. Above, Ch.4., p. 55.

7. Above, Ch.4., pp. 75-76.

8. The E.P. did, though, use a full barrel at Myin-pya-gu and Hpet-leik, but never on a large temple ambulatory.

9. Above, Ch.4., p 77.

10. Above, Ch.4., p. 76; see Luce *O.B.E.P.*, I, p. 347.

11. Some of which have been extracted.

12. Above, Ch.4, p. 71.

13. Originally translated by Pe Maung Tin and Luce in *B.B.H.C.*, I, pt.I, pp.18-19; here quoted from Luce's revised version in *O.B.E.P.*, I, pp. 86-7.

14. *B.B.H.C.*, I, pt.I, p. 24.

15. These now seem to have disintegrated. See Luce, *O.B.E.P.*, III, Pl.373 a,b.

16. Tharba Gate Inscription, trans, in *Epig.Birm.* Vol.III, pt.I.

17. *G.P.C.*, pp.127-8.

18. *G.P.C.*, p.128.

19. Above, Ch.4, p. 66.

20. Luce, *O.B.E.P.*, I, p.407.

21. Ba Shin, *The Loka-hteik-pan.*

22. *ibid.* pp.22-3. Also see Luce *O.B.E.P.*, p.385.
23. For discussion on painting styles see above, pp. 60-61, 64, 73-4.
24. There is no extant inscription for this temple and therefore such a dating is based on style alone.
25. Luce, *O.B.E.P.*, I, pp.412.
26. Above, pp. 81-2.
27. Luce, *O.B.E.P.*, I, p.417.
28. Luce, *O.B.E.P.*, I, p.418.
29. *G.P.C.*, p.134. The chronicle believed Narathu's assassins to be agents of the king of Pteikkara.
30. Wickremasinghe, "Ceylon's relations with South-East Asia with special reference to Burma." Also see Aung Thwin, "The problem of Ceylonese-Burmese relations in the 12th century and the question of interregnum in Pagan: 1165-1174 A.D."
31. Aung Thwin, "The question of an interregnum...", p.67, cites epigraphic evidence that proves that Sithu I was still reigning in 1169 and says, "The famous Ajawlat inscription, recorded in 1165 A.D. showed generous endowments being made to the *sangha* as if everything were normal. Also see: Hall, Kenneth R., *Maritime trade...* p. 203-4.
32. Translated in *B.B.H.C.*, Vol.I, pt.II, pp. 239-255.
33. Luce, *O.B.E.P.*, I, p.417.
34. *G.P.C.*. pp.127-8.
35. Above, p. 84.
36. Yule, *Mission to Ava...*
37. If ever included on the original Ananda.
38. Luce, *O.B.E.P.*, I, p.422.
39. Their now rebricked incision is still visible on the west side of the ambulatory.
40. Luce, *O.B.E.P.*, I, p.422.
41. Luce, *O.B.E.P.*, III, Pl. 411b.
42. *ibid.* p.421. Note that in 1343 the Dhamma-yan-gyi was associated with Sithu, not Narathu, however, which Sithu is not indicated.
43. Above, p.44.
44. Below, Ch.6, pp. 95 and 98.
45. Above, Ch.4, p. 55.
46. Verbal communication from U Aung Kyaing; Luce, *O.B.E.P.*, I, 280, 410.
47. Above, Ch.4, p. 103.

CHAPTER SIX

1. Pierre Pichard, "Les monuments sur le plan pentagone à Pagan." And below, pp. 121-123.
2. The first restoration visit was in the time of Kyanzittha (1084-1113) which lead to decorative innovations on the Wetkyi-in Kubyauk-ngè temple, above p.75, and the second was under Nadaungmya (1211-34) who built the Maha-bodhi temple, below, p. 99. It was most likely following this second visit that a new wave of *sikhara* types appear at Pagan and more numerously at Salé.
3. Below, p.124.
4. Though often set in a slight recess or niche.
5. Than Tun, "Religious buildings in Burma." p.71.
6. Than Tun, "Mahakassapa and his tradition."
7. Duroiselle, "The Ari of Burma and Tantric Buddhism." pp.81; *G.P.C.*, pp.59-60, and p.70 which laments on their *droit de seigneur*!
8. Duroiselle, "The Ari of Burma..." pp.82,84.
9. Than Tun, *ibid..* U Bo Kay believes 'Ari' to be derived from *ariya*, 'the victorious'. Neither U Bo Kay nor Dr Than Tun believe the sect was either Mahayanist or Tantric.
10. Robert Mayer directed me to the Tantra text *Kriyasamuccaya* which states: "A most serious gross offence arises from spending more than seven days with the Sravavaka."
11. Zwalf, *Buddhistm art and faith.* Pl.71.
12. *G.P.C.*, p. 143-5. Below, pp. 96-97.
13. Aung Thwin, *Pagan...*
14. Which may be contrasted by the shoddiness of Konbaung craftmanship. For example, the Konbaung left a wide mortar filled gap between their bricks whilst those at Pagan tightly interlock. Even the Pagan monuments dating from the early 14th century, after the dynasty's fall, reveal good workmanship; for example, the Thisa-wadi, Ch.7, p. 124, and E. Zanthi, Ch.7, p. 126.
15. Bennet, "The 'Fall of Pagan'..." pp.15-16.
16. Duroiselle, "Mongol frescoes at Pagan."
17. Pe Maung Tin, "Buddhism in the inscriptions of Pagan." pp. 63-4.
18. U Bo Kay believes the 'destruction' of Pagan occured as late as the early 18th century during the Mon-Burmese wars. He cites a protective prayer the Buddhist *tabena-sha* might invoke to annul the effects of epigraphic curses, before settling to work on the destruction of a shrine.
19. Even the main image at the Thatbyin-nyu was added in the 14th century. Post-Pagan dedications at Pagan are too numerous to list here and in their entirty could be the subject of a separate volume. Some description and illustration of Konbaung mural painting at Pagan may be found in Ono Toro and Wenck.
20. Pe Maung Tin, "Buddhism in the Inscriptions of Pagan." p.64. Than Tun, *The Buddhist Church....*pp.80-1; also see Huber, "Le fin de la dynastie de Pagan."
21. Pagan style images were also copied. Recently one was spotted in a prestigious London art dealer's gallery; it was on sale as 'Pagan Period'.
22. *G.P.C.*, p.147.
23. I did not personally count the number of cells on account of the undergrowth, but was assured that this figure was correct by one of the monks.
24. *G.P.C.*, p.147.
25. *G.P.C.*, p.144.
26. No actual Pyu monument survives with a *harmika*, though two relief sculptures of convexly shaped stupas have the *harmika.*
27. For example, Nos. 1831 and 566 East Zanthi Nga-myet-hna (above, p 126).
28. Luce, "Greater temples of Pagan."
29. Quaritch Wales, *Old Burma-early Siam.*
30. *G.P.C.*, pp.142, 154. *Glimpses...* p.29.
31. *Glimpses.* p.29.
32. *ibid.*, p.29
33. The *G.P.C.*, p.142, says of Sithu II, "Likewise he built a work of merit with two hollow storeys and an upwards winding stair and called it by the name Ka-dawpallin." However, the Dhamma-yan-gyi was also said to be hollow but, on recent investigation, proved solid throughout the core; above, Ch.5, p. 90.
34. *G.P.C.*, p. 154.
35. Above, p. 95.
36. Note that such conservatism may only be applied to the colossal temple, on the scale of the Sulamani or Hti-lo-min-lo, middle and small size temples exhibit a far greater experimental and innovative spirit.
37. Below, Ch.3, pp. 75 and 80-81.
38. U Mya, *Votive tablets...*, I, Pl.46.
39. Yule, *Narrative...*, p.35.
40. Above, p. 90.
41. Than Tun, "Religious buildings...,' p72.
42. Whitbread, "Medieval Burmese wall paintings...," pp. 88-92; also see Ba Shin, Whitbread and Luce, "Pagan, Wetkyi-in Kubyauk-gyi...," pp.167-9.
43. Whitbread, *ibid.* pp.168-9.
44. Below, p. 116.
45. Thomann was to write the first book on Pagan, *Pagan ein jahrtausend tempelkunst,* published in 1923.
46. Whitbread, "Medieval Burmese wall paintings..," p.120.
47. Luce mentions these paintings in his

work on Early Pagan but talks of 25 rather than 28 buddhas; this I presume to be a typological error. *O.B.E.P.*, I,p.247.

48. The text followed here was the *Buddhavamsa* (trans., by I.B.Horner, *The minor anthologies of the Pali Canon Part III...*)

49. Above, Ch.3, pp. 71-74.

50. Below, Ch.7, pp. 129 and 134.

52. Taw Sein Ko, *A.S.I.*

53. *Pictorial guide...*, p.34.

54. Below, Ch.5, p. 81.

55. *G.P.C.*, p.171.

56. Aung Thwin, *Pagan...*, pp. 172-176; Than Tun, "Social life in Burma, AD 1044-1287," p.41.

57. Above, Ch 5, p. 87.

58. Above, Ch.5, p. 92.

59. Below, Ch.7, pp. 127-8.

60. Luce includes the stupa in his work on Early Pagan stating "The date of this great stupa is open to question....its distinctive character, fine workmanship and magnificent glazed work suggest to me a date near the begining of the 12th Century A.D." and goes on to discuss the inscription dated to 1204/5 A.D. which he admits could refer to the building of the stupa.

61. For example, Nos. 58, 19, 20/4.

62. Above, pp. 95-6.

63. W. Braxton Sinclair, "Monasteries of Pagan," pp.1-4.

64. Below, pp. 113-4, and above Wu-tha-na-daw.

65. Luce, *O.B.E.P.*, I, p. 391.

66. Above, p. 111.

67. The exception to this being the Kondaw-gyi (No.122), and E.Zanthi (No.300); below, Ch.7, pp. 126 and 138.

68. *Lonely planet guide: Burma.*

69. Below, Ch.7, pp. 119-20.

70. Below, Ch.4, p. 74-5.

71. For example monument nos. 58, 19, 20/4 in the Shwe-zigon vicinity.

72. For example the Abe-ya-dana or Alopyé. Above, Ch.4, pp. 60 and 77.

73. As at Kyasin and the Myinkaba Kubyauk-ngè, above, pp. 105 and 113-4; see Luce, *O.B.E.P.*, I, p.391, for Kyasin.

74. With the exception of monastery block houses, for example No.232

75. Above, pp. 109-10.

76. On *ok-taik* in the Shwe-zigon enclosure (No.20/4) also wooden slot holes about its base, suggests a circumambulatory wooden extension from the brickwork.

77. Above, p. 96.

78. Above, Ch.4. p. 45.

79. As at Kyasin, below, pp. 113-4, and

Tha-bai-mauk (No.363) to the east of the Sulamani.

80. Luce, *O.B.E.P.*, I, pp. 391-397. A description of the temple was also included in the *Pagan newsletter* for 1987.

81. Luce, *O.B.E.P.*, I, p. 391.

82. *ibid.* p. 391.

83. Below, Ch.7, p. 109.

84. Above, Ch.5, p. 92.

85. Whitbread, "Medieval Burmese wall paintings...," pp. 88-92.

86. I am grateful to U Aung Kyaing for pointing this out to me; for the cosmological background to this see Q.Wales, *The universe around them*, pp.51-2.

87. Which U Aung Kyaing also directed me to.

88. The most impressive post-Pagan por trayal of Mount Meru is at Hpowindaung, most likely dating from the mid 18th century, where a whole rock face has been carved into this image.

89. Below, Ch.7, p. 134

90. U Bo Kay, p. 300.

91. Below, Ch.7, pp. 129-32.

92. Above, p. 46

CHAPTER SEVEN

1. U Aung Kyaing.

2. Below, Ch.6, p. 101.

3. Above, Ch.6, p. 108.

4. *G.P.C.*, p. 154.

5. "Revived" because the Pyu knew about the *harmika*, including it in relief scenes of stupas, now in Hmawza museum.

6. As at the Hsin-pya-gu pair of stupas; above, Ch.6, p. 109.7. No.1790, above, Ch.6, p. 108, and about one Ceylonese-type stupa at Minnanthu.

8. Above, Ch.4, pp. 41-2.

9. Above, Ch.4, pp. 43-4.

10. "Dhammarajika pagoda stone inscription," trans. by Pe Maung Tin and G.H.Luce in *B.B.H.C.*, Vol.III, 1963, p.137.

11. *ibid.* p. 136.

12. Above, Ch.3, p. 32.

13. Now in the Archaeology Dept. museum at Hmawza.

14. Pierre Pichard, "Les monuments...," pp. 306, 339.

15. The Pe-na-tha-gu is described below, pp. 117-8, for Min-o-chantha see Luce's illustration, *O.B.E.P.*, III, Pl.263 and text, I, pp.276-7.

16. Below, p. 102-3.

17. Above, Ch.3, p. 75.

18. No.354.

19. Above, p. 124.

20. Like at the Kondaw-gyi, where the hallextends out further out from the

shrine base.

21. Local people jokingly call it the *pyat-thana hpaya* or 'problem pagoda', a pun on the word *pyatthat.*

22. *G.P.C.*, p.156.

23. Than Tun, *The Buddhist church...*, pp.62-66.

24. Than Tun, "History of Buddhism in Burma, A.D. 1000-1300." p.133.

25. Aung Kyaing, ပုဂံခေတ်ဗိသုကာလက်ရာမြာ p.15.

26. The finest examples, both dating from the Nyaung-yan Period, being at Minkin and Myaing.

27. Above, p. 11.

28. Above, p. 11.

29. Duroiselle, "The Ari of Burma..." p. 82; Than Tun, "Report: the study and preservation of Pagan", p. 77: "With Mahayanist pictures in the Abeyadana and here at the Paya-thon-zu, at the time of Pagan's fall, we want to correct the tradition that Pagan religion was pure Hinayanist."

30. Ray, *Sanskrit Buddhism...*, pp.51-61.

31. Than Tun, *The Buddhist church...*, later published as "Mahakassapa and his tradition."

32. Of interest is the fact that two nearby temples are called East and West Kassapa.

33. Ray, *op.cit.* p. 52.

34. See discussion of Abe-ya-dana paintings, above, Ch.4, pp. 60-61

35. Zwalf, *Buddhism, art and faith.* Pl.171.

36. Below, p. 134.

37. Braxton Sinclair, "Monasteries of Pagan", pp.1-4.

38. *Glimpses...*, p.55.

39. *Glimpses...*, p.54.

40. Duroiselle, "The Ari of Burma...," p.83.

41. Above, Ch.6, p. 108.

42. *ibid.* p.82.

43. Though this may be explained by fading caused by the brighter light in the Paya-thon-zu east *gu*, where the colouring is lighter in tone than the central *gu* which is far darker; the painting's colouring here tending towards reds and blues as at the Nanda-ma-nya. Below, p 108.

44. Nos.3, 19, 20/4, 58 in the Shwe-zigon vicinity, and the Sa-thin-gu, below, p. 137.

45. Above, Ch.6, pp. 109-10.

46. The other nine were last sighted on sale in a Rangoon shop, destined for resale through the usual diplomatic channels, to plush commercial galleries and their conscienceless clients.

BIBLIOGRAPHY

ABBREVIATIONS

A.R.	Annual Report
A.S.I	Archaeological Survey of India
B.B.H.C.	Bulletin of the Burma Historical Commission
B.E.F.O.	Bulletin de l'Ecole Francais de Extrême-Orient
J.B.R.S.	Journal of the Burma Research Society

Aung Thaw. *Historical sites in Burma*. Ministry of Union Culture, Rangoon, 1972.

Aung Thwin, Michael. *Pagan the origins of modern Burma*, University of Hawaii Press, Honolulu, 1985.

"Kingship, the Sangha and Society in Pagan." In: *Explorations in Southeast Asian history: the origins of Southeast Asian statecraft*, edited by Kenneth R. Hall and John K. Whitmore, Ann Arbor, 1976, pp.107-148.

"The problem of Ceylonese-Burmese relations in the 12th century and the question of an interregnum at Pagan, 1165-1174 A.D." *Journal of the Siam Society* LXIV, pt. I, 1976, pp.53-74.

Ba Shin, *Bohmu. Lokhateikpan*. Burma Historical Commission—Ministry of Union Culture, Rangoon, 1962.

Ba Shin, Whitbread and Luce, "Pagan Wetkyi-in Kubyauk-gyi, an early Burmese temple with ink glosses." *Artibus Asiae* , XXXIII, pt.III,1971.

Bennet, Paul J. "The 'Fall of Pagan': continuity and change in 14th century Burma." *Conference under the Tamarind tree: three essays in Burmese history*. Yale University University Monograph Series, no. 15., Yale Univerity Press, New Haven, 1971.

Blagden, C.O. "The 'Pyu' inscriptions." *Epigraphica Indica*, XII, 1913-14, no.16. pp.127-32; reprinted in *J.B.R.S.*, VII, pt.I, 1917, pp.37-44.

Buddhadatta, A.P. Mahathera. *Concise Pali-English dictionary*. The Colombo Apothecaries Co., Colombo,1949.

Coedès, George. *The Indianised states of Southeast Asia*, [Paris 1964] ; English Edition, Honolulu 1971.

Crawford, John. *Journal of an embassy from the Governor General of India to the court of Ava in the year 1827*. London, 1829, p.129.

Duroiselle, Charles. *A guide to the Mandalay Palace*. Superintendent of Government Printing, Rangoon, 1925.

"The Hledauk pagoda and its relics." *A.S.I.-A.R.*, 1911-12, pp.149-51 [Pl.LXIX].

"Pictorial representations of the Jatakas in Burma." *A.S.I.-A.R.*, 1912-13, pp. 87-119 [Plates L-LX].

"Mongol frescoes at Pagan." *A.S.I-A.R.*, 1912-13, pp.146-148.

"The stone sculptures in the Ananda Temple at Pagan." *A.S.I.-A.R*, 1913-14, pp.63-97; reprinted in *J.B.R.S.*, Vol. VII, pt. II, 1917, p.194.

"The Ari of Burma and Tantric Buddhism." *A.S.I.-A.R.*, 1915-16, pp.79-93.

The Ananda Temple. Memoirs of the Archaeological Survey of India, No.56, Delhi, 1937.

"Somingyi stupa", *A.S.I.-A.R.*, 1936-7, pp.221-3.

"The Bodhisattva Maitreya in Burma." *J.B.R.S.*, II, pt.I, 1912, pp.101-2.

Duroiselle, Charles and Blagden, C.O. *Epigraphica Birmanica* Vols. I-V, Rangoon 1919-1936; reprinted Rangoon, 1960.

Forchammer, Emil. *Pagan I. The Kyaukku Temple*. Rangoon, 1891; reprinted as: *Report on the Kyaukku Temple at Pagan*. Rangoon, 1919.

Glimpses of glorious Pagan, Department of History, University of Rangoon, The Universities Press, Rangoon, 1986.

Grunwedel, Albert. *1.Glasuren von Pagan. 3.Pasten aus Pagan. 4.Skulpturen aus Pagan*. Veroffentlichungen aus dem Konliglichen Museum für Völkerkunde, Berlin, V Band. Dietrich Reimer, 1897.

Guillon, Emmanuel. *L'armée de Mara au pied de l'Ananda*. Editions Recherches sur les Civilisations, Memoir no.60, Paris,1985.

Hall, Kenneth R. and Whitmore, John K. "Southeast Asian trade and the Isthmian struggle, 1000-1200 A.D." In: *Explorations in South East Asian history: the origins of Southeast Asian statecraft*, edited by Kenneth R. Hall and John K. Whitmore, Ann Arbor, 1976, pp.107-148.

Hall, Kenneth R., *Maritime trade and state development in early Southeast Asia*. University of Hawaii Press, Honolulu, 1985.

Harvey, G.E. *A history of Burma: from the earliest times to 10 March 1824: the beginning of the English conquest*. Frank Cass and Co., London, 1925; reprinted by same in London,1967.

Horner, I.B., *The minor anthologies in the Pali canon part III: chronicle of the buddhas (*Buddhavamsa*) and Basket of Conduct (*Cariyapitaka*)*. Pali Text Society, London, 1975.

Huber, Edouard. "Les bas-reliefs du temple d'Ananda a Pagan". *B.E.F.O.*, XI, 1911, pp.1-5 [5 photos].

"Le fin de la dynastie Pagan." *B.E.F.O.*, IX, 1909, pp.633-680.

Luce, G.H. "The greater temples of Pagan." *J.B.R.S.*, VII pt.III, 1918, p.189.

"The smaller temples of Pagan." *J.B.R.S.*, X, pt.II, 1920, pp.41-49.

"A Cambodian invasion of Lower Burma—a comparison of Burmese and Talaing chronicles." *J.B.R.S.*, XII, pt.I, 1922, pp.39-45.

"Burma's debt to Pagan." *J.B.R.S.*, XXII, 1937, pp.120-127.

"The ancient Pyu." *J.B.R.S.*, XXVII, pt III, 1937, pp.239-253.

"Economic life of the early Burman." *J.B.R.S.*, XXX, 1940. pp.283-335. Reprinted in *J.B.R.S.* 50th Anniversary Publications Vol.II, 1960, pp.323-374.

"A century of progress in Burmese history and archaeology." *J.B.R.S.*, XXXII, 1949, p.79-94.

"Mons of the Pagan dynasty." *J.B.R.S.*, XXXVI, pt.I, 1953, pp.1-19.

"The 550 Jatakas in Old Burma." *Artibus Asiae*, Vol. XIX, pts. 3 and 4, 1956, pp.291-214.

"Notes on the peoples of Burma in 12th-13th centuries A.D." *J.B.R.S.*, XLII, pt.I, 1959, pp. 52-74.

"Old Kyaukse and the coming of the Burmans." *J.B.R.S.*, XLII, pt.I, June 1959, p.75-109.

"Dvaravati and Old Burma." *Journal of the Siam Society,* LIII, 1965, pp.139-152.

Old Burma-early Pagan. Vols.I-III, Locust Valley, New York, 1969.

Phases of pre-Pagan Burma languages and history. 2 Vols., Oxford University Press, 1985.

Luce, G.H. and *Bohmu* Ba Shin. "Pagan Myinkaba Kubyauk-gyi temple of Rajakumar (1113 A.D.) and the Old Mon writings on its walls." *B.B.H.C.*, Vol. II, 1961, pp.277-416.

"Aspects of Pagan history—late

period." *In memoriam Phya Anuman Rajadhou*, ed. Tej Bunnag and Michael Smithies, Bangkok, 1970, pp.138 -146.

Luce, G.H. and Pe Maung Tin. *Inscriptions of Burma*. 5 Portfolio Vols. Rangoon University Press and Oxford University Press, 1933-1956.

Marco Polo. *The travels*. Trans. R. Latham, Penguin Modern Classics, London, 1958.

Mya, U. "A note on the Buddha's footprints in Burma." *A.S.I.-A.R.*, Part I, 1930-34, and Part I pp.320-331.
"Note on the Nanpaya Temple and the images of Brahma carved on the pillars, Myinpagan, Pagan." *A.S.I.-A.R.*, 1934-35, pp.101-106.

Mya Mu, Daw. "The kalasa pot." *J.B.R.S.*, XXII, pt.II, 1932, pp.97-98.

Nai Pan Hla. "Gordon Hannington Luce 1889-1979." *J.B.R.S.*, LXII, Pts. I and II, 1979.

Okell, John K. *A guide to the Romanisation of Burmese*. Royal Asiatic Society, London, 1971.

Ono, Toru. *Pagan: mural painting of the Buddhist temples in Burma*. Kodansa Publications, Tokyo, 1978, Pl.159.

Pagan newsletter. UNESCO, Bangkok and Pondicherry, 1981-1987.

Pe Maung Tin. "Women in the inscriptions of Pagan." *J.B.R.S.*, XXV 1935, pp.149-159. Reprinted in *J.B.R.S.* 50th Anniversary Publications, Vol.II, Rangoon, 1960, pp.411-421.
"Buddhism in the inscriptions of Pagan." *J.B.R.S.*, XXVI, pt.I, 1936, pp.52-70. Reprinted in *J.B.R.S.* 50th Anniversary Publications, Vol.II, Rangoon, 1960, pp.423-441.

Pe Maung Tin and G.H. Luce. *The Glass Palace chronicle of the kings of Burma*, London, 1923.
Selections from the inscriptions of Pagan. Department of Oriental Studies, University of Rangoon, Publication no.1, Rangoon, 1928.
"Inscriptions of Burma. Portfolio I, Plates 1 and 2. Pagan, Shwegugyi Inscription, edited and translated." *B.B.H.C.*, I, pt. I, 1960, pp.1-28.
"Inscriptions of Burma. Portfolio I, Plates 3,4,5 (Kyaukse Myingondaing and Pagan Dhamma-yangyi inscriptions), edited and translated." *B.B.H.C.*, I pt.II, 1960, pp.231-255.
"Inscriptions of Burma. Portfolio I, Plates 6 to 20." Vol.III [not distributed, copy in library of E.F.E.O., Paris, and in collection of the author].

Pichard, Pierre. "Les monuments sur le plan pentagone à Pagan." *B.E.F.E.O.*, Vol.LXXIV, Paris 1985, pp.305-36 [24

plates and 70 photos.]

Quaritch Wales, H.G. *Early Burma-Old Siam, a comparative commentary*. Bernard Quaritch, London, 1973.
The universe around them: cosmology and cosmic renewal in Indianized South-East Asia. Arthur Probsthain, London, 1977.

Ray, Niharranjan. *Brahmanical gods in Burma*. Calcutta, 1932.
Sanskrit Buddhism in Burma. H.J.Paris, Amsterdam, 1936; reprinted by Department of Religious Affairs, Rangoon, 1985.
"Lokantha and other Mahayana gods in Burma." *Buddhistic Studies*, Vol.I, Calcutta, 1931.
"Paintings at Pagan." *Journal of Indian Society of Oriental Art*, 1938, pp.138-48.

Scott, J.G. and J.P. Hardimann, eds. *Gazeteer of Upper Burma and the Shan States*. 5 Vols. Supt. Gov. Printing, Rangoon,1900-01.

Seidenstucker, K. *Sud-buddhistiche studien. I. Die Buddha-legende in der skulpturen des Ananda-Temples zu Pagan. Mitteilungen aus dem Museum für Völkerkunde in Hamburg IV*. Hamburg, 1916.

Shorto, H.L. "The Gavampati tradition in Burma." Dr. R.C. Majumadar Felicitations Volume Ed. H.B. Sarkar, Calcutta 1970, pp.15-30.
"The stupa as a Buddha icon in South East Asia." In: *Mahayana Art after A.D.900*, ed. Watson, Colloquies on Art and Architecture of Asia, 2, University of London, London, 1974.
"The devata plaques on the Ananda basement." In: *Essays offered to G.H. Luce*. ed. Ba Shin, et.al., Ascona 1966, pp.156-165.

Sinclair, W.Braxton. "Monasteries of Pagan." *J.B.R.S.*, X, pt.I, 1920, pp.1-4 [6 plates].

Smith, Bardwell L. "The Pagan period (1044-1287): a bibliographic note." *Contributions to Asian studies*, XVI, E.J. Brill, Leiden, 1981., pp.112-130.

Snellgrove, David, et.al. *The image of the Buddha*. London, 1978.

Spiro, Melford E. *Buddhism and society: a great tradition and its Burmese vicissitudes*. Harper and Row, New York, 1972.

Stargardt, Janice. "Social and religious aspects of royal power in Burma from inscriptions from Kyanzittha's reign." *Journal of the Social and Economic History of the Orient*, Vol.XIII, pt. III, 1970, pp.289-308.
"Burma's economic and diplomatic relations with India and China from early medieval sources." *Journal of*

the Economic and Social History of the Orient vol.XIV, pt.I, 1971, pp.38-62.

Strachan, Paul, ed. *Essays on the history and Buddhism of Burma by Professor Than Tun*. Kiscadale Publications, Arran, Scotland, 1988.

Symes, Michael. *An account of an embassy to the kingdom of Ava, sent by the Governor-General of India in the year 1795*. London, 1800.

Tambiah, Stanley J. *World conqueror and world renouncer*. Cambridge University Press, London, 1977.

Taw Sein Ko. *Archaeological notes on Pagan*. Supt. Gov. Printing, Rangoon, 1926.
"Some excavations at Pagan." *A.S.I.-A.R.*, 1905-06, pp.131-134.
"Chinese antiquities at Pagan." *J.B.R.S.*, I, pt.I, 1911.
"The plaques found at the Hpeitleik pagoda, Pagan." *A.S.I.-A.R.*, 1906-7, pp.127-136 [illustrations and ground plan].

Thin Kyi, Daw, "The old city of Pagan." In: *Essays offered to G.H.Luce*, eds. Ba Shin, Jean Boisellier and A.B. Griswold, Ascona 1966, Vol.II , pp.179-188.

Than Tun. *The Buddhist church in Burma during the Pagan Period (1044-1287)*. University of London Ph.D. thesis, 1955.
"History of Burma 1300-1400." *J.B.R.S.*, XLII, pt. II, 1959, pp.119-33; reprinted in *B.B.H.C.*, Vol.I, pt.I, 1960, pp.39-57 and in Paul Strachan, ed. *Essays ...*
"Mahakassapa and his tradition." *J.B.R.S.*, XLII, pt.2, 1959, pp.99-118 and in Paul Strachan, ed. *Essays ...*
"Pagan restoration." *J.B.R.S.*, LIX, pts. I and II, pp.49-69 [27 plates].
"Review of G.H. Luce, Old Burma-early Pagan." Mandalay University Mimeograph, 1974.
"Social life in Burma, A.D. 1044-1287." *J.B.R.S.*, XLI, pt.I, 1958, pp.37-47 and in Paul Strachan, ed. *Essays ...*
"Religion in Burma, A.D. 1000-1300." J.B.R.S., XLII, pt.I, 1959, pp.47-69 and in Paul Strachan, ed. *Essays ...*
"Religious buildings in Burma, A.D. 1000-1300." *J.B.R.S.*, XLII, pt.II, 1959, pp.71-80 and in Paul Strachan, ed. *Essays ...*
"Report: the preservation and study of Pagan." *Study and preservation of historic cities of South East Asia—research report*, eds. Y.Ishizawa and Y.Kono, Institute of Asian Cultures-Sophia University, Tokyo, 1986, pp.78-84.

Thomann, Th. *Pagan ein jahrtausend*

Buddhistichen Tempelkunst. Stuttgart, 1923.

Tongkamawan, Cham. "A Tai inscription in the museum at Pagan." Trans. A.B.Griswold, *Artibus Asiae* Vol. XXIV, 1961, pp.249-252.

Tin Lwin. "Old Burmese painting." *Oriens Extremus,* vol. XXI, 1974, pp.237-259.

Tinker, Hugh. "The Place of Gordon Luce in research and education in Burma during the last decades of British rule." *Journal of the Royal Asiatic Society,* 1985, pt.II, pp.174-190.

Traditional Burmese architecture. Pagan Period. [Portfolio volume of architectural drawings.] Department of Higher Education, Ministry of Education, Rangoon, 1986.

Whitbread, K.J. "Medieval Burmese wall paintings from a temple in Pagan now in the Hamburgisches Museum fur Volkerkunde, Hamburg." *Oriens Extremus,* Vol. XVIII, pt.I, 1971, pp.85-122.

Wickremasingh, Sirima. "Ceylon's relations with South East Asia, with special reference to Burma." *Ceylon Journal of Historial and Social Studies,* Vol.III, 1960, pp.38-58.

Win Maung, Tampawaddy. *Iconography of certain periods.* Trans. E. Bagshawe, 1975 [unpublished; copy at SOAS.]

Yule, Henry. *Mission to the court of Ava in 1985.* Reprinted Oxford University Press, 1968.

Zimmer, Heinrich. *The Art of Indian Asia.* Vol.I - Text, Vol.II - Plates, Bollingen Series XXXIX, Pantheon Pooks, New York, 1955. [Completed and edited by Joseph Campbell.]

Zwalf, W. *Buddhism, art and faith.* Thames and Hudson, London, 1986.

INDEX

Abe-ya-dana, 33, 34, 39, 47, 54, 60, 61, 70, 72, 74, 77, 84, 94, 102, 131
Abeyadana, 10, 59
abhayamudra, 21, 26, 64, 70
Abhidhamma, 73, 84
Athinkhayar, 137
Ajawlat, Middle Princess, 83, 87
Ajanta, 55, 61, 73, 102, 104, 131
Alaungsithu, 79
Aleya-gu, 137
Alopyé, 77-78
Alopyé, 41, 55, 72, 76, 78
amalaka, 16, 42, 57, 60, 98
Ananda, 65-71
Ananda Kyaung-taik, 22, 30
Ananda Museum, 104
Ananda, 5, 26, 28, 29, 33, 52, 53, 56, 57, 60, 62, 64, 66, 67, 72, 79, 81, 82, 85, 88, 89, 106, 108
Anandasura, 127, 128
anantasayin, 34, 39, 41
anantapannya, 134
Anantasura, 125
Anawrahta, 7, 8, 9, 10, 17, 26, 27, 28, 32, 33, 37, 39, 41, 42, 43, 45, 46, 48, 52, 53, 54, 49, 57, 61, 73, 76, 77, 118, 119, 124
anda, 14, 15, 16, 41, 42, 57, 60, 91, 96, 97, 99, 103, 108, 121, 124,
andagu, 21, 27, 31
Anglo-Burmese War, First, 2
Anglo-Burmese War, Second, 3
Aniruddhadeva, Sri, 33
Annam, 7
Anotatta, 116
Apwar, 137
Arahan, Shin, 8, 33, 70, 134
arhat, 74, 105, 124
Arakan, 8, 31
Arakanese, 7, 21-2, 52
Archaeological Survey of India, 1, 4, 41
Archaeology Department, 6, 19, 41, 69, 73, 89, 110, 129
Ari, 94, 130
Arimaddanapura, 7, 121
Arimettaya, 32
Army of Mara, 102
Arranavasi, 94, 129, 130
Asoka Maurya, 8, 74
Assam, 8
athwat, 16
Attack and Defeat of Mara, 26, 60, 64, 66, 74, 116, 134, 136
atthatthana, 27, 28
Aung Kyaing, Minbu U, 25, 34, 44, 118, 128
Aung Thwin, Michael, 11, 87, 94
Ava Period, 22, 25, 70, 89, 90, 109, 138

Ava periods, 31
Ava, 2, 21, 44, 62
Avalokitesvara, 31
Avici, 101
Aye Hlaing, Ko, 89
Ba Shin, *Bohmu*, 1, 5, 38, 73, 83
Badon, 45
Bagshawe, L.E., 25
Bangarh, 50
Baruci, 113
Bassein, 87, 96
Baw-baw-gyi, 9
Bayinnaung, 57
Be-be, 9, 16, 39
Bengal Engineers, 3
Bengal, 7, 24, 27, 31, 47, 65
Bengali, 28, 29, 59, 74
Berlin Völkerkunde Museum, 4
bhadrakalpala, 16, 20, 22, 32, 52, 57, 123, 133
bhakti, 17, 20, 21
Buddhavamsa, 117, 133, 136
bhumisparsa buddha, 26, 64, 132
bhumisparsamudra, 21, 23, 24, 25, 26, 31, 32, 44, 46, 53, 59, 61, 64, 69, 81, 90, 106, 111, 114, 123, 131, 132, 137
Bhuvaneswar, 17
bilu, 50, 53, 58, 66, 67, 89
Bimbisara, 56, 84
Blagden, C.O., 5
Bo Kay, U, 5, 28, 47, 64, 71, 90, 117, 124
Bo-ta-taung, 34
Bodaw, 103
bodawin, 26, 28, 30, 31, 33, 46, 52, 56, 62, 64, 67, 81, 84, 102, 131, 134, 136
Bodawpaya, King, 2, 71
Bodh Gaya, 24, 68, 76, 81, 93, 99, 100, 105, 119
bodhi, 84, 124, 132
Bodhisattva, the, 68
bodhisattva, 10, 16, 20, 23, 29, 31, 32, 33, 34, 41, 50, 56, 61, 62, 64, 66, 74, 76, 78, 131, 132, 135
bodhisattvas, 60
Bogyoke-mi, 99, 109, 120
Bogyoke-mi kubyauk, 119-120
Brahma, 21, 34, 43, 47, 48, 68, 71, 74, 81, 108, 135
Brahmaloka, 84, 120
Brahmanic, 8, 9, 13, 14, 21, 34, 39, 49, 61
Brahmans, 43
Buddhahood, 23
Buddhapada, 101, 136
Buddhavamsa, 9, 64, 75, 84, 131
Bu-hpaya, 38
Bu-hpaya, 6

Bu-le-thi, 91
Burma-Ceylon Relations, 96
Burma Circle, 4
Burmanisation, 79
cakka, 55
cakkavatti, 11
cakkavatti, 31, 32
Calcutta Museum
Cambodia, 87
Cambodian, 7
Cansu, 91
Ceylon, 15, 45, 54, 56, 61, 66, 93, 94, 96, 121, 122, 130
Ceylonese, 10, 23, 28, 67, 73, 79, 83, 87, 92, 108, 126, 134
chattrâvali, 16, 17, 42, 57, 92, 96, 97
Chauk, 22, 30, 116, 119, 120
China, 40
China road, 8
Chindwin, 7, 8, 121
Chinese, 37, 129
chinthé, 53, 60, 66, 67, 71, 92, 99
Circuit House, 7
Cola, 9
Conception of the Buddha, 60
Craganajore, 39
Crawfurd, John, 3
Culavamsa, 73
Curzon, Lord, 4
dagaba, 97
dana, 69
Deer Park at Sarnath, 26, 81, 115, 131, 133
Descent from Tavatsima, 56, 108, 115, 131, 133
deva, 53, 60, 66, 81, 82, 111, 114, 117, 131, 132, 133, 135
Devangala, 87
Devangala Inscription, 87
devi, 135
dhamma, 10, 11, 13, 16, 31, 32, 130
Dhammaram, 91
Dhammasala, 125
Dhamma-yan-gyi, 82-91
Dhamma-yan-gyi, 1, 25, 32, 79, 83, 85, 86, 93, 95, 98, 111
Dhamma-yazika, 121-4
Dhamma-yazika, 4, 14, 20, 25, 100, 102, 120
dhamma-yon, 20, 41, 105, 112, 125, 128
dhammaraja, 11, 99
Dhanapala, 102
dharmacakra, 26, 56, 60, 69, 76, 111, 117
dharmacakramudra, 26, 64, 70, 78, 81, 92, 106, 108, 114, 115, 132, 133, 135
dhyana, 26, 64, 124, 131
dhyanamudra, 25, 26, 31, 44, 60, 64,